Bluecoats and Tar Heels

NEW DIRECTIONS IN SOUTHERN HISTORY

Series Editors
Peter S. Carmichael, West Virginia University
Michele Gillespie, Wake Forest University
William A. Link, University of Florida

BLUECOATS & TAR HEELS

Soldiers and Civilians in Reconstruction North Carolina

MARK L. BRADLEY

THE UNIVERSITY PRESS OF KENTUCKY

Scholarly publisher for the Commonwealth,
serving Bellarmine University, Berea College, Centre College of Kentucky, Eastern
Kentucky University, The Filson Historical Society, Georgetown College, Kentucky
Historical Society, Kentucky State University, Morehead State University, Murray State
University, Northern Kentucky University, Transylvania University, University of
Kentucky, University of Louisville, and Western Kentucky University.
All rights reserved.

Editorial and Sales Offices: The University Press of Kentucky
663 South Limestone Street, Lexington, Kentucky 40508-4008
www.kentuckypress.com

13 12 11 10 09   5 4 3 2 1

Library of Congress Cataloging-in-Publication Data

Bradley, Mark L.
  Bluecoats and Tar Heels : soldiers and civilians in Reconstruction North Carolina /
Mark L. Bradley.
    p. cm. — (New directions in southern history)
  Based on the author's thesis (Ph. D.)—University of North Carolina, Chapel Hill.
  Includes bibliographical references and index.
  ISBN 978-0-8131-2507-7 (hardcover : alk. paper)
  1. Reconstruction (U.S. history, 1865–1877)—North Carolina. 2. Civil-military
relations—North Carolina—History—19th century. 3. Soldiers—North Carolina—
History—19th century. 4. Peacekeeping forces—North Carolina—History—19th
century. 5. United States. Army—History—19th century. 6. Violence—North
Carolina—History—19th century. 7. Social conflict—North Carolina—History—19th
century. 8. North Carolina—Social conditions—19th century. 9. North Carolina—
Politics and government—1865–1950. I. Title.
  F259.B73 2009
  975.6'041—dc22   2008038543

 Member of the Association of
American University Presses

To the memory of my parents,
John and Audrey Bradley

CONTENTS

ILLUSTRATIONS

ACKNOWLEDGMENTS

Many people and institutions have helped to make this book possible. I am especially grateful for all the wonderful resources available at the University of North Carolina at Chapel Hill. In expressing my thanks, it is only appropriate that I start at Louis Round Wilson Library, since I spent so much of my research time there. My thanks go to John White, Laura Brown, and the rest of the staff of the Southern Historical Collection, and to Harry McKown and the rest of the North Carolina Collection staff. I am grateful to Patricia Dominguez, the head of Collection Development, and to the circulation and interlibrary service staff of Walter R. Davis Library for their assistance.

This book is based on my doctoral dissertation, and as such, many people at UNC-Chapel Hill gave me invaluable assistance. The staff of the Graduate School helped me obtain funding for dissertation research and writing. Above all, I thank Steve Boone, the Director of Fellowships and Tuition Awards, and Rachell Underhill, the External Fellowship Coordinator. My thanks go to the administrative staff of the History Department, especially Pamela Fesmire, Jackie Gorman, and Violet Lentz, for keeping me on track. I also thank Professor Jacqueline Hall and the students in my dissertation design class for their comments and suggestions. Special thanks to my good friends and fellow grad students Michael Allsep, Maj. John Hall, Robert Richardson, and Michael Weisel for their advice, encouragement, and good company.

Generous funding from several sources has enabled me to complete my dissertation with few distractions. I am grateful to the History Department for providing me with a Mowry Fellowship for initial research expenses. I am likewise thankful for two additional UNC grants: a Holsenbeck Grant that provided funds for microfilm from the National Archives, and a Faherty Grant that helped with general research expenses. I am grateful for a Gilder Lehrman Grant that enabled me to spend a week at the New York Public Library. My thanks to H. G. Jones, Robert Anthony, and the rest of the North Caroliniana Society for generously providing me with two Archie K. Davis Research Fellowships. Thanks also to the U.S. Army Center of Military History for a generous fellowship that covered most of my research expenses for one year. I am thankful for a Dolores Zohrab Liebmann Dissertation Fellowship that enabled me to devote two uninterrupted years to writing my dissertation.

I am grateful for the help I received at numerous archives and libraries across the country. I particularly thank Dr. Richard J. Sommers and his staff at the U.S. Army Military History Institute for making my visit so enjoyable and productive. Thanks also to archivists at Bowdoin College in Brunswick, Maine; the Indiana Historical Society in Indianapolis, Indiana; the State Archives in Raleigh, North Carolina; and the National Archives in Washington, D.C., for going above and beyond the call of duty.

A special thanks to Terrell Armistead Crow for providing me with transcripts of several articles by Mary Bayard Clarke that did not appear in the volume of Clarke papers Terri co-edited with Mary Moulton Barden. Thanks also to Catherine Bishir for sharing her insights into the conciliatory efforts of Col. James V. Bomford, the commander of the Post of Raleigh during Military Reconstruction, and to Henry Mintz for helping me plot my research strategy for the National Archives.

My thanks go to Harry W. Pfanz, John R. Kirkland, James E. Sefton, Joseph G. Dawson III, William L. Richter, Craig Jeffrey Currey, and Robert J. Zalimas Jr., for their studies on the U.S. Army in the South during Reconstruction.

I am grateful to the members of my dissertation committee, William L. Barney, Joseph T. Glatthaar, William C. Harris, Don Higginbotham, Richard H. Kohn, and Harry L. Watson for their invaluable comments and suggestions. I cannot thank Professor Barney enough for his guidance. I thoroughly enjoyed working under his direction and am grateful for all his help. Thanks also to Professor Alex Roland of Duke University for reading most of my dissertation and for describing the army's complex task as "Mission Impossible."

A special thanks to Ed Bearss for taking time from his busy schedule to read my dissertation. Because of his efforts, I feel a bit less anxious about sending my manuscript into the world. Many thanks to my good friend Mark Moore for interrupting his own writing projects to create a map for my book. I am grateful to my colleagues at the U.S. Army Center of Military History in Washington, D. C., for sharing their knowledge and expertise. During work on the manuscript, I could always rely on two close friends: Peter Cozzens for his advice and encouragement, and Leny Sagastizado for her kindness and unfailing good cheer.

A special thanks to my good friend Peter S. Carmichael of West Virginia University. As an editor of the University Press of Kentucky's New Directions in Southern History series, Pete became an early and enthusiastic advocate of my manuscript. My thanks also to Pete's two coeditors, Michele Gillespie of Wake Forest University and William A. Link of the University of Florida. I am grateful to the two readers who evaluated my manuscript for UPK; their comments and suggestions resulted in a better book.

Many thanks to the staff of the University Press of Kentucky for their efforts in bringing my book into the world. I am grateful to the director, Stephen M. Wrinn, for explaining the publication process at UPK and answering my many questions. I am indebted to Joyce Harrison and Ann Malcolm of the editorial staff for their patience and professionalism.

A special thanks to my grandfather, James Jackson Hagan, for making the long-ago Civil War come alive. Thanks also to my brothers, Bill and Jim, for being my best friends. Most of all, I am grateful to my parents, John and Audrey Bradley, for their love, support, and encouragement. This study is dedicated to their memory.

Prologue

TAKING ON
MISSION IMPOSSIBLE

In his semiautobiographical novel, *A Fool's Errand*, Albion W. Tourgée sought to explain the failure of postwar Reconstruction in the South. Few persons had been more dedicated to its success. In the fall of 1865, the Union officer-turned-carpetbagger attorney settled in Greensboro, North Carolina, where he aroused considerable controversy as a champion of the freedpeople. In 1868, he served as the delegate for Guilford County in the state constitutional convention and coauthored the new state legal code. A few years later, as a superior court judge in a Ku Klux Klan hotbed, he received numerous death threats for attempting to bring Klansmen to justice. His best-selling novel appeared in 1879, two years after the Compromise of 1877 had signaled the end of Reconstruction.

Speaking through his fictional counterpart, Col. Comfort Servosse, Tourgée argued:

> I begin seriously to fear that the North lacks virility. This cowardly shirking of responsibility, this pandering to sentimental whimsicalities, this snuffling whine about peace and conciliation, is sheer weakness. The North is simply a conqueror; and, if the results she fought for are to be secured, she must rule as a conqueror. Suppose the South had been triumphant, and had overwhelmed and determined to hold the North? Before now, a thoroughly organized system of provincial government would

have been securely established . . . because the people of the
South are born rulers. . . . In this the North fails. She hesitates,
palters, shirks.[1]

For all its hyperbole, Colonel Servosse's bitter critique contains much
truth. From the start, a spirit of moderation pervaded northern Reconstruction policy. When President Andrew Johnson unveiled his Reconstruction plan in May 1865, it proved far more lenient than almost anyone
in either the North or the South had anticipated, given his earlier pledge
to punish traitors. To reenter the Union, southern states merely had to repeal their secession ordinances, ratify the Thirteenth Amendment ending
slavery, and repudiate their war debt. If Johnson's program denied amnesty to fourteen classes of ex-Confederates, the president nevertheless
granted a pardon to nearly any person who applied for one. Along with
the pardons, the president restored confiscated southern lands to their
former owners, dimming freedpeople's hopes of receiving "forty acres
and a mule" from the federal government. As a result, most ex-slaves
remained dependent on their former masters for their livelihood. Johnson thus attempted to build a broadly based constituency by appeasing
southern whites while keeping freedpeople in a servile position.

Presidential Reconstruction revived the spirits of ex-Confederates
throughout the South. The collapse of the Confederacy in April 1865
had filled white southerners with dread and despair, while the presence
of Union occupation troops in many southern towns and communities
served as a continual reminder of their defeat. In North Carolina, nearly
every household mourned the loss of a loved one or a friend who had
died while in the Confederate army. From a white military-age (eighteen
to forty-five) population of 115,000 males, the Tar Heel State mobilized
125,000 soldiers. About 40,000, or one-third, were killed in action or
succumbed to wounds or disease.[2]

Financial and material losses in North Carolina were catastrophic.
The passage of Union and Confederate forces through the state during
the final weeks of the war wreaked untold havoc on civilians in their
path. Defeat wiped out all property in slaves, all state bonds, and most
state bank stock. Four years of war on a shoestring had left the state's
railroads in a dilapidated condition, and the rail companies had no capital to finance their repair. To fill the vacuum left by the collapse of state
and local government, the Union command in North Carolina declared
martial law, yet lawlessness prevailed in some rural areas for months and

even years. Although faced with the formidable task of rebuilding their businesses, homes, and lives, most white Tar Heels seemed resigned to their fate and ready to start anew.

Encouraged by the former Rebels' apparent resignation, the War Department in Washington rapidly demobilized the large and costly army of occupation. By the end of 1865, only a token force remained in North Carolina to preserve law and order. Under Johnson's mild Reconstruction plan, North Carolina and other former Confederate states were on the verge of rejoining the Union.

From the perspective of northern Republicans, however, Presidential Reconstruction had gone terribly awry, for Johnson appeared to place greater emphasis on conciliating former enemies than on punishing traitors. With the president as their champion, ex-Confederates recovered their equilibrium by late 1865. The fall elections revealed that southern whites still looked to their wartime leaders, and reports from northern observers in the South indicated that violence against blacks and white Unionists was on the rise. The southern state legislatures passed so-called Black Codes to keep freedpeople in a condition as close to slavery as the lawmakers dared. Left to their own devices, ex-Confederates seemed stubbornly unrepentant, and Johnson appeared content to let them remain so.

Determined to preserve the fruits of victory, the Republican majority in Congress moved to replace Johnson's plan with their own. In 1866, Congress passed the Civil Rights and Freedmen's Bureau bills over presidential vetoes in order to negate the Black Codes and ease the former slaves' transition to a free labor economy. Later that year, Congress passed the Fourteenth Amendment to safeguard freedpeople's rights against Johnson's vetoes and other political maneuvers. Acting on the president's advice, every southern state except Tennessee rejected the amendment.

In March 1867, Congress responded by passing the Reconstruction Act over yet another presidential veto. The measure divided the ten recalcitrant southern states into five military districts and placed a general in command of each district. A supplementary act specified the procedure for forming new state governments and regaining admittance to Congress. The steps included drafting and approving by popular vote a constitution that both granted adult male suffrage and ratified the Fourteenth Amendment.

Members of the southern elite viewed Congressional—or Military—Reconstruction as a threat to their status and authority. In North Carolina,

Conservative leaders such as Zebulon B. Vance and William A. Graham sought to attract popular support by pledging to maintain "White Man's Government." Conversely, dissident newspaper editor and former provisional governor William W. Holden led a coalition of blacks, scalawags (native whites), and carpetbaggers (northern whites) that became the state Republican Party. Holden thus hoped to regain the power he had briefly held under presidential appointment before being voted out of office in late 1865. The new party depended heavily on black voters; according to the 1860 U.S. Census, blacks comprised one-third of the state's nearly one million residents. While Conservative candidates played the race card, Republicans appealed to their diverse constituency by espousing an array of reforms that included equal civil and political rights for all citizens, no more property qualifications for jury duty or office-holding, popular election of judges and other public officials, free public education, abolition of corporal punishment, and uniform taxation.[3]

The rank and file of each party believed they had as much at stake in the political struggle as their leaders. Conservatives regarded blacks as lesser beings and sought to keep them in an inferior caste. Many believed that freedmen should not own land or other property, and most opposed granting them citizenship. When the Republicans rose to power in 1868, thousands of Conservatives across the state formed local vigilante units known collectively as the Ku Klux Klan. Klansmen were political terrorists who employed any means necessary—including arson, whipping, and murder—to restore Conservatives to political dominance and relegate blacks to servile status.

Carpetbaggers such as former Union general Joseph C. Abbott had settled in North Carolina to establish homes, businesses, and, in some cases, political careers. Abbott owned and managed a sawmill near Wilmington. In 1868, he was elected to the U.S. Senate. Scalawags such as former Confederate officer William Blount Rodman believed the Republican Party offered the best hope for personal advancement and for North Carolina's economic recovery. A prominent attorney, Rodman served as a delegate to the 1868 state constitutional convention and coauthored the new state legal code. Blacks such as the former runaway slave and fiery young orator Abraham H. Galloway depended on the Republican Party to secure their civil and political rights, especially the right to vote. With the onset of Military Reconstruction, their aspirations for land ownership revived. Above all, Republicans of both races relied on the U.S. Army to protect themselves and their families from vindictive Conservatives determined to restore the old political and racial hierarchy. The freedpeople's gains meant little unless they could live and work in safety. The army, however, often proved slow in coming to their aid.

In addition to protecting blacks and white loyalists, the army's mission included implementing federal policy, peacekeeping, and conciliating former Confederates. As Colonel Servosse could have told them, occupation commanders discovered that accomplishing the first three objectives often rendered the fourth impossible. Given the violence, lawlessness, and terrorism that plagued the state from 1865 to 1871, it is remarkable—if not altogether surprising—that army officers refused to abandon moderation for a more coercive policy.

In North Carolina, the process of conciliation began in April 1865 with the generous preliminary surrender agreement drafted by Maj. Gen. William T. Sherman, a Union commander better known for his devastating marches through Georgia and the Carolinas. Although the authorities in Washington rejected Sherman's initial terms as too liberal, the Union commander continued to advocate a conciliatory policy toward the South. Other recent Reconstruction studies begin in 1863 or even earlier, but in this work I start with the negotiations at Bennett Place in April 1865, because that is when the transition from war to peace in North Carolina truly began.

Army officers maintained a policy of moderation even during Military Reconstruction, when postwar civil-military relations in North Carolina were often contentious. In performing their duties with discretion and impartiality, several post commanders became popular with local whites, and the latter showed their gratitude by petitioning district commanders to retain federal troops in their communities.

The end of Military Reconstruction and drastic troop reductions relegated the army to a supporting role in maintaining law and order. For two years, the army stood by as the Ku Klux Klan's reign of terror spread across the state. The army's delayed intervention resulted largely from policy decisions in Washington, but several high-ranking army officers deserve a share of the blame for failing to act even when they had the authority to do so. In 1871, the army at last suppressed the Klan in North Carolina, but only after the nightriders had succeeded in restoring the Conservatives to power. Acting with characteristic restraint, the federal judiciary punished only a handful of the guilty as a warning to the rest.

Even as they combated the Ku Klux Klan and other outlaws, federal officers in North Carolina attempted to conciliate their former enemies.

Most did so because they identified more readily with local whites than with the freedpeople. After all, racism was almost as pervasive in the mid-nineteenth-century North as it was in the South. As the occupation force shrank, army officers increasingly favored moderation over severity in their dealings with southern whites. They relied on conciliation to soften lingering sectional animosities, to ease the transition from martial law to civil government, and to reduce the need for force in maintaining order. Few officers relished occupation duty in the South, for the complex challenges rendered such duty obnoxious. After two years of Reconstruction duty in North Carolina, Col. Nelson A. Miles welcomed the news of his transfer to the western frontier. "It was a pleasure to be relieved of the anxieties and responsibilities of civil affairs," Miles recalled four decades later, "to hear nothing of the controversies incident to race prejudice, and to be once more engaged in strictly military duties."[4]

Recent studies of Reconstruction in Louisiana, Mississippi, and South Carolina portray the ongoing resistance of former Confederates as a continuation of the Civil War by other means. This description also holds true for North Carolina, with the difference that Tar Heel Conservatives ceased using violence as a tool of counterrevolution about six years earlier than did reactionary forces in southern states with more firmly entrenched Republican governments. The ensuing peace facilitated the process of conciliation in North Carolina. By the mid-1870s, the Redeemer Democrats—or former Confederate leaders—had established "home rule" in the Tar Heel State. As a result, they felt secure enough to reciprocate the federal soldiers' conciliatory gestures. Thereafter, bluecoats participated in public ceremonies with Confederate veterans and found that white society had at last opened its doors to them. After a dozen years of taking on "Mission Impossible"—the juggling act that combined protecting blacks and conciliating former Confederates—the army abandoned the freedpeople for the sake of sectional reconciliation.[5]

Chapter One

THE WARRIOR AS PEACEMAKER

Sherman and the Bennett Place Negotiations

Of the eleven states that comprised the Confederacy, North Carolina was the last to secede from the Union. Only after the fall of Fort Sumter and President Abraham Lincoln's call for seventy-five thousand troops to suppress the rebellion did North Carolina succumb to the "secession mania" that had already swept the Deep South states. But Unionism and other forms of anti-Confederate dissent were far from extinguished in North Carolina. Although the state furnished more than 120,000 men to the Confederate army, Unionist sympathizers hid out in the eastern swamps and in the mountains bordering Tennessee. Many North Carolina Unionists—in the east, they were called "buffaloes," and in the west, "tories"—actively resisted the Confederate government as guerrillas; others, including several thousand former slaves, enlisted in federal regiments. In 1864, a burgeoning peace movement briefly threatened to carry North Carolina out of the Confederacy. The state's central counties, or "Quaker Belt," became a haven for Unionists, deserters, and draft dodgers, many of them preying on helpless civilians. In early 1865, the problem became so acute that a force of six hundred troops was transferred from the frontlines in Virginia to round them up. The bitterness and rancor resulting from the conflict between Tar Heel Unionists and Confederates would persist long after the Civil War had officially ceased, resulting in an ongoing cycle of violence and bloodshed.

Despite the presence of federal troops along its coast for most of the war, North Carolina remained a strategic backwater until the conflict's final months. While the major campaigns and battles raged elsewhere, the Union army contented itself with chipping away at the Tar Heel State's coastline or with making an occasional foray across the western border of the state. In January 1865, however, the federal juggernaut began its invasion of North Carolina in earnest. Fort Fisher fell on January 15, closing Wilmington as a blockade running port and thus severing "the Lifeline of the Confederacy"—so-called because Gen. Robert E. Lee's Army of Northern Virginia had long relied on that entrepôt as its sole source of supplies from the outside world. For nine months, Lee's army had defended Richmond, Virginia, the Confederate capital, but the closing of Wilmington rendered the fate of both Richmond and the Confederacy's principal field army precarious at best. Wilmington itself fell on February 22.

During the first week of March, three Union forces were poised to overrun North Carolina. After a devastating march through South Carolina, Maj. Gen. William T. Sherman's army of sixty thousand troops was winding northward into the vast longleaf pine forests of the Tar Heel State, while Maj. Gen. John M. Schofield's thirty-thousand-man force was marching inland from New Bern and Wilmington toward a junction with Sherman at Goldsboro. At Greeneville, Tennessee, Maj. Gen. George Stoneman was preparing to lead his four-thousand-strong cavalry division on a destructive raid through the western part of the state. In mid-March, the Confederate army in North Carolina under Gen. Joseph E. Johnston attempted to crush elements of Sherman's and Schofield's forces at Wyse Fork, Monroe's Crossroads, Averasboro, and Bentonville, but the Southerners lacked the numerical strength to defeat even a part of the federal force. After the junction of Sherman and Schofield at Goldsboro, the heavily outnumbered Johnston rested his army near Smithfield, anxiously awaiting Lee's order to join him. Both Lee and Johnston believed their only hope lay in combining and then crushing Sherman before he could reach the forces commanded by the Union army's general-in-chief, Lt. Gen. Ulysses S. Grant, besieging Richmond and Petersburg. There was just one problem: Sherman's 90,000 effectives alone equaled the Confederates' combined strength, with Grant fielding an additional 115,000 troops. By the spring of 1865, only a miracle could save the Confederacy.

Governor Zebulon B. Vance of North Carolina had seen the handwriting on the wall for several months. On January 18, 1865, Vance wrote

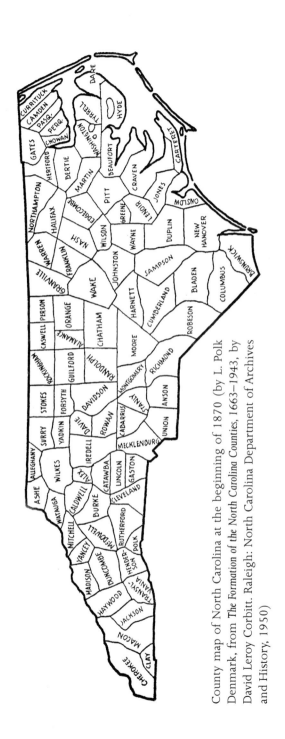

County map of North Carolina at the beginning of 1870 (by L. Polk Denmark, from *The Formation of the North Carolina Counties, 1663–1943*, by David Leroy Corbitt. Raleigh: North Carolina Department of Archives and History, 1950)

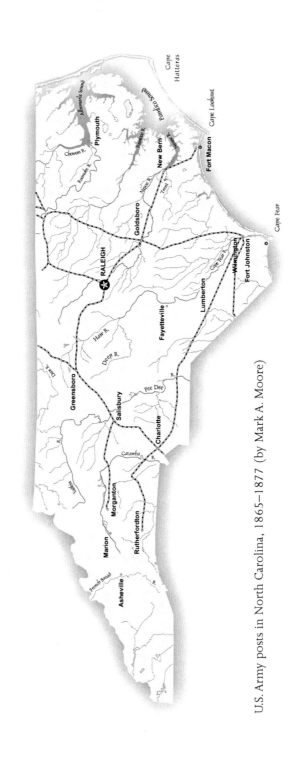

U.S. Army posts in North Carolina, 1865–1877 (by Mark A. Moore)

Georgia governor Joseph E. Brown that their chief duty was "to hold the demoralized and trembling fragments of society and law together and prevent them from dropping to pieces until the rapidly hastening end of our struggle shall be developed." Vance, however, was powerless to prevent the disintegration of his state's social and legal fabric resulting from the presence of the contending armies. The closing days of the war brought untold suffering and privation to thousands of North Carolinians, underscoring Sherman's declaration, "War is cruelty, and you cannot refine it." Both Union and Confederate armies lived off the land, prompting former North Carolina governor Charles Manly to condemn the "horrid deeds" and "atrocious acts" of Yankees and Rebels alike. "Between the two fires desolation, plunder, & actual starvation await us," Manly wrote. "God help the country." In mid-April 1865, anxious Tar Heels held out scant hope for generous terms from the hated Sherman, yet that is precisely what the Union commander offered his defeated foe, much to the astonishment of outraged Northerners.[1]

Shortly before dawn on April 12, 1865, two riders galloped up to Sherman's headquarters in the courthouse square at Smithfield, North Carolina. They bore momentous news from Grant: Lee had surrendered the Army of Northern Virginia at Appomattox Court House on April 9. Grant's message quoted verbatim the surrender terms, which permitted Lee's officers and men to return home, "not to be disturbed by the U.S. authorities as long as they observe their parole and the laws in force where they reside." Sherman was overjoyed at the news that signaled the collapse of the Confederacy. "I hardly know how to express my feelings, but you can imagine them," he wrote Grant. "The terms you have given Lee are magnanimous and liberal." Sherman added that should Johnston "follow Lee's example[,] I shall of course grant the same." Unfortunately for Sherman, Johnston's Army of Tennessee appeared to be retreating more rapidly than he could pursue. On the morning of the twelfth, the Confederates were camped beyond Raleigh, the state capital, about thirty miles to the northwest and well beyond Sherman's grasp. Although he outnumbered the Confederates by more than three to one, Sherman realized that he could not compel Johnston's surrender. The question that now confronted Sherman was this: Would Johnston capitulate, or would he allow his army to disperse into guerrilla bands? Sherman feared that if Johnston chose the latter course, the war could be protracted indefinitely.[2]

On the evening of April 12, as Union columns converged on Raleigh,

Sherman met with a delegation from Governor Vance. The two representatives, University of North Carolina president David L. Swain and Confederate senator William A. Graham, bore a letter from Vance requesting "a personal interview . . . for the purpose of conferring upon the subject of a suspension of hostilities, with a view to further communications with the United States, touching the final termination of the existing war." Vance's letter indicated that the Tar Heel governor was anxious to negotiate separate peace terms, and it reminded Sherman of a proposal he had made to Governor Joseph E. Brown of Georgia the previous September. Sherman had offered to pay for his army's supplies and cease his policy of destruction if Brown ordered the withdrawal of all Georgia troops from the Confederate army. Although Brown did not respond, Sherman believed that the Georgia governor would have cooperated but for fear of reprisal. Recalling President Abraham Lincoln's encouragement of the Brown peace overture, the general therefore decided to repeat the experiment with Vance. "I will aid you all in my power to contribute to the end you aim to reach," Sherman wrote Vance, "the termination of the existing war." Even after Vance fled Raleigh upon receiving word of Graham and Swain's capture, Sherman offered him and other government officials safe passage to the state capital and promised to retain Vance as governor.[3]

On the morning of April 13, Union soldiers entered Raleigh, and Sherman established his headquarters at the Governor's Palace. Meanwhile, Sherman's Confederate counterpart, General Johnston, was at Greensboro eighty miles to the west trying to convince a defiant President Jefferson Davis that "it would be the greatest of human crimes for us . . . to continue the war." After questioning Johnston's second-in-command, Gen. P. G. T. Beauregard, and then polling his cabinet, Davis realized that only he and Secretary of State Judah P. Benjamin still advocated fighting on. The Confederate president reluctantly yielded to the majority and dictated a message to Sherman, requesting a cease-fire "to permit the civil authorities to enter into the needful arrangements to terminate the existing war." Johnston signed the letter and ordered it sent at once to Sherman in Raleigh. But Davis had no intention of negotiating with the Lincoln government and resumed his southward flight even before the arrival of Sherman's reply.[4]

Johnston's dispatch reached Sherman's headquarters at midnight on April 15. Sherman informed Johnston that he was "fully empowered to arrange with you any terms for the suspension of further hostilities" between their armies. Ignoring Johnston's request for a cease-fire "to

Maj. Gen. William T. Sherman (Library of Congress)

permit the *civil authorities*" (italics added) to negotiate, Sherman wrote, "I undertake to abide by the same terms and conditions as were made by Generals Grant and Lee at Appomattox Court-House on the 9th instant." Sherman also promised to secure a general cease-fire from Grant, and he assured Johnston, "I really desire to save the people of North Carolina the damage they would sustain by the march of this army through the central or western parts of this state." In a letter to Grant and Secretary of War Edwin M. Stanton, Sherman stated that he would offer Johnston the same terms Grant had given Lee and be "careful not to complicate any points of civil policy."[5]

Due to a subterfuge on the part of the Union cavalry commander, Brig. Gen. Judson Kilpatrick, Sherman's message did not reach Johnston until Easter Sunday, April 16. Kilpatrick tried to convince Sherman that Johnston had engineered the delay to make his escape. But Sherman refused to be taken in and noted that Johnston "could not stop the movement of his troops till he got my letter, which I hear was delayed all day yesterday by your adjutant's not sending it forward." Sherman's faith in Johnston's sincerity was repaid when he received a dispatch from the Confederate cavalry commander, Lt. Gen. Wade Hampton, proposing a conference halfway between Kilpatrick's headquarters at Durham's Station and Hampton's headquarters at Hillsborough. "The war is over—occupation's gone!" Sherman blurted, quoting Shakespeare's Othello.[6]

On the morning of April 17, as Sherman was boarding a train en route to his conference with Johnston, a coded message from Stanton arrived at the depot announcing Lincoln's assassination. Sherman ordered the telegraph operator to keep the message confidential until his return, and the federal commander likewise said nothing about it to his subordinates. Instead, Sherman waited until he met with Johnston at the James Bennett farmhouse about five miles west of Durham's Station. According to Sherman, beads of sweat formed on Johnston's brow as he read Stanton's message, and the Confederate commander pronounced Lincoln's death "the greatest possible calamity to the South." Sherman said that he dreaded "the effect of this act on the country at large and on the armies," particularly his forces camped around Raleigh.

When Johnston reminded Sherman that his mission was to arrange an armistice to enable the civil authorities to negotiate, the latter objected because the U.S. government refused to recognize the Confederacy. Nevertheless, Sherman told Johnston that he wanted to spare the South further devastation, and he spoke in a tone that the Confederate commander believed "carried conviction of sincerity." Sherman thereupon offered Johnston the terms that Grant had given Lee at Appomattox Court House. Johnston conceded that Grant's terms were indeed generous—to a surrounded foe, that is. He then noted that his army was camped around

Greensboro, eighty miles west of Sherman's army at Raleigh. Why not negotiate for the surrender of all the remaining Confederate forces, Johnston suggested, and make one job of it? Sherman was skeptical and asked how he proposed to guarantee the surrender. Johnston replied that he could obtain President Davis's personal authorization.

The two men discussed possible surrender terms. Sherman said that he had recently conferred with Lincoln, and the late president had been anxious to get the southern men back to their homes as soon as possible. The Union commander added that the northern people harbored no vindictive feelings against the southern soldiery, though they felt far less charitable toward Davis and other southern political leaders. It soon became apparent to Johnston that Sherman would refuse to grant amnesty to Davis and his cabinet, an essential condition for the obvious reason that Davis would likely regard it as such. For his part, Sherman remained doubtful of Johnston's ability to fulfill his end of the bargain. The generals ended their conference around mid-afternoon to give Johnston time to communicate with Davis and enable Sherman to reach Raleigh before word of Lincoln's assassination could spread. They agreed to meet again at the Bennett house at noon the next day.[7]

When Sherman returned to Raleigh, he discovered that news of Lincoln's assassination had already spread throughout the capital. A crowd of angry soldiers met him at the depot, shouting: "Don't let Johnston surrender!" According to an Illinois major, "The army is crazy for vengeance. If we make another campaign it will be an awful one. . . . We hope Johnston will not surrender. God pity this country if he retreats or fights us." That night, Sherman strengthened the guard patrolling Raleigh, posted pickets on all roads into town, and ordered all unauthorized soldiers found on the streets arrested and jailed. The Union commander spent an anxious night riding through the camps of his armies, calming his men. He later claimed that without his efforts, "Raleigh would have been destroyed." Indeed, one of Sherman's subordinates, Maj. Gen. John A. Logan, had to threaten a mob of his men with cannon fire at point-blank range to prevent them from laying waste to the capital.[8]

Given the vengeful temper of their men and the daunting prospect of pursuing "a dissolving and fleeing" foe, it was hardly surprising that Sherman's subordinates urged him to grant generous terms to Johnston. One general even suggested that if it became necessary, Sherman should offer Jefferson Davis a seagoing vessel to make his escape. Although he did not mention it at the time, Sherman may have recalled his promise to Mayor James M. Calhoun of Atlanta the previous September: once peace was at hand, "you may call on me for anything—Then will I share with you the last cracker, and watch with you to shield your homes & families against danger from every quarter." Sherman's conciliatory attitude was bolstered by his conversations with Lincoln at City Point in March. Sherman recalled that the late president "contemplated no revenge—no harsh measures, but quite the contrary, and that [the Rebels'] suffering and hardships in the war would make them the more submissive to Law." Although Sherman's decision to offer his enemy generous terms was based on strategic considerations, it was also consistent with his previous thinking.[9]

While Sherman conferred with his generals, Johnston consulted two Confederate cabinet members, Secretary of War John C. Breckinridge and Postmaster General John H. Reagan, at Hampton's headquarters near Hillsborough. The Confederates stole a march on Sherman by drafting their own preliminary surrender terms: in return for disbanding the Confederate army and recognizing the Constitution and the authority of the U.S. government, the incumbent southern state governments would be retained; the personal, political, and property rights of the southern people would be preserved; they would receive universal amnesty for their participation in the war. As Johnston knew all too well, the third and last provision was the one Sherman had vetoed during their first meeting.[10]

When the two commanders met at Bennett Place on April 18, Johnston assured Sherman that he now had authority to surrender all remaining Confederate forces, but he wanted written assurance that the constitutional rights of his soldiers would be respected. Sherman replied that Lincoln's amnesty proclamation of 1863 guaranteed a full pardon for all soldiers below the rank of brigadier general, and the Appomattox terms embraced all general officers, including Robert E. Lee. Johnston nonetheless insisted on written guarantees for his men. He also requested that Breckinridge be allowed to participate in the negotiations. Sherman initially refused because Breckinridge was a Confederate cabinet officer, but when Johnston said that he was also a major general in the Confederate army, Sherman relented.[11]

Johnston then read Reagan's "Basis of Pacification" aloud to Sherman, commenting that it differed from the terms previously discussed only insofar as it granted the Confederates universal amnesty. Sherman was unimpressed, finding Reagan's paper "so general and verbose" that he deemed it "inadmissible." Johnston nevertheless handed him the document to study. Breckinridge expatiated on the Reagan terms for several minutes, and then Sherman took out pen and paper and drafted his own surrender agreement. Sherman wrote so rapidly that Johnston believed he had come prepared to grant the very terms in Reagan's paper. Once he had finished, Sherman looked up and said, "Gentlemen, this is the best I can do." As the two Confederates read the agreement, they thought it too good to be true, and in fact, they were right.[12]

Although Sherman had dismissed the Reagan document as too verbose, his own "Memorandum or Basis of Agreement" ran twice the length of the Texan's, for Sherman was offering the Confederates even more than they had requested. First, the Confederate soldiers would be permitted to retain their arms and deposit them in their respective state arsenals for use in peacekeeping. Second, in addition to retaining the existing southern state governments, Sherman proposed that cases involving conflicting state governments established during the war (such as the newly formed state of West Virginia) be decided by the U.S. Supreme Court. This condition went far beyond Reagan's simple guarantee of existing southern state governments. Third, the southern people would retain their personal, political, and property rights as defined by the constitutions of the United States and the individual states. Because Sherman omitted any mention of slaves on the grounds that slavery was already dead, Reagan and other Confederates argued that the property clause of his agreement left "the peculiar institution" intact. Fourth, the southern people would receive universal amnesty for their part in the war as long as they lived in peace and obeyed the law. Because Sherman listed no exceptions, the amnesty presumably included Jefferson Davis and his cabinet. Johnston later boasted that Sherman "had accepted, virtually, the terms I had offered in writing. They included general amnesty without naming individuals or classes."[13]

Sherman had indeed given Johnston all he wanted and more. Unlike Grant, Sherman chose to decide both political and military issues in his agreement, despite his usual aversion to political matters. Just a few weeks before, Sherman had assured his father-in-law, Thomas Ewing, "You need not fear my committing a political mistake, for I am fully conscious of the fact that I would imperil all by any concessions in that direction." Yet Sherman had decided to enter the political minefield in the aftermath of Lincoln's assassination; he did so for four reasons.[14]

First, the idea of ending the war "by one single stroke of the pen" appealed to Sherman's flair for the dramatic. Second, Sherman believed that he was fulfilling Lincoln's wishes as expressed to him at City Point. Although they probably did not discuss specific terms, Sherman inferred that Lincoln favored a conciliatory policy enabling the southern states to resume their peacetime status as soon as possible. Sherman had just learned of Maj. Gen. Godfrey Weitzel's call of the Virginia legislature, permitting that body to meet while Richmond was under federal occupation. The call implied that Lincoln had favored retaining Confederate state governments, at least until others could be elected or appointed. Sherman also recalled Lincoln's encouragement of his efforts to communicate with Georgia Governor Joseph E. Brown the previous September, and the general inferred that the late president would have approved of his decision to negotiate on political and military matters. But Sherman could not have been more mistaken. Unknown to him was a message Lincoln had dictated to Stanton in early March instructing Grant "not to decide, discuss, or confer upon any political question. Such questions the President holds in his own hands, and will submit them to no military conferences or conventions." Oddly enough, neither Stanton nor Grant had thought to transmit this message to Sherman, and Lincoln did not discuss it with him at City Point. Third, Sherman dreaded the prospect of pursuing Johnston's smaller and more mobile army, only to see it break up into guerrilla bands. By granting generous terms, Sherman hoped to avoid a protracted guerrilla war and the necessity for a large and costly occupation force in the South.[15]

Fourth, and most important, Sherman believed that he was fulfilling his promise to aid the South once it laid down its arms. By virtue of his years spent in the South both before and during the war, Sherman regarded himself as better qualified than most northern politicians to decide on what terms the South should reenter the Union. He especially distrusted the motives of the radical Republican faction in Congress, for the radicals appeared eager to impose a harsh reconstruction on the South to suit their own agenda, which included exploiting the freedmen as voters. In a letter to a friend, Sherman bluntly revealed his contempt for Washington politicians: "I would rather serve 4 years in the Singsing Penitentiary than in Washington & believe I would come out a better man." Contrary to most northern politicians, Sherman believed that the best means of securing a lasting peace was to bypass reconstruction altogether and let the southern whites determine their own fate.[16]

Sherman realized that he had delved into political matters beyond his authority as a military commander. He inserted a clause at the end of his agreement stating that he and Johnston pledged to obtain the prompt approval of their "respective principals" before carrying the terms into effect. In the meantime, there would be a cease-fire; hostilities could resume only after either commander had given the other forty-eight hours' notice. That evening, a euphoric Sherman returned to his headquarters in Raleigh and immediately sent one of his staff officers to Washington, D.C., with his agreement. The Union commander was supremely confident that his terms would be approved. "I can hardly realize it," Sherman confided to his wife, "but I can see no slip. The terms are all on our side."[17]

While Sherman awaited word from President Andrew Johnson, his subordinates attempted to soften the hardships imposed on inhabitants by his armies. Union Maj. Gen. Henry W. Slocum, the commander of the Army of Georgia, redistributed his General Orders No. 8 and ordered the Raleigh newspapers to print it. The order had first appeared on March 7 as his army was entering the Tar Heel State after cutting a destructive swath through South Carolina. The document noted that North Carolina was one of the last states to secede and had retained a strong Unionist element. "It should not be assumed that the inhabitants are enemies to our government," the order read, "and it is hoped that every effort will be made to prevent any wanton destruction of property or any unkind treatment of citizens."[18]

Union Maj. Gen. Oliver O. Howard, the commander of the Army of the Tennessee, likewise published General Field Orders No. 15, prohibiting the taking of animals or provisions from civilians without authorization from corps or division commanders. "Great disregard has been shown in many instances to the orders heretofore issued on this subject," the order read, "and many of the poor people of the surrounding country are entirely deprived of their provisions and of their animals, which are worthless to us, but are invaluable to them." Howard enjoined his subordinates to prevent the robbery of civilians by holding officers in charge of foraging details strictly accountable. He ordered the arrest of all men found outside camp without permission and offered to provide guards for citizens living within five miles of Raleigh. One of Howard's subordinates, Maj. Gen. John A. Logan, also issued an order directing that all wagons, tents, and knapsacks be searched for such contraband as women's clothing, watches, jewelry, shotguns, and silver plate. Logan stipulated that the inspections were to occur simultaneously and in the presence of a strong guard. The inspectors were to confiscate all unauthorized property. The depredations of unauthorized foragers, or "bummers," in Franklin County led Howard to send a detachment after the outlaws. Howard urged "all citizens beyond the lines . . . to afford our officers in charge of patrols and guards every possible facility for bringing to justice these marauders and stragglers, who are a disgrace to our army and to our country." Both Howard and Slocum ordered their commissary officers to distribute rations to needy families and several state institutions.[19]

The orders from Slocum and Howard indicate that the Union high command attempted to prevent the wholesale pillaging and robbery of North Carolina civilians. The commanders' influence extended only as far as the picket line, however, and efforts to curb infractions beyond that point largely failed. Sherman conceded that "it is idle to promise to protect the whole country, it can only be done partially," given the impossibility of providing guards for every home and farm in the countryside. In reply to a letter from David L. Swain appealing for aid to destitute citizens living near Chapel Hill, Sherman pledged that once "war ceases, and I think that time is at hand, all seizures of horses and private property will cease on our part, and it may be we will be able to spare some animals for the use of the farmers of your neighborhood." Much as he had promised Mayor Calhoun of Atlanta the previous September, Sherman assured Swain that once peace was made, "we will accept it and be the friends of the farmers and working classes of North Carolina, as well as actual patrons of churches, colleges, asylums, and all institutions of learning and charity."[20]

While Sherman and his subordinates held out the olive branch to Tar Heel civilians, the mood in Washington after Lincoln's assassination seemed far from conciliatory. Sherman learned from northern newspapers that the new commander in Richmond, Maj. Gen. Edward O. C. Ord, had been ordered to withdraw permission for the Virginia legislature to meet, boding ill for the article guaranteeing existing state governments. Northern papers also accused Jefferson Davis and other southern civilian leaders of complicity in the assassination plot. Sherman warned Johnston of the "changed feeling about Washington arising from this new and unforeseen complication," yet the Union commander still believed that there was "enough good sense left on this continent" for cooler heads to prevail. Although Sherman remained hopeful that his terms would be approved, he also braced himself for their rejection. Unaware of the furor gripping Washington, Sherman expected the authorities in the nation's capital to regard his agreement as a well-meaning attempt to reunite the country in a spirit of conciliation. Sherman would soon discover that he could not have been more mistaken.[21]

Early on the morning of April 24, 1865, General Grant arrived at the Governor's Palace in Raleigh to inform Sherman that President Johnson had rejected his terms and had ordered him to resume hostilities. Grant also showed his subordinate a letter from Secretary of War Edwin M. Stanton instructing the general-in-chief to "direct operations" in North Carolina, which angered Sherman. Grant then showed him another dispatch bearing Stanton's signature. The letter was dated March 3, 1865, and it was addressed to the general-in-chief, informing him that the president "wishes you to have no conference with General Lee, unless it be for the capitulation of General Lee's army or on some minor and purely military matter." Sherman later remarked that if Stanton had sent him the message sooner, it "would have saved a world of trouble."[22]

On April 24, Sherman sent Johnston two dispatches, the first ending the truce in forty-eight hours as agreed, and the second announcing that Sherman had received orders to undertake no civil negotiations and to include only Johnston's troops in the surrender. "I therefore demand the surrender of your army on the same terms as were given General Lee at Appomattox, . . . purely and simply," Sherman wrote. The dispatches arrived at Johnston's headquarters late that afternoon, about an hour after the Confederate commander had received President Davis's approval of Sherman's original terms. Johnston proposed another cease-fire to resume negotiations, and he stated that the Appomattox terms were inadequate. "The disbanding of General Lee's army has afflicted this country with numerous bands having no means of subsistence but robbery," Johnston wrote, "a knowledge of which would, I am sure, induce you to agree to other conditions."[23]

Sherman agreed to meet Johnston at the Bennett farm on April 26. Ignoring Stanton's order to "direct operations," Grant remained behind in Raleigh, but Sherman brought several of his lieutenants, including Maj. Gen. John M. Schofield, his second-in-command. The third conference inside the Bennett house began inauspiciously, for Johnston refused Sherman's offer of the Appomattox terms. While Sherman conceded the necessity of supplementary terms to provide for Johnston's men, he doubted that such an agreement would be approved in Washington. After further discussion proved fruitless, Sherman summoned Schofield to resolve their impasse. Schofield suggested drafting a surrender document virtually identical to the Appomattox agreement to satisfy President Johnson and a second document containing special terms for General Johnston's troops. Under Schofield's "Terms of a Military Convention,"

Johnston's men were "permitted to return to their homes, not to be disturbed by the United States authorities so long as they observe their obligation and the laws in force where they may reside." Schofield thus copied Grant's amnesty clause almost verbatim. This condition subsequently placed Grant and Sherman in the position of defending former enemies against northern jurists and politicians eager for revenge. As a point of honor, the federal commanders were determined to prevent any treason trials against former Confederate soldiers paroled under their agreements.[24]

Schofield's "Supplemental Terms" allowed the Confederates to retain their field transportation, as well as their private property, permitted one-seventh of the men to retain their arms for use in hunting and self-defense, and provided troops from the Trans-Mississippi with waterborne transportation to their homes. Schofield also provided rail transportation to homeward-bound ex-Confederates wherever possible. Sherman even offered Johnston a quarter-million rations from his coastal warehouses. "Now that war is over, I am as willing to risk my person and reputation as heretofore to heal the wounds made by the past war," Sherman wrote, perhaps recalling both his ill-fated "Memorandum" and his promise to share his last cracker with Mayor Calhoun of Atlanta. Sherman's gesture moved a grateful Johnston to reply that it "reconciles me to what I had previously regarded as the misfortune of my life—that of having had you to encounter in the field." In response to Sherman's order to cease all foraging, Johnston wrote, "The enlightened and humane policy you have adopted will certainly be successful."[25]

No sooner had Grant departed for Washington with the April 26 surrender agreement than northern newspapers condemning Sherman's first agreement with Johnston arrived at the North Carolina capital. Stanton himself led the assault in the pages of the *New York Times*, insinuating that Sherman had openly defied his civilian superiors by drafting a surrender agreement that granted the Rebels far more than they "had ever asked in their most prosperous condition." Stanton's news bulletin ensured the unanimity of the northern press in condemning Sherman's terms as a betrayal of Union war aims. Even Sherman's wife Ellen thought her husband had been too lenient to "perjured traitors," as she called her husband's former U.S. Army comrades in Confederate gray. Fortunately for Sherman, the North's outrage at his conciliatory terms proved as brief as it was violent. At the Grand Review in Washington, D.C., one month later, cheering throngs hailed the general as a conquering hero.[26]

Sherman nevertheless was deeply stung by the North's hostile reaction to his conciliatory terms, and he did not soon forget it. The general directed much of his anger and resentment at Stanton, whom he publicly snubbed during the Grand Review. Describing himself as thoroughly "untamed and unconquered," Sherman continued to assert that his first agreement was the best means of reuniting the country, for it relied on the southerners themselves to rebuild their devastated region, and it acknowledged that the war's devastation had already punished them sufficiently. "No matter what change we may desire in the feelings and thoughts of people South, we cannot accomplish it by force," the general wrote his brother, Republican senator John Sherman of Ohio, in September 1865. Sherman believed that a harsh Reconstruction policy would necessitate a substantial occupation force in the former Confederate states, and he doubted that the North would want to maintain a large peacetime army "to hold them in subjugation." He came to regard the presence of *any* federal troops in the South as "obnoxious to our ideas of Self Government." In November 1865, Sherman commented that President Johnson was "drifting toward my terms to Johnston. He cannot help it, for there is no other solution." Sherman believed that conciliation was the only viable means of restoring the South to the Union, and he regarded his "Memorandum" as the best blueprint for peace.[27]

In truth, Sherman's controversial first agreement was soon forgotten amid the victory celebrations in the North, and few Southerners became aware of the document—which is hardly surprising, given the confusion that reigned throughout the South after Lee's surrender. For all his good intentions, Sherman remained the most hated Yankee among white Southerners. Even the notorious Maj. Gen. Benjamin F. "Beast" Butler ran no better than a close second to "Uncle Billy." Raleigh author Mary Bayard Clarke expressed an opinion shared by most Southern women when she wrote, "Savage Sherman . . . had not the first conception of civilized warfare." He made war on defenseless women and children, she argued, "justifying his conduct by saying the South could never be conquered until the spirit of its women was broken." Clarke noted that Sherman's barbarous mode of warfare had "rendered him the object of deep, bitter, and burning hatred wherever he has gone."[28]

While Clarke's assessment was typical, some Tar Heels nonetheless gave the devil his due. In her 1866 history, *The Last Ninety Days of the War in North Carolina*, Chapel Hill resident Cornelia Phillips Spencer devoted several chapters to condemning Sherman's hard-war policy, yet she conceded that "General Sherman alone, of all the prominent men and leaders" of the North, "was at that time possessed of the requisite ability and statesmanship and magnanimity to . . . seize the opportunity . . . for an equitable adjustment of our difficulties." Spencer contended that had Sherman's first agreement been ratified, "the happiest results would have followed, and an immense amount of trouble, expense, and evil would have been avoided by the whole country." Speculating that Sherman may have been motivated by remorse for his past conduct, Spencer declared, "in the civil policy he has always advocated toward the South, he has shown himself at once generous and politic." While Spencer could not have been more mistaken as to Sherman's motives, she was one of relatively few white Southerners who viewed Sherman as a generous victor as well as a ruthless practitioner of "hard war."[29]

In March 1867, when confronted with the grim prospect of Military Reconstruction, the editor of the *Wilmington Dispatch* fondly recalled Sherman's first agreement and condemned "the shortsightedness of President Johnson" in refusing to ratify terms that "would have rid the arena of politics of much embittered strife which has since brought both sections nigh unto entire ruin." The editor predicted that Sherman would be North Carolina's military governor, and he was "pleased to believe" that if the general was "stained with an infamy that cannot be effaced, he at least has the merit of wisdom and forecast, and is not wholly abandoned to a thirst for vengeance." In truth, Sherman wanted no part of occupation duty in the South, and he managed to avoid serving there during the postwar years.[30]

Having completed his work in North Carolina, Sherman departed Raleigh on April 28, 1865, after announcing "a final agreement with General Johnston which terminates the war as to the armies under his command." As a parting gesture, Sherman authorized his army commanders to loan surplus wagons and draft animals and issue supplies to needy citizens "to relieve present wants and to encourage the inhabitants to renew their peaceful pursuits and to restore the relations of friendship among our fellow-citizens and countrymen." Sherman ordered the Army of Georgia under Slocum and the Army of the Tennessee under Howard to march to Washington, D.C., leaving Schofield in command of the Department of North Carolina. Kilpatrick's cavalry and the Army of the Ohio would serve as the occupation force in the Tar Heel State. It now remained to be seen if Schofield and his subordinates would pursue Sherman's conciliatory policy.[31]

Chapter Two

MILITARY RULE BY DEFAULT

Schofield's One-Month Regime

As the occupation commander in North Carolina, General Schofield presided over a state that lacked a civil government. President Andrew Johnson's repudiation of Sherman's first agreement had made it clear that the governor, the General Assembly, and other state and local officials would not be permitted to resume their former duties. Unlike Arkansas, Louisiana, Tennessee, and Virginia, the Old North State possessed no Lincoln-sponsored, Unionist government to fill the vacuum. In mid-1862 Lincoln had appointed a native Tar Heel, Edward Stanly, as military governor, but in January 1863, the proslavery Stanly resigned in protest over the Emancipation Proclamation. Disappointed over the absence of loyal sentiment in Union-held areas of North Carolina, Lincoln decided against replacing Stanly and installing a Unionist government. North Carolina therefore would remain under martial law until the resumption of civil government in the Tar Heel State. Much to Schofield's annoyance, President Johnson failed to act during the critical first month after the surrender. Shortly after assuming command, an impatient Schofield wrote that the people of North Carolina were willing to accept almost any plan "which promises a definite settlement." Schofield believed that Johnson was squandering an irretrievable opportunity to conciliate North Carolinians by swiftly restoring their state to the Union. In truth, the opportunity was not as golden as Schofield supposed.[1]

Maj. Gen. John M. Schofield (Library of Congress)

Thirty-three-year-old John McAllister Schofield possessed considerable experience as a wartime occupation commander in Missouri, Tennessee, and North Carolina. Perhaps this was only fitting, for the portly, balding Schofield more closely resembled a deskbound bureaucrat than a warrior. A West Point graduate (class of 1853), Schofield served as Brig.

Gen. Nathaniel Lyon's chief of staff in the 1861 Battle of Wilson's Creek. For the next two-and-a-half years, Schofield saw little field service and spent much of that time commanding the Department of Missouri, an administrative post. Beginning in May 1864 he commanded the Army of the Ohio under Sherman during the Atlanta Campaign, and in late 1864, he led the Twenty-third Corps under Maj. Gen. George H. Thomas in Tennessee. In repulsing Gen. John Bell Hood's Army of Tennessee at Franklin, Schofield dealt the Confederates a crippling blow. Two weeks later, Schofield participated in the Union attacks that nearly annihilated Hood's army at Nashville. In early 1865, Schofield and his Twenty-third Corps were transferred to North Carolina by rail and ship. On his arrival, Schofield assumed command of the Department of North Carolina. As noted in chapter 1, Schofield's shrewd advice to Sherman and Johnston to draft two surrender agreements neatly resolved the commanders' dilemma and indicated that Schofield possessed the skill to effect a smooth transition from war to peace in the Tar Heel State.[2]

On April 27, 1865, Schofield issued two orders that heralded a new state of affairs within his department. General Orders No. 31 announced an end to the war in North Carolina: "It is now the duty of all to cultivate friendly relations with the same zeal which has characterized our conduct of the war." Schofield urged soldiers and civilians alike to "cordially unite in honest endeavors to accomplish this great end." The commanding general offered protection to all law-abiding citizens, whereas "those who disturb the peace or violate the laws will be punished with the severity of martial law." Schofield also promised to issue provisions and loan captured draft animals and wagons to the destitute. Until a civilian constabulary could be recruited, Schofield assigned his soldiers a new peacekeeping role. Their mission was "to secure the interests of the U.S. Government and protect the people until a civil government can be established in harmony with the Constitution and laws of the United States."[3]

General Orders No. 32 declared all slaves free by virtue of the Emancipation Proclamation and stipulated that it was the army's duty to ensure their freedom. Schofield exhorted former slaveholders to pay their freedmen a fair wage and advised erstwhile slaves to continue working for their former masters. Should this prove impossible, Schofield warned, the freedpeople must find work elsewhere and avoid congregating in towns and military camps, for they would "not be supported in idleness."[4]

After Sherman's departure, Schofield's first item of business was to parole Johnston's army in accordance with the final surrender agreement. On April 29, Schofield learned from Johnston that most of his cavalry was riding off in defiance of the agreement and the Confederate commander was powerless to stop them. Schofield feared that the deserters "will give us no little trouble, and keep the country in a disturbed condition for a long time. But we must deal with them as best we can." The two generals arranged the distribution of paroles and the collection of arms. On April 30, Schofield would send staff officers and parole forms to designated sites on the North Carolina Railroad. Every officer and man in Johnston's command would receive a parole form. Brigade commanders would retain the paroles of their men for as long as possible to preserve a semblance of organization during the homeward journey.[5]

The issuing of paroles began on May 1. On the following day, Schofield and Twenty-third Corps commander Maj. Gen. Jacob D. Cox traveled by rail from Raleigh to Johnston's headquarters at Greensboro. Aware of depredations committed by Lee's hungry and footsore veterans as they passed through North Carolina en route to their homes, Schofield told Johnston that he would fulfill Sherman's promise of a quarter-million rations to the Confederate troops, let them keep their wagons and teams, and furnish them with railroad transportation wherever possible. For his part, Johnston assured Schofield that his men were laying down their arms with the intention of keeping their paroles in good faith. That night, Governor Zebulon B. Vance met with Schofield and learned from the general that neither the governor nor any other state official would be retained in office. Vance thereupon surrendered himself, but Schofield informed the ex-governor that he had no orders for Vance's arrest. In that case, Vance replied, he would rejoin his family at Statesville and remain there should the general wish to summon him.[6]

On May 3, Schofield returned to Raleigh, leaving Cox in command at Greensboro. Cox had brought only one regiment, the 104th Ohio Infantry, in deference to Johnston, who feared that a large Union presence might result in bloodshed. After glimpsing the unruly Confederate multitude at Greensboro, Cox immediately summoned the 9th New Jersey Infantry to assist the Ohioans in keeping the peace and guarding the immense stockpile of arms and accoutrements. The rest of Cox's Twenty-third Corps and two brigades of Kilpatrick's cavalry would begin arriving within a few days—and not a moment too soon. One of Schofield's staff officers, Col. William Hartsuff, noted that the Confederates at Greensboro were "raising the devil." The situation appeared volatile.[7]

Fortunately for all concerned, no hostilities between Yankees and Rebels erupted. On the contrary, most Confederate units simply stacked their arms—unlike the surrender at Appomattox, no Union soldiers were present—and then began their journey home. A notable exception was the 104th Ohio's relief of the town's Confederate garrison. First, the Confederate commandant, Brig. Gen. John D. Kennedy, formally turned over the Post of Greensboro to the commander of the 104th Ohio, Lt. Col. William J. Jordan. Then, as details of the 104th arrived at their new posts, they were met by soldiers from Kennedy's South Carolina brigade, the Confederates stacking arms while the Ohioans looked on. At the conclusion, the former enemies shook hands and wished each other well, though there were a few grumblers on either side.[8]

On May 4, the 9th New Jersey arrived at Greensboro and immediately went on guard duty to assist the 104th Ohio. At dawn the next day, two companies of the 9th boarded a train for Salisbury and Charlotte, the first of Schofield's troops sent to either point. Lt. David Kille's Company I reached Salisbury at 10:30 A.M. to collect Confederate arms and ammunition. Kille's company completed its task within a few days and returned to Greensboro. Capt. Morris C. Runyan's Company G traveled on toward Charlotte and soon found its task far more difficult than Company I's had been.[9]

Captain Runyan and his company had to abandon their train at a creek just north of Concord because Union Maj. Gen. George Stoneman's cavalry had destroyed the bridge. They also discovered that the raiders had cut the telegraph lines to Salisbury and Greensboro. As they crossed the creek en route to Charlotte, Runyan and his men knew they were on their own; for much of their march, they were surrounded by hundreds of homeward-bound Confederates.[10]

When Runyan reached Charlotte late on the afternoon of May 7, he found the town in a state of chaos. Bands of lawless Confederates roamed the streets, terrorizing the citizens. "Drunkenness and disorder generally" were "the order of the day," Runyan reported. Assuming command of the Post of Charlotte, Runyan immediately placed guards at the powder magazine and warehouses, formed around-the-clock patrols, issued provisions to starving soldiers and civilians, and banned the sale of alcohol. By this means, the Union soldiers soon restored order.[11]

While inspecting a warehouse, Runyan made a startling discovery when he uncovered stacks of captured U.S. flags and regimental colors and eighty-odd boxes containing Confederate documents. Learning that

Joseph E. Johnston was in town and had keys to the warehouse, Runyan requested the former Confederate general to meet him. Johnston informed the captain that the boxes in question contained papers of the Confederate War Department. Johnston reported the abandoned documents to Schofield, who sent his quartermaster to Charlotte to retrieve them. Not only had Runyan and his company established order at Charlotte quietly and without bloodshed, but also they had preserved a priceless cache of source material for future generations of historians.[12]

As Runyan's experience at Charlotte had demonstrated, Schofield's top priority was to restore security and stability in his department. In addition to the exodus of freedpeople and white refugees into North Carolina's already overcrowded towns, thousands of Confederate deserters and paroled veterans passed through the Tar Heel State en route to their homes. Lawlessness prevailed in much of the state. Numerous citizens' committees urged Union occupation commanders to send troops to their communities to protect them from marauders. Several of the bolder outlaw bands preyed on soldiers as well as civilians. Near Fayetteville, desperadoes robbed a squad of the 13th Pennsylvania Cavalry. A detachment of picked men under Capt. Michael O'Shea pursued the outlaws and surrounded their camp on the South Carolina border. Col. Thomas T. Heath reported that the robbers "were desperate characters, fought hotly, and asked no quarter. Not one of their number escaped the penalty of their crimes." The soldiers' possessions were found on the bodies of the slain outlaws.[13]

In early May, Schofield deployed his forty-six thousand troops across North Carolina. The Tenth Corps and Heath's cavalry brigade under Maj. Gen. Alfred H. Terry occupied the eastern half, while the Twenty-third Corps and Jordan's and Atkins's cavalry brigades under Maj. Gen. Jacob D. Cox held the western half. On the coast, Brig. Gen. Innis N. Palmer commanded the District of Beaufort and Brig. Gen. Joseph R. Hawley the District of Wilmington. A native Tar Heel, Hawley had moved with his family to Connecticut when he was eleven. Schofield ordered his command to "visit all parts of the State, disperse or capture all bands of guerrillas and marauders, and collect all military arms," except weapons exempted by the April 26 surrender terms. He further directed his subordinates to organize a civilian police force in each county within their districts. All recruits had to take a loyalty oath, as well as an oath to "preserve the peace" and "obey all lawful orders of the military authorities." The police would hand over all those under arrest "to the nearest military post for trial by military commission." Schofield's last provision left no doubt that North Carolina remained under martial law.[14]

During the final days of April and the first week of May, thousands of Union soldiers marched to their new posts; their conduct en route was strictly regulated. Brig. Gen. Charles J. Paine's marching orders were typical, but his command was not. Paine commanded a division of U.S. Colored Troops (USCT)—the only black foot soldiers in Schofield's occupation force. They were to march sixty miles from Raleigh to Goldsboro. Paine ordered the commanding officer of the lead brigade to post a guard at each house along the route, with instructions to remain until the column had passed and to "allow no one to interfere with the persons or property of the residents." No animals, food, forage, or other property was to be taken without permission from Paine himself. No firing of weapons or straggling would be permitted, and officers were to arrest all violators. Paine directed that the march be "conducted as if in a friendly country," the as if indicating that he anticipated a less than friendly reception from the citizens along the soldiers' route.[15]

At Smithfield, Paine's men found the Neuse River bridge burned, compelling them to wade a stream that was chin-deep in places. Many of the soldiers stripped and crossed nude, their uniforms hanging from their bayonets. "I was much amused to see the secesh [secessionist] women watching with the utmost intensity, thousands of our soldiers, in a state of nudity," wrote Chaplain Henry M. Turner of the 1st USCT. "I suppose they desired to see whether these audacious Yankees were really men, made like other men, or if they were a set of varmints. So they thronged the windows, porticos and yards, in the finest attire imaginable." As the nude soldiers strode past "the feminine gazers," it appeared to Turner that the black men were telling the white women: "Yes, though naked, we are your masters." Even with their clothes on, the black soldiers often caused white bystanders to stare in mute disbelief. "The rebel party steps to one side," Chaplain Turner observed during the march into Goldsboro, "and onward goes the negro van, looking neither to the right or left." The onlookers gazed "at these magic lords, swaggering on in their exultant conquest," and seemed "to be musing as to whether they are actually in another world, or whether this one is turned wrong side out, until they finally resume their equilibrium."[16]

Despite the experience of Paine's troops, the new marching orders reflected the changed attitude of both soldiers and civilians now that peace had returned to North Carolina. Pvt. Leonard A. Boyd, an Illinois soldier in the all-white Twenty-third Corps, noted "a great change in our marching from Raleigh" to Greensboro: "Not a thing disturbed, hardly an onion pulled." Contrary to Paine's expectations, Boyd found "the citizens pleasant all the way from the fact of the war being over." Because they were white, Boyd and his comrades doubtless met with a much friendlier reception than did Paine's soldiers.[17]

Although most Union soldiers behaved themselves while on the march, the conduct of the 10th Ohio Cavalry proved the exception. While clearing away some brush to make camp near Company Shops in Alamance County, several men of the 10th found $57,000 in gold buried in boxes marked, "Bank of Commerce, New Berne, N.C." The finders shrewdly divided the money with several of their officers and claimed the coin as spoils of war—though the war had been over in North Carolina for more than a week when they made their discovery. Bank of Commerce officials therefore appealed to General Kilpatrick for assistance, and Kilpatrick ordered his inspector, Capt. Edward R. Brink, to recover the gold. Meanwhile, Schofield learned of the affair and termed Brink's recovery effort "a farce." He ordered Kilpatrick to arrest all suspects and recover the money: "Do not let the disgrace of such an affair as this attach to your command." Only $16,000 of the gold was recovered, in part because Kilpatrick allowed three of the suspects to escape. Kilpatrick's mishandling of the affair casts suspicion on his role in the theft.[18]

Once the troops had reached their stations, their commanding officers began sending out detachments to confiscate arms and raise local police companies. Maj. George F. Towle accompanied one such detail of Pennsylvania soldiers from Raleigh to Pittsboro, the Chatham County seat. As the column approached the town, Towle decided to ride ahead and reconnoiter. A small black boy astride an ox preceded him. The boy shouted, "The Yankees are coming. The Yankees are coming." As Towle rode down the main street of Pittsboro, the residents rushed to their doors, making the major feel "much more conspicuous than I cared to be." Towle halted at the courthouse, and he soon found himself surrounded by curious townspeople. He assured the citizens that the soldiers were not going to arrest anyone or destroy the town. Towle learned that Sherman's notorious bummers had not visited Pittsboro, making his detachment the first Yankees the locals had seen. This might explain why the major "was most kindly treated" during his stay. He found the town "quiet and sleepy but comfortable looking" but detected "no Union sentiment here whatever."[19]

If Towle could find no Unionists in Pittsboro, 324 citizens never-theless deemed it expedient to take the oath of allegiance, reported the commander of the detachment. A New York officer stationed at Greens-boro likewise commented on the willingness of Tar Heel civilians "to conform quietly to the new order of things." Col. William H. Walling of the 142nd New York Infantry commanded a detachment sent to raise a local police force at Hillsborough. Walling wrote that the citizens "treated me very kindly and one of them remarked if they could always meet such Yankees as I had with me they would have no more war with them on any account." Capt. James McCartney commanded a company of the 112th Illinois Infantry sent to protect Stokes County on the Virginia bor-der. Finding the residents "as pleasant and hospitable as any people I have ever seen anywhere," McCartney rode alone through the sparsely settled countryside unarmed and "in perfect safety." From Wilmington, General Hawley reported, "the general sentiment of the people hereabouts is ex-pressed by about these words: 'For God's sake, tell us what we must do and we'll do it.'"[20]

The experiences of many Union occupation troops suggested that North Carolinians were resigned to the outcome of the war, but other sol-diers detected signs of recalcitrance. The commanding officer at Franklin-ton in Franklin County confided to his superior that it required "all his forbearance at times to endure the arrogance and insolence daily exhib-ited by a part of the community." In Greensboro, Col. Thomas J. Hen-derson attended a citizens' meeting at the Guilford County Courthouse. "It was a dull, cold, lifeless meeting," a disappointed Henderson wrote: "The people did not meet the occasion with a becoming spirit—there was no feeling, no enthusiasm, and one could hardly realize that they were just emerging from under the dark cloud of war into the glorious sunlight of peace." Henderson concluded that "they are not fully purged of their disloyalty—they are still clinging to slavery as if they could retain it." Believing that the citizens needed to hear "words of truth and sober-ness," Henderson accepted their invitation to address them in a second meeting a few nights later. The general spoke "very plainly and earnestly," informing his audience "that they were responsible for the calamities which had come upon them, that there was no hope and ought not to be for slavery." The sooner they "addressed themselves to the great work of resuming their former relations to the Government, of restoring law and order and of building up their state under the new order of things," Hen-derson counseled, "the better it would be for them, the Nation, and the

World." As he doubtless expected, Henderson observed that some in the audience "were most offended & thought I was severe," but, he insisted, "it was what they needed." Several weeks later, Henderson noticed an improved attitude among the citizens of Greensboro. They were holding Union meetings and "acknowledging slavery as dead," yet, Henderson conceded, "there are those who give up the Institution very unwillingly, and especially the women."[21]

In at least one instance, hostilities erupted between soldiers and civilians. Near Clinton in Sampson County, a detachment of the 1st USCT briefly skirmished with a band of mounted guerrillas, who avoided capture by outracing their pursuers. The commander of the detachment, Capt. H. P. Thompson, reported seeing several other guerrilla bands, but they fired no more shots. Another matter of concern to Union occupation commanders was vigilante justice dispensed by volunteer home guard companies. One such company, the Columbus Union Regulators, arrested alleged wrongdoers and then tried them in their own kangaroo court. The commander of the District of Wilmington, Brig. Gen. Joseph R. Hawley, reported that another Columbus County company recently had crossed into South Carolina and shot nine men who reputedly were guerrillas and robbers. "I shall endeavor to put an end to such summary transactions," Hawley assured Schofield. But Hawley added that "the citizens are all very anxious to get information, instructions, and advice, and it seems to me that judicious counsel will do much to hasten a complete pacification."[22]

Much to Schofield's dismay, there was as yet no guidance from Washington. "I hope the Government will make known its policy as to organization of State governments without delay," Schofield wrote Sherman on May 5. "Affairs must necessarily be in a very unsettled state until that is done. The people are now in a mood to accept almost anything which promises a definite settlement." Schofield viewed the fate of the freedpeople as "the question of all," and "the all-important question" requiring "prompt and wise action to prevent the negro from becoming a huge elephant on our hands. If I am to govern this State," Schofield asserted, "it is important for me to know it at once. If another is to be sent here it cannot be done too soon, for he will probably undo the most of what I shall have done." When combined with his warning to the ex-slaves that they would "not be supported in idleness," Schofield's "elephant" statement indicates that he regarded the freedpeople rather than the ex-Confederates as the source of his problems. The general shared at least one assumption with the former slaveholders. He believed emancipation had rendered the freedpeople an indolent labor force content to subsist indefinitely on government rations until compelled to work for their livelihood. Like other commanders in the South, Schofield nonetheless realized that blacks had to be protected, for they could easily be neglected, exploited, or abused by hostile whites.[23]

Schofield's concern prompted him to issue an order specifying the obligations of both the freedpeople and the ex-slaveholders. He directed that in child rearing, parents and guardians were to assume the authority and responsibility once held by their former masters. In the absence of parents or other relatives, ex-masters would serve as guardians for minors, the sick, and the aged. Persons not yet twenty-one remained under the control of their parents or guardians and were therefore expected to contribute to the support of their families. Former masters could not evict or neglect the aged, the sick, or the young, and able-bodied adult freedpeople were likewise prohibited from abandoning their families and living in idleness. Independent adults were free to move wherever they could find employment, but they would receive no support from the government or their former masters unless they worked. In negotiating wages with their employers, laborers should expect to receive for the present only modest pay or a share of the crop. Schofield enjoined all soldiers and white civilians to inform the freedpeople of their new rights and responsibilities, and he ordered all army officers and county police chiefs to enforce the regulations.[24]

Schofield's order also implemented a mechanism for relocating the thousands of refugees inundating North Carolina. Although Congress had recently established the Bureau of Refugees, Freedmen, and Abandoned Lands—or Freedmen's Bureau—to handle such matters, it had not yet set up shop in North Carolina. Much as other Union generals had done during the war, Schofield created his own interim freedmen's agency. He directed each district commander to appoint a commissioned officer as superintendent of freedmen and several assistants "to take charge of all the freed people in his district, who are without homes or proper employment." The superintendents' task was threefold: arrange the return of refugees to their homes; secure food, shelter, and work for the homeless; and hear all complaints involving freedpeople and report the facts to their district commanders, who had authority to settle the disputes.[25]

Although Schofield's order set forth the obligations of freedpeople and former masters alike, his repeated admonitions to the ex-slaves against idleness revealed his true preoccupation. To encourage refugees to return to their homes, Schofield directed local commanders to provide them with railroad passes and rations, but he cautioned that they must not be given passage to Raleigh or the coast, "nor be permitted to congregate about towns or camps, there to live in idleness," a familiar refrain in Schofield's orders and dispatches.[26]

Schofield was too fixed in his prejudices regarding "idle" freedpeople to consider that many were flocking to the towns in search of protection or lost family members and would willingly return to work once they were reassured on both counts. Others were "trying out" their freedom by traveling at their own discretion, a privilege rarely granted to slaves. In 1867, a Freedmen's Bureau official reported that he received few complaints of "lazy" freedpeople in his district. At the end of the war, he recalled, many former slaves "could not realize that they really were free so long as they remained at their old homes, and a perfect mania seemed to possess them to go some where or anywhere so they could enjoy this new found liberty." The bureau official noted that most freedpeople eventually returned to their "old neighborhoods, satisfied with the experience they gained in their wanderings." According to the head of the Freedmen's Bureau in North Carolina, "the great mass of colored people have remained quietly at work upon the plantations of their former masters during the entire summer" of 1865. In August, the issue of rations declined from 215,285 to 156,289. By October, only 5,000 of the state's 350,000 freedpeople were receiving government rations. In any event, the government discouraged long-term dependency by ensuring that the rations were barely sufficient to keep the recipients alive.[27]

On May 7, Schofield received a letter from U.S. Supreme Court Chief Justice Salmon P. Chase at Morehead City. At President Johnson's behest, Chase was on an inspection tour of the southern states. An advocate of giving black men the vote, Chase recommended that North Carolina voters be registered under the state's first constitution to give voting rights to all free citizens. In a May 10 letter to General Grant, Schofield contended that Chase's proposal would "lead to disastrous results." The amended constitution barring free men of color was still in force, the general argued, "and no power on earth but the people of the State can alter it . . . without first altering or else violating the Constitution of the United States."[28]

Schofield further contended that most freedmen were illiterate and ignorant of law, government, and even "the meaning of the freedom that has been given them." He noted that they were "much astonished when informed that it does not mean that they are to live in idleness and be fed by the Government." Although Schofield conceded that blacks were "docile, obedient, and anxious to learn," he advised that they should be educated before being given "an equal voice" in government. He asserted that if southern whites "did not rebel against it, it would only be because rebellion would be hopeless. A government so organized would in no sense be a popular government." Grant agreed with Schofield that the adoption of black suffrage might trigger widespread violence in the South. Both generals advised waiting until blacks had become qualified voters. In doing so, they sought to conciliate southern whites.[29]

In his letter to Grant, Schofield outlined a plan of reconstruction for North Carolina. The department commander recommended appointing a military governor who would declare the state's antebellum laws and constitution in force as long as they did not conflict with the U.S. Constitution or any wartime presidential proclamations. The military governor would command the state's occupation force, appoint temporary sheriffs and other officials, and call an election for delegates to a state convention. Schofield would require the convention to repudiate secession, abolish slavery, resume federal-state relations, and order the election of a governor and state legislature. The acts of the convention would then be submitted to the people for ratification. Should the convention fail to accomplish its requisite tasks, Schofield recommended dissolving it and placing the state once more under military government "until the people should come to their senses." Should Chase's black suffrage proposal be adopted, Schofield indicated that he was "not the proper person to carry it out." Grant agreed with Schofield's views, but he reminded his subordinate that "the military authorities can do nothing but keep the peace" until the federal government introduced its reconstruction plan.[30]

Although Schofield could not restore civil government in North Carolina, he was authorized to resume trade in the Tar Heel State. He prohibited only the sale of arms, ammunition, and other contraband of war. Schofield directed his subordinates to encourage the resumption of trade in their districts by protecting merchants, customers, and their goods. While sections of the state's railroads and telegraph lines remained under military control, Schofield permitted the rest to be owner-operated as long as all company officers and employees swore a loyalty oath. Schofield even ordered his subordinates to reappoint twelve loyal justices of the peace for each county within their commands.[31]

Given the lack of guidance from Washington, it is hardly surprising that Schofield and his subordinates occasionally exceeded their authority, as in the case of a provost court in New Bern established by the department commander. After reports reached the War Department that the court was trying civil cases, Schofield received peremptory orders to limit the court's jurisdiction to military affairs.[32]

Schofield nevertheless wielded his authority with restraint, even when provoked by what he considered "intolerable ingratitude" on the part of John L. Pennington, the editor and publisher of the *Raleigh Progress*. The general rebuked Pennington for an editorial that criticized the military authorities in Raleigh for using private homes and offices after the close of hostilities. "We have the right to grumble," the *Progress* asserted, but Schofield thought otherwise. "If you or any other citizens feel aggrieved by the conduct of any in the army," he informed Pennington, "your remedy is to apply to me or other commanders having jurisdiction in the case. The public is not the tribunal authorized to judge of such matters, and their public discussion will not be tolerated." Offered the choice of either printing Schofield's letter or suspending publication of his newspaper, Pennington published the letter and thus escaped with a warning.[33]

Concerning Vance and other wartime state officials, Schofield believed that it was "wiser to treat them with contempt than to make lions of them." In late April, Schofield had even considered retaining Vance as governor. In mid-May, however, President Johnson ordered Vance's arrest and confinement at Old Capitol Prison in Washington, D.C., and Schofield had to comply. He relayed the order to General Cox at Greensboro. Like Schofield, Cox privately disapproved of Vance's arrest, believing a general amnesty the best means of pacifying the South. But orders had to be obeyed. Cox instructed Kilpatrick to send a squadron of cavalry to arrest Vance at Statesville, where the ex-governor was staying with his family. Vance was arrested on May 13, his thirty-fifth birthday; he was freed on July 6 to care for his ailing wife.[34]

Acting in the spirit of General Orders No. 31, Schofield attempted to relieve the postwar suffering of North Carolinians. In response to an appeal from the citizens of Fayetteville, Schofield authorized the shipment of fifteen thousand rations to the town, which had been stripped of provisions by Sherman's army. Throughout the month of May, he issued free rations to civilians, and in June, ordered thirty days' meat and flour distributed to persons deemed "absolutely destitute." The general also permitted his subordinates to loan surplus draft animals to needy farmers. To prevent the spread of disease in Raleigh, Schofield ordered the relocation of refugees from cramped quarters in town to camps and abandoned barracks in the suburbs.[35]

Schofield's subordinates took similar steps to aid North Carolinians, but chaotic conditions often made their task difficult. During the first few weeks after Johnston's surrender, Greensboro teemed with thousands of paroled Confederates, former slaves, and indigent whites, including women "laying around the streets in perfect vulgarity," observed Lt. Redmond F. Laswell of the 120th Indiana Infantry. "Evry thing is quiet in Camp but not so in town," Laswell continued. "There are so many country women laying around on the streets that it keeps a continual uproar with the [Confederate] soldiers." Laswell also resented the fact that many former Rebels were "getting some of Uncle Sams grub to live on after trying to kill all of his boys inother day." The Union army's issue of provisions to ex-Confederates resulted in short rations for the bluecoats, which only added to their resentment. A disapproving federal officer watched a continual procession of "Rebel officers" ride through town wearing their side arms and behaving "haughty and insolently." The Union soldiers at Greensboro nevertheless remained under strict orders to avoid confrontations with their former enemies; aside from apprehending outlaws, they managed to comply.[36]

The commander at Greensboro, General Cox, agreed with Schofield that it was better to exercise restraint than rule with an iron fist. Cox furnished safeguards and provisions to those who requested them, encouraged local businesses to reopen, and directed civic officials to resume their duties. The general also ordered Greensboro's streets cleaned and swept, contracting unemployed blacks to do the work. Many townspeople chipped in by tidying up their yards and homes. The commandant of the Post of Raleigh, Col. George F. Granger, likewise ordered soldiers and civilians to cooperate in cleaning up the state capital's streets, public grounds, and private residences, and he distributed rations to needy citizens.[37]

In North Carolina's western counties, outlaw bands roamed the countryside, robbing, looting, and killing with impunity—that is, until the arrival of Union troops. The desperadoes consisted of Union deserters, former Confederate soldiers, and local civilians, with the gangs sometimes masquerading as federal or home guard units. "At first we were threatened by armed mobs of Confederate soldiers, deserters &c,"

wrote Lincolnton resident David Schenck, "but, the Yankees put them down where they were, and in our town we dispersed a large mob by promptly arming our citizens and defying their power." After they arrested nine of the ringleaders, the soldiers and civilians quickly restored order in Lincolnton. A grateful Schenck praised the discipline of the federal troops, noting that "under their control and power we live in peace and quiet."[38]

In response to reports of outrages by guerrillas in Henderson and Transylvania counties, Cox ordered Kilpatrick to send a detachment there to "hunt out" the desperadoes and "pacify" the region. Cox suggested that "an example of an execution by drumhead court-martial would, I think, be necessary to make all banditti understand that they are in fact outlaws." The assignment fell to Maj. William C. Stevens and one hundred officers and men of the 9th Michigan Cavalry. In addition to pacifying the two western counties, Stevens had orders to confiscate all firearms and then organize and arm a few local police companies.[39]

When Stevens and his detachment arrived at Hendersonville, they "met with a warm reception . . . , the citizens being greatly pleased to have some troops here." He learned that "quite a number of robberies and several murders" had been committed during the past month, but that no outrages had been reported within the past ten days. Stevens reported that Unionists had committed most of the recent crimes to avenge past wrongs suffered at the hands of Rebels. The major found his situation "rather a peculiar one," in that former Confederates complained to him of recent depredations, while Unionists reported crimes committed against them during the war. Stevens noted that many accusers were friends or relatives of persons allegedly "killed by home guards for their disloyalty to the so-called Confederate government." Presented with a host of unsubstantiated charges from Unionists and ex-Confederates, Stevens decided that the most evenhanded policy was to make no arrests at all. Within a few weeks of his arrival, Stevens shifted his attention from suppressing outlaws to mediating the "difficulty" between the freedpeople and their former masters. He believed that it would "take some time" before the ex-slaves "are made to learn that freedom does not mean plenty to eat, drink & wear with nothing to do." As the "judge and jury for three or four counties," Stevens spent most of his day adjudicating disputes over horses and mules or in defining "the status of the negro, which is not a very pleasant task." Like Schofield, Stevens soon discovered that the fate of the freedpeople was "the all-important question," even though the major presided over a region with few blacks. Stevens also shared Schofield's assumption that the ex-slaves would not work unless they were compelled to do so.[40]

Many Union soldiers had expected to fight partisan bands after the war, but they were "much disappointed, and agreeably so," wrote Col. Thomas J. Henderson, "that the Guerrilla warfare which it was anticipated would give us so much trouble has hushed up as suddenly and surprisingly as the Great War itself." Now that the war was over in North Carolina and all violent resistance to federal authority apparently had ceased, the occupation troops settled into the dull routine of camp life. Their duties consisted mainly of guard detail and company drill. "This quiet duty is getting tiresome," Col. Thomas J. Jordan wrote his wife: "The total want of excitement is too common place, after the active campaigns just closed." The return of peace also meant tighter regulations for the enlisted men. Illinois Pvt. Benjamin W. Todd complained that "the officers are very strict since the fighting is done[.] They put on a great deal of style. We have to come out with our shoes blacked and our arms as bright as Silver[.]" Many enlisted men understood the necessity of strict discipline during wartime, but they believed that with the arrival of peace, their officers could afford to relax discipline "nearly if not quite to the point of having no discipline," wrote Lt. William A. Ketcham of the 13th Indiana Infantry. Most officers disagreed, Ketcham noted, and the loftier their rank, the less inclined they were to share the privates' viewpoint. The officers reasoned that the Union was now restored and discipline should therefore "be much closer and sharper in order that nothing should be done that would create friction between the soldiers of our army" and the former Confederates who were once again their fellow citizens. Another reason for strict discipline was that boredom and homesickness had induced many soldiers to drink heavily. As a result, brawling had become "a common diversion" among the men, observed Sgt. Edmund J. Cleveland of the 9th New Jersey Infantry.[41]

"We count the days till we can return [home]," Lieutenant Ketcham wrote his aunt in Indiana. "I have felt more homesick since [Johnston's] surrender than I have at any time since I have been in the army except whilst I was in the Hospital." According to Ketcham, the soldiers believed that, having "put down the rebellion," they "ought to be permitted to go home." Most bluecoats viewed the prospect of occupation duty with repugnance. "I don't like the idea of being a soldier in my own country," Capt. Dwight Fraser of the 128th Indiana Infantry wrote his sister, "and for the purpose of making the people respect the Laws now that there are no rebellious armies in the field. It looks now as if we ought to get away from these people right off," Fraser contended. "I think they have had all the war with the North that this and the next generation will want, and if we let them alone I am sure that they will behave."[42]

Some of the occupation commanders appeared no more eager than the privates to remain on duty in the Tar Heel State. Responding to a citizens' petition calling for his appointment as military governor of North Carolina, Brig. Gen. Innis N. Palmer wrote President Johnson that he had "no desire to have my name presented to you as an applicant for any position connected with the Government of this State." Upon hearing a rumor that he was to replace Schofield, Maj. Gen. Alfred H. Terry asked General Hawley at Wilmington to sound out Chief Justice Chase on the subject and "to 'stamp upon it' at once" if the rumor proved true.[43]

Anxious to comply with the desire of homesick volunteer soldiers, the War Department began demobilizing Schofield's occupation force in late May. Longstanding distrust of large peacetime armies and a determination to avoid the heavy financial burden of maintaining such a force were the most compelling reasons for rapid demobilization, but Stanton and Grant were also confident that Regular Army units would be sufficient to replace the volunteer regiments in the former Confederate states. Of course, demobilization could not move rapidly enough to suit the volunteer troops, but the process succeeded in reducing the occupation force in the Tar Heel State from 43,948 in June 1865 to 2,209 in January 1866.[44]

To enable the white troops to return home as quickly as possible, the War Department retained most of the black regiments, especially those from southern states. In June, there were forty-eight white and ten black regiments in North Carolina; by September, there were six black and only five white regiments. Like their white comrades, many black troops in the Tar Heel State suffered from homesickness. Sgt. N. B. Sterrett of the 39th USCT observed that most soldiers in his regiment thought it "unjust" that they should remain behind, "exposed to diseases and hardship," while the white soldiers returned home. In a letter to the *Christian Recorder*, Sterrett admitted, "we would like to return to our families and homes," but he counseled his comrades, "Wait patiently, men! God will see that justice is done us." This policy was not as unjust as it might appear, for most of the white soldiers had entered the army before their black comrades.[45]

Schofield authorized District of Wilmington commander Hawley "to use the colored troops as you think best, so as to relieve the white troops from duty [on the coast] where they would be exposed to disease." Schofield also believed that prolonged garrison duty had left the white troops "in a bad state of inefficiency and disorganization." He therefore heeded Hawley's advice to move the white soldiers inland or, better still, to muster them out before summer. While the order appears callous, the two generals acted in the belief that southern blacks were better acclimated to the sweltering climate of coastal North Carolina than were northern whites. On June 1, Schofield directed that one brigade of Paine's division of black troops be sent to the District of Wilmington and the other two brigades to the District of Beaufort to relieve the white soldiers on duty there.[46]

The diary of a New York soldier stationed at New Bern underscores Schofield's concern about transferring the white troops from the coast. According to Pvt. Charles A. Tournier of the 3rd New York Light Artillery, several of his comrades had already been sent home "on account of sickness and the hospitals are full as hot weather comes on." Upon hearing a rumor that a regiment of black soldiers was to relieve his unit, Tournier concluded, "we will soon be on a transport bound for home. I have enjoyed being a soldier while in health . . . but the last days [have been] rather hard ones for me for I now have chills and fever and . . . I remain quietly in my shanty." On the day of the black troops' arrival, Tournier wrote: "They are all southern born. Men born in slavery and used to the climate. They look strong and healthy [and] thoroughly enjoy wearing the uniforms and handling the guns." Tournier then observed with apparent regret that he and his white comrades "will not have the freedom to run around the city after the darkies go on duty."[47]

Schofield's and Hawley's assumptions about the black soldiers' resilience to extreme heat and humidity soon proved mistaken. "We have bin a Surfring [suffering] in Terrable condision," a black private in New Bern complained to Secretary of War Stanton. "We have men that bin on [guard] Duty now fo Near two months havent bin Releve . . . & we have bin a careing [carrying] has high as five & Six men to the Hospital in a Day." The frustrated soldier told Stanton that he and his comrades "Expected to be Treated as men but we have ben treated more Like Dogs then men."[48]

General Grant meanwhile decided to muster out the northern black regiments and retain the southern regiments. He believed that the government should continue to feed, clothe, shelter, and pay the southern-

Governor William W. Holden (Courtesy of the North Carolina State Archives)

born black soldiers rather than turn them loose on a devastated South. Grant also knew that the army still needed them as occupation troops.[49]

On May 29, President Johnson issued two proclamations outlining his Reconstruction policy. Given Johnson's pledge to punish traitors, the conditions were surprisingly lenient. The first proclamation granted amnesty to all ex-Confederates except those who fell into fourteen classes, but the excluded men could apply for a presidential pardon. The second proclamation appointed William W. Holden, the longtime editor and publisher of the Raleigh-based *North Carolina Standard*, provisional governor of North Carolina. Holden had been the unsuccessful candidate of the state's so-called peace faction in the 1864 gubernatorial election against the ever-popular incumbent, Zebulon B. Vance, a former Conservative ally. Although Holden had called for a convention to consider separate state action regarding the war, he stopped short of publicly advocating North Carolina's return to the Union. Johnson nevertheless regarded him as the Tar Heel State's most trustworthy wartime Unionist. While Holden had his advocates among the state's leading politicians, many Vance supporters condemned Holden as a traitor. Several *Standard* editorials that had appeared after Johnston's surrender—particularly one that called for a $25,000 reward for Vance's capture—only deepened the Conservatives' enmity for the new provisional governor. In conciliating his numerous political enemies, Holden faced a daunting task.[50]

Johnson's second proclamation also provided a mechanism for the state to resume its former relations with the federal government. Holden would call a convention consisting of delegates elected by loyal citizens "for the purpose of altering or amending" the state constitution. At minimum, the convention had to declare the secession ordinance null and void and abolish slavery. The proclamation required all voters and electors to take an amnesty oath and meet the qualifications set forth by the state constitution in force before May 20, 1861, the day North Carolina passed its secession ordinance. In short, no freedmen could vote for delegates. The convention would determine the qualifications for electors and the eligibility of officeholders. The proclamation officially restored the authority and functions of federal law, federal tax and customs collectors, federal courts, and the U.S. Post Office within the Tar Heel State. Aside from Johnson's appointment of a civilian governor, his Reconstruction plan was almost identical to Schofield's.[51]

Of greatest interest to Schofield, no doubt, was the paragraph regarding the military's role in Presidential Reconstruction. The department commander and his officers and men were to "assist the said provisional governor in carrying into effect this proclamation." They were also "to abstain from in any way hindering, impeding, or discouraging the loyal people from the organization of a State government as herein authorized." That was all—Johnson's proclamation was silent on martial law and lacked a clear definition of the army's role. The president's vague

instructions all but ensured a conflict between the provisional governor and the military commander over their respective powers. In the
absence of specific guidelines, the department commander regarded his
authority as supreme within North Carolina until the resumption of civil
government.[52]

Despite the considerable authority he still wielded, Schofield was
disappointed at being passed over as military governor. The general later
wrote that he disagreed with Holden's appointment on constitutional
grounds, arguing that temporary military government was the "only
lawful substitute" for "popular civil government." On June 4, Schofield
applied for a leave of absence, informing Grant that North Carolina was
"so perfectly quiet that the presence of troops seems almost unnecessary." Anxious as Schofield was to obtain his leave, it is hardly surprising
that the general painted a rosy picture of the situation in North Carolina.
In truth, Schofield's department was quiet only *because* of the presence
of federal soldiers, and their removal might have plunged the state into
chaos. On June 20, Schofield turned over his command to General Cox
and then departed the Tar Heel State with no intention of returning.[53]

Schofield left North Carolina in far better condition than he had
found it. Law and order were nearly restored, agriculture and trade were
beginning a slow recovery, and state and local governments were being reestablished. Lacking instructions from Washington, Schofield had
improvised his own ad hoc recovery program. He provided for paroled
Confederate soldiers, fed and sheltered refugees, loaned draft animals to
destitute farmers, formed local police companies, created his own bureau of freedmen's affairs, issued guidelines for freedpeople and their
former masters, and continued the unofficial policy of conciliation begun by Sherman. Schofield's successors faced a formidable task, however,
for white North Carolinians were not as amenable to the new order as
Schofield and other federal commanders had supposed. Only by inter-
acting with the state's citizenry would bluecoats grasp the difficulty of
reconciling whites to the new state of affairs while protecting the rights
of freedpeople.

Chapter Three

An Uncertain Relationship

The Interaction of Soldiers and Civilians in 1865

With the surrender at the Bennett farm, the U.S. Army's role in North Carolina abruptly shifted from conqueror to peacekeeper, the bluecoats' erstwhile foes becoming their fellow countrymen once more. The trauma of defeat left white North Carolinians briefly disoriented and despondent; some Union commanders erroneously interpreted their apparent passivity as resignation to the new state of affairs. Federal soldiers therefore made a concerted effort to conciliate their former enemies—in some cases, even before the surrender became official. The former Confederate commander in North Carolina, Joseph E. Johnston, noted that Union occupation troops treated Tar Heel civilians "as they would have done those of Ohio or New York." Many Confederate veterans responded favorably to the bluecoats' friendly overtures, encouraging hopes for a swift reunion of the two sections. Nevertheless, many white Tar Heels, especially women, remained defiantly irreconcilable. "Can we ever live in peace with the desecrators of our homes & the murderers of our Fathers, Brothers & Sons [?]" wrote Hillsborough resident Elizabeth Collier: "*Never*." A Fayetteville woman declared that her hatred of "the Yankees" was "deeper and more bitter now that we are conquered than while we were fighting them."[1]

A further complication arose when it became clear that white North Carolinians would not tolerate black occupation troops in their midst. They accused the black soldiers of insolence and brutality and of filling the freedpeople's heads with absurd notions of political and social equality. Rumors also spread that blacks were plotting an insurrection to kill white landowners and seize their property. Conversely, many whites—including some federal soldiers—demonstrated their hostility to freedpeople by openly beating, killing, or otherwise abusing blacks. The army meanwhile attempted a seemingly impossible juggling act—conciliating white Tar Heels while protecting the freedpeople's rights.

In North Carolina, the first opportunity for Union and Confederate soldiers to meet as friends rather than as foes came during the cease-fire in mid-April, when Sherman sent his initial surrender agreement to Washington for approval. Raleigh's Capitol Square served as a gathering place for Yankees and homeward-bound Rebels, the bluecoats often sharing their rations with the men in butternut and gray. Union Brig. Gen. Manning F. Force reported that a squad of Confederate cavalry brought some stragglers from his command to his headquarters near Raleigh. "The [Confederate] Sergeant in charge said that they and Kilpatrick's [Union] cavalry patrol together, under the same orders," Force wrote. During the truce, the area around Durham's Station was neutral ground. Federals and Confederates met there to swap horses, run footraces, and shoot at targets rather than at each other. At night they sat around campfires telling stories and smoking tobacco plundered from a local factory. A Michigan cavalry officer observed a similar détente in the streets of Chapel Hill. "There are quite a number of confederate Officers here from Lee's army," the officer wrote his sister, "and could you see them visiting and riding out with our Officers you would hardly believe they had been opposed to each other in deadly warfare for four years." During the war, similar encounters had frequently occurred inside the no man's land separating the contending armies, where enemies had met in defiance of orders to converse and exchange newspapers, coffee, tobacco, and other articles. Given this wartime precedent, the ease with which many Yankees and Rebels made the postwar transition from adversaries to fellow countrymen came as no surprise.[2]

Soldiers such as Lt. Nicholas De Graff of the 115th New York Infantry felt ambivalent about their former enemies. "Of course now we are all friends," he wrote, "but it comes very hard to treat them with any respect when we think of the sorrow and woe they have entailed on themselves and the nation." Some blue-gray encounters became ugly, such as the confrontation at Bennett Place between Union cavalry commander Judson Kilpatrick and his Confederate counterpart, Wade Hampton. As the two men argued, "words grew hot," recalled an eyewitness, "both parties expressing a desire that the issue of the war should be left between the cavalry." In contrast, Johnston's engineering officer, Maj. John Johnson, spent much of his time at the Bennett farm talking shop under a tall oak tree with Sherman's chief engineer, Col. Orlando M. Poe. Johnson also chatted with another Sherman staff officer, Maj. Henry Hitchcock. When the time came to part, Johnson said, "Good-bye, Major—hope we shall meet again!" to which he added in a low voice, "*in the right way.*"[3]

The rapid rapprochement of many recent enemies in blue and gray was facilitated by the common hardship, suffering, and danger they had endured during the war, forging a bond that transcended sectional animosities. As a result, Union and Confederate veterans who met often chose to set aside their differences and treat each other with courtesy and respect. Capt. Dwight Fraser of the 128th Indiana Infantry boarded at the home of some "bitter Rebels," including three brothers who had served in the Confederate army. "It seems odd for us to be sitting daily at the same table and talking about the war," Fraser mused. "I can not help feeling sorry for many of the young men, and will not causelessly wound their feelings." George P. Collins, a former staff officer in Johnston's army, appealed to the local post commander, Col. Jones Frankle, after a Union army quartermaster seized his wagons, mules, and farm tools. Collins was pleased to find Frankle "very much a gentleman & inclined to do all he could to help." Thanks to Frankle's intervention, Collins managed to recover his wagons, mules, and most of his tools. At Collins's request, several of Frankle's subordinates paid "a friendly visit" to Somerset Place, the Collins family plantation, and lectured the black laborers on the dangers of idleness. About a month later, Collins met Frankle during a trip to New Bern. The colonel greeted him as if he "had been an old friend & companion."[4]

Whereas the often harmonious interaction of Union and Confederate soldiers seemed to presage a rapid reconciliation of North and South, the behavior of southern white women indicated a lengthier and more tortuous road to reunion. At first glance, the federals found the young women polite if somewhat aloof. According to Raleigh author Mary Bayard Clarke, the women "meekly submit for the time, and acknowledge that the force of circumstances obliges them to be polite outwardly, when in their hearts they are saying very naughty words." Indeed, the soldiers soon discovered that beneath the ladies' civil exterior lurked a grim defiance. An Indiana officer was briefly quartered in the home of former *Raleigh Confederate* editor Duncan K. McRae, who had fled town on the Union army's approach. McRae's wife and daughters had remained behind, however, and the statements of one of the girls would have made her father proud. When they first met, Miss McRae informed the Union officer that she would not even give him a cup of water to relieve his "dying agonies." As they became better acquainted, her opinion of the officer improved to the extent that she told him: "I *would* give you a cup of water to soothe your dying agonies, and as you are a Yankee, I wish I had the opportunity to do so."[5]

Although federal officers sometimes met with open hostility, most were eager to conciliate white North Carolinians. Even so, Mary Bayard Clarke noted that some officers "had not a spark of generosity, and were to the last degree rude and insulting." One such case involved Capt. John B. Gilbert of the 6th Connecticut Infantry, who accosted a woman at a Wilmington theater. "I am going home with you to-night," Gilbert reportedly told her, "and am going to sleep with you." Soon afterward, Gilbert was arrested and tried by a general court-martial for "conduct unbecoming an officer and a gentleman." Although the witnesses could not agree on whether Gilbert was drunk, they all testified that the captain had insulted the woman. Gilbert was found guilty and dishonorably discharged from the service.[6]

Clarke hastened to add that "acts of courtesy and kindness" on the officers' part "were more numerous . . . than the reverse." But she added that the Yankees soon discovered that they had to conquer every southern woman they met, for each was convinced that "the only gentleman . . . in the United States army, is her Colonel, Captain, or Major, who, when she was in trouble, was as kind to her 'as if he had been a Confederate.'" Clarke noted that the behavior of white women when in the presence of federal officers ranged from "timidly conciliating" to "boldly defiant." For her part, Clarke relished bantering with Union officers. She began conversing with them as a means of gathering material for magazine articles and soon found that she enjoyed the company of several officers, especially Col. George F. Granger, the commandant of the Post of Raleigh. Clarke's behavior so scandalized her sister, Frances Miller (with whom Clarke and two of her children were living), that Miller ordered Clarke to receive no more Yankee officers or speak to them from her window. Miller conceded that they had to be "decently polite" when the officers called, but that they could "certainly manage to do so" without encour-

William J. Clarke and Mary Bayard Clarke (Courtesy of the North Carolina State Archives)

aging more visits. Reminding Clarke that her husband, Confederate Col. William J. Clarke, was still a prisoner of war at Fort Delaware, Miller described her sister's behavior "as an insult to Bro. William while he is in a northern prison to have his wife entertain for 4 hours one of his jailors." Clarke evidently ignored Miller's ultimatum, for she was soon compelled to leave her sister's house. After her eviction, Clarke supported herself and her children by writing magazine articles.[7]

Clarke's case proved the exception to the rule, for southern white women expressed their defiance and hostility by ostracizing federal soldiers of all ranks. In most North Carolina households, husbands yielded to their wives in the matter of social arrangements. So implacable were the women that as late as 1872, when fewer than four hundred federal troops were stationed in North Carolina, Capt. V. K. Hart, the post commander at Lincolnton, complained to a reporter "of the lack of social attentions to himself and his wife." Whenever possible, white women simply avoided contact with the hated Yankees. In Wilmington, a Confederate veteran observed, "the ladies keep very quiet & are seldom out of doors, and then, they go hurriedly and deeply veiled." A Union officer told the ex-Confederate "with much indignation" that he had recently called on a young woman "with whom he had been quite intimate before the war, but was informed she was 'not at home' though he saw her at a window as he was approaching the house."[8]

In May 1865, an entire community of white women shunned Union soldiers. At Goldsboro, officers of Paine's division decided to hold a ball in the town hall. They printed about one hundred invitations and left them at the homes of the "best families in the town," wrote Capt. John McMurray of the 6th USCT. The officers hired musicians and decorated the hall. On the night of the dance, they arrived at the hall in their dress uniforms and waited for the young women of Goldsboro to arrive. "But they never came," McMurray recalled. "One lone female put in an appearance" and then left after a few minutes. The ball proved to be an enormous embarrassment for the organizers, who were continually reminded of the fiasco by their comrades. The fact that the officers commanded black troops probably accounted for the wholesale boycott of the dance.[9]

Even when contact with federal soldiers appeared unavoidable, many white women somehow managed to shun them. "I got into a real nest of yankees last week," Raleigh resident Laura Craven informed a friend, when she was invited to her aunt's house. Upon her arrival, Craven learned that a federal colonel and his family as well as a lieutenant were boarding there. During her stay, "two yankee wimmin and their escorts" called on the colonel and his wife, and the lieutenant brought in six of his fellow officers. Craven reported that she and her friends—including "several confed boys"—"formed ourselves into a party in one corner, had our own music[,] conversation, and amusements. It was real laughable,"

Craven commented, "the fact that there is not alkali enough in the south to make water and oil mix was plainly demonstrated that night."[10]

Some white women expressed their contempt for federal officers in no uncertain terms and in public places such as Yarborough House, Raleigh's finest hotel. "Our little secesh dancing girls have mortifyed some of their friends by insulting a Federal Major & his lady . . . by refusing their hand and otherwise insulting them," noted one dismayed onlooker, who witnessed the incident inside the hotel's ballroom. "It is said they are hurt about it." Some Union officers were no less forceful in expressing their resentment at being snubbed. When excluded from an ice cream party at the house where he was quartered, the commander at Salisbury retaliated by ordering his brass band to stand on the veranda and play "Yankee Doodle" until the party broke up. A Union major stationed at nearby Lexington described the women he met as "the worst rebels I ever saw[.] The men appear to be well enough satisfied," he commented, "but the women are rampant & can smell a Yankee through a brick wall."[11]

Not content with shunning federal soldiers, white women also castigated them for turning to freedwomen for companionship. A disgusted Catherine Ann Edmondston noted that the federals held nightly balls at Raleigh's Guion Hotel, "& that the *Yankee Officers* dance with *the negro women!*" From Graham, a woman reported, "We have a sweet mess of Yankees here. They hug & kiss the niggers, promenade the street with them, & carry the black babies in their arms. Ain't this enough to make a Christian cuss, &c." Given the soldiers' miscegenational behavior, she concluded, "in ten years . . . there would not be a white man in Yankee land."[12]

There were exceptions to the widespread animosity of white Tar Heel women, especially in the state's heavily Unionist western counties. The commanding officer at Hendersonville, Maj. William C. Stevens, proudly reported to his sister that "the young union ladies of this county publicly presented to me and my command a very nice [U.S.] Flag which they had made for that purpose"—perhaps the first such postwar presentation in North Carolina if not the entire South. Afterward, the major went on a carriage ride with the two women who had presented the Stars and Stripes. A popular dinner guest with the area's prominent families, Stevens boasted that he would need a month to fulfill all his social engagements. Buncombe County resident Mary Brown befriended a federal captain who was later wounded and robbed by bushwhackers. She was angered to learn that many citizens of Asheville "rejoiced" at the captain's misfortune. "Not so with us," Brown asserted, "we sympathized with him & fought many battles for him when his enemies assailed [him] be-cause he was a 'Yankee.' . . . I think some of the people of Asheville make themselves appear *very ridiculous* in their scornful manner toward the Fed-erals," Brown continued. "Certainly they fail maintaining Southern *dignity & honor* in such a course." In Raleigh, an Indiana surgeon was moved by the southern hospitality lavished on him to comment, "that they excel our folks in this respect is beyond a doubt."[13]

Some federal soldiers married North Carolina women. By far the most notorious Yankee–Tar Heel union was the marriage of Union of-ficer Smith D. Atkins to Ella Swain, the daughter of University of North Carolina president David L. Swain. One of the wedding guests, Cornelia Phillips Spencer, noted that, while there "were a number of gallant ex-Confederate soldiers" in attendance, "very very few people went to the wedding—tho' very general invitations were issued and a grand supper [was] prepared." Spencer reported that the townspeople expressed "[a] good deal of bitter feeling" about the "Yankee wedding." Rumor had it that "invitations were *spit upon* in one or two of the houses." One week after the wedding, the couple left for Freeport, Illinois—Atkins's home-town—where they would live. The gossips then had a field day. "It was told from mouth to mouth and believed all over North Carolina," Spen-cer later wrote, "that Ellie Swain went to Illinois loaded with finery and jewels stolen from the women of states farther south, and given to her by her husband." Spencer believed the Atkins-Swain wedding "was the principal agent in alienating public affection and confidence" from the university and its president. While Spencer probably exaggerated the fall-out, Ella Swain's marriage to a "Yankee officer" did generate considerable resentment against the once-popular ex-governor Swain.[14]

In contrast to the notoriety of the Atkins-Swain union was the ex-ample of Maj. Clinton A. Cilley, a Harvard-educated, Union war hero who served in postwar North Carolina as a headquarters staff officer and Freedmen's Bureau official before returning to civilian life. Remaining in the state, Cilley established a law firm with a former Confederate of-ficer, married the daughter of a prominent citizen, and settled in Lenoir, a small town in western North Carolina. Cilley soon emerged as a civic leader, receiving an appointment as a superior court judge and then be-coming Lenoir's first mayor. Unlike more notorious Union army veterans who settled in the Tar Heel State, Cilley managed to avoid controversy and thus faded into obscurity after his death in 1900.[15]

During his brief tenure as an occupation commander in North Carolina, Maj. Gen. Jacob D. Cox was as admired and respected as Cilley later became. Letitia Morehead Walker, the daughter of John M. Morehead, a former governor and an ex-president of the North Carolina Railroad, called Cox "a most courteous and elegant man." The Presbyterian minister at Greensboro, Jacob Henry Smith, and his wife found the general "intelligent, cultivated, reasonable, and just."[16]

Nothing could have placed white North Carolinians' reaction to Cox in starker relief than the frosty reception accorded Brig. Gen. Judson Kilpatrick. The general and his adjutant traveled with two women they referred to as their wives but who wore privates' uniforms and answered to the names "Charley" and "Frank." Kilpatrick's host at Durham's Station described the women as "vulgar, rude and indecent, but fitting companions for a man of General Kilpatrick's character." Adding further spice to the scandal, Kilpatrick's mulatto laundress insisted that she was carrying the general's baby. Not surprisingly, Kilpatrick lacked Cox's consummate tact, and his inflammatory remarks to white North Carolinians ensured his notoriety but won him few friends.[17]

The behavior of most Union soldiers fell within the spectrum of sociability that separated the boorish Kilpatrick from the courtly Cox. Some Tar Heels even admitted as much. "We are getting along very quietly," a Raleigh resident wrote ex-governor Zebulon B. Vance, "the city was never more orderly, the Ohio troops here are very clever, and we find Military rule not so bad as we feared." The mayor and commissioners of Fayetteville sent a letter of appreciation to the town's post commandant, Col. Michael Kerwin, when word arrived that he would soon be mustered out. They praised the colonel for rescuing Fayetteville from the brink of anarchy without oppressing the people in the process. "Your administration has been characterized by a happy blending of gentleness and firmness," the letter read, "by gentleness you have won the hearts of our people; by firmness you have secured respect for legitimate authority."[18]

The postwar occupation force in North Carolina nevertheless contained its share of miscreants. Despite the official ban on foraging, soldiers continued to roam the countryside and rob civilians, though army safeguards rendered the townspeople relatively safe. From Morganton, Tod R. Caldwell reported to Governor Holden that the garrison there had "become a terror" to the people, "robbing and plundering both white and black." Caldwell warned that unless the department commander acted soon, "our people will have to resort to bushwhacking for self-protection." Some victims believed that the federal troops who had robbed them were members of an organized theft ring. After four soldiers way-laid Fayetteville resident W. G. MacRae on a country road, he reported the robbery to the post commander, Col. Michael Kerwin. Soon afterward, several more brazen robberies occurred on the streets of Fayetteville and resulted in one arrest, but Kerwin's seemingly half-hearted investigation produced no suspects in MacRae's case. A disgusted MacRae concluded that the colonel "went halves with his damned cut throats." Needless to say, the above-mentioned encomium to Kerwin did not bear MacRae's signature.[19]

A handful of federals committed murder or rape. Like many other bored and homesick soldiers, Pvt. Henry Anderson of the 9th Michigan Cavalry and two comrades rode out into the country one day and got drunk. A new recruit, Anderson had been with his regiment only a few weeks. While drunk, Anderson met two civilians in a buggy and demanded their money. When they refused, he shot and killed one of them. An army court-martial tried and convicted Anderson of murder and sentenced him to be shot. When asked if he had anything to say, Anderson replied that strong drink was the reason for his having to face a firing squad, and he exhorted his comrades never to "become so drunk as not to know what they were doing." Anderson's advice apparently fell on deaf ears, for crimes attributable to drunkenness were all too common among those committed by occupation troops in North Carolina.[20]

Some of the crimes were fairly harmless, as in the case of a "shamefully intoxicated" regimental surgeon who insulted several officers at a Salisbury hotel "in the presence of ladies," but who escaped punishment because of irregularities in his court-martial proceedings. More serious were the charges against Capt. John S. Bowles, the commanding officer at Morganton, whose penchant for prostitutes and public drunkenness culminated in his arrest for indecent exposure. Although the court-martial found Bowles guilty as charged, the captain's punishment consisted merely of a reprimand from the department commander. From the commander's headquarters at Raleigh came a rebuke of another kind: "Conduct more degrading to a gentleman, or more prejudicial to good order and military discipline, cannot well be imagined; and a court which passes such offences by, with a simple reprimand, can have little consideration for the interests of the service, and no appreciation of its duty." Much to the commander's disgust, Bowles was released and honorably discharged.[21]

Like Bowles, Lt. James H. Simpson of the 120th Indiana Infantry was convicted of making "a public exhibition of himself . . . in the streets of Raleigh" and in camp while he was inebriated. Simpson was fined one month's pay, which was later remitted, and thus escaped with a warning from the department commander. Less fortunate was Capt. John F. Deveraux of the 6th USCT, who was cashiered because his chronic drunkenness repeatedly rendered him unfit for duty. Deveraux was far from alone, for other officers were cashiered for the same reason. Privates found guilty of drunkenness typically were fined one to three months' pay or were sentenced to at least thirty days' confinement at hard labor. Despite the threat of severe punishment, soldiers indulged in heavy drinking to overcome boredom and homesickness. Drunken and disorderly conduct therefore remained a chronic problem for occupation commanders in North Carolina.[22]

Most commanders realized that punishing soldiers for drunkenness was largely ineffective and concluded that they had to regulate the supply of alcohol. The post commander at New Bern, Lt. Col. Augustus S. Boernstein, pronounced the "infamous liquor traffic" as "always at the bottom of difficulties, rows and riots." In Greensboro, the post commander prohibited the sale of alcohol to soldiers without his special permission and required distillers to post a $1,000 bond. The provost marshal at Wilmington decided to make an example by punishing several civilians for selling whiskey to soldiers. He confiscated their stock and fined them large sums or tied them up by the thumbs before town hall "in company with their customers." One bootlegger was paraded about town in an open cart while wearing a placard that read, "I sold rum." When this failed to alleviate the problem, the post commander at Wilmington prohibited the sale of alcohol without exception. The post commander at Raleigh issued similarly draconian orders, prohibiting all merchants and sutlers from selling alcohol to anyone. Despite the stringent regulations and the threat of severe punishment, the commanders' attempts at prohibition failed because the demand for alcohol was simply too great, yet this did not discourage their successors from repeating the experiment.[23]

Alcohol was not the only commodity that forged a commercial bond between soldiers and civilians. The quantity and quality of army rations seldom satisfied the bluecoats, so the local citizens supplied them with lemonade, soft bread, butter, milk, eggs, cakes, pies, cherries, strawberries, and rice in exchange for coffee, sugar, or greenbacks. An Indiana soldier observed that although the locals disliked the Yankees, they "like the Yankee money firstrate." As price-gougers, Tar Heel entrepreneurs soon proved themselves the equals of army sutlers. Some bluecoats bypassed the cash nexus altogether and raided citizens' dairies, orchards, henhouses, or gardens. This sometimes proved fatal to the thief, as in the case of a light-fingered Union soldier who was caught plundering a vegetable garden and then was shot to death by the owner, a former Confederate officer.[24]

In addition to the cash nexus, many bluecoats shared another bond with two-thirds of the Tar Heel populace: their whiteness. This bond became more apparent as large numbers of white troops departed the state and black soldiers formed an ever-increasing percentage of the occupation force in North Carolina. White North Carolinians found this trend alarming—in fact, most found the presence of *any* black soldiers intolerable. At first, a handful of local newspapers advocated giving the African American troops the benefit of the doubt. The *Raleigh Progress* noted that during the war, "the great mass" of the southern people had "vehemently opposed" making Confederate soldiers of their slaves "because we thought the colored man incapable of that high discipline and training necessary to make good soldiers." But the *Progress* conceded that "in this, as in many other things, many of us were no doubt mistaken." In defending the use of black occupation troops, the *Wilmington Herald* cited the tradition of African American soldiers dating back to the War of Independence and the War of 1812. The *Herald* described the black troops stationed at Wilmington as "splendidly disciplined" and "modest and respectful." Since their arrival, the *Herald* observed, the town had been "remarkably quiet, the street fights and disturbances so common" during the white soldiers' tenure "having entirely ceased."[25]

But there were few advocates of African American troops among white North Carolinians. Within a few weeks of the black soldiers' arrival at Wilmington, New Bern, and other coastal towns, white citizens began complaining about their presence. Wilmington resident John MacRae found it easier to bear the "evils" of the sickly season than "the negro soldiery that it has pleased our very good masters to place over us to insult abuse and annoy our citizens." MacRae supposed that the black troops were stationed in the South to "humble" white civilians, but in doing so, he wrote, the northern authorities "are not likely to increase our love or respect for them." A Sampson County minister noted that the people were "troubled here by the presence of Negro troops," and he expressed surprise that the commanders "do not know better than to be sending them about the country. No policy c[oul]d be worse." So odious were the black soldiers that former state supreme court chief justice Thomas Ruffin blamed Maj. Gen. Darius N. Couch's "large black division or corps" for ravaging his Alamance County plantation while they were en route to Greensboro. In truth, Couch's division consisted entirely of white soldiers; the nearest black troops were then at Goldsboro one hundred miles to the east.[26]

White North Carolinians feared and despised black soldiers because they shattered the familiar stereotype of the "servile negro." The soldiers were armed, uniformed, and disciplined; they were proud and assertive; they protected the local freedpeople and served as both their counselors and role models. When freedmen began to advocate universal male suffrage, outraged whites accused black soldiers of encouraging them. For white Tar Heels, the presence of African American troops evoked the reality of Confederate defeat far more graphically than any number of white Union soldiers could have.[27]

Even a well-meaning black soldier could enrage a former slaveholder by unconsciously violating the old racial etiquette. A prominent Goldsboro man was furious because a "nigger soldier" had bowed to him and said "good morning" as he sat on his veranda. The man complained of the "infraction" to a Freedmen's Bureau official, explaining that he had never submitted to such a gross indignity before because he had forbidden his slaves to speak to him first. Most black troops, however, were well aware of the hostility they inspired. Sgt. N. B. Sterrett, an African American soldier stationed at Kinston, frequently overheard the white townspeople "calling in all manner of names that were ever applied to the Deity, to deliver them from the hands of the *smoked Yankees*." Black occupation troops despised the former slaveholders in equal measure and longed to see them suffer for their presumed cruelty. While his regiment was camped on the Henry Nutt plantation near Wilmington, Sterrett was taken to the whipping post, "where, I am informed, many a poor soul had his death wound inflicted upon him." Regarding the plantation owner, Sterrett quipped, "I think it is time that that Nutt were cracked." The racial tension occasionally erupted in violence. In July 1865, one of Sterrett's comrades was killed by a local white man. Later that year, two privates in the 37th USCT were wounded by ex-Confederates in Wilmington and Morehead City. The mutual enmity of African American soldiers and ex-slaveholders offered scant prospect of peaceful coexistence. Indeed, the coastal region's white leadership agreed almost unanimously that the black soldiers had to go.[28]

In a letter to Governor Holden, Alfred M. Waddell, a Wilmington resident and a former Confederate officer, complained that "although our people behave with remarkable propriety, the frequent and indeed daily outrages perpetrated by [black troops], or by other negroes instigated by them, have excited serious and well-grounded fears for the safety of our unarmed and defenceless people. . . . Unless there is a change for the better," Waddell warned, "it will inevitably result in massacre." He blamed northern "teachers and preachers" and black soldiers for encouraging the freedpeople to "believe that all the property is theirs of right and that every day of delay in the assertion of their rights is rendering their claims weaker." Although Waddell admitted that neither he nor his family had been mistreated, he claimed that black "soldiers insult and curse the most respectable ladies in Wilmington in the presence of the so-called negro citizens," and that they "continually arrest, in violation of orders, unoffending citizens even when walking the streets with ladies." Waddell stated that the people of Wilmington did not wish "to interfere with the negroes in any way, but there is a very strong indisposition to be placed at their mercy." He asked Holden to urge the military commander to transfer the African American soldiers, for their removal would calm the white residents' fears "and do away with the evil influence exerted upon our colored citizens."[29]

Waddell's comments regarding insolent and undisciplined black soldiers were typical. White citizens invariably claimed that they were victims of unprovoked outrages at the hands of brutal African American troops and impressionable local freedpeople who fell under their malevolent sway. The reports were often based on hearsay and lacked such essential details as names, places, and dates. The petitioners usually attributed the unrest to the blacks' unrealistic demands for political and social equality and property in the form of "forty acres and a mule." Unless the black soldiers were immediately withdrawn, the writers warned, the "inevitable" result would be a "massacre" of the defenseless white citizens. White North Carolinians were accustomed to viewing racial conflict in apocalyptic terms, thanks to decades of paranoia regarding the possibility of slave insurrections. Although largely irrational, their fears were nonetheless genuine. During the war, rumors of slave uprisings usually brought swift punishment of the accused. As recently as December 1864, white Tar Heels had uncovered an alleged slave insurrection plot in several southern counties and had summarily executed the ringleaders. The presence of black troops on the North Carolina coast would soon help to trigger another insurrection scare involving the former slaves.[30]

Holden promptly sent Waddell's letter, along with a similar missive penned by John Pool, a former state senator, to General Cox, the department commander. Cox assured Holden that he had issued "stringent orders" to his subordinates commanding the coastal districts, which, the general hoped, "will prevent any like outrages in the future." Dissatisfied with Cox's assurances, Waddell and several other citizens traveled to Raleigh and delivered a petition to the general requesting the removal of the black troops from Wilmington.[31]

A few days later, Cox received orders to turn over his command and report to the War Department in Washington for orders. Cox must have considered the timing fortuitous, for the issue of unwanted black soldiers was rapidly escalating into a headache that his successor, Brig. Gen. Thomas H. Ruger, would inherit. Shortly after Ruger's accession to department command, an editorial appeared in the *Wilmington Herald* (which had advocated black occupation troops just one month earlier) blaming the baleful influence of the town's garrison for the "fearfully demoralized" state of the black civilian populace. "We are really slumbering on a volcano," the editorial warned: "The general eruption is likely to occur at any time. In such an event the whites will be at the mercy of the blacks." The commanding officer at Wilmington, Col. J. Worthington Ames, investigated the *Herald*'s allegations and found them "absurdly false." Instead, Ames noted, the editorial had "greatly excited the [white] populace & placed the blacks in great peril."[32]

Nevertheless, a few days later, Ruger received a message from Holden accompanied by a letter from the mayor and commissioners of Wilmington and a memorandum headed "Notice this!" The Wilmington officials implored Holden to secure the removal of the black garrison from their town with even greater urgency than Waddell had the previous month. In addition to the inflammatory *Herald* editorial, the officials' letter was prompted by the enclosed statement of a freedman to a Union hospital steward, in which the former revealed "a conspiracy among the colored race to murder all the white race" in order to seize the property of the ex-slaveholders after the federal troops had departed. The officials, however, believed that the insurrectionary freedpeople would in fact be "aided and abetted by United [States] Colored Troops, and further encouraged by their Preachers and Teachers, who are generally denizens of the North." They detected "a somewhat dictatorial spirit" among the blacks and feared that "a riot, or something even worse" was imminent. Holden therefore urged Ruger to arm the Wilmington police force at once.[33]

Instead, Ruger ordered the commander of the District of Wilmington, Col. Samuel A. Duncan, to investigate the civilians' dire reports. On July 26, 1865, Duncan informed Ruger, "I deem the fear of a negro insurrection here utterly groundless, & absurd in the extreme." Duncan also dismissed allegations that black soldiers were frequently drunk and disorderly in the streets of Wilmington, yet he admitted, "individual cases of drunkenness do arise among them." The colonel likewise conceded that blacks were sometimes insolent and domineering, but he accused whites of being far more so, "both in their manners and their words & actions."[34]

On the heels of Duncan's report came a second letter from the mayor and commissioners of Wilmington informing Holden of fresh outrages on the part of black troops and once more urging their immediate removal from the town. The most recent incidents involved violent confrontations between Wilmington police and black soldiers and civilians. A similar letter from the mayor of New Bern also reached the governor at this time. Deeming the situation critical, Holden decided to bypass Ruger and appeal directly to President Johnson for action. The governor blamed the presence of African American troops for the racial strife and suggested that they be transferred to the relative isolation of the coastal forts. Perhaps it was no coincidence that a petition signed by several dozen citizens of Edenton arrived on Johnson's desk about the same time as Holden's letter, complaining of mistreatment at the hands of the garrison stationed in their town and requesting the black soldiers' removal. In his reply to Holden, Johnson informed the governor that Maj. Gen. George G. Meade was making an inspection tour of the South and suggested that Holden consult with Meade regarding the disposition of troops in North Carolina.[35]

During July and August 1865, several clashes between black soldiers and white policemen erupted in Wilmington and New Bern. Contrary to the accusations of local officials, the police bore as much blame as the occupation troops for provoking the altercations. After one such scrape, the commander of the District of New Bern (formerly the District of Beaufort), Brig. Gen. Charles J. Paine, decided to make an example of two policemen and ordered them arrested and tried by a military commission. The two men were convicted of assaulting a sergeant in the 4th USCT and sentenced to one month at hard labor. Since their arrest, Paine noted, "there has not been the slightest trouble" in New Bern. To prevent future collisions, Col. Nathan Goff Jr., the commandant of the Post of Wilmington, replaced the town's provost guard (or military police) and instructed his subordinates to confine the remaining soldiers to their camps outside town. Only one man per regiment would be permitted to visit Wilmington each day to pick up mail and run other errands for his unit. These restrictions coincided with Goff's order prohibiting the sale and distribution of alcohol in Wilmington. Although aimed at different antagonists, Goff and Paine's measures proved equally effective. For all the sound and fury, the fighting between police and occupation troops was mercifully brief and resulted in few casualties.[36]

Far more alarming were the clashes between white soldiers and black soldiers, for their confrontations often threatened to escalate into full-blown riots. In July 1865, Wilmington was the scene of at least two collisions between white soldiers attempting to rescue their comrades and the black provost guards who arrested them. The two white regiments involved, the 13th Pennsylvania Cavalry and the 2nd Massachusetts Heavy Artillery, were each enjoying a brief stopover in town. The horse soldiers were heading home, and the artillerymen were en route to a new post. The incidents occurred at two of the busiest places in town, the Wilmington and Weldon Railroad depot and the corner of Front and Market streets. In both cases, only the timely intervention of a few officers prevented bloodshed, for many of the soldiers converging on the crowded scenes were both armed and drunk. At Kinston, some white soldiers hopped off their train during a brief stop and raided a nearby army bakery guarded by black soldiers. The guards refused to yield and were saved only by the blowing of the train whistle. At Goldsboro, a fistfight broke out when several white soldiers at the depot insulted some black civilians, causing several black soldiers "to return the cursing compliment," noted an eyewitness. A more serious conflict occurred at Morehead City, in which a white officer shot and killed a black soldier during a scuffle. The confrontations revealed that many white occupation troops in the Tar Heel State were no more willing than white North Carolinians to treat African Americans as equals, even if they wore the same uniform. More collisions would have occurred had the military commanders failed to keep white and black soldiers segregated as a matter of policy. Unaware of this practice, Holden sought to calm citizens' fears by advising the president to station white troops near large concentrations of black troops. Johnson ignored the governor's misguided advice.[37]

The discipline of black regiments stationed in North Carolina was comparable with that of white regiments, in that it varied from unit to unit. A U.S. Army inspector who admitted to being "a little skeptical" about the capabilities of black soldiers, "unhesitatingly" pronounced a company of the 37th USCT "one of the very best companies in the service." As might be expected given his prejudice, the inspector lauded the company commander and his "system of instruction and discipline," but rated the enlisted men as merely average black soldiers.[38]

Most of the black occupation troops in North Carolina were veterans of the Petersburg and Fort Fisher–Wilmington campaigns, and ten of them were Medal of Honor recipients. Their discipline was often superior to that of white troops who had grown soft after several years of garrison duty on the North Carolina coast. Nevertheless, an army quartermaster characterized the black soldiers detailed as laborers as "almost worthless." The officer estimated that it took "three times [longer] to load cars or unload vessels with enlisted colored troops [than] it does with citizen colored labor or white troops." But he blamed the problem on white officers who failed to discipline their black troops. Like their white counterparts, African American soldiers committed crimes such as assault, robbery, rape, and murder. Local newspapers publicized these cases to illustrate the unsuitability of black soldiers for occupation duty. In reporting the "diabolical murder" of a white citizen and the arrest of four black soldiers accused of the crime, the *Wilmington Journal* editorialized, "The perpetrators must be brought to justice. A little stretching of hemp would have a salutary effect." The defendants were acquitted after a lengthy trial.[39]

Black troops staged several mutinies in North Carolina; the deadliest involved a company of the 37th USCT. The mutineers killed a lieutenant and a private who were trying to subdue them. Justice was swift: four of the ringleaders were tried for mutiny, convicted, and executed by a firing squad.[40]

White soldiers were also guilty of mutiny. The most notorious case involved twenty-eight soldiers of the 12th New York Cavalry stationed at Tarboro who forcibly released four of their comrades from confinement. The mutineers were dishonorably discharged with loss of pay and bounties and sentenced to one year's imprisonment at hard labor, which was later commuted by President Johnson.[41]

Several mutinies went unreported, including an incident in which soldiers of Col. John C. McQuiston's brigade stormed the commissary at

Charlotte, demanding an increase in their provisions after several days of half-rations. According to a soldier from another brigade, McQuiston soon arrived and met the mutineers' demands to prevent a full-scale riot. "So the next morning thay got plenty of rations," grumbled the soldier, "while we did not get any except a fiew hard tack." Although white troops behaved no better than black troops, racial prejudice caused white officers and civilians to overlook their offenses and condemn those of black soldiers.[42]

During the war, white officers and their black troops had been bound together by a common purpose—to preserve the Union and free the slaves—but victory abruptly severed that bond. Two postwar confrontations involving black soldiers and white civilians revealed that some Union officers, when intervening in such conflicts, deemed the color of a man's skin more important than the color of his uniform. Beginning on July 5, 1865, an order issued by the commandant of the Post of Wilmington prohibited ex-Confederates from wearing any "buttons, badges, [braids] or other insignia of rank," yet permitted them to continue wearing gray uniform clothing. The order warned that violators would be subject "to the unpleasant necessity of being stopped wherever found" and having the insignia removed. Several days after the order took effect, a black soldier passing through the Wilmington marketplace accosted a white citizen in gray who was violating the order and demanded in the name of the provost marshal that he remove his jacket buttons. The citizen replied that he was unaware of the order. An officer standing nearby overheard the exchange and rushed over to the two men. By this time, a crowd of freedpeople had gathered to witness the encounter, expecting the officer to support the private. To the onlookers' surprise, the officer grabbed the soldier by the collar and kicked him several times before driving the hapless private back to camp. Whereas the soldier believed he was merely performing his duty, the officer found the image of a black man publicly humiliating a white man intolerable.[43]

The second incident also occurred in Wilmington and involved Sgt. John W. Benson of the 6th USCT, who attempted to arrest a white woman after she had pointed a revolver at his head. Word of the incident spread quickly, for when Benson arrived at her house, the woman was shielded by a cordon of officers who refused to let the sergeant take her to the provost marshal's office. Benson retaliated by sending a letter of complaint to the *Wilmington Herald*, which agreed to print it—but only as a paid advertisement. The letter proved far more expensive than anticipated, for it cost Benson his stripes and some jail time for "insolence to commissioned officers."[44]

The punishment meted out to black soldiers sometimes resembled the abuse masters inflicted on their slaves, as in the near-fatal choking of a soldier in the 37th USCT by his commanding officer, Maj. William A. Cutler. Cutler justified his action by explaining that the soldier tried to resist arrest, but Cutler's superior ruled that his action was unnecessary because the prisoner was under a strong guard. In another incident, Pvt. James L. Gant of the 27th USCT complained of being excessively disciplined by his company commander for talking back to his sergeant. The captain repeatedly struck Gant and then gagged him with a bayonet "so tight," the private wrote, that the gag "broke out my Jaw tooth." To intensify his agony and humiliation, Gant was tied up by his thumbs before the captain's headquarters for ninety minutes. The incident may have led to a mutiny in the 27th USCT just two weeks later, in which soldiers attempted to free several comrades being punished for misconduct. The court-martial records indicate that at least one of the prisoners was hung up by his thumbs. The mutiny was soon quelled and the ringleaders were sentenced to lengthy terms at hard labor.[45]

The mistreatment of black soldiers extended beyond physical abuse. According to Lt. Col. John A. Campbell, the assistant adjutant general for the Department of North Carolina, African American soldiers were "defrauded of very large sums of money" by dishonest state bounty agents, army paymasters, and even their own officers. Exploiting black privates was easy enough, Campbell noted, for most of them were illiterate and inexperienced in financial matters. "This is a very common practice," Campbell asserted, "and pay-day for [black troops], in multitudes of cases, has never come." When testifying before Congress, Campbell recommended that the War Department appoint a special commission "to pursue every case of this kind of fraud to a final issue." The army attempted to rectify the injustice after the war, but many blacks never received fair compensation.[46]

While black soldiers received harsh treatment from their officers, black civilians became the victims of white troops who apparently forgot the enthusiastic welcome freedpeople had given them when they entered New Bern, Wilmington, Raleigh, and many other North Carolina towns. The chaplain of the 1st USCT, Henry M. Turner, contended (with probable exaggeration) that "not one in twenty" white soldiers "will do justice to the colored man." Instead, Turner wrote, "many . . . will curse, threaten, and, as I learn, even whip colored persons, where they think they can escape detection, to gratify some 'secesh belle,' or to keep the good will of some Southerner who can keep a good table. I have been told over and over, by colored persons," Turner continued, "that they were never treated more cruelly, than they were by some of the white Yankees." "Sallie," an African American teacher in Wilmington, complained that "Yankee Soldiers" continually victimized her black students. "Scarcely a day passes but some one is molested," she wrote. Freedpeople who managed to earn a "dime or two . . . are robbed by these lawless desperadoes. . . . One or two [students] have been killed." The officers were aware of their soldiers' crimes, she maintained, yet they did nothing to bring the culprits to justice. Not surprisingly, when three regiments of black troops arrived at Wilmington to replace the white garrison, the freedpeople rejoiced. "We have so long been annoyed by 'rebs' in the garb of Union soldiers," "Sallie" wrote, "that it was almost like the transition from slavery to liberty, to feel that we had those around us who would be our protectors indeed."[47]

In Raleigh, gangs of soldiers robbed and vandalized black-owned businesses and beat the proprietors. As soon as he learned of the soldiers' Raleigh-based crime ring, General Ruger ordered all troops temporarily confined to camp, and he warned that further offenses would compel him to make the town permanently off-limits. The freedpeople on Roanoke Island complained that white occupation troops stole from them with impunity and that any attempt to resist invariably resulted in a trip to the guardhouse. The victims, many of them family members of black soldiers, appealed to the commander, Col. T. F. Lehmann, for help, but he ignored their complaints. A white resident of Warrenton noted the daily spectacle of freedmen hanging by their thumbs on the Main Street sidewalk, punished by the local commander for various minor offenses. "It reminds me forcibly of the fable of the wolf & the Shepherds," the citizen remarked. "'What a fuss there would be if we were to do this thing.'"[48]

Freedpeople were defrauded by unscrupulous quartermaster and commissary officers who promised both rations and cash wages to entice black laborers to work for them. When the workers demanded payment, the officers insisted they had never promised them greenbacks. A Freedmen's Bureau official believed that "such treatment of Freedmen by officers of the U.S. Government" would result "in the destruction of the implicit faith which they have had in the Government and its officers, and the increase among them of the disinclination to work." The official deemed the exploitation of black laborers by unprincipled army officers as the greatest obstacle to making the former slaves "honest and industrious citizens."[49]

Reports from across the state indicated that white North Carolinians were committing outrages upon freedpeople reminiscent of the punishment formerly meted out to slaves. Col. Thomas T. Heath reported that "woman whipping is common" in parts of Wake County and that "orders forbidding the lash are hooted at." He stated that "five wealthy planters" had "brutally & outrageously pounded black women, formerly their slaves, until life was nearly extinct" and that a sixth planter had shot a freedman to death simply because he no longer desired his services.[50]

Other federal commanders found similar reports either exaggerated or unfounded. In August 1865, the Wilmington Herald published reports from Fayetteville of whippings by the sheriff and other white citizens, with several blacks dying as a result of their punishment. The Herald also reprinted a letter from Fayetteville mayor Archibald McLean denying the rumors. General Ruger nevertheless directed several officers, including Col. J. Worthington Ames, to investigate the whipping rumors, along with reports that teachers were being driven from freedpeople's schools. "I am happy to say," Ames informed Ruger, "that I believe all reports [of outrages] to be false." Ames reported that Fayetteville and the surrounding countryside were "unusually quiet" and the white citizens "loyal and well disposed towards the Freedmen." The colonel left a post commander but no garrison at Fayetteville. The mayor and the police nevertheless obeyed the officer's orders "with zeal," and the freedpeople seemed to be gaining confidence in the local authorities. "The desire to avoid a garrison of colored troops is a powerful spur to good conduct," Ames commented.[51]

About the time of Ames's investigation, Governor Holden received a letter from a Unionist named J. C. Williams alleging that former slaveholders in Sampson County were attempting to revive "the peculiar institution" with the cooperation of the local police, who chased ex-slaves with hounds, confiscated their property, and hung them up by the thumbs until they promised to return to their former masters. Holden sent Williams's letter to Ruger, who, in turn, ordered Colonel Ames to investigate the allegations. Ames directed Maj. Samuel C. Oliver of the 2nd Massachusetts Heavy Artillery to take two companies and proceed to Sampson County. Oliver's investigation uncovered no evidence of attempts to coerce freedpeople back into slavery. "I must say that however much the people of this county have been opposed to the United States . . . ," Oliver reported, "they seem now loyally disposed."[52]

When a white missionary and a black minister at Goldsboro accused his soldiers of abusing blacks, Col. Joseph C. Abbott insisted that "it is hardly possible . . . these things could have occurred to the extent complained of" by the two men. Although conceding that "lawless soldiers" had "annoyed" the freedpeople of Goldsboro, Abbott refused to believe that his provost marshal remained unaware of so many outrages. He therefore concluded that the two men's "statements are largely based upon the exaggeration of the Negroes." The reluctance of federal officers such as Ames, Oliver, and Abbott to credit the accusations of freedpeople and white Unionists indicates both a determination to be impartial and skepticism regarding the accusers' veracity. A diehard Confederate living in Wilmington noted that although he admitted to being an "incorrigible" Rebel when questioned by Union soldiers, "I find I am more respected than those who have suddenly become so intensely Union & loyal. They are looked upon with distrust & suspicion." Army quartermaster general Montgomery C. Meigs instructed his chief subordinate in North Carolina to beware of self-proclaimed Unionists filing claims for property confiscated by the army. "There are so many cases of simulated loyalty presented in connection with claims," Meigs wrote, "that the mere taking [of] the oath of allegiance is not of itself sufficient proof of loyalty." Meigs ruled that the claimant had to present evidence of his loyalty in the form of documents or personal references before any money would be paid to him.[53]

Most occupation commanders attempted to steer clear of civil conflicts whenever possible, but they were sometimes compelled to intervene in even religious matters. When black members of Wilmington's Front Street Methodist Church decided to secede, they contended that the church legally belonged to them. Not surprisingly, the white members contested their claim. In an effort to placate the disputants, the post commander issued an order allowing each congregation use of the church for one-half of the Sabbath. Although the arrangement satisfied neither party, General Ruger refused to decide the case, well aware that his ruling would only generate further controversy. "This matter will remain as it is until the civil law decides it," Ruger announced. "If the two congregations cannot worship together they must divide the Sabbath Day between them as at present."[54]

Despite the bluecoats' efforts at conciliation, white Tar Heels viewed federal occupation troops as unwelcome strangers blocking their rightful return to power. The freedpeople, however, distrusted the white civil authorities and believed that the Union soldiers—their own outrages notwithstanding—were all that stood between them and a return to slavery or something akin to it. The white soldiers disliked the situation as much as the civilians did, for they viewed their war-fighting task as finished and had no desire to remain in the South as peacekeepers. The process of conciliation nevertheless continued as military commanders began relinquishing authority to the provisional government during the summer of 1865.[55]

Chapter Four

THE RETURN OF CIVIL GOVERNMENT

Shortly after assuming command of the Department of North Carolina, General Ruger began transferring authority to the state's civil officers. Ruger nevertheless was barraged with complaints from Governor Holden concerning troublesome black soldiers and the military's improper interference in civil affairs. Holden also maintained that civil authority reigned supreme in the Tar Heel State. Ruger disagreed, however, asserting that martial law remained very much in force, enabling him to intervene in civil affairs as he saw fit. The two men had to resolve their differences before civil government could be restored in North Carolina.

Thirty-two-year-old Thomas Howard Ruger was born in New York and raised in Janesville, Wisconsin. He graduated third in the West Point class of 1854 and received an appointment to the U.S. Army Corps of Engineers but resigned his commission soon afterward to practice law in Janesville. In June 1861, Ruger rejoined the army as lieutenant colonel of the 3rd Wisconsin Infantry and became its colonel the following September. In 1862, Ruger and the 3rd Wisconsin served in the Union force that "Stonewall" Jackson repeatedly defeated in the Shenandoah Valley and at Cedar Mountain. Later that year, Ruger commanded a Twelfth Corps brigade at Antietam and was promoted to brigadier general soon afterward. In 1863, he continued as a brigade commander at Chancellorsville and temporarily led a division at Gettysburg. Ruger's brigade

Brig. Gen. Thomas H. Ruger (Library of Congress)

was among the Twelfth Corps units sent to the Western Theater that fall to aid in raising the siege of Chattanooga, Tennessee. During the 1864 Atlanta Campaign, Ruger commanded a brigade in the Twentieth Corps. He was later transferred to the Twenty-third Corps and rose to division command under General Schofield in Tennessee. Ruger's division played a crucial role in repulsing the Confederate assaults at Franklin. In January 1865, he accompanied Schofield to North Carolina, where his command participated in the Battle of Wyse Fork.

A West Point classmate, Maj. Gen. Oliver O. Howard, described Ruger as a "deliberative, cautious, and yet fearless" man who tended to dig in his heels when pressed. Although obstinacy had served Ruger well on the battlefield, he found it less useful in resolving peacetime disputes. Still, Ruger's legal expertise was rare among the army's occupation commanders in the South and gave him a considerable advantage in negotiating the complexities of postwar occupation. But it remained to be seen if the youthful Ruger could meet the challenge of overseeing the transition from military to civil government in North Carolina.[1]

On July 5, 1865, Ruger announced that Governor Holden had appointed mayors and commissioners for eighteen North Carolina towns, with more to follow. As soon as the mayors indicated their readiness to govern, the federal garrisons would withdraw, with small detachments remaining to guard public property and inspect railroad trains. Ruger instructed his post commanders to assist in preserving order when called on by the mayors and to ensure that their men obeyed "all lawful ordinances and rules of the towns." He prohibited any laws or official actions that violated the freedpeople's rights, warning that such violations would lead to a resumption of "exclusive military control" in the offending communities. On July 6, Ruger announced that the Tar Heel State would be divided into five military districts. Four days later, he issued a circular reminding his district and post commanders that the transfer of authority did not relieve them of responsibility for the sanitary condition of towns within their commands, nor did it remove the liquor traffic from their "exclusive control." By the end of July, most local governments were functioning. Wilmington resident Armand De Rosset nevertheless continued to describe the Union occupation as "an overwhelming military despotism," even as he hailed the return to office of Mayor John Dawson and the town commissioners.[2]

Whereas Ruger's order restoring local governments met with widespread approval, other military orders proved less popular, such as the one requiring former Confederate officers "to remove all badges, military buttons, braid, cord, or other articles designating rank." Unable to afford civilian clothing, most ex-Confederates had to improvise. Charlotte Grimes sewed black cloth over the brass buttons of her husband Bryan's uniform—"in mourning for the Confederacy," the former general told her. Soon afterward, Charlotte sold several of her silk dresses to enable him to buy a suit of civilian clothes. Many gray-clad veterans simply ignored the order until they were forced to comply. No less obnoxious to ex-Confederates was the directive requiring wedding couples to take the oath of allegiance along with their marriage vows. When that unpopular order was rescinded, the *North Carolina Standard* commented that any bride was now free to marry "without taking the oath of allegiance, except to her spouse."[3]

The transition from military to civil government progressed smoothly enough in most North Carolina towns and communities. In Greensboro, the post commandant turned over the issuing of government rations to Mayor William L. Scott because the officer deemed Scott "more competent to decide who are needy." At Scott's request, Ruger halted the post sutlers' sale of liquor in Greensboro because it violated a local ordinance prohibiting trade monopolies. In late September, Tar Heel Unionist Daniel R. Goodloe reported from Henderson in Granville County that "not the slightest sign of disturbance exists" since the removal of federal troops from the area.[4]

New Bern proved a conspicuous exception, however, as military and civil authorities clashed over prerogatives there. On July 22, federal soldiers at New Bern entered an illegal casino and seized the gambling equipment in obedience to orders from Ruger. In reply to Holden's letter protesting the seizure, Ruger stated that, while the post commander at New Bern had handed over the reins of government to the civil authorities, this did not prevent the military from intervening in civil affairs when necessary. Ruger also cited an order from General Grant authorizing the seizure. "No license to keep gambling houses will be recognized by the military authorities," Ruger informed Holden, "and orders have been given to break up such establishments."[5]

On July 23, the post commander at New Bern, Lt. Col. Augustus S. Boernstein, sent Mayor John T. Hough a copy of Ruger's circular to remind him that the military still controlled the town's liquor trade and retained responsibility for its sanitary condition. Boernstein notified the mayor that he intended to "suppress" New Bern's "infamous liquor traffic," and he called attention to the "filth" that had recently accumulated on some of the town's streets. Boernstein's missive triggered a vitriolic reply from John M. Davies, New Bern's acting mayor and a former assistant surgeon for the 9th New Jersey Infantry. Davies began by challenging Boernstein's authority to control the sale of liquor in New Bern, and he accused army officers of being among the worst violators in "the infamous traffic in liquors and the demoralizing practice of gaming." The officers "thereby disgrace the uniform they wear," Davies maintained. He also urged Boernstein to "see that the Military at this Post conform to our Sanitary Regulations, which they daily violate." Davies reserved his harshest criticism for the "lazy negro soldiers who loaf around the streets of the town," suggesting that if they "were kept in camp and drilled, there would be few 'rows' occurring in" New Bern. Davies sent a letter to President Johnson, urging that "all negro troops be immediately removed" from New Bern. Despite Davies's efforts, Boernstein's regiment was retained because the soldiers were needed to guard the government warehouses.[6]

Although Ruger had restored civil government in much of North Carolina, he regarded the state as still under martial law. According to Ruger, the provisional governor was not the state executive but merely a "civil agent" appointed by the president to facilitate the restoration of civil law and the resumption of federal-state relations. In the meantime, Ruger asserted, the military assumed responsibility in four areas: "acts of hostility to the Government, supervision of the public press & public speakers, the protection of the freedmen in their new rights, & also the preservation of public order." Given Ruger's narrow definition of the provisional governor's authority and the wide latitude the general assigned to the military, a confrontation with Holden over their respective powers was all but inevitable.[7]

The controversy began in late July when Holden requested that the military remand to civil custody a white man accused of murdering a former slave. The commander of the District of Raleigh, Brig. Gen. Adelbert Ames, refused because "the enormity of the crime" demanded a prompt trial before a military commission. Despite this setback, the governor remained undeterred. A few days later, Holden requested that Ruger turn over three white men accused of assaulting a freedman. The governor noted that the trial would be held in Person County, where civil law was in force and a competent judge had been appointed. "This is a matter in which I conceive the civil courts have sole and exclusive jurisdiction,"

Holden maintained, "and I have every confidence that strict and impartial justice will be administered."[8]

Ruger took a different view of the situation, however. He refused to comply with Holden's request on the grounds that martial law remained in force in North Carolina. Until the "complete restoration" of civil law, the general contended, "military tribunals have jurisdiction in all that relates to the preservation of order, including the trial and punishment of those guilty of acts of violence." Ruger further asserted that military commanders did not have to await the summons of civil authorities to quell disturbances and punish the guilty, nor were they required to obey writs of habeas corpus issued by state courts. He noted that, before the military's arrest of the three assault suspects, "no civil court had taken cognizance of the matter," and he was aware of several recent murders of blacks in which no investigation had been made. Ruger believed that violence against blacks was increasing because whites had shaken off the "apparent apathy and stuper" stemming from defeat and now sought vengeance against their former slaves. Expressing little faith in the current effectiveness of civilian grand juries, Ruger maintained that "the restraining influence of prompt trial and punishment of offenders" by military commissions "is the only adequate remedy for the existing evil."[9]

Holden disagreed with Ruger's understanding of the situation and informed the general that he was submitting the case to President Johnson. The governor also ordered the opening of county courts throughout the state to deflect Ruger's criticism that civil justice was moving too slowly. Johnson, however, did not have to intervene. While awaiting the president's ruling, Holden met with Ruger to discuss the situation in North Carolina. The two men reached agreement on the jurisdiction of civil and military law in the state. Until the state laws were revised to admit freedpeople's testimony in trials involving white citizens, military commissions would try cases involving blacks, while the civil courts would try cases involving only whites. Ruger's superior, Maj. Gen. George G. Meade, approved the compromise and assured Holden, "When ever the laws of the state and the practice of the courts are such as to leave no doubt the freedman will have justice done him[,] there will be no occasion for the use of military courts, except for purely military offenses."[10]

Despite Ruger's guarantee of swift justice for the freedpeople, the records of the military commissions indicate that barely more than one-half the white suspects were even tried, compared with nearly all the black suspects. The records covered an eight-month period from John-

ston's surrender to the end of 1865. During that span, the military re-
corded 113 crimes committed by whites against blacks and 85 crimes
committed by blacks against whites. White crimes were predominantly
violent, with fourteen murders and sixty-two assaults heading the list.
Black crimes were mainly theft-related, including fourteen burglaries,
eighteen larcenies, and just one murder case. Black suspects nevertheless
found military justice more implacable than did their white counterparts.
The military hanged one black for rape but executed no whites, not even
among those convicted of murder. In thirty-three cases, white suspects
were not tried, among them some unnamed "Citizens of Hillsboro" who
had murdered a black man. In five cases, the record indicated that the
white suspects "could not be found," including a Granville County mob
guilty of "lynching a freedman for rape." Nine white men arrested for
"assault and breaking up [a] Freedmen's meeting" were released upon
giving their bond "to keep the peace."[11]

Among black defendants, only one man was listed as "not tried" and
a second as "could not be found," while five managed to escape from
jail. Twenty-two black suspects were "turned over to the civil authorities"
for trial. The remaining blacks found guilty by the military commissions
often faced stiffer jail sentences than did white criminals. Four murder
cases involving white suspects were not even tried, and in one of the
few murder trials that resulted in conviction, upon Ruger's recommendation President Johnson commuted defendant Archibald Baynes's sentence
from execution by hanging to ten years' imprisonment at hard labor. In
contrast, two black defendants convicted of larceny were each sentenced
to three years at hard labor with a ball and chain attached to the left
leg. In short, military commissions meted out unequal punishment to
white and black North Carolinians, conveying a far different message
than the one Ruger had intended. When a white woman named Temperance Neely was merely fined $1,000 for murdering a former slave,
Ruger pronounced the sentence "entirely inadequate for the crime of
which the prisoner is found guilty. It is a dangerous precedent to establish, particularly at this time, that a human life can be taken almost
entirely without provocation or extenuating circumstances and without
fear of a greater punishment than a fine." Within three days of Neely's
sentencing, a citizens' group took up a collection and paid her fine. Some
Union commanders viewed the situation as critical. From his headquarters at Lexington, General Kilpatrick warned: "Unless examples are made
at once, and every case promptly investigated . . . , the negro will be at the

mercy of his former master, who will not hesitate to murder him on the slightest provocation." Kilpatrick's grim prediction proved all too true.[12]

Ruger received numerous reports confirming his belief that white outrages against blacks were increasing. One such report from Col. Thomas T. Heath, the commander of the District of West North Carolina, was typical. On his arrival at Morganton, Heath "found great injustice being practiced pretty generally on the freedmen." In some cases, Heath noted, former masters banded together and drove off their ex-slaves without paying them for their labor, or they "shamefully" abused the freedmen "for slight or imaginary offenses." Two of the victims were shot. Heath returned all evicted freedmen to their homes and informed blacks and whites alike that they must obey "the orders of the Government," but the outrages continued. The state head of the Freedmen's Bureau remarked that complaints of cruelty to freedpeople crossed his desk every day, borne out by his first quarterly report, which included a lengthy recital of outrages. On August 3, he reported more than one hundred complaints against white employers for dismissing their black laborers without pay after the harvest.[13]

Some blame for the increase in outrages on freedpeople must be placed at Ruger's doorstep, for he might have mitigated this trend had he mandated harsher sentences on convicted whites. As the department commander, Ruger possessed the authority to establish guidelines for stiffer sentences in cases of violent crime, but he chose not to. Instead, he often sought clemency for whites convicted of capital offenses, much to the dismay of the U.S. Army's judge advocate general, Brig. Gen. Joseph Holt. In a letter to President Johnson, Holt argued that, if granted, Ruger's recommendation of leniency for Baynes and other whites guilty of "barbarous murders" would "be followed by the most deplorable consequences." Holt indicated that North Carolina "now enjoys a pre-eminence in murder, especially as committed upon the weak, submissive, unarmed, and defenceless."[14]

The withdrawal of federal troops from much of the Tar Heel State left local police companies in control, and some began assuming extralegal authority. "It is extremely difficult to procure judicious and politic action on the part of the local Police, and in some instances impossible," complained one district commander. In Caswell County, local police arrested a man for killing a former slave and then tried him. Their verdict was "justifiable homicide." The military later intervened, "retried" the man, and found him guilty of murder.[15]

Some police companies bore a striking resemblance to the old slave patrols. The commander of the Post of Kinston, Maj. Edward M. Fuller, reported that the police of Pitt County allegedly were "maintaining a regular patrol day & night on the highway and no colored person is allowed to leave the neighborhood or hire to any one without permission in writing from their former master." Fuller described the captain of the Pitt County police, Tilman R. Cherry, as "a Speculator in Negroes before the war, a violent secessionist during the rebellion and but little if any better now." In response to complaints that local police were abusing their authority, Ruger ordered his district commanders to "remove objectionable persons and appoint others in their stead. No man who has been an active supporter of the rebellion, either by his counsel or acts, will be appointed a policeman." It was one thing for Ruger to issue this order and quite another for it to be executed, however, especially in counties where most able-bodied white males were veterans of the Confederate army. The War Department's rapid withdrawal of occupation troops and Ruger's failure to establish a precedent of swift and impartial justice encouraged white North Carolinians to reassert their former ascendancy over the blacks.[16]

On August 30, 1865, Holden informed Ruger that he had issued a proclamation calling a convention to meet in Raleigh on October 2. A statewide election of delegates was set for September 21. Ruger issued an order prohibiting officers and men from visiting the polls or from leaving camp unless absolutely necessary. At the request of civil officials, commanding officers were to "render all needful assistance" in preserving order; in the event of a "serious disturbance," officers were authorized to act even if not called on to do so. Ruger promised severe punishment for those who attempted "by force, to prevent an orderly and quiet election." The department commander, however, lacked sufficient troops to enforce the order throughout the state, as a major disturbance in a central North Carolina town demonstrated.[17]

On election day, several hundred freedpeople gathered in the Concord town square to hear a speech by the local Freedmen's Bureau official. As the crowd waited, a group of white men carrying firearms, clubs, and stones attacked the blacks and stampeded them through the streets, severely injuring dozens and driving the remainder out of town. Unable to stop the violence, the town officials implored the military to restore order. Colonel Heath immediately sent a detachment of two officers and twenty men by train, but they arrived too late to prevent the rioters from accomplishing their objective. It soon became apparent that the attack on the freedpeople was planned. The commanding officer at Concord arrested the ringleaders and shipped them to Morganton for trial. "This is the out cropping of a spirit which I have detected for some time, wherein the white people cherish the purpose and intent of exterminating the black race," Heath commented with understandable exaggeration. The colonel reported that a recently elected delegate in the Concord area "has openly excited the people by harangueing them to the effect that 'he was in favor of colonizing them (the freed people) six feet due east and west.'" To restore order, Heath transferred a company of soldiers from Charlotte to Concord.[18]

Eight of the ringleaders were charged with rioting and assault and battery and were tried by a military commission. Of the six men found guilty, five received prison sentences ranging from fifteen days to four months, and one was fined $30. Contrary to Ruger's promise of severe punishment for those who rioted on election day, a military court once again dealt leniently with whites found guilty of violent crimes against blacks.[19]

During the election canvass, the military also sought to prevent collisions between Unionists and ex-Confederates, particularly in the District of West North Carolina. When Heath learned that one of the Buncombe County candidates for the state convention was bringing a large contingent of armed Confederate veterans to his debates to intimidate his rivals, the colonel issued a stern warning: "If armed men shall continue to frequent your meetings[,] you will be prohibited from holding such meetings and all such men will be arrested and imprisoned." No federal troops were present to protect candidate W. H. Herbert, who complained of being "most cruely beaten by a mob of lawless men" during his canvass of Cherokee County. In response to Herbert's appeal for a detachment of Union soldiers to restore order, Ruger indicated that troops could not easily be supplied in such a remote area, and he recommended that a local police company be formed instead. At the time, Cherokee County was overrun with outlaws from Tennessee and Georgia, and the sheriff refused to act without the aid of federal troops. According to Heath, many of the Holden-appointed magistrates in the western counties were "unpardoned rebels" who had victimized Unionists—or "tories"—during the war and appeared determined to do so indefinitely. Among the most notorious was Thomas Walton of Burke County, who allegedly issued a written warning "to a union man to leave the country or be shot for his unionism." A magistrate in McDowell County reportedly notified returning Union army veterans "to leave the country or be killed." Maj. J. M. Pierce of the 128th Indiana Infantry informed Holden that a Randolph County Unionist was "shamefully beat and maltreated" as the county sheriff and a justice of the peace looked on. A band of armed men entered the town of Hendersonville and beat or drove off several citizens who had assembled to take the amnesty oath. The town officials were too intimidated to intervene.[20]

Some "tories" were themselves the perpetrators of outrages. Heath reported that veterans of two Union regiments raised in western North Carolina—the 2nd and 3rd Mounted Infantry—had returned home from Tennessee and begun a "reign of terror" against their ex-Confederate neighbors. Maintaining law and order in this region was a daunting task, for Heath had only the 5th Ohio Cavalry to patrol seventeen counties "in a wild country, among a class of people of lawless proclivities."[21]

As the ongoing conflict in western North Carolina degenerated into postwar feuding between Unionists and former Rebels, other forms of lawlessness presented no less a problem for the occupation troops stationed there. Heath reported that horse theft was commonplace in his district. Even the colonel's own mount was stolen by a deserter from the 10th Michigan Cavalry, who also confessed to killing nineteen Tar Heels since the surrender. Some of the thieves claimed to be confiscating horses for the U.S. government, while others were actually given the job by the army. Horse theft increased markedly after the fall harvest, when Ruger ordered the collection of army livestock that Schofield had loaned to needy farmers in May. Heath noted that Kilpatrick had delegated the collection of government stock to citizens who reputedly were "the worst men" in his district. The post quartermaster at Charlotte may have been the greatest horse thief of all, "scouring the country for twenty or thirty miles around Charlotte," Heath reported, and sometimes crossing into South Carolina to collect animals allegedly belonging to the government. "In many cases an only horse or mule is taken from a poor man," Heath wrote, "thus leaving him with no team to work his land or haul his corn." He noted that the quartermaster was in the habit of "cursing and damning citizens, and refusing to let them produce evidence to show the animal was their private property." Heath directed the overzealous quartermaster to cease his confiscation efforts at once.[22]

But the damage was already done. Contrary to Schofield's generous policy of loaning government horses and mules to needy farmers, many army quartermasters performed their collection duty in strict obedience

to orders and without regard for the circumstances. Although some confiscated horses bore the "US" brand, many had, in fact, been sold to
civilians at army sales or by individual Union soldiers, and others had
been nursed back to health after the federals had swapped their broken-
down animals for the citizens' fresh mounts. Conceding the hardship and
inequity resulting from the army's confiscation policy, Ruger ordered
his quartermasters to hold all collected animals long enough to enable
claimants to substantiate ownership.[23]

In addition to keeping the peace and dispensing justice, the military
monitored North Carolina's newspapers and public speakers. On July
21, 1865, Ruger ordered the Salisbury Union Banner to suspend publication
because of a "disloyal" editorial that accused the department commander and other generals of dictating the freedpeople's rights and thereby
obviating the need for a state convention. Referring to Ruger's orders
prohibiting the wearing of Confederate insignia and regulating the sale
of alcohol, the editorial charged that the occupation commanders had
"assumed the power to say what we shall drink and wear." An indignant
Ruger dismissed the editorial's accusations as "false," noting that an order "prohibiting the wearing of insignia and badges of rank, by persons
lately officers of the insurgent forces, and one for the prevention of the
sale of liquor, as a police regulation, cannot honestly be construed as assuming 'the power to say what we shall drink and wear.'"[24]

A week after the suspension, J. J. Bruner, the owner of the office and
presses of the Banner, informed Ruger that his son-in-law was the editor
of the paper and that he had no prior knowledge of its content. Bruner
promised the general that if he were allowed to resume publication, "it
will be done on my own responsibility, and with the honest purpose
of promoting the peace & harmony of the Country." Ruger accepted
Bruner's explanation and lifted the suspension on July 31. To prevent
further misunderstanding, the department commander issued an order
reminding North Carolinians that the state remained under martial law.
"Until the restoration and full operation of civil laws," Ruger announced,
"publishers of newspapers, as well as public speakers, will be subject to
the restrictions existing under military rule, and will not be permitted to
discuss and criticise the acts of the military authorities with that freedom
allowed where civil law is in full operation." Although no Tar Heel newspaper dared criticize Ruger's order, only a few, such as the pro-Holden
North Carolina Standard, expressed support for it.[25]

Several newspapermen were arrested for violating Ruger's restrictions, including the publisher of the *Goldsboro News* and an editor of the *Fayetteville News*; both were charged with using "seditious and treasonable language" and were briefly jailed. Perhaps the most notable such case involved Robert P. Waring, the editor of the *Charlotte Carolina Times*. A military commission tried Waring for "publishing and circulating disloyal and seditious writings within a District under Martial Law." The offending editorial declared that the South was languishing "under a more grinding despotism than has heretofore found a place upon the face of the earth." The officers composing the tribunal were not amused at being described as "despots." They found Waring guilty as charged and fined him $300. The editor managed to pay the fine within five days of his conviction and thus avoided a six-month prison term. Although Ruger's suspension order curtailed the use of "seditious and treasonable language" in North Carolina newspapers, it won him few friends among white Tar Heels. In February 1866, General Grant assumed the responsibility of censoring southern newspapers, relieving Ruger and other department commanders of an unpleasant and thankless task.[26]

In accordance with Holden's August proclamation, the state convention met in October 1865 and wasted no time in passing ordinances that prohibited slavery and repealed North Carolina's secession ordinance. Contrary to Holden's expectations, however, the delegates engaged in a lengthy debate over repudiating the state's war debt. At Holden's request, President Johnson ordered that the debt be repudiated "finally and forever." The morning after the arrival of Johnson's message, the delegates passed the repudiation measure by a voice vote. The issue nevertheless cost Holden the support of political allies such as Jonathan Worth, who decided to oppose Holden in the upcoming gubernatorial election. The convention also established a state militia and scheduled an election for November. Qualified voters would choose a governor, state legislators, U.S. congressmen, and some local officials. The state appeared well on its way to completing the president's Reconstruction program, but it remained to be seen if the Republican majority in Congress would endorse Johnson's lenient plan.[27]

The U.S. Army remained in the background during the convention and the election, though ready to act in case of an emergency. Fortunately for all concerned, there were few disturbances on election day. At Morganton, Lt. Col. R. K. Miller received a request for a detachment to restore order at the polls. Voting was interrupted when a large crowd gathered

around the election officials' table after a voter's qualifications were challenged. Miller immediately sent a detail to the scene, and the soldiers
soon restored order.[28]

In the gubernatorial election, Holden lost to Jonathan Worth, the
state treasurer. Worth was elected by an alliance of Conservatives, the
dominant political faction in North Carolina since 1862, and former secession Democrats, who were united in their opposition to Holden. The
Conservative-Democratic coalition was determined to wrest power from
Holden, win control of the first General Assembly elected after the war,
and restore as much of the old order as possible. Although Worth regarded Ruger as "a good lawyer and an intelligent and upright man," the
department commander would find the newly elected governor far less
inclined to cooperate than Holden had been. On the contrary, Worth's
first order of business was to secure the army's speedy removal from
North Carolina and pass legislation to regulate the freedpeople. Holden
remained in office until December 28.[29]

As with the governor and the department commander, personnel of the
U.S. Army and the Freedmen's Bureau in North Carolina often considered
their partnership a marriage of inconvenience. In any event, the assistant
commissioner—or state head—of the Freedmen's Bureau, Col. Eliphalet
Whittlesey, received a cordial welcome from army officers on his arrival
at Raleigh in June 1865. Whittlesey observed that the officers "seem glad
that somebody is sent to take from their shoulders a work & responsibility which they do not know what to do with." A Yale graduate and former Bowdoin College professor, Whittlesey was himself an army officer.
During the war, he had served under Maj. Gen. Oliver O. Howard, the
commissioner of the Freedmen's Bureau. Whittlesey announced that the
bureau's mission consisted of four tasks:

1. To aid the destitute [of both races], yet in such a way as not to
   encourage dependence
2. To protect freedmen from injustice
3. To assist freedmen in obtaining employment and fair wages for
   their labor
4. To encourage education, intellectual and moral

Whittlesey knew that the Freedmen's Bureau could accomplish its ambitious goals only with the army's cooperation. An agency of the War

Department, the Freedmen's Bureau relied on the army for most of its personnel. The War Department's General Orders No. 102 instructed all commanding officers to "make such temporary details of officers and soldiers as may be required" by the bureau's assistant commissioners and to render them or other bureau officers "any aid that may be required by them in the discharge of their official duties." But the rapid demobilization of the occupation force in the South made fulfilling this order difficult at best.[30]

Whittlesey divided the state into four districts—the Eastern, Central, Southern, and Western—headed by a superintendent. Each district included several local bureau offices—or subdistricts—run by assistant superintendents with authority to try citizens accused of minor crimes and impose fines and jail sentences. They could also arrest felony suspects but were required to turn them over to the military for trial. Local bureau agents spent most of their workday as arbitrators in disputes or contract negotiations between black laborers and their white employers, often handling dozens of cases per day. The bureau never seemed to have enough agents to handle its caseload.[31]

Whittlesey soon discovered that his greatest bureaucratic headache was constant personnel turnover, thanks to the rapid mustering out of the army officers who served as his field agents. He reported that his organization had nearly been "broken up" three times during its first three months of operation. In October, more than one-half of the agent posts remained vacant. Whittlesey hired northern civilians to fill some of the positions, and he even tried a few Tar Heels but was disappointed with the experiment. Most civilian agents expressed open contempt for freedpeople that boded ill for their ability to deal fairly with their black charges. "The affrican race are naturally lazy have no forecast," was the blunt assessment of William B. Bowe, the civilian bureau agent for Caswell County. A Virginia native and longtime resident of Caswell, Bowe's low opinion of blacks was hardly surprising. Although Whittlesey preferred to appoint army officers, they often proved disappointing as well. "Even these, after being mustered out, are not as efficient as when in the military service," Whittlesey wrote: "They fail to command respect. They do not inspire the freedmen with confidence."[32]

Whittlesey, however, could ill-afford to turn down anyone willing to accept a position as Freedmen's Bureau agent. On August 21, he learned of yet another muster-out of white troops and asked Ruger for a company of enlisted men to replace them. In a letter to Commissioner Howard, Whittlesey asked, "What am I to do for men[?] Only four Regiments of White troops remain in the State. I am crippled entirely." Whittlesey warned that the bureau employees still on duty were "overworked, and will soon break down" unless they received immediate assistance. Howard responded to Whittlesey's message by urging Ruger—an old West Point classmate—to provide the Freedmen's Bureau whatever personnel he could spare. Complying with Howard's request proved all but impossible, for three weeks later, the War Department ordered Ruger and other department commanders in the South to muster out all regiments of black troops raised in the North. The order removed four USCT regiments from North Carolina, and many of the departing officers were Freedmen's Bureau agents. Ruger informed Howard that he would do what he could to provide Whittlesey with new personnel, but he explained that it often required detaching company officers from their commands due to the remoteness of many bureau offices. "I will give the matter due attention," Ruger told Howard, who must have found the lukewarm response less than reassuring.[33]

Despite his own personnel concerns, Ruger could have been more candid with Howard and Whittlesey. On September 19, while the Freedmen's Bureau was struggling to replace departing personnel, Ruger informed his superior General Meade that the occupation force in North Carolina could again be safely reduced. Ruger reported that he had 3,227 white troops and 4,524 black troops. He recommended keeping the former at their present strength while eliminating about one-half of the latter. Ruger suggested that the remaining African American soldiers be used for guard duty at several coastal forts and depots. At Ruger's recommendation, two more USCT regiments were transferred from North Carolina, once again compelling Whittlesey to plead for new bureau agents.[34]

In any event, the black soldiers' departure overjoyed white Tar Heels. Ruger announced the transfer a few days after he wrote Meade. Holden had forwarded a letter from a Kinston resident complaining of abuses suffered at the hands of black troops stationed there. Encouraged by the news of the muster-out of northern black regiments, Holden suggested: "Now that the rebellion has been suppressed . . . it does seem to me that a great and magnanimous government like ours, is not obliged to keep colored troops in our midst." One week later, Ruger notified Holden that he had removed the black troops from Kinston.[35]

Ruger cited three reasons to justify the use of white soldiers rather than black soldiers for occupation duty. First, even the most loyal of the southern whites despised black soldiers. Second, the black troops amply reciprocated the whites' antipathy. Third, Ruger feared that the mutual hatred of white civilians and black soldiers might trigger a race riot. Ruger nevertheless conceded that the black soldiers' behavior had been no worse than that of their white counterparts: "The acts complained of, if committed by white troops, would probably not have been the cause of formal or persistent complaint." He believed that most complaints arose because white citizens simply wanted to get rid of black soldiers rather than from misconduct on their part.[36]

Ruger's decision disappointed Whittlesey for more than personnel reasons. The Freedmen's Bureau relied on the U.S. Army to protect its employees and the freedpeople, and to enforce the bureau's policies and rulings. After spending six months in North Carolina, Whittlesey concluded that "the white people in this State are not yet ready to treat the black men justly," and he argued that "our military force ought to be *increased, not decreased.* In some districts," Whittlesey maintained, "I could not now safely travel in U.S. uniform."[37]

Whittlesey had ample reason to express concern. If there was anything more galling to white North Carolinians than the presence of African American troops, it was Freedmen's Bureau officials dictating how they should treat their black laborers. Halifax County plantation mistress Catherine Ann Edmondston criticized local bureau agents for their constant meddling in freedpeople's affairs: "No sooner are the negroes seemingly contented & beginning to work steadily than some Major, Capt, or Lieut in the Free negro service with more time than brains announces a Speech to the Freedmen in Halifax, when 'down goes the shovel & hoe' and presto away they all start to drink some new draught from the 'Free Spring,' & they come home with their heads so filled with their fancied rights . . . that discipline & order are at an end for days."

For Lincolnton attorney and planter David Schenck, it made no difference whether officers served with the army or the bureau—their impact on the freedpeople was equally pernicious. Schenck complained: "The effect of their occupation is to make the negroes insolent and idle and protect them in their meaness. If the officer follows the precedent of his brethren a negro's testimony is as good as a white man's and every complaint he lodges against his employer or former master, subjects such person to the annoyance and disgrace of going before the Yankee commander to answer said negro's charge and there to have no more dignity or respect than is shown the Negro." Schenck's comments illustrate the difficulty that bureau agents faced when arbitrating contracts or disputes between whites and blacks: treating the freedman as an equal party in such negotiations was tantamount to insulting his white counterpart.[38]

Some bureau agents managed to please Tar Heels of both races, however, by bringing fairness and stability to potentially volatile labor relations. Greensboro resident M. S. Sherwood conceded that while "there is much anxiety to get rid of the Freedmen's Bureau" in some parts of the state, there was little hostility to the bureau in his hometown. Sherwood credited bureau officer Capt. Asa Teal of the 124th Indiana Infantry for this state of affairs. He described Teal as an "intelligent, moral, honorable gentleman . . . who has the nerve and the disposition to do *equal justice* between white and black, and between blacks." According to Sherwood, Teal had done more good than "one of our own citizens could have done in his place; and at the present, I seriously doubt whether either the whites or blacks would be bettered by the withdrawal of the Bureau." The mayor of Greensboro, William L. Scott, concurred with Sherwood's assessment and requested that Teal be retained. Unfortunately for all concerned, Teal was mustered out after just a few months at his post. Worse yet, Teal's successor proved incompetent, but the citizens of Greensboro managed to have him removed. Much to the citizens' relief, Teal later returned to the Greensboro subdistrict as a civilian agent. Soon afterward, a bureau inspector reported that the area's "freedmen were industriously working and were protected in their interests."[39]

Many freedpeople were reluctant to sign contracts with white employers, fearing entrapment in a situation like their former servitude or that federal land would be denied them once it became available. To disabuse blacks laboring under this delusion, Whittlesey issued a circular stating that anyone who refused to enter into a contract on that basis was mistaken because the government owned no land in North Carolina and therefore had none to give away. Whittlesey's statement was true to the extent that President Johnson had no intention of distributing confiscated lands to blacks, restoring it instead to ex-Confederates who received presidential pardons. The circular advised freedmen to work hard and save their wages in order to buy their own property. Most white North Carolinians endorsed this advice, secure in the belief that few blacks would save enough to buy their "forty acres and a mule." Those same whites also believed that the freedpeople were plotting to seize their land, and no amount of assurances from the U.S. Army or the Freedmen's Bureau could convince them otherwise.[40]

Rumors of a freedmen's Christmas insurrection plot circulated throughout North Carolina and other southern states during the summer and fall of 1865. In late June, white vigilantes in Halifax County surprised a midnight gathering of unarmed black men and captured several. Under interrogation, the prisoners confessed to a plot to seize the lands of their former masters at Christmas. The vigilantes turned over their terrified prisoners to the local Freedmen's Bureau official, who immediately released them. On August 7, Freedmen's Bureau official Lt. Col. Dexter E. Clapp reported that white citizens throughout his district feared a freedmen's insurrection, but he believed the real danger lay in the overreaction of the county police. In Nash County, Clapp wrote, the police "have dealt with the persons suspected of this in a manner both cruel and calculated to produce the very evil dreaded." Clapp concluded that there was "not the slightest indication of any danger of insurrection on the part of the freedmen." Regardless of the circumstances, many white North Carolinians were convinced that a vile conspiracy was afoot. "Much fear is expressed by various Southern people of an insurrection among the Freedmen," bureau commissioner Howard wrote Whittlesey on September 16. "Now I do not credit one half the stories I hear, but in order to quiet apprehension, please secure from the Department Commander if you can, an order for patrolling the country wherever you, and he, may deem it necessary." In short, Howard recommended that Ruger and Whittlesey reassure white Tar Heels by placing troop detachments where they most feared an insurrection. And that is the policy Ruger adopted.[41]

In a November 11 circular to Freedmen's Bureau employees, Howard sought to defuse the potentially explosive situation by denying rumors that the U.S. government planned to confiscate lands from southern whites and distribute them to the freedpeople during the holidays. Howard ordered all bureau employees "to take every possible means to remove so erroneous and injurious an impression" and to instruct the freedpeople "to look to the property holders for employment." Above all, Howard hoped to mollify concerned white property owners, but as the holiday season approached, they grew increasingly anxious. In early December, several North Carolina newspapers heightened the tension by publishing reports of a foiled insurrection conspiracy in Mississippi, as well as graphic accounts of blacks murdering whites in Jamaica during the Morant Bay Rebellion.[42]

Whites in the eastern counties most feared insurrections, for the largest concentration of the state's freedpeople resided there, with blacks outnumbering their white neighbors in many areas. In mid-December, Holden received several urgent letters from the region, which he forwarded to Ruger. A message from Greene County stated that two local merchants had received at least fifty requests from freedmen for gunpowder—needless to say, no orders were filled—and that one man had offered "$5.00 per lb. rather than not get it." The writer claimed that the militia and most of the police lacked weapons and ammunition while many of the freedpeople were armed. From Elizabeth City a citizen reported that "the people were very much alarmed about negro insurrections." The freedmen were said "to be drilling nights, & showing other indications of hostility to the whites." The writer urged Holden to request "at least one company of white soldiers sent to this town immediately."[43]

On December 13, the state senate's committee on military affairs met with Ruger and requested that he provide the state militia with arms and ammunition, but the general refused on the grounds that he lacked the authority to do so. Ruger also told the committee members that he could find no evidence of an insurrection plot by the freedpeople. In case of a disturbance, he continued, the white occupation troops and the county police (aided by the people, if necessary) would be sufficient to preserve order throughout the state. Ruger noted that he had moved the remaining black troops to the coastal forts and that white soldiers were now stationed at Wilmington and New Bern. As a precaution, Ruger dispatched a company of white soldiers to both Edenton and Elizabeth City, two potential flash points on the coast. Although he dismissed the likelihood of an insurrection, Ruger nonetheless wanted troops on hand to prevent a collision between euphoric blacks celebrating the holiday season and nervous whites who might misinterpret their actions. Ruger also directed that Whittlesey instruct his agents "to caution the Freedmen that they must keep within proper limits in their holiday festivities." Despite Ruger's assurances that he had matters well in hand, the Wilmington Dispatch spoke for many white Tar Heels when it alleged that the department commander's insufficient precautions demonstrated "an utter blindness" to the grave danger posed by a freedmen's insurrection.[44]

The two companies sent to Edenton and Elizabeth City belonged to the 28th Michigan Infantry, whose commander, Col. William W. Wheeler, also headed the District of New Bern. Ruger instructed Wheeler that the detachments' objective was "to guard against any possible trouble by the freedmen in that section of the State during the holidays, of which there seems to be apprehension on the part of the people of that section." The company commanders should tell the freedpeople "that all must observe the law and remain quiet and peaceful," Ruger continued. In the event of trouble, the troops "will promptly suppress any outbreak." He hastened to add that his orders were merely precautionary and that no holiday celebration by the freedpeople should "be mistaken for, or allowed to be acted on by timid people, as an evidence of intended insurrection." The holidays were free of disturbances, so on January 3, 1866, the two companies returned to New Bern as ordered. The rest of the state was likewise peaceful. In Wilmington, Brig. Gen. George Crook permitted the town's freedpeople to hold an Emancipation Day parade on January 1, which the *Wilmington Herald* described as a "harmless enjoyment." Similar parades were held in Fayetteville, Halifax, and New Bern. "All admit that a more quiet and orderly Christmas has never been enjoyed" in North Carolina, wrote Whittlesey. Thus ended the Christmas insurrection scare of 1865.[45]

The surest indication of Ruger's opinion regarding the scare was his steady reduction of troop strength in his department until just three volunteer regiments—two white and one black—remained at the end of 1865. Between June and December 1865, roughly 42,000 troops departed from North Carolina, leaving Ruger with an occupation force of 2,209—a reduction of 95 percent. At first glance, Ruger's troop transfers appear irresponsible, given that the restoration of civil law in the Tar Heel State remained far from complete. But as the avowed purpose of Reconstruction was to restore civil government in the former Confederate states, Ruger expected the county police to assume a more active role in preserving law and order. On December 19, he therefore authorized the formation of county military companies to augment the police. Above all, the general realized that the volunteer soldiers' distaste for postwar occupation duty rendered them increasingly unreliable.[46]

Ruger knew that his troops were homesick, bored, and often undisciplined. Citizens at Morganton complained of outrages committed by soldiers of the 5th Ohio Cavalry. The regimental commander's flagrant misconduct resulted in his court-martial and conviction on several charges. District commander Heath reported that desertions in the 5th Ohio had reached epidemic proportions. He ascribed the cause to "an unreasonable and over weaning desire" on the part of the deserters "to get out of the service and return to their homes." The desertions continued until the regiment was mustered out in late October. The 128th Indiana Infantry replaced the 5th Ohio, but problems arising from low morale persisted. The commander of the 128th, Lt. Col. R. K. Miller, reported that his men were "quite restless and desire to be mustered out." The soldiers had not been paid for five months, and many of them had "great need of their wages to maintain their families at home," Miller noted.[47]

Discipline all but collapsed in Company B of the 128th Indiana while it was stationed at Greensboro in the fall of 1865. Ruger received several affidavits and a petition signed by more than a hundred townspeople attesting to numerous outrages committed by soldiers and complaining that the commanding officer had made no effort to investigate the crimes or arrest the perpetrators. The papers noted that one of the victims, Walter Green, had suffered a fractured skull and was not expected to live (he later recovered, however). In a dispatch to Ruger, the post commander, Capt. Frank M. Hinton, stated that he had promptly investigated all crimes reported to him and arrested the guilty parties, including Green's assailants. Hinton admitted that he had been aware of "an ill feeling existing between the citizens and Soldiers," but he held each side equally responsible for the disturbances.[48]

In response to the citizens' complaints, Ruger sent his inspector general, Maj. Norris J. Frink, to Greensboro to investigate. In his report, Frink described Company B's conduct as "disgraceful" and their appearance as "unsoldierly." He noted that it was commonplace "to see drunken and noisy soldiers in the streets" day and night, and that it was "no uncommon thing to hear them cursing their officers in public places." The men frequently insulted and abused the citizens they met. "Robbing and stealing are a nightly pastime at this point," Frink wrote. Few of the perpetrators had been arrested and punished, and the officers appeared indifferent to the situation; some were probably fearful of chastising their men. Ruger therefore ordered his judge advocate, Maj. Francis E. Wolcott, to try Hinton on charges of "incompetency and neglect of duty" and to prefer charges against the men accused of assaulting Green. By making an example of disorderly soldiers, the general hoped to discourage further misconduct on the part of his troops. The soldiers who assaulted Green were convicted of assault and battery and sentenced to sixty days at hard labor. But Hinton apparently was never tried, for there are no court-martial records bearing his name.[49]

A few months later, Ruger learned of outrages perpetrated by a second detachment of the 128th Indiana serving as the garrison for Asheville. Complaining of drunken soldiers rampaging through the streets at all hours, about a hundred townspeople petitioned Ruger to either remove the garrison or send "a commander *who can and will control his men.*" Ruger also received complaints that prostitutes were living with soldiers of the 28th Michigan Infantry stationed at Goldsboro. In Wilmington, meanwhile, a corporal and three privates of the 37th USCT stood trial for murdering a white citizen.[50]

Ruger was understandably eager to replace his volunteer soldiers with (so he hoped) more disciplined regulars, but the latter remained in short supply. Only after the arrival of four companies of the 5th U.S. Cavalry and six companies of the 8th U.S. Infantry in the spring of 1866 could he authorize the mustering out of his two remaining white volunteer regiments. A Salisbury resident liked the change from volunteer soldiers to regulars: "Among professional soldiers, order and discipline are rigidly enforced," "Raptim" asserted in a letter to the *Raleigh Progress*. The writer noted that volunteer officers, on the contrary, were "apt to wink and connive at the petty misdemeanors" of men who would once more be their "neighbors and social equals" when they returned home.[51]

As 1865 drew to a close, soldiers and civilians in North Carolina could reflect on a year filled with momentous events. The war was over, the Union was preserved, slavery was abolished, and the work of Presidential Reconstruction was under way. For their part, the occupation troops assumed the tasks of preserving order and conciliating their former enemies. While military commanders and civilian authorities often disagreed over their respective powers and prerogatives, they nevertheless managed to resolve most of their differences. The U.S. Army compromised on the issue of judicial authority and appeased white citizens by removing black soldiers from their midst. Despite accusations of "military despotism," the army administered martial law with restraint, providing the stability that the provisional government needed to function.

Events in Washington, however, soon complicated the army's mission. In early December, the Thirty-ninth Congress met in Washington and debated Johnson's mild Reconstruction program. The Republicans enjoyed a substantial majority in both Houses, and they demanded unmistakable proof that the South accepted the consequences of defeat—namely, the failure of secession and the end of slavery. Instead, the northern solons found irrefutable evidence that the South remained openly defiant. Many newly elected southern congressmen had held high office in the Confederacy, and numerous reports from the South indicated that northerners and native Unionists were persecuted and that freedpeople were denied their basic rights. The Republican majority in Congress therefore decided not to seat the congressmen from the former Confederate states and to establish a Joint Committee on Reconstruction to investigate conditions in the postwar South. Thus began the struggle between Congress and the president over Reconstruction policy. The army would find itself plunged squarely in the middle.[52]

Chapter Five

THE STRUGGLE FOR CIVILIAN SUPREMACY

The new governor of North Carolina, Jonathan Worth, took pride in his record as a steadfast Union Whig. "The preservation of the Union has been the polar star of my political life," he declared in June 1866. As a first-term state legislator in 1831, Worth denounced nullification, a doctrine granting a state the right to reject a federal measure it deemed unjust. Three decades later, as a six-term veteran of the General Assembly, he struggled to keep North Carolina in the Union until the state's secession on May 20, 1861. Although Worth feared that secession would prove suicidal, he yielded to the ties of home and family and remained loyal to the Old North State. In December 1862, he was elected state treasurer and served in that capacity until Johnston's surrender. A less than enthusiastic supporter of the Confederate war effort, Worth drafted an anonymous petition in 1864 calling for a state convention to consider peace negotiations with the North. Although his petition failed to sway Governor Zebulon B. Vance, who advocated fighting on for southern independence, Worth continued to support the peace movement clandestinely to the end of the war.[1]

Sharing similar antiwar views with Vance's archrival Holden, Worth remained on good terms with the *Standard* editor and, in June 1865, was appointed treasurer in Holden's provisional government. The two men split over Holden's support of the repudiation of North Carolina's war debt. Soon afterward, Worth announced his candidacy in the fall guber-

Governor
Jonathan Worth
(Courtesy of the
North Carolina
State Archives)

natorial race. Worth's conservatism appealed not only to ex-Union Whig
colleagues such as Vance and William A. Graham—aptly renamed "Conservatives" during the war—but also to former secession Democrats,
longtime political adversaries who now threw their support to Worth
because of his commitment to restoring as much of the old order as possible. The Democrats regarded him as far more dependable than Holden,
whose frequent shifts of political allegiance smacked of rank opportun-
ism. During the war, the Conservatives and the Democrats had discovered
that they could compromise when necessary. Although most Conservatives had protested what they perceived as the Confederate government's
unconstitutional encroachment on state sovereignty, they had shared the
secession Democrats' commitment to southern independence.[2]

Thanks to the support of the newly forged Conservative-Democratic coalition, Worth was elected by a substantial majority, despite losing several Unionist counties to Holden—including Worth's home county of Randolph. Holden's success in the staunchly Unionist counties was due to his continued popularity as the peace candidate for governor in 1864. Despite his success with Unionist voters, Holden lacked the broadly based support needed to defeat Worth.[3]

The victorious Worth rode a mandate to restore as much of the status quo antebellum as possible. Whereas Holden had appointed a high percentage of "new men" to local offices, Worth's appointees reflected his intention to keep the traditional state elite in positions of authority. Among other conservative measures, Worth advocated upholding minimum property qualifications for governors and state legislators, favored creditors by recommending the repeal of a postwar stay law, and opposed granting the right to vote or hold office to freedpeople, a viewpoint the governor shared with many federal occupation commanders in the South. He also supported abolishing the state's common school system because of fears that the Freedmen's Bureau would require the state to fund schools for black children as well. Worth intended to adhere to President Johnson's Reconstruction plan, which promised a swift restoration of North Carolina to the Union and an early departure of U.S. Army and Freedmen's Bureau personnel.[4]

Above all, the state's political leaders planned to restore control of the black workforce during the upcoming session of the General Assembly. Although the Thirteenth Amendment had abolished slavery, Conservative legislators sought to consign blacks to a subservient position resembling "the peculiar institution" in all but name. In the meantime, Worth would attempt to prevent the army and the bureau from interfering in civil government, even if it meant having to make a few temporary legal concessions to racial equality. Unfortunately for Worth and the Conservative-Democratic coalition, the Republican-dominated Congress was maneuvering to supplant Presidential Reconstruction with a far more radical plan.

Worth believed that the Republicans' rejection of Johnson's Reconstruction program revealed a fundamental flaw in their political strategy. Instead of courting their natural allies in the South—the former Union Whigs—the Republicans in Congress appeared to be snubbing them. The governor accused the Republicans of having forgotten the crucial distinction between the Union Whigs and the secession Democrats—or

"Southern Disunionists," as he dubbed them. Worth wished to remind Republican congressmen that the former Whigs had attempted to preserve the antebellum Union, while the extremists of both sections sought to destroy it. He now charged the radical Republicans—or "Northern Disunionists"—with trying "to accomplish what the secession[ist]s could not effect." The governor viewed the radicals' sabotaging of Presidential Reconstruction as the present danger to the Union, for their action kept the nation divided and perpetuated sectional hatreds. Once again, Worth perceived himself as a true believer engaged in a desperate struggle to save the Union from extremist heretics.[5]

Worth wasted no time in defending his state against what he regarded as "military despotism." During the first week of 1866, several North Carolina newspapers reported that President Johnson had suspended collection of a tax authorized by the state convention to pay the expenses of the new state government. Worth immediately telegraphed Johnson for confirmation, and the president replied that he had issued no such order. A few days later, the sheriff of New Hanover County informed Worth that Brig. Gen. George Crook, the commander at Wilmington, had prohibited him from taxing a local merchant "until the proper tribunal decides on the legality of the tax." Wishing "to avoid . . . any jarring between the Civil & Military authorities," Worth requested that Ruger explain why the military had intervened when citizens were now able to challenge the tax in the newly reopened state courts, yet the governor neglected to mention that the judge for Wilmington was not yet seated.[6]

Ruger explained that he had ordered the tax suspended because the merchant in question was reportedly assessed for a period during which he was trading under a special license granted by the U.S. Treasury Department and for which he had paid a federal tax. Ruger acted in the belief that the merchant was not liable for state taxes while paying a tax to trade in "Insurrectionary Districts" and while there were no civil courts to appeal to for an injunction. "From your note," Ruger wrote Worth, "I infer that the Civil Court has that power [to grant an injunction]. If such is the case I would be glad if you would so state." Ruger then instructed Crook "that so soon as the Civil Courts are established and a Judge qualified . . . , all military control of the matter will cease and the case will be left to the decision of the Civil Courts." The department commander sent a copy of his order to Worth. The matter did not end there, however, for the state courts were slow to convene. When Ruger intervened in a similar case in

New Bern, Worth conceded that the taxpayers' legal recourse should have been "more expeditious," but he expressed the hope that the legality of state taxes and other civil measures would not thereafter "rest on the opinion of the General who may at the time have military command." Believing that Worth still failed to grasp his rationale, Ruger repeated his reasons for suspending the state tax in certain instances and then reassured the governor that the sheriffs could collect the tax in all other cases. Once more, Ruger informed Worth that as soon as the state courts announced their readiness to hear the exceptional cases, the department commander would revoke the restraining order on the sheriffs.[7]

Worth also had to contend with the troublesome presence of African American soldiers on the coast. In December 1865, several outrages allegedly committed by black troops stationed at Morehead City prompted white residents to clamor for the soldiers' removal. The residents sent two petitions to Worth, who passed them on to Ruger. The general ordered one of his subordinates to investigate the petitioners' allegations; in the meantime, he permitted no black soldiers to leave Fort Macon unless under the command of a white officer. The investigation led to the arrest of four soldiers accused of raping a sixteen-year-old black girl. Convinced of their guilt, Worth expected the accused to be convicted and executed, but he was soon distressed to learn that an army court-martial had acquitted the four soldiers. Both Ruger and his judge advocate, Maj. Frank Wolcott, also believed that the defendants' guilt had been established beyond a reasonable doubt. "It is a shame that such an aggravated offense should go unpunished," Wolcott wrote. A reluctant Ruger ordered the four soldiers to report to their company.[8]

Meanwhile, Worth urged President Johnson to withdraw the remaining black troops from the state. Much to his chagrin, Worth soon learned that the War Department had kept the 37th USCT in North Carolina because most of the soldiers were native Tar Heels. Most of the 37th remained in the state until February 1867—the last volunteer regiment to be mustered out in the Tar Heel State.[9]

The governor also received reports of outrages committed by black civilians. On January 15, 1866, Worth sent Ruger a letter from a citizen who reported that bands of lawless freedmen were terrorizing residents of Craven County. The governor requested that Ruger apprehend the outlaws and bring them to trial. He also asked for authorization to arm the Craven County militia, but Ruger refused on the grounds that "the generally quiet conduct of the freedmen" rendered such measures unnecessary.

Ruger no doubt assumed that the militia would merely oppress innocent blacks. He assured Worth that the commander at New Bern would bring the guilty to justice and thus discourage further crime. Ruger also insisted that civil law enforcement officers assume a more active role.[10]

In late January, Worth learned that the crime wave in Craven County had induced many frightened citizens to flock to New Bern for protection. The report noted that the perpetrators were recently returned black army veterans. "Having become accustomed to get their living without labor during their service in the army," the report continued, "they doubtless feel no inclination to resort to labor to secure a living so long as they can obtain it by plundering the unprotected inhabitants living within their reach."[11]

Although reports of lawless blacks contained much truth, the accusers failed to mention that numerous whites had likewise turned to crime for their livelihood. On January 8, 1866, Col. Eliphalet Whittlesey, the state head of the Freedmen's Bureau, informed Ruger "that a band of men in Pitt County calling themselves Regulators, are committing depredations and keeping the citizens in a state of excitement and terror." Two months earlier, Whittlesey reported, the gang had raided Washington, the Beaufort County seat, killing a freedman and severely wounding a white man. At the local bureau superintendent's behest, the county sheriff had persuaded three of the outlaws to surrender, but they later escaped from jail. On learning of the breakout, Whittlesey took personal charge of the pursuit. He received a mounted force from the district commander but failed to track down the desperadoes. Several citizens he met along the way claimed that the outlaws had fled the state. Yet Whittlesey later heard that the bandits had voted in Greenville during the recent state election and had helped to organize a local militia company. In the meantime, one of the outlaws reportedly had killed a black man and severely wounded another. "The police have made no efforts as far as I can learn, to arrest them," Whittlesey wrote Ruger, "& it is reported that they boast of their ability to defend themselves against any police or Yankee force." A pattern had emerged in which civil law enforcement officers failed to bring criminals to justice due to apathy, fear of reprisal, or sympathy with the outlaws. In his annual report for 1866, Col. Allan C. Bready of the Freedmen's Bureau reported that "not a single arrest" had been made in his district for crimes against blacks without the bureau's intervention.[12]

The Regulators derived their name from a pre–Revolutionary War vigilante organization consisting of piedmont farmers who sought to end what its members regarded as injustice at the hands of greedy colonial officials. Although the original Regulators had met defeat at the hands of Royal Governor William Tryon's militia, they nonetheless served as the inspiration for a subsequent generation of North Carolinians who considered themselves in the grip of an oppressive "foreign" government. The later Regulators stemmed from bands of Confederate guerrillas and renegade "buffaloes" that had roamed the state's war-torn eastern counties. They sometimes behaved as their eighteenth-century counterparts had. Regulators robbed a Johnston County tax collector, seized court documents from the sheriff of Pitt County, and ransacked the county courthouse at Greenville. In all three cases, the bandits wore masks. Regulators usually rode in disguise, often blacking their faces in minstrel-show fashion. Alluding to the third incident, the *Wilmington Journal* quipped that the gang had acted "a little ahead of any 'Bill for the relief of the people.'" The *Journal* attributed the deed to the outlaws' "desire to protect themselves from what they thought was oppression—the oppression of merciless creditors." But the *Journal* hastened to add that the perpetrators were no better than "regular highwaymen."[13]

Indeed, despite their name, the Regulators of Presidential Reconstruction were above all robbers and vandals who increasingly focused their criminal activities on freedpeople. Bureau agents contended that the outlaws acted in the belief that blacks should not be permitted to own property. The Regulators' victims soon adopted a fatalistic attitude regarding their plight, for neither the civil nor the military authorities seemed willing or able to protect them. "The freedmen who suffer from these outrages, either quietly submit, or leave the neighborhood, as they have found from experience the utter uselessness of entering complaint," observed a Freedmen's Bureau official at Wilmington. A Boston minister named James Thurston visited Goldsboro and found a similar situation there. "Again and again, colored people have told me they dare not go to the Bureau for help," Thurston informed Republican senator Henry Wilson of Massachusetts, "for if they did so, their lives would be in imminent danger." Most of the Regulators' crimes were not reported to the army or the bureau. "From the immunity enjoyed by these Regulators, their organization and number have greatly increased," reported Capt. Allan Rutherford, the supervisor of the bureau's Southern District, "so that in some sections citizens fear to speak of the matter to their neighbors or friends, not knowing but that they may belong to them."[14]

Perhaps the Regulators' most blatant flouting of military authority involved a ruse in which some of them posed as local police "confiscating" firearms and other private property under army orders. Responding to complaints of widespread marauding near Wilmington, district commander General Crook issued a circular directing the police to confiscate "all arms belonging to private individuals who are disturbing or likely to disturb the peace of the community." The order backfired, for reports soon reached the Freedmen's Bureau superintendent at Wilmington that unauthorized "persons acting under this order" far exceeded Crook's instructions, confiscating not only "Fire arms of all kinds," but also "Horses, Mules, Carts, Wagons, &c." Worse yet, instead of turning over their haul to the district quartermaster as directed, the impostors either kept the property or distributed it among their friends.[15]

Some local police either colluded with the Regulators or were members themselves. On February 20, 1866, Whittlesey sent Ruger a letter complaining of outrages committed by the Johnston County police from an unlikely source—the police captain for that county. "I learn from officers at Wilmington that similar outrages are committed in Sampson & Duplin Counties," Whittlesey wrote. "The police of these counties are not only inefficient, but are often engaged in robbing freedmen and others who sympathize with them." As in the case of the Memphis and New Orleans riots of 1866, law enforcement officers not only refused to protect the freedpeople, but some of them also numbered among their assailants.[16]

In at least one instance, some concerned North Carolinians decided to take matters into their own hands when they realized that the local authorities either could not or would not protect them. In response to the Regulators' outrages, a group of Jones County residents met at Trenton and drafted a set of resolutions establishing "a vigilance and safety committee for the protection of our lives, homes and property against assassins, robbers thieves &c." The resolutions proposed the formation of a biracial night watch for Trenton with authority "to arrest all . . . suspicious characters who may be found prowling about said town at unseasonable hours." One of the signers, William H. Bryan, sent the resolutions to the governor for his authorization, but Worth replied that he lacked the power to grant the petitioners' request.[17]

Among other crimes, Regulators assaulted several Union veterans who had settled in the eastern part of the state, and they (as well as other outlaws) threatened or assaulted several Freedmen's Bureau agents. The bureau agent for Murfreesboro, Lt. George S. Hawley, reported that while he was riding down the town's main street, a white man with a double-barreled shotgun confronted him. Cocking both triggers, the man threatened to shoot Hawley and defied the military authorities to arrest him. Much to Hawley's relief, several citizens managed to wrestle the gun from the man's hands before he could carry out his threat. Authorities later arrested the man for assaulting two freedmen and firing into the house of a third. The accused secured his release by posting a $500 bond, a sum that Hawley deemed "entirely insufficient," given the gravity of the man's alleged offenses. After he was assaulted by "three ruffians," Lumberton bureau agent William H. H. Birnie pressed charges for assault and secured a trial by military commission because he distrusted the civil courts. Although the men were convicted, the commission merely fined them $50 each. A third bureau official, Col. Allan C. Bready, was attacked in the Raleigh boarding house where he lived and nearly killed by a man armed with a revolver. When it became apparent that neither the sheriff nor the police were pursuing the suspect, Bready asked the post commander to intervene.[18]

Not surprisingly, many Freedmen's Bureau agents in remote locations requested troops to protect them and enforce their rulings, but often to no avail. "The number of troops in the State is so small that a large guard . . . cannot be spared," Whittlesey informed Capt. H. H. Foster, the agent for Duplin County. Whittlesey therefore cautioned Foster to avoid "provoking any violence or opposition" among the whites or risk being "overpowered." Foster must have found Whittlesey's advice of doubtful utility, given that many local whites found the agent's mere presence intolerable.[19]

A few U.S. soldiers became victims of Regulators. On January 27, 1866, Lt. John E. Kenyon of the 28th Michigan Infantry was mortally wounded while commanding a mounted detachment sent from New Bern to Pitt County to arrest eight men charged with murdering a freedman and raiding Washington two months earlier. Kenyon managed to arrest seven of them, but they escaped soon afterward. Two nights later, Kenyon and his squad found the gang barricaded inside the home of the reputed leader, Reddick Carney. After his surrender demand was refused, the impetuous Kenyon entered the house alone and was shot while ascending the stairs. Kenyon's men were so unnerved by their commander's shooting that they abandoned their mission and returned empty-handed to New Bern. A large force hurried to Pitt County to apprehend the outlaws, but the gang had vanished into the countryside.[20]

On May 10, 1866, Capt. Hugo Hillebrandt, the Freedmen's Bureau chief for Lenoir County, received a complaint from a freedman named Stephen Parker that a horse belonging to him had recently been stolen and was now in the possession of Harper Williams, a white man. Hillebrandt assigned Cpl. Henry Callicott the task of presenting Williams with a summons to appear at the Freedmen's Bureau office with the horse in question and an explanation as to how he came to possess it. On May 11, Callicott and Parker traveled to Williams's farm, and the corporal left the summons at the front door when he found that Williams was away. Soon afterward, Callicott and Parker were confronted by a white youth named Nathan W. Roberts, who was pointing a rifle at them. When Callicott reached for his revolver, Roberts shot the corporal. Parker fled the scene and only learned later that Callicott was dead. On receiving the news, Hillebrandt telegraphed to New Bern for troops, having been warned that the area where Callicott fell was controlled by a large band of horse thieves and that Roberts probably was one of them. By the time the detachment recovered Callicott's mutilated corpse, Roberts had vanished. The civil authorities in Lenoir County made no investigation of the murder. Both Ruger and his successor, Brig. Gen. John C. Robinson, pursued several leads but failed to apprehend Callicott's killer.[21]

As the above incidents suggest, federal soldiers found chasing Regulators a frustrating—and sometimes deadly—business. If Ruger attributed the Regulators' outrages to "a few desperate men," Freedmen's Bureau officials' reports of widespread violence and anarchy suggest a far different situation. For the month of July 1866, the assistant commissioner reported forty-nine cases in which whites had committed violent crimes against blacks, in contrast to just one case in which a freedman had assaulted a white man. Yet the reticence of the Regulators' victims makes determining the full extent of Regulator crime next to impossible. Suffice it to say that the civil authorities lacked either the resources or the will to subdue the Regulators, and the army refused to intervene unless called on to do so, which remained unlikely as long as Worth was governor.[22]

In Raleigh, Worth and other state political leaders deemed securing control of their black workforce a far more pressing issue than the Regulator crime wave. Deprived of the slaveholder's prerogative, they turned to legislation. When the General Assembly met in January 1866, legislators rewrote some old laws and passed several new ones intended to restrict the freedpeople's rights. These and similar laws passed by other southern state legislatures became known collectively as the "Black Codes." While North Carolina's Black Code proved more liberal than those of other southern states, the laws nonetheless placed freedpeople under virtually the same discriminatory restrictions as antebellum free blacks. The state's lawmakers sought to clothe the doctrine of white supremacy in the benevolent guise of paternalistic concern for the blacks' welfare. Insisting that there was no "disposition to deny to [blacks] any of the essential rights of civil or religious freedom," Worth nevertheless asserted that "restraining measures are necessary to prevent pauperism, vagrancy, idleness, and their consequent crimes." Under the state's Black Code, freedmen could not testify in court against whites, serve on juries, or intermarry with whites. The laws also discriminated in such matters as mobility, vagrancy, apprenticeship, contracts, weapon ownership, and punishment for assault with intent to commit rape, a capital offense only when the assailant was a black man and the victim a white woman.[23]

Northern Republicans concluded that the Black Codes were an underhanded attempt to resurrect slavery in the South. In Congress, the Republican majority responded with two bills in early 1866, designed to protect freedpeople from southern white oppression. The Freedmen's Bureau bill extended the life of the agency and authorized military tribunals to intervene in cases involving blacks who were denied rights enjoyed by whites or who faced unequal punishment for the same crime. The Civil Rights bill was even more ambitious, conferring citizenship on all native-born Americans except Indians and defining their rights under federal authority. The bill authorized federal judicial and law enforcement officers to prosecute state or local authorities suspected of denying citizens their rights. One week after the two bills were reported to the Senate, the War Department issued General Orders No. 3, instructing commanders in the South to protect army and Freedmen's Bureau personnel and native loyalists from civil prosecution for acts committed under military authority. The order also embraced blacks "charged with offences for which white persons are not prosecuted or punished in the same manner or degree." The army was charged with protecting the rights enumerated in the two bills. The emphasis in federal policy toward the South clearly had shifted from conciliation of ex-Confederates to protection of blacks and white Unionists. But President Johnson was determined to overturn the Republicans' Reconstruction program.[24]

After receiving General Orders No. 3, Ruger notified Worth of its effect on potential civil trials involving freedpeople. "In cases where there is no distinction either as to [presenting] evidence or punishment between whites and blacks," the general explained, "the Civil Courts will not be interfered with." But Ruger failed to explain the procedure in cases where there *was* discrimination. After conferring with Ruger, Whittlesey drafted a set of guidelines for the respective jurisdiction of civil, military, and bureau courts. On February 16, these and other directives appeared as Circular No. 1. First, trials in civil courts were permissible if the testimony of black witnesses was admitted and the punishments were the same for whites and blacks. Second, in cases where white citizens were accused of crimes against blacks, bureau or military authorities would assume jurisdiction because state law prohibited blacks from testifying in those instances. Third, bureau officers would try cases involving crimes punishable under state law by a maximum $100 fine or thirty days' imprisonment, while military commissions would try all cases in which punishments exceeded that ceiling.[25]

Fearing the indefinite protraction of "military rule" if the state's discriminatory laws were not repealed, Worth urged the General Assembly to draft a law admitting black testimony, which became the ninth section of "an act concerning negroes and persons of color or of mixed blood." Much to Worth's dismay, a proviso was added stipulating that the law would not take effect until jurisdiction over the freedpeople was fully remitted to the civil courts. The condition was a none-too-subtle hint to Freedmen's Bureau courts and military tribunals to relinquish control over the civil judiciary. The bill further stipulated that in cases involving whites alone, black testimony was admissible only with the consent of both parties. Worth lobbied hard to have the proviso stricken, but to no avail. On March 10, 1866, the bill passed with the proviso intact.[26]

Uncertain as to the effect of the new law on the state's courts, Whittlesey consulted Worth and several other state legal experts. Whittlesey thus remained uncertain whether "the effect is to restore freedmen to all common-law rights"—as Worth maintained—"or to leave them in the same position as before." Convinced that "the negro has very little chance of getting his due before the Civil Courts of N.C. at present," Whittlesey met again with Ruger, and the two men decided to continue using Circular No. 1 as a temporary expedient. Both Ruger and Whittlesey pledged "to turn over the whole matter of criminal jurisdiction to the civil courts" as soon as the state laws were changed to admit black testimony and mandate the same punishment for whites and blacks. Having failed to sway the legislature, Worth now planned to convince the delegates at the upcoming state convention to make the necessary changes in the law.[27]

In late January, the Congressional Joint Committee on Reconstruction began its hearings on conditions in the South. The subcommittee for North Carolina interviewed eleven witnesses from that state; only three were army personnel. For some reason, Ruger did not testify but Whittlesey did. At the close of his interview, Whittlesey suggested that if the Freedmen's Bureau were to remain in North Carolina, it must have the army's ongoing protection. Otherwise, bureau agents could not safely perform their duty in much of the state. Whittlesey thought an occupation force of "three thousand to four thousand men scattered across the State" would suffice—roughly a doubling of the occupation force. Unsolicited advice from a former Union officer named George F. Granger was even more categorical. A resident of Wilmington and a onetime commander of the Post of Raleigh, Granger urged Reconstruction Committee member Thaddeus Stevens to ignore white Southerners' appeals to withdraw the military and restore civil law. "In my humble opinion," Granger wrote, "no law can be Established here at present Except that law which is Enforced by United States troops, at the point of the bayonet." The bulk of the testimony indicated that military occupation must continue in the South to protect blacks, Northerners, and native loyalists.[28]

During the Joint Committee hearings, Congress passed the Freedmen's Bureau and Civil Rights bills. President Johnson vetoed both bills because he deemed them unconstitutional and because the bills would require "a permanent military force" to enforce them. The vetoes all but guaranteed a bitter struggle between the president and Congress over Reconstruction policy. For his part, Johnson remained supremely confident that he would triumph in the end. Johnson's vetoes and his Washington's Birthday speech—in which he accused radical Republican leaders Thaddeus Stevens and Charles Sumner of treason—likewise encouraged many Southerners to believe that he would soon deliver them from military rule. "The people here are exultant," Whittlesey informed Freedmen's Bureau head Oliver O. Howard. "They think our occupation is gone." The *Charlotte Western Democrat* advised its readers to adopt "a prudent, quiet course . . . until the President conquers the [radical] faction at the North and secures equal rights for us." Several related incidents gave Conservative-Democrats in North Carolina further cause for optimism.[29]

While the president and Congress wrangled over Reconstruction policy in Washington, an army war crimes tribunal in Raleigh provoked a similar confrontation between civil and military authorities there. The defendant was John H. Gee, a former Confederate major and commandant of Salisbury Prison. Gee was charged with violating the laws of war in his mistreatment of more than ten thousand Union prisoners that had jammed the six-acre stockade in late 1864. One appalling statistic looms above all others: just over one-third of the inmates at Salisbury died within its walls. No other Civil War prison could match that horrific mortality rate—not even the notorious Andersonville prison in Georgia. This chilling fact seemed to augur that Gee would share the fate of Henry Wirz, the former commandant of Andersonville. After a military commission in Washington convicted him of war crimes, Wirz was hanged the previous November.[30]

Gee's trial began on February 21, 1866, with the judge advocate's reading of the charges and specifications. Afterward, Gee's two attorneys, D. P. Holland and John Wilder, argued that their client should not be tried, for he was paroled under the surrender terms agreed on by Sherman and Johnston. The commission ruled that Gee's parole did not absolve him from crimes committed in violation of the laws of war. On the following day, Gee's attorneys claimed that he had also been pardoned under President Johnson's amnesty proclamation of May 29, 1865. Once again, the commission ruled against the defendant, citing the sixth exception to the president's amnesty proclamation, which denied pardon to anyone who had treated Union prisoners contrary to the laws of war.[31]

As the trial entered its eighth week, Gee's attorneys once more turned to a presidential proclamation for their client's salvation. On April 2, 1866, Johnson declared the insurrection over and peace restored throughout the United States save Texas (which was excluded because it had not yet completed the president's Reconstruction program). The proclamation further stated that martial law, military tribunals, and occupation forces should not be allowed during peacetime, leading many Southerners, including an editorial writer for the *Raleigh Sentinel*, to assume that "the work of re-construction is complete, so far as it lies in the power of the States and of the President."[32]

Contrary to the understanding of the *Sentinel* writer, Johnson's procla-

mation did not dissolve the Freedmen's Bureau and end military occupation with the stroke of a pen. Even so, commanders in the South were
uncertain as to how the document affected their jurisdiction. In response
to an inquiry from the assistant commissioner of the Freedmen's Bureau
for Georgia, Secretary of War Edwin M. Stanton notified the department
commanders in the South that Johnson had authorized him "to inform
you that the President's Proclamation does not remove martial law or
operate in any way upon the Freedmen's Bureau in the exercise of its
legitimate jurisdiction." Stanton added, however, that it was "not expedient" for the commanders "to resort to military tribunals in any case
where justice can be attained through the medium of civil authority." The
secretary probably issued the above directive in response to the U.S. Supreme Court's preliminary ruling in Ex parte Milligan, which prohibited the
trial of civilians by military commissions while civil courts were open.
The Supreme Court's ruling on the Milligan case appeared one day after
Johnson's proclamation and supported his statement regarding the juris-
dictional limits of military courts during peacetime. The timing suggests
that the president was apprised of the court's decision before its release.
At Johnson's behest, Stanton rendered the Milligan ruling official army
policy in General Orders No. 26.[33]

On April 10, attorney D. P. Holland petitioned Judge Daniel G. Fowle
of the state superior court in Raleigh for a writ of habeas corpus to release Gee on the grounds that, by virtue of the president's proclamation,
"martial law is abolished" and "civil law [is] restored in full force" in
North Carolina. Holland argued that the military commission trying Gee
was now "illegal" and should therefore immediately surrender his client
to the civil authorities. On the eleventh, Judge Fowle granted Holland's
petition and issued a writ of habeas corpus to Ruger, but the general
refused to surrender Gee because he was "detained as a prisoner under
authority of the President of the United States." On learning of Ruger's
refusal to honor Fowle's writ, Holland applied for an attachment against
the general. Assuming that Ruger would not submit to arrest by a civil
officer, Fowle decided to continue Holland's motion until April 28, perhaps hoping that President Johnson would intervene in the defendant's
favor before the deadline. The judge also ruled that the president's intention was to restore the supremacy of civil law during peacetime, thereby
restricting those tried by military courts to U.S. armed forces personnel,
which Gee clearly was not. Yet Fowle justified his continuance by allowing that he may have misconstrued the president's meaning and therefore

needed time to further review the case. Fowle notified Worth of Ruger's refusal to surrender Gee. The governor, in turn, sought Johnson's intervention, pleading that he was "impotent to give any assistance to the judiciary in enforcing its decisions."[34]

The War Department meanwhile notified Ruger that because the Gee trial had begun before the president's proclamation appeared, he was to see the trial to its conclusion but suspend execution of the sentence until the judge advocate general in Washington had reviewed the trial records. On the eve of Fowle's decision regarding Ruger's refusal to surrender Gee, Johnson informed Worth that the general had instructions to complete the Gee trial, for the president had not intended his proclamation "to interfere with" existing military commissions. Fowle was unaware of Johnson's message to Worth when he handed down his decision at 10 A.M. on April 28. By virtue of the president's proclamation that the insurrection was at an end, Fowle ruled, Gee was entitled to a writ of habeas corpus and Ruger was legally bound to comply. The judge directed the sheriff of Wake County to serve an attachment against Ruger if he refused to honor the writ. Once again, Ruger neither accepted the writ nor submitted to arrest. Gee's trial thus continued without interruption.[35]

The military tribunal demonstrated its impartiality by avoiding the partisan chicanery that had marred the Wirz trial. The commission was also thorough. The Gee trial consumed fifty-seven days spanning four months, during which more than one hundred witnesses were cross-examined; their testimony generated almost four thousand pages of hand-written trial transcripts. After weighing the evidence, the commission unanimously acquitted Gee of all charges and specifications. While Gee's hometown newspaper proclaimed the local hero's acquittal "a vindication of the South," the *Raleigh Sentinel* believed the verdict demonstrated "that military men can rise above the heat and fury of bloody fratricidal war to do justice to innocence, virtue and humanity." In all probability, Gee's acquittal resulted from the consensus that the hanging of one notorious scapegoat was sufficient expiation for the Confederacy's inhumanity to Union prisoners.[36]

In its findings, the commission attached no responsibility to Gee "other than for weakness in retaining [his] position when unable to carry out the dictates of humanity." The commission instead blamed certain unspecified "higher authorities of the Rebel Government" for the appalling conditions inside Salisbury Prison. But the commander in North Carolina at the time of Gee's release, Brig. Gen. John C. Robinson, disagreed with the commission's findings. Robinson believed that Gee "had it in his power to relieve much of the suffering of the prisoners under his charge." He concluded, "there seems to have been more anxiety to prevent the escape of prisoners of war than to preserve their lives."[37]

Gee remained in military custody while Brig. Gen. Joseph Holt, the army's judge advocate general, reviewed the trial proceedings. Maj. Eugene A. Carr, the post commander at Raleigh, meanwhile informed Robinson that Gee was "suffering very materially from his confinement, and from the extreme heat of his room." The attending physician told Carr "that if they didn't hurry up the review of the proceedings in Gee's case they would not find him alive." Despite the doctor's dire prognosis, Gee managed to hold on. On July 5, three weeks after Gee's acquittal, an order from President Johnson secured his release.[38]

Ruger probably would have held a second war crimes tribunal in Raleigh had it not been for the president's April 2 proclamation. On September 13, 1865, Freedmen's Bureau agent Capt. William H. Doherty informed Ruger that in February 1864, twenty-two Union soldiers from North Carolina were publicly hanged in Kinston by order of the area's ranking Confederate general, George E. Pickett, and that Pickett's subordinate, Robert F. Hoke, had presided over the executions. Lacking a parole and fearing prosecution for his role in the Kinston executions, Pickett had fled to Canada. Ruger, meanwhile, instructed Doherty to convene a board of inquiry and interview witnesses. On November 8, Doherty reported that he had proof that Pickett and Hoke were guilty of executing Union soldiers who were wrongly accused of being Confederate deserters. Doherty recommended that the two former Confederate generals be arrested and tried by a military commission. On December 30, Judge Advocate General Holt advised Stanton to arrest Pickett and Hoke at once. Holt also recommended that Ruger continue the investigation into the Kinston hangings. The second board of inquiry convened on January 17, 1866. Two months later, the board ruled that only Pickett bore sufficient responsibility to be tried for war crimes.[39]

On March 12, a concerned Pickett asked an old West Point chum and Mexican War comrade, Ulysses S. Grant, to intercede for him. Four days later, Grant wrote President Johnson on Pickett's behalf. The general-in-chief requested that Johnson extend clemency to the former Confederate, for his trial would inevitably raise the question of whether the U.S. government was violating "its contract entered into to secure the surrender of an armed enemy." Grant also wrote a parole prohibiting Pickett's arrest

Gen. Ulysses S. Grant (Library of Congress)

unless ordered by the president or the secretary of war. Johnson took no direct action on Grant's request, but his April 2 proclamation—not to mention Grant's parole and the Milligan ruling—made a military trial of Pickett unlikely. In any event, the federal government never formally charged him with war crimes.[40]

There were also instances of Union officers honoring their onetime enemies. Perhaps the warmest tribute a federal officer paid to a former adversary during the first year after the war was that of Col. William W. Wheeler, the twenty-five-year-old commandant of the District of New Bern and the president of the military commission that tried Gee. In granting the request of a citizens' committee to hold a benefit concert for the widow of Stonewall Jackson, Wheeler assured the committee that the U.S. military authorities "can never object to a charitable action. All soldiers owe a tribute to gallantry and honor. It is presumed that every officer of this command will esteem it a privilege to be permitted to engage with you in the assistance of a lady whose husband was so respected and renowned."[41]

The Gee trial and the investigation of Pickett and Hoke revealed two utterly opposed viewpoints among army officers involved in the cases. Officers such as Judge Holt and Captain Doherty evinced a fierce determination to make the former Rebels pay for their supposed crimes, whereas officers such as General Grant and Colonel Wheeler exhibited a forbearance that resulted in the unanimous acquittal of the commandant of the war's deadliest military prison and the extension of amnesty to the alleged murderer of twenty-two Union prisoners. For every officer who cried for vengeance, there was another who acted with quiet magnanimity. Even as Presidential Reconstruction came under increasing fire in the North, army officers continued to practice conciliation in the South.

In April 1866, Congress passed the Civil Rights bill over Johnson's veto. The news reached North Carolina as state authorities and army and Freedmen's Bureau officers were attempting to sort out the freedpeople's status in the civil courts. State bureau chief Whittlesey accused the courts of imposing harsher punishment on blacks than on whites. "It is true that the law makes no distinction on account of color," Whittlesey informed Freedmen's Bureau head Oliver O. Howard, "but in the practical application[,] colored men are publicly whipped and white men discharged on the payment of a small fine, or giving bonds for future good conduct." Whittlesey condemned the "barbarous punishment" because of its inherent cruelty, as well as "its brutalizing influence upon the community." The colonel also maintained that public whippings tended to "excite a riotous spirit" among freedpeople who regarded the practice "as a relic of slavery." Bureau official Capt. Allan Rutherford claimed that several courts in his district convicted white Unionists on "trumped up charges" and then whipped them in order to drive them off. But Whittlesey and Rutherford failed to cite the most far-reaching consequence of whipping: the state law disfranchised anyone sentenced to corporal punishment.[42]

In March, Whittlesey received a letter from Wilmington bureau officer Charles J. Wickersham, reporting that he had suspended the public whipping of several freedmen under sentence of the New Hanover County court. On learning of the punishment, Wickersham had sent two armed orderlies to the courthouse to inform the sheriff that the whipping was suspended pending an investigation of the proceedings. Wickersham justified his action by noting that the judge had prohibited black testimony on behalf of the defendants and that a white man convicted of the same crime was released on good behavior. The bureau officer reported that his action "produced the most intense excitement not only in the Court Room but in the street" and that the local authorities threatened to arrest him and his orderlies for obstruction of justice. Whittlesey approved Wickersham's action. He also urged Ruger to issue an order forbidding "the infliction of this barbarous punishment."[43]

When Whittlesey learned that a freedman was publicly whipped in Raleigh for stealing a pair of shoes, he protested to superior court judge Daniel G. Fowle. Whittlesey explained that federal law prohibited military commissions from imposing whipping sentences. Most whites charged with felonies appeared before military tribunals, Whittlesey noted, whereas most black defendants had to face civil courts. He argued that this resulted in "unjust discrimination against the negro race." Whittlesey requested that Fowle suspend further punishment pending orders from either Ruger or Howard.[44]

Fowle replied that the civil courts were sentencing both whites and blacks to whipping, and he cited a few examples. The judge indicated that he had already discussed the situation with Ruger, and while the general disapproved of public whipping, he assured Fowle that the military would not interfere as long as the civil courts "impartially administered" the punishment. Fowle suggested that Whittlesey remove the inequality by turning over all the bureau's cases to the civil courts. The judge ridiculed the idea that military and bureau courts be retained solely because the state law prohibited blacks from testifying in trials that involved only whites.[45]

Whittlesey was chagrined to learn from Fowle that Ruger had decided not to intervene in the whipping controversy. "Having no command," Whittlesey lamented to Howard, "I have no power to put a stop to" the whippings. Howard appealed to Ruger on Whittlesey's behalf. The bureau director noted that the department commanders in South Carolina and Florida had already prohibited whipping in their states. He indicated that Stanton and Grant had approved the generals' action, but that they preferred "the initiative be taken by the Dept. Commander in whose jurisdiction such barbarity is practiced." Howard suggested that Ruger "take such action as may be necessary to prevent the infliction of this kind of punishment." A few days later, Ruger received the secretary of war's authorization to do precisely what Howard had recommended. On April 9, Stanton notified Ruger that he had received a complaint from the mayor of Wilmington regarding Wickersham's suspension of whipping as a punishment for larceny. Stanton indicated that the issue of corporal punishment "cannot safely be regulated at Washington," but should be placed under Ruger's jurisdiction, thus conferring a responsibility on the general that he gladly would have conceded to the war minister.[46]

Ruger decided to retain whipping as a punishment for three reasons. First, because the state lacked a penitentiary, whipping functioned as the sole penalty for larceny and other serious crimes. Second, the state law on public whipping was nondiscriminatory—at least in theory. Third, Ruger had no intention of repealing a state law, however odious, by military edict, even with Stanton's approval.[47]

Six weeks after his epistolary debate with Fowle, Whittlesey's tenure as assistant commissioner of the Freedmen's Bureau for North Carolina came to an abrupt end. On May 15, 1866, the War Department relieved Whittlesey and ten of his subordinates from duty and placed them under arrest. The charges, ranging from embezzlement to criminal negligence, stemmed from a report issued by Maj. Gen. James B. Steedman and Col. Joseph S. Fullerton after their inspection tour of the Freedmen's Bureau in North Carolina. The officers made the investigation at President Johnson's behest. Not content with his veto of the Freedmen's Bureau bill, Johnson sought to discredit bureau personnel by uncovering widespread corruption and incompetence, thereby demonstrating that southern blacks and their former masters would be better off without the bureau.[48]

The president had chosen his inspectors well, for Steedman and Fullerton found much to condemn and little to commend in North Carolina. The inspectors alleged that Whittlesey was guilty of conflict of interest in his part ownership of a Pitt County plantation run by Horace James, a civilian bureau official serving without pay. Worse yet, Steedman and Fullerton accused Whittlesey of covering up the shooting death of a freedman who had worked on his plantation. During the summer of 1866, an army court-martial tried the defendants. Several were convicted and dismissed from the service, but James was acquitted of all charges. Whittlesey's court-martial proved far more protracted than the others. The trial dragged on for two months, mainly because Steedman and Fullerton were unable to testify. The delay was intentional—the two officers never did materialize—for Johnson wanted to keep the scandal in the public eye to discredit his political opponents before the crucial midterm elections in the North. Whittlesey was at last found guilty of one of the two charges against him, but his punishment was simply a mild reprimand from Howard, who then appointed his protégé to a staff position at his Washington headquarters. Whittlesey thus emerged from the bureau scandal relatively unscathed though bitter at the apparent injustice done to him.[49]

On July 16, 1866, Congress passed a revised Freedmen's Bureau bill over Johnson's veto. Although he had failed to terminate the bureau, the president was confident that the scandal in North Carolina would compel the War Department to fill vacant bureau positions with army officers whose thinking was more in line with his own. Johnson was not the first to favor such a restructuring of the bureau. In December 1865, Grant had recommended replacing bureau officials with army officers. He noted that the army and the bureau operated as separate entities; as such, "one does not necessarily know what the other is doing or what orders they are acting under." Grant's solution was to send all of Commissioner Howard's orders through the department commanders and to appoint every army officer in the South a Freedmen's Bureau official. Such an arrangement would ensure the prompt execution of orders and "secure uniformity of action," rendering the old bureau hierarchy redundant. In their report, Steedman and Fullerton likewise recommended that "the services of the officers of the bureau be dispensed with . . . , and that these duties be performed by the officers commanding the troops in the department." The inspectors contended that the change "would relieve the government of the large and, in our opinion, unnecessary expense of supporting a superfluous number of officers and employees." Although Howard was willing to accept a military commander as assistant commissioner if he were the "right kind of man," he was far from agreeable to the wholesale replacement of bureau officials with army officers.[50]

On May 21, Ruger succeeded Whittlesey as the assistant commissioner for North Carolina while remaining the state's military commander. The War Department meanwhile restructured the geographical commands in the South. Ruger's department was renamed the Military Command of North Carolina, and he now reported to Maj. Gen. Daniel E. Sickles, the commander of the Department of the Carolinas. Howard's inspector general, Col. William E. Strong, reported that Ruger "seems well pleased with his new position and is taking hold of freedmen's affairs with great earnestness and vigor." Strong noted that the general planned to conduct monthly inspections of the bureau's officers and agents, "and all who are worthless and inefficient will be disposed of and replaced by others."[51]

Before Ruger could begin cleaning house, he was transferred from the Tar Heel State. He left on June 20, having served as department commander for a year and assistant commissioner for barely a month. Shortly after his departure, the *Raleigh Sentinel* stated that "no Federal officer has been among us, who has borne himself better . . . than Gen. Ruger." The *Sentinel* described Ruger's manner as "frank, polite and gentlemanly." While noting that a few of the general's decisions appeared "harsh and incorrect" to some, the *Sentinel* contended that no one ever accused him of being "domineering or tyrannical." This was high praise indeed from a Conservative newspaper that openly opposed the military occupation of the state.[52]

Ruger's replacement, Brig. Gen. John Cleveland Robinson, would also serve a dual role as the state's bureau head and military commander. The stocky, heavily bearded Robinson was forty-nine and an alumnus of West Point. He left the academy to study law but secured an appointment as second lieutenant in 1839, the year he would have graduated. A veteran of the Mexican and Third Seminole Wars, Robinson also participated in the Mormon Expedition. Robinson commanded Fort McHenry during the riot that erupted in Baltimore on April 19, 1861, as Union troops passed through the city en route to Washington, D.C. With a garrison of just sixty men, he managed to intimidate the pro-secession mob into leaving the fort alone. During the war, Robinson rose to division-level command in the Army of the Potomac, receiving the nickname "Old Reliable" from his men. On May 8, 1864, Robinson was leading a charge in the Battle of Spotsylvania Court House when a minié ball shattered his left knee. Robinson's leg was amputated soon afterward, putting an immediate end to his field service. After his recovery, Robinson was transferred to the Veteran Reserve Corps, consisting of officers and men too incapacitated by wounds or illness for frontline duty yet able to serve elsewhere. This was Robinson's first occupation command assignment. As such, he was something of an unknown quantity, but that would soon change.[53]

On July 3, Robinson sent Worth several copies of General Orders No. 3, and he requested that the governor distribute them to the state's judges and solicitors. Robinson expressed the hope that there would be "no clash between the Military and Civil authorities in the State" and no need to remove state officials for violating the order. Robinson's closing statement revealed his assumption that North Carolina remained under martial law.[54]

Worth regarded the order as simply one more capricious military decree. "You do not explain what . . . in your opinion made it necessary to communicate this order so long after the date of its issue," he wrote. The governor sent copies of General Orders No. 3 to the state's judges as directed, but he gave Robinson two reasons why he had advised them to ignore it. First, Worth maintained that the state constitution's separation of powers clause prohibited the governor from instructing judicial officers about their responsibilities. Second, Worth noted that the Civil Rights bill covered the same ground, and he regarded that law as supreme. In any event, he added, judges should not be governed by military orders during peacetime. Worth thus denied Robinson's contention that martial law remained in force. The governor also indicated that he was sending a copy of Robinson's letter to the president in order to learn "to what extent . . . the military authorities of the United States have a supervisory power over the judiciary of this State." Worth's letter to the president provoked a prompt response. At Johnson's behest, the War Department prohibited Robinson from suspending civil officials on his own responsibility.[55]

On July 12, Worth assumed the offensive. Having received General Orders No. 3, the governor now sent Robinson a copy of the state laws pertaining to freedpeople as revised by the recent state convention, along with a letter indicating that those laws no longer discriminated against blacks. Worth now expected the civil courts to be given "exclusive jurisdiction in judicial matters relating to freedmen." The following day, Robinson informed Worth that he was issuing the state bureau's General Orders No. 3 (not to be confused with the War Department's Gener-

Brig. Gen. John C. Robinson (Library of Congress)

al Orders No. 3) directing bureau personnel to refer all cases involving freedpeople to the civil courts with the exception of labor contracts approved by bureau agents. While Robinson's order relinquished most of the bureau's judicial authority to the civil courts, it also contained a caveat: if the civil authorities proved unable or unwilling to arrest and try persons charged with crimes, military officers were directed to make the arrests and confine the accused "until such time as a proper judicial tribunal may be ready and willing to try them." Robinson's order quoted the army's General Orders No. 44, which Grant recently had issued to secure justice for freedpeople and white loyalists.[56]

Worth considered Robinson's latest order a victory for civil law in North Carolina, but he felt in no mood to celebrate. In Washington, the Republicans appeared to have a firm grip on federal legislation, and Worth dreaded the result. Having overturned the president's veto of the Civil Rights and Freedmen's Bureau bills, Congress next passed the so-called Howard Amendment—named after its chief sponsor, Senator Jacob Howard—in June. (To avoid confusion, the Howard Amendment will henceforth be referred to as the Fourteenth Amendment.) The five-section amendment constituted the North's peace terms to the defeated South. The first section restated the Civil Rights bill in terms that established the supremacy of the federal government in defining and protecting the rights of its citizens. The second section allowed the states to continue determining voter eligibility but reduced congressional representation in proportion to the number of adult males denied the franchise. The provision thus penalized any southern state that barred freedmen from voting. The third section barred persons from federal or state office who had supported the rebellion after taking an oath to uphold the Constitution. This affected most of the South's political leadership, for nearly every Southerner who had held any civil or military office before the war had taken the oath. The fourth section renewed the government's commitment to pay the federal war debt, repudiated the Confederate debt, and denied compensation for the loss of slave property. The fifth section granted Congress the power to enforce the amendment.[57]

Although the Fourteenth Amendment omitted such radical measures as land confiscation and voting rights for black men, Worth and many other white Tar Heels deemed it a humiliating imposition of the victorious North's will. The provision Worth found most objectionable disqualified him and other ex-Union Whig leaders from holding office, yet left onetime fire-eating secessionists eligible as long as they had held no public office before the war. "If we were voluntarily to adopt this amendment," Worth declared, "I think we would be the meanest and most despicable people on earth. Nobody in this State that I have heard of, except a few Holden men per se, will vote for it."[58]

Confident of defeating the Fourteenth Amendment's proponents in the upcoming midterm election, Johnson openly advised his southern supporters to reject it. In an effort to forge a bipartisan coalition of moderates and conservatives, Johnson formed the National Union Party to oppose the Republicans in the midterm elections. To attract northern voters, he undertook a late-summer campaign tour of northern cities. Johnson's so-called "Swing around the Circle" was a fiasco, his speeches often degenerating into incoherent harangues. Although Johnson's tirades cost him at the polls, they did not determine the election of 1866. The outcome revealed that northern voters overwhelmingly favored the Fourteenth Amendment, and there was little Johnson could have done to dissuade them. The Republicans also secured a two-thirds majority in both Houses, enough to override Johnson's vetoes and thereby supplant the president's Reconstruction plan with their own.[59]

On July 21, Robinson answered Worth's query as to his reason for issuing General Orders No. 3 at such a late date. He explained that General Ruger had been compelled to intervene on several occasions when men entitled to protection under General Orders No. 3 were arrested for no other crime than demonstrating their loyalty to the U.S. government. Robinson expressed surprise that Worth was unaware of the persecution of Union soldiers and loyal civilians, for "the subject formed a matter of discussion in the late State Convention." The general asserted that, as long as the state remained under martial law, he would "permit no person to be persecuted or punished" whom he was "required by orders to protect."[60]

Shortly after assuming command, Robinson had ordered his judge advocate, Maj. Frank Wolcott, and Maj. Eugene A. Carr of the 5th U.S. Cavalry to investigate reports of outrages against native Unionists in the state's western counties. Both officers admitted that their investigation was hindered by the vast amount of ground they had to cover in the allotted two weeks. Within that span, however, they managed to gather enough evidence to indicate that some "tories" were the victims of crimes, ranging from theft to murder, and that others had been charged with crimes that were, in fact, legitimate acts of war. The officers reported that the grand jury of the Caldwell County Superior Court had found 180 true bills of indictment: 145 were against Unionists, and the other 35 were for petty offenses. Wolcott stated that the grand jury members in each of the counties he visited were "notoriously disloyal" to the U.S. government, and he accused them of looking the other way whenever former Rebels committed crimes against "tories." He cited the case of Austin Coffee, who was summarily executed by the Watauga County Home Guard on suspicion of harboring Confederate deserters and escaped Union prisoners. Wolcott noted that the perpetrators were "well known" but "no steps have been taken to prosecute them."[61]

Robinson sent copies of the officers' reports and the accompanying documents to Worth. Among the papers were petitions from Clay, Stokes, and Forsyth counties appealing for relief from persecution by vengeful ex-Confederate neighbors. Worth dismissed these petitions as the work of "dirty birds willing to foul their own nests to reek [wreak] vengeance on others." The governor maintained that the petitions and Robinson's "ex parte investigation" were part of an "extensive" conspiracy to prove "that a Union man cannot have justice" in the state courts. The intent of the conspiracy, Worth believed, was to establish military rule in North Carolina. On July 27, Worth wrote the president, asking if the state was under martial law.[62]

Worth meanwhile received a letter from William P. Bynum, the solicitor for one of the judicial circuits in which Wolcott and Carr had traveled. Bynum refuted many of the officers' allegations. As for the Austin Coffee case, he indicated that a grand jury had indicted the suspects for murder, and the trial was scheduled for the fall term. Bynum noted that the actual number of true bills was closer to 40 than 180, and that he was unaware of the loyalties of the accused. He admitted, however, that grand juries in his district had ignored true bills that should have resulted in criminal indictments. Bynum believed that if any wrong was done, it was during this preliminary stage. "So soon after the termination of the war, it is natural that there should be some bitterness of feeling," Bynum wrote, "and under such influences, that there should be occasional acts of wrong and injustice in making indictments and presentments." But Bynum maintained that when such cases came before a judge in his district, "not a solitary instance has occurred where parties have been convicted." Bynum's letter strengthened Worth's conviction that the conduct of the state's judges and solicitors was beyond reproach, even if jurors or magistrates sometimes proved unreliable.[63]

Acting on Wolcott and Carr's recommendation, Robinson ordered a second investigation in late July. This time, however, he allowed the governor to choose a civilian, William S. Mason, to assist Wolcott. Not surprisingly, the two men disagreed on nearly every aspect of the investigation. In each of the counties Mason and Wolcott visited, they found a secret organization known as the "Heroes of America," or "Red Strings," from the insignia worn by its members. During the war, Tar Heel Unionists had established the Heroes of America as a mutual aid society. After the surrender, the organization continued to defend members against persecution while promoting the election of loyalists to political office. Wolcott reported that the Red Strings outnumbered the ex-Confederates in the western counties and that the latter were forming local militia units for self-defense. He believed that "political militia companies" would "continue the hatreds and prejudices engendered by the war" and lead to "open violence."[64]

Mason, however, reported that the companies in question were organized in accordance with the state's militia law and that membership was open to anyone. As for the Heroes of America, Mason alleged that some members were "bad men" who had joined during the war "to cloak their acts of wrong and violence." Mason concluded that the numerous indictments against both Unionists and former Confederates would "necessarily serve to keep alive violent neighborhood hostilities" in the western counties.[65]

The Wolcott-Mason investigation bolstered Robinson's conviction that Unionists were being persecuted and yet reaffirmed Worth's belief that the civil officials were acting properly. The general continued to send Worth petitions from loyal citizens seeking protection, and in each case, the governor replied that the petitioners' allegations would not hold up in court. In one instance, Robinson asked Worth to furnish proof as to why the army should not intervene in several cases involving Union veterans who maintained they were wrongly arrested. The governor replied that he lacked the authority to requisition such evidence, for it could only be obtained in a proper trial. "I am sorry," an exasperated Robinson wrote Worth, "that I am to look to your Excellency for no assistance in protecting former Union soldiers and other loyal citizens."[66]

In addition to conflicts between Unionists and ex-Confederates in the western counties, white soldiers and black soldiers in the Tar Heel State often clashed. The *Salisbury Old North State* reported that a group of homeward-bound black veterans collided with some regulars at Morganton and were driven from the town. In Raleigh, the chaplain and several soldiers of the 37th USCT were walking down the street when a club-wielding white infantryman struck a black sergeant over the head, knocking him unconscious. Ten days later, a white enlisted man insulted another sergeant in the 37th as he disciplined one of his men. The commander of the 37th USCT, Capt. Charles H. Whitney, informed post head-quarters that "incidents are occurring daily of insults and abuse towards the colored soldiers from the white." He requested "that measures may be taken to prevent such occurrences in the future." So far, segregation had provided the only remedy for racial conflict in the army. For all their reputed discipline, regulars tended to be just as unruly as the white volunteer soldiers had been.[67]

Lawless conditions in western North Carolina received far more notoriety than outrages against Unionists in the eastern part of the state. By far the most notable case was the trial by military commission of J. L. McMillan and Neill McGill, former members of the Bladen County Home Guard charged with the brutal murder of Union scout Matthew P. Sykes. Although the commission found the two men guilty of war crimes and sentenced them to hang, it recommended mercy on their behalf. The case became a cause célèbre among Tar Heel Conservatives in late 1865. More than a dozen petitions, including one signed by all fifty members of the state senate, appealed to President Johnson for executive clemency. Judge Advocate General Joseph Holt argued that granting clemency to the guilty parties would "compromise the future safety of those who in the rebellious States were true to our flag in the midst of war." Despite Holt's plea for severity, Johnson granted the petitioners' request and pardoned the two men.[68]

To end war-related persecutions, the General Assembly passed the Amnesty Act in December 1866. The act extended a general amnesty to civil officials and military personnel for acts of war committed in the state but omitted civilians who had served as Union scouts, spies, or guides or who had resisted Confederate conscription. They remained subject to prosecution for acts that were legitimate under the laws of war but criminal under the state's peacetime laws. The Amnesty Act thus failed to end the persecution of white loyalists.[69]

In August, amid reports of outrages against Unionists, Robinson received a letter from Lt. Edward B. Northrup, the bureau agent for Bladen County, recounting his futile attempt to prosecute a white man for the brutal beating of a freedman. Northrup reported that the hearing was held in his office before the local justice of the peace and that the room was filled with angry citizens, several of whom drew their revolvers and threatened the agent's life. Much to Northrup's dismay, the magistrate dismissed the charges against the accused because the plaintiff was too severely injured to testify. Robinson sent Northrup's letter to Worth. He warned that another such incident would compel him to resume jurisdiction in cases involving freedmen and to use federal troops to protect bureau officials from "outrageous insults and threats of violence." Worth replied that the incident as recounted by Northrup was "entirely at variance with the generally orderly conduct of the people of North Carolina." The governor maintained that neither Northrup nor anyone else in the state would need a military escort if "he behaved himself with propriety."[70]

Facing the threat of military intervention, Worth once more appealed to the president for a ruling on the status of martial law in North Carolina. Although Worth had not received an answer to his July 27 letter to Johnson, he took heart in the president's proclamation of August 20 declaring the insurrection over in Texas (the only southern state omitted by his April 2 proclamation) and civil authority restored throughout the United States. Worth assumed that the proclamation ended martial law in North Carolina and that the president would soon revoke General Orders Nos. 3 and 44. But he was soon disappointed. Choosing to remain noncommittal, Johnson directed Stanton to inform Worth that he would review any charges of military interference in civil affairs when given the necessary information.[71]

Another dispute between the civil and the military authorities arose over the apprenticeship of black children and adolescents. The ostensible purpose of apprenticing minors of either race was to rescue orphans and abandoned children from destitution by providing them with homes, jobs, and a rudimentary education. In return, the children provided their guardians with cheap labor until they reached maturity. But the apprenticeship section of the Black Code contained three discriminatory clauses: ex-masters had preference in binding out their former slaves, black children whose parents did not work full-time could be bound out, and black girls could remain apprenticed until the age of twenty-one, a term three years longer than that of white girls.[72]

In the hands of unscrupulous operators, apprenticeships assumed all the features of slavery. From November 1865 to February 1866, the Sampson County court bound out 479 black children to their former masters. The judge ordered local police to seize the children, even though many had jobs and were living with their parents or other family members. The local bureau agent informed Whittlesey of the compulsory apprenticeships, and the state bureau head concluded that most of the children had been kidnapped. He immediately notified Ruger, who, in turn, ordered a company of troops to Sampson County to return the children to their homes.[73]

In October 1866, the apprenticeship issue resurfaced when Robeson County planter Daniel L. Russell complained to Worth that Capt. Allan Rutherford of the Freedmen's Bureau had canceled the indentures of Harriet and Eliza Ambrose, two teenage black girls bound out to him. Worth asked Robinson to explain why Rutherford had nullified the decision of a county court. Robinson replied that the court had violated the state apprenticeship law in binding out the Ambrose girls. He noted that the girls' parents were willing and able to support them and that Russell had kept them in jail while the court processed the indentures. "It looks to me like a reestablishment of slavery under the mild name of apprenticeship," Robinson commented.[74]

Worth made no attempt to defend Russell's actions, but he contended that the civil courts should have been allowed to rectify the injustice. Robinson ignored Worth's suggestion, for he assumed that the girls would still be bound out to Russell had it not been for the bureau's intervention. Whenever "I have reason to believe that injustice is done to the humblest freedman," Robinson informed the governor, "it becomes my duty to protect him, and I shall not hesitate to use the power delegated to me for that purpose." In response to Robinson's declaration, Worth urged the General Assembly to remove the discriminatory clauses in the apprenticeship law, which it did in November 1866. The state supreme court meanwhile ruled that a legal technicality invalidated Russell's indentures, and the Ambrose girls were soon reunited with their parents.[75]

The gravest threat to civil authority in North Carolina during the first year of Worth's administration was General Sickles's General Orders No. 15, which prohibited public whipping as a punishment for crime. Sickles's order accomplished what Ruger had refused to do six months earlier—repeal the state's whipping law—but its impact was short-lived. Worth protested to President Johnson that Sickles's order appeared "to rest on the assumption that the Military Commandant of the Department has a right to suspend or annul such laws of the States within his command as he may deem inhumane or unwise." The governor once more argued that, by virtue of the president's August 20 proclamation, civil law had supplanted martial law in the state. He also noted that the state law mandated whipping as the sole penalty for larceny, bigamy, and other serious crimes. Should Sickles's order be upheld, many crimes in North Carolina would perforce go unpunished. Worth also headed a delegation to Washington and personally pleaded his case to the president.[76]

On December 8, Robinson's replacement, Col. James V. Bomford, informed Worth that a freedman at Salisbury had recently undergone a punishment of "thirty nine lashes on the bare back." Bomford asked Worth to urge the civil courts to cease defying Sickles's order, but the governor refused on the grounds of separation of powers. Oblivious to the controversy, the courts continued doing business as usual—that is, until the military intervened. During Worth's absence, Bomford ordered his adjutant, Maj. Daniel T. Wells, to halt the whipping of a freedman at Raleigh. Wells arrived as the sheriff was administering the lashes; he immediately halted the proceedings and took the freedman, Cornelius Walters, into custody. Judge Fowle responded by issuing a writ for Walters and an arrest warrant for Bomford, which the colonel ignored. Bomford and Worth then agreed to a compromise: the civil authorities could retain Walters if they withheld punishment pending instructions from the president.[77]

On December 19, Worth telegraphed Bomford from Washington that the president had revoked Sickles's order. Seeking to prevent a "collision" between the civil and military authorities, Bomford requested that Worth postpone execution of the punishment until "the proper orders" had reached his headquarters. The orders arrived soon afterward, and Bomford surrendered Walters to the tender mercies of the sheriff. In issuing General Orders No. 15, Sickles had underestimated the resourcefulness of Worth and his Conservative allies. The revocation of Sickles's order ranks as Worth's greatest triumph in his struggle with the military authorities in North Carolina. It also proved to be one of his last such victories.[78]

No sooner had the Christmas insurrection scare of 1865 subsided than white North Carolinians began glimpsing signs of an impending Armageddon in 1866. The mayor of Williamston, Abner S. Williams, informed Worth that the freedmen of Martin County had organized a secret society called "the League." The society was probably a branch of the "Equal Rights League," a freedmen's political organization forming throughout North Carolina. Williams stated that the members went to their meetings heavily armed and reportedly planned "to burn the town for the purpose of pillage and other unlawful acts." From Enfield, John F. Bellamy wrote the governor that the freedmen of Edgecombe County were holding "mass meetings" in which they drilled and maneuvered with firearms. "The ostensible purpose of these meetings are a strike for higher wages," Bellamy stated, "but I believe the real design is to organise for a general massacre of the white population." Bellamy urged that the meetings be stopped and the blacks disarmed.[79]

Worth sent copies of the letters to Bomford with the request that he investigate the allegations. The colonel assigned the task to two Freedmen's Bureau agents. After making a thorough investigation of conditions in Martin and Edgecombe counties, they reported that the freedpeople were "quiet and law abiding" and there was no cause for alarm. Worth conceded that Williams had made his allegations "without due inquiry and upon insufficient grounds." As for the Bellamy complaint, the governor wondered if "the assemblage of a like number of white men under the circumstances set forth" would have excited greater concern on Bomford's part. Worth advised that Bomford exercise due caution and "prevent such assemblages in future."[80]

If rumors of imminent freedmen's insurrections proved false, the Regulator crime wave remained all too real. In September 1866, General Sickles decided that his command should assume a more active role in law enforcement than General Orders No. 44 permitted. To counteract the Regulators and other outlaw bands, Sickles issued General Orders No. 7. The order prohibited ad hoc "organizations of white or colored persons bearing arms" from acting as paramilitary units or exercising extralegal authority. It warned that the army would treat Regulators as guerrillas and summarily punish them upon capture. The order authorized post commanders to use civilian posses to apprehend the outlaws. Sickles also prohibited Confederate veterans from forming organizations that perpetuated "military or civil organization engaged in the Rebellion" or that commemorated "any of the acts of the insurgents prior to the final surrender."[81]

General Orders No. 7 failed to intimidate the outlaws. If anything, they became even bolder. On October 29, the commandant of the Post of New Bern, Lt. Henry E. Hazen, reported that outlaws of both races were committing outrages in several eastern counties. One gang burned a cotton gin and thirty bales of cotton belonging to John G. Colgrove, a northern-born planter. "These outrages are becoming of most frequent occurrence," Hazen wrote, "and the civil authorities can not, or will not, arrest the perpetrators." After further reflection, Hazen concluded that the gangs "are too formidable to be put down by the civil authorities."

He requested that Robinson send a company of cavalry to New Bern to track down the desperadoes. The general refused to grant Hazen's request, however, apparently because the two companies of cavalry in the state could not be spared elsewhere.[82]

One Regulator band added a multiple murder to its catalog of crime. On December 20, 1866, a white woman was gang-raped in Greene County. Four days later, six black men and one white man were charged with the crime and jailed at Snow Hill, the county seat. Soon after their incarceration, the victim identified three of the inmates as among her assailants. At midnight on January 8, 1867, a gang of outlaws took the keys from the jailor, removed the prisoners from their cells, and then executed them at a nearby creek. The seven inmates were later found with their heads split open. Despite the victim's identification of three suspects, the Freedmen's Bureau official who investigated the incident, Lt. Robert Avery, could find no evidence that linked the murdered men to the rape. Avery, however, learned that four of the victims were Union veterans. The lieutenant suspected that the jailor knew the identity of the two men who took the jail keys. He also believed that enough Snow Hill residents were involved in the conspiracy that "any effort openly made to discover these murderers would prove abortive."[83]

The Snow Hill lynching exemplifies the Regulators' audacity and reveals that some of them were political terrorists in addition to being bandits and vandals. Terror served the Regulators well in subduing their victims, enabling them to achieve local dominance. Whether the crime was the murder of black army veterans or the destruction of a northern planter's property, the objective was the same: eliminate the opposition or intimidate it into mute acquiescence. It came as no surprise that the Regulators served as a model for the Ku Klux Klan and that some members later became Klansmen.

The numerous outrages committed against blacks and white Unionists during the past year revealed the decision of former Confederates to wage guerrilla warfare against a more vulnerable foe than the federal occupation force. The consequences of defeat—including the emancipation of North Carolina's more than 300,000 slaves, the conquering army's ongoing presence in the state, the widespread death and devastation caused by the war, and the resulting economic dislocation—induced some embittered Tar Heels to seek revenge for their misfortune. These ex-Confederates discovered that using violence to settle an old score with a Unionist adversary or to put an "insolent" freedman in his place seldom entailed punishment or retribution; hence, both the outlaws and their crimes rapidly multiplied. For Confederate veterans unable or unwilling to adapt to peacetime civilian life, the Bennett Place surrender had served as a truce—a much-needed opportunity to rest and reorganize before resuming hostilities.

By early 1867, the Regulators had become so formidable that many white citizens in the eastern counties feared the consequences. On January 10, the *Tarboro Southerner* reported that outlaws in Greene and Pitt counties had organized into "regular companies" and defeated the state militia. Alleging the inability of the state authorities to halt the depredations, the *Southerner* appealed to the federal authorities for help. The editorial infuriated Worth. He wrote the editors, calling attention to the "mischief" they had wrought by conveying the impression "that our people are lawless, and our State authorities impotent or grossly remiss." The governor denied that the state government was incapable of subduing the desperadoes, insisting that "no government can protect a people too cowardly to expose the names of those who maltreat them." What made the *Southerner* editorial particularly galling to Worth was its appearance in a Conservative paper rather than an opposition daily such as Holden's *Standard*. "Nothing I have seen in any Radical Journal," Worth wrote, "furnishes so much pablum to those who would reduce us to a territorial condition." Newspapers throughout the state joined the *Southerner* in publicizing the Regulator crisis, but Worth dismissed the accounts as exaggerated or false.[84]

The worse the Regulator crime wave became, the more firmly Worth denied the state government's inability to cope with the emergency. Worth assumed that if he requested federal assistance—and thus conceded the state authorities' failure to restore order—he would provide the U.S. Army and the Freedmen's Bureau with an excuse to interfere in state affairs. The governor therefore denied any justification for keeping federal troops or bureau agents in the state. In obstructing efforts to publicize the widespread violence against blacks and white loyalists in North Carolina, Worth effectively shielded the wrongdoers and thereby made himself a part of the problem.

The civil authorities' failure to subdue the Regulators at last compelled the army to intervene. On February 18, 1867, Colonel Bomford sent Worth a report from Capt. Allan Rutherford, the supervisor of the bureau's Southern District. Rutherford indicated that bands of Regulators were roaming "at will" through several counties in his district and that the civil authorities were "either unable or unwilling to arrest and punish the men belonging to these bands." Bomford asked Worth "to make any suggestion" he could "as to a remedy" and to cooperate with the army "in breaking up an organization ruinous to both the social and political status of the State."[85]

Rather than offer a solution, Worth repeated his assertion that the victims "did not know or would not disclose the names" of the outlaws. The governor maintained that he could not call out the militia because no magistrate or sheriff had failed to perform his duty. "If you think the presence of your troops" in the eastern counties "will embolden the parties wronged to expose the malefactors," Worth wrote, "I shall be gratified to have you send them." Worth thus offered his belated support to Bomford.[86]

On February 20, acting department commander John C. Robinson responded to the Regulator crisis by issuing General Orders No. 17, a pointed reiteration of Sickles's Regulator order. Citing the inability of civil authorities in the Carolinas "to capture or disperse" the Regulators, Robinson directed post commanders "to use every means at their disposal to rid the country of these banditti." If the outlaws resisted arrest, the order stated, they were to "be treated as 'guerrillas' and summarily punished." It now remained to be seen how soon the army could suppress the Regulators.[87]

Judging from the situation that confronted Capt. Royal T. Frank, the post commander at Wilmington, the bluecoats' short-term prospects appeared grim. Frank reported that he could send only one sergeant and six enlisted men after a band of twenty-five Regulators terrorizing the countryside. Worse yet, the soldiers were poorly mounted and armed with Springfield rifle-muskets, an unwieldy weapon on horseback. Frank requested that Bomford send him some good horses and a shipment of breech-loading carbines and revolvers, which were much easier for horsemen to handle than the infantry's muzzle-loading rifles. In the meantime, Frank held "but little hope of good results," yet he assured Bomford that "no pains will be spared to overtake and punish" the outlaws.[88]

Worth, in contrast, soon became preoccupied with what he considered a far graver crisis than the Regulator crime wave. On March 2, 1867, Congress passed the Reconstruction Act over Johnson's veto and thus placed North Carolina and nine other former Confederate states under military rule—the penalty for the states' failure to ratify the Fourteenth Amendment and protect blacks and loyal whites from the kind of organized violence perpetrated by the Regulators. Tennessee was excluded because it had already ratified the amendment and rejoined the Union. The act divided the South into five military districts and directed the president to appoint a general to command each district. North Carolina and South Carolina formed the Second Military District. General Sickles assumed the command and retained his headquarters at Charleston, South Carolina.[89]

Passed on March 23, the Second Reconstruction Act specified the procedure that the ten Southern states had to follow to reenter the Union. The act authorized the district commanders to call elections for each of their states to decide on a constitutional convention and elect delegates. This raised the possibility of voters choosing delegates for a convention that would not meet. The commanders would appoint three-man boards of registration for each voting district. All male citizens were eligible to vote except those disqualified by the Fourteenth Amendment or a felony conviction; all voters had to take an oath affirming their qualifications. For the convention measure to be approved, a majority of the state's registered voters had to vote in the affirmative. Should this occur, the convention would meet and draft a new constitution guaranteeing suffrage for freedmen. Once the state had ratified the constitution and the Fourteenth Amendment, Congress would review its action. If approved, the state's U.S. representatives and senators would be seated, signifying readmission to the Union. At that point, Congress would declare Military Reconstruction finished in that state.[90]

Throughout 1866, Worth had maintained a running battle with the military authorities to restore civil government and had won several impressive victories. But the establishment of Military Reconstruction negated his successes, placing the state under military rule and reducing the civil government to provisional status. Worth deemed the Reconstruction Acts unconstitutional, but when it became apparent that the U.S. Supreme Court would not intervene, he decided that open resistance was futile. The governor concluded that "obedience no longer becomes degradation—but sensible prudence." Worth consoled himself with the thought that resistance on his part would only "result in putting the executive power in hands likely to use it more oppressively than I would." Sharing the governor's resignation, R. J. Powell, a North Carolinian living in Washington, expressed the hope that "our loyal people will accept the Situation, and in good faith do what is required of them." The *Raleigh Sentinel* believed that the people wanted "peace and quiet, and a speedy restoration of the Union, and they are ready to do what they are bidden by the Congress to do, in order to secure it." Adopting a severer tone, the *Wilmington Journal* advised its readers to "respect the law" and do everything possible "to so control events" that the Tar Heel State "may still be saved from greater infamy."[91]

Although many North Carolinians dreaded the prospect of Military Reconstruction, former Confederate general (and West Point graduate) D. H. Hill claimed to have no such fear because he trusted "*the honor of the American soldier*" to serve as a bulwark against the vindictiveness of Pennsylvania Representative Thaddeus Stevens and other radical congressmen. "The military ruler has no partisans to reward, and no enmities to gratify," Hill wrote in the pages of his Charlotte-based monthly, *The Land We Love*. "The fair presumption is that he will be just and impartial, having no controlling motive but a sense of duty." The *Charlotte Western Democrat*, on the other hand, took a more cynical view of the situation. "In the present anomalous state of affairs," the *Democrat* argued, "we believe it would be better for the people to accept military rule, and have their grievances and difficulties settled altogether by military authority rather than pay the expense of a civil government that cannot enforce its laws or protect them."[92]

Regardless of their attitude toward Military Reconstruction, white North Carolinians would soon discover that a new and harsher set of Reconstruction laws did not mean that army officers in their state had abandoned conciliation as an instrument of policy. In turn, the occupation soldiers would often find their conciliatory gestures reciprocated by grateful civilians.

Chapter Six

MILITARY RECONSTRUCTION UNDER SICKLES

The commander of the Second Military District, Maj. Gen. Daniel Edgar Sickles, ranks as one of the more flamboyant characters to tread the American public stage of his time. A lawyer, Tammany Hall Democrat, and U.S. congressman before the war, Sickles created a scandal in 1859 when he murdered his young wife's lover, Francis Barton Key, the son of "Star Spangled Banner" composer Francis Scott Key. In true tabloid fashion, Sickles was acquitted by reason of temporary insanity—a precedent-setting verdict—and then forgave his wife. During the secession crisis, Sickles defended the action of the departing southern states and supported President James Buchanan's policy of nonintervention. The firing on Fort Sumter changed all that: Sickles became a War Democrat, raised a brigade of infantry, and secured an appointment as a brigadier general in the Union army. By 1863, Sickles was a major general commanding the Third Corps of the Army of the Potomac. Despite the lack of a military education, Sickles proved to be a capable, if quarrelsome, corps commander. But at Gettysburg on July 2, Sickles's decision to disobey orders and advance his corps to high ground three-fourths of a mile beyond the Union army's main line nearly proved disastrous. Sickles paid dearly for his rashness: as he witnessed the rout of his corps, a Confederate cannon ball smashed into his right leg. The mangled limb was immediately amputated, and Sickles returned to Washington a battle-scarred hero. After his recovery, Sickles made an inspection tour of the occupied South for

Maj. Gen. Daniel E. Sickles (Library of Congress)

President Lincoln. The general reported that war profiteers and corrupt Union officers had entered into an unholy alliance in Memphis and other occupied towns, and he warned of the intense hatred that Southerners felt for the North. After the war, Sickles commanded the Department of South Carolina; in June 1866, North Carolina was added to his jurisdiction. Sickles's expanded command was first designated the Department of the Carolinas, then the Department of the South, and finally the Second Military District.[1]

When he believed the situation warranted decisive action, Sickles often exercised his authority without fear of the consequences, much as he had on that second of July at Gettysburg. In at least two instances during 1866, he issued orders that overrode federal or state laws. Sickles's order mandating summary punishment for captured Regulators denied the prisoners a trial in the civil courts and thus violated the U.S. Supreme Court's *Milligan* ruling. His order prohibiting whipping as a punishment overturned several North Carolina statutes. Whereas the War Department sustained the Regulator order, President Johnson revoked the whipping ban after it had aroused a storm of protest in the Tar Heel State.

A similar fearlessness is evident in Sickles's orders issued during Military Reconstruction. On March 21, 1867, Sickles officially assumed command of the Second Military District, which he announced in General Orders No. 1. The order also laid the ground rules for Sickles's military administration. Sickles reiterated that civil government in the Carolinas was merely provisional "and subject to the paramount authority of the United States," which the general believed he embodied. Although Sickles believed that the disability clause of the Fourteenth Amendment justified "the removal of *nearly Every Civil Officer in these States,*" he permitted them to remain in office because he could find few qualified replacements. State and local laws likewise remained in force as long as they did not conflict with the U. S. Constitution, federal laws, presidential proclamations, or Sickles's own orders.[2]

The reaction of Governor Worth and other Conservative-Democrats— or Conservatives, as they were usually called—to General Orders No. 1 was mixed. If Sickles appeared content to leave the civilian leadership and the state laws as he found them, he also seemed prone to intervene in civil affairs. Sickles allowed the civil courts to continue as before but reserved the right to refer certain cases to military tribunals. The general directed post commanders to arrest suspects that the civil authorities failed to bring to justice and to try the accused before a military commission. He also ordered commanders to report the failure of civil officials to perform their duty. Sickles's frequent intervention in civil affairs led to repeated conflicts with state and, ultimately, federal authorities.[3]

In issuing General Orders No. 3, which established a quarantine of all ports in the Carolinas, Sickles demonstrated a readiness to intervene in matters unrelated to Military Reconstruction. Another such directive was General Orders No. 25, which prohibited the manufacture—but not the sale or consumption—of grain alcohol in the Second Military District. Both orders were based on sound reasons: the former to prevent the spread of infectious diseases, and the latter to minimize the hardship resulting from a poor grain harvest in the preceding year. For all Sickles's good intentions, the two orders met with a hostile reception—especially the ban on alcohol production, which proved both difficult and dangerous to enforce in some areas of North Carolina. Claiming that it was "altogether unsafe to attempt breaking up" illegal stills in his district, J. B. Weaver, a collector for the Bureau of Internal Revenue in western North Carolina, requested—and promptly received—a company of the 5th U.S. Cavalry to assist him. Several local officials attempted to obstruct Weaver by charging him with illegal search and seizure, but their efforts failed to stop him.[4]

A related provision in General Orders No. 12 prohibited the sale of alcohol to soldiers, sailors, or marines. Offenders would be brought to trial before a military commission and, after conviction, either fined between $50 and $100 or imprisoned for up to two months. Aware that this order would prove impossible to enforce without a financial incentive, Sickles rewarded informants with one-fourth of the fine. The order curtailed the sale of alcohol to soldiers but failed to stop it because the demand was too great.[5]

Two more of Sickles's general orders provoked bitter controversy and divided North Carolinians along both class and racial lines. In General Orders No. 10, Sickles introduced several far-reaching economic and legal changes, ranging from debtor relief to gun control. Declaring that the "general destitution prevailing among the population of this military district . . . demand[s] extraordinary measures," Sickles abolished the collection of personal debts incurred between December 19, 1860 (the date of South Carolina's secession) and May 15, 1865. He suspended the collection of debts incurred before December 19, 1860, and mortgage foreclosures for twelve months. Sickles also prohibited imprisonment for debt and abolished the collection of debts incurred in the purchase of slaves. General Orders No. 10 infuriated elite creditors, none more than Governor Worth, who had made a good living before the war as a lawyer collecting debts for wealthy clients. Tar Heel creditors also took issue with the date December 19, 1860, noting that North Carolina had not seceded until May 20, 1861. On the other hand, Sickles's stay law pleased the largely anonymous but far more numerous debtors in the state.[6]

The remainder of General Orders No. 10 covered a wide array of controversial legal matters. The order outlawed the carrying of deadly weapons, abolished the death penalty for burglary and larceny, and reaffirmed a previous order issued by General Robinson "prohibiting the punishment of crimes and offences by whipping, maiming, branding, stocks, pillory, or other corporal punishment." The weapons ban proved especially onerous to Carolinians who hunted for a living and to civil law enforcement authorities. One month later, Sickles responded to their complaints by permitting "the use of fowling pieces for hunting game upon one's own premises," and he authorized post commanders to grant permission to local law officers "to carry arms when absolutely necessary." As a replacement for corporal punishment, Sickles suggested that Worth urge the General Assembly to vote for construction of a state penitentiary—a costly initiative that at first met with a lukewarm response.[7]

General Orders No. 32 was as sweeping an edict as General Orders No. 10 and proved even more detestable to Worth and other Conservative leaders. The order removed all property qualifications for public office and made all current taxpayers eligible jury members as long as they were not disfranchised under the Reconstruction Act. Worth regarded Sickles's order as a democratic Pandora's box. "Nearly all the whites, however ignorant or vicious, and nearly every negro without any other test of fitness than he has paid a tax are to be placed on the jury list," Worth lamented to President Johnson. The governor probably was speaking for the state's elite class rather than for the majority of North Carolinians when he commented, "I need not describe the horror of our people at the idea of having their character, laws and property in the keeping of juries thus constituted."[8]

Among other provisions, General Orders No. 32 prohibited racial and class discrimination on public transportation and rendered violators liable to civil lawsuits and trial by military tribunals. The order also required civil officials and private citizens to assist post commanders when summoned; refusal to do so was punishable by a fine and imprisonment. Still another provision limited the sale of alcohol in quantities of less than one gallon to innkeepers. Capt. James J. Van Horn, the commandant of the Post of New Bern, reported that some of the town's disreputable liquor dealers were obtaining licenses and setting up shop in shanties with room for a few beds at most. "I am confident that the sole object of the parties referred to . . . is to sell liquor by the small quantity," Van Horn wrote. Believing that Sickles "intended no such trifling with G. O. No. 32," Van Horn suspended the dealers' licenses and sought the commanding general's approval. Sickles, meanwhile, issued a circular warning that civil officials who issued licenses to illicit dealers would lose their authority.[9]

These and other orders issued by Sickles formed a new—albeit temporary—legal code for North Carolina that resulted in fundamental economic, social, judicial, and political changes. To underscore the supremacy of his edicts, Sickles stated in the final paragraph of General Orders No. 10 that any law in force within his district, "inconsistent with the provisions of this General Order, is hereby suspended and declared inoperative." Many Conservatives shared the viewpoint of Beaufort lawyer and former General Assembly member John M. Perry regarding Sickles's assumption of legislative authority. "All our laws are only laws as far as Gen Sickles chooses," Perry wrote, "and I confess that I don't care to participate in legislation that may be annulled at the caprice of the military."[10]

Among the many disapproving Conservatives was superior court judge Augustus S. Merrimon, who resigned because he believed his oath of office forbade him from upholding military orders that overrode state laws. Although he sympathized with Merrimon, Worth initially refused his resignation on the grounds that it might induce other judges to follow suit. Worth also hoped to persuade Merrimon to reconsider. To that end, he attempted to arrange a meeting in Raleigh between Sickles and the state's superior court judges. In a telegram to the governor, Sickles replied that he was too busy to travel to Raleigh. He expressed his regret over Merrimon's resignation but advised Worth to convene the Council of State and choose a replacement. After conferring with his advisors, Worth accepted Merrimon's resignation and appointed a new judge. Sickles approved both decisions, yet he could not resist commenting that he deemed Merrimon's decision "untenable."[11]

Perhaps the aspect of Sickles's code that Worth and his Conservative colleagues found most objectionable was its leveling spirit. For the first time, the landless "dregs of society" (to use Worth's phraseology) could

enjoy full participation in the state's civil affairs. Sickles's reforms heralded the radical revolution that Worth had dreaded since the passage of the
Reconstruction Act. Yet Worth believed that Sickles had far exceeded his
legal authority. "Did Congress mean to establish a military despotism?"
Worth asked President Johnson. The anticipated reply to the governor's
rhetorical question clearly was "no." According to Worth, Congress had
drafted the Reconstruction Act in response to the inability of the former
Confederate states to preserve law and order, and it had designated the
army to restore peace and stability in the South. Noting that the act had
left the southern state governments intact to serve as local extensions of
the federal government, Worth argued that Congress therefore intended
civil government in the South to remain supreme in all matters outside
the army's law enforcement mission. In short, Worth's narrow interpretation of the Reconstruction Act could scarcely have differed more from
Sickles's. "Congress has declared all existing government in these [south-
ern] states illegal," Sickles maintained. "Surely, Congress intended to establish some government. What has been established, if it be not military
government, is nothing."[12]

Perhaps the most controversial case of military intervention in North
Carolina during Sickles's tenure involved the murder of Fayetteville resident Archibald Beebee, a freedman charged with the attempted rape of a
young white woman. After his arraignment, Beebe was shot in the head
as the sheriff led him through an angry mob back to his jail cell. At the
coroner's inquest the next day, two witnesses identified William J. Tolar
as the man who had fired the fatal shot, but the verdict handed down
was that Beebee had been killed "by the hands of some person unknown
to the Jury." The civil authorities of Fayetteville made no further investigation of Beebee's murder. The apparent consensus was that justice had
been served.[13]

Army and Freedmen's Bureau officers arrived at a different conclusion, however. After an investigation of the Beebee murder by Lt. Robert
Avery of the Freedmen's Bureau, Sickles ordered the arrest of Tolar and
four other suspects on May 11, 1867. Among those arrested was Duncan
G. McRae, the magistrate who had indicted Beebee the day he was murdered. McRae's arrest was made on the strength of an eyewitness's testimony that he had incited the mob to kill Beebee. Denied bail, McRae was
jailed at Fort Macon pending his trial in Raleigh. The post commandant
at Fayetteville, Maj. Milton Cogswell, meanwhile notified Sickles that he
had made a thorough investigation of the case and concluded that McRae

was in his office preparing Beebee's commitment papers when the freed-man was shot. Cogswell therefore recommended that McRae be freed at once. Instead, McRae was taken to Raleigh and tried as an accessory to murder. The testimony of McRae's accuser proved so unreliable, however, that the prosecutor dismissed her and dropped the murder charge against the defendant.[14]

Like the John H. Gee war crimes trial the year before, the army con-ducted the Beebee murder trial with impartiality and thoroughness. The trial lasted over two months, and more than sixty witnesses testified. The defendants were ably represented by five of the best criminal lawyers in the state. Defense attorney Samuel F. Phillips argued that, under the Civil Rights bill, his clients were entitled to a trial in a civil court, because the Beebee murder had occurred on February 11, 1867, three weeks before the Reconstruction Act had become law. Few persons in the courtroom would have missed the irony of the Civil Rights bill being cited on behalf of white men charged with murdering a black man. The prosecution countered that the second Freedmen's Bureau bill provided for trials be-fore military tribunals if the crimes in question involved white assailants and black victims, and the commission ruled in their favor.[15]

Defeated in their bid to move the trial to a friendlier court, the de-fense team attempted to contradict or discredit the witnesses for the prosecution. More often than not, the witnesses for the defense instead contradicted themselves or other defense witnesses, whereas more than a dozen prosecution witnesses testified that they had seen Tolar shoot Bee-bee and that two other defendants, Thomas Powers and David Watkins, had helped him. The charges against the fifth defendant, Samuel A. Phil-lips (no relation to the attorney of the same name), were dropped when it became clear that he, like McRae, was not involved in Beebee's murder. After weighing the evidence, the commission found Tolar, Powers, and Watkins guilty of murder and sentenced them to hang. The sentence was then mitigated to fifteen years' imprisonment at hard labor by Sickles's successor, Brig. Gen. Edward R. S. Canby.[16]

The Conservatives' response to the military commission's verdict was by now a familiar ritual, the precedent having been set by the McMillan-McGill case of 1865. The president received numerous letters and peti-tions urging him to pardon the convicted men, and Johnson, standing on the foundation of the U.S. Supreme Court's 1866 ruling in the Milligan case, duly complied with their request. Having spent just over a year in jail, Tolar, Powers, and Watkins were set free. Once again, the army's attempt to punish white North Carolinians for murdering Unionists or blacks was defeated by a presidential pardon.[17]

An important consequence of the Beebee case was Sickles's decision to replace most of Fayetteville's civil officials and establish a provost court there. Sickles took drastic action because he regarded the inconclusive Beebee murder investigation as symptomatic of the local authorities' intent to deny justice to the freedpeople. In Sickles's view, the Reconstruction Acts bound him to protect blacks' civil liberties. The removals included Mayor Thomas J. Curtis, County Coroner Isham Blake, seven town commissioners, four constables, and three magistrates. In a letter that appeared in several North Carolina newspapers, Curtis complained that not even President Johnson dared "to restrain Gen. Sickles and his petty subalterns in the exercise of despotic, arbitrary, and unlawful power," a sentiment doubtless shared by many white Tar Heels. Worth later informed the president that Sickles had refused the civil authorities' request to prosecute the defendants in the Beebee case, but the governor neglected to mention that the town officials had done nothing for three months after the coroner's inquest and only lurched into action when the military arrested the suspects.[18]

Sickles also replaced the civil court at Fayetteville with a provost court, which proved as controversial as the removal of the town officials. Worth described the three civilian judges as "respectable mechanics" without any legal training or experience, yet the governor received few complaints regarding their administration of justice. In any event, Sickles kept the judges on a short leash. The post commander determined their docket, which consisted of lesser crimes, and they needed Sickles's approval to impose prison terms or fines greater than $100.[19]

Sickles intervened in the civil affairs of Beaufort, Morehead City, New Bern, Tarboro, and other North Carolina towns. In addition to appointing or removing mayors and other civic officials, he suspended local elections and tax collection. Sickles also placed local law enforcement personnel under the supervision of post commanders. On April 12, Capt. Royal T. Frank, the post commander at Wilmington, dismissed two police officers for brutality. Frank informed the mayor that "nine tenths of all the shooting stabbing &c which has been committed in this City in the last eight or ten months has been committed by the police." Several of Frank's soldiers numbered among the victims.[20]

At the request of concerned citizens in Jones County, Sickles authorized a thorough housecleaning of law enforcement officials there. On

April 26, 1867, a group of Jones County residents met at Trenton and drafted a set of resolutions condemning the Regulators' outrages and the inaction of local law enforcement officers. The citizens sent the petition to Sickles, who then referred them to Capt. James J. Van Horn, the local post commander. Van Horn reported that the petitioners "correctly represented" conditions in Jones County "with perhaps some exaggeration." But the captain indicated that he had received no complaints from Jones County since late March, when he had sent a detachment there. Van Horn nevertheless reported that the sheriff, Thomas Wilcox, and other civil authorities in Jones County were "very remiss" in executing their duties, "particularly so in rendering assistance to the military authorities." The post commander therefore recommended replacing Wilcox and seventeen magistrates with the persons named in the Trenton resolutions. Sickles authorized Van Horn's recommendations but stipulated that the appointees must be able to take the Ironclad Oath, affirming that the swearer had never taken up arms against the Union or otherwise aided the rebellion. Among Van Horn's appointees was Sheriff Orson R. Colgrove, a northern-born victim of the Regulators and the driving force behind the Trenton resolutions.[21]

Sickles's actions struck his Conservative critics as despotic. Their perception of Sickles was skewed, however, particularly in the matter of appointments and removals. At first, he acted on the recommendations of his post commanders; later, he relied heavily on Worth's judgment. In answer to a request from the governor to retain the sheriff of Randolph County, whose term of office had expired, Sickles granted Worth the power to appoint civil officials as long as they were not disqualified under the third section of the Fourteenth Amendment. For the rest of his tenure, Sickles employed this policy with few exceptions.[22]

If the situation in Jones County appeared to be improving, residents of neighboring Lenoir County believed that conditions there were rapidly deteriorating. In a petition to Governor Worth, the citizens complained that "some of the most atrocious acts of lawlessness known in the annals of crime have been perpetrated in our midst . . . and [are] fearfully on the increase. . . . Highway robbery, murder, arson, theft, and other crimes and misdemeanors, are of such frequent occurrence, as to intimidate even the most resolute." The petitioners informed Worth that "some 12 or 15" of the alleged outlaws had been arrested and confined in the county jail at Kinston, but "a large number" of them were still at large. Fearing that they might attempt to free their partners, the citizens urged Worth to call a special session of the superior court to bring the prisoners "to speedy trial."[23]

In a letter that arrived soon after the petition, Freedmen's Bureau official H. H. Foster cited allegations that three large gangs of Regulators were rampaging through several eastern counties. Foster reported that the first gang was all-white, the second was all-black, "and the third (and by far the worst) is made up of both whites and blacks." He also noted that Jones County was "overrun with 'Regulators," contradicting Captain Van Horn's assessment. The county even lacked a jail, compelling the authorities to hold the prisoners in the jail of neighboring Lenoir County. Foster warned that until the remaining desperadoes were brought to justice, "the country in this section at least is ruined."[24]

The Lenoir County petition and Foster's letter spurred Worth into action. On May 18, 1867, the governor notified Colonel Bomford of the crisis and requested that a detachment of troops be sent to Kinston to guard the county jail. He also offered a reward for the capture of the Regulators still at large and directed Judge Edward J. Warren to open an extra session of the Lenoir County superior court as soon as possible. Worth meanwhile continued to argue that the crisis was "not attributable to the civil authorities, but to the failure of parties injured and others, to furnish the specific information to the civil officers which would authorise the authorities to act." Worth thus hoped to conceal the fact that the Regulators remained at large because many law enforcement officers either feared or sympathized with them.[25]

Bomford relayed Worth's request to Maj. Charles E. Compton, the commandant of the Post of Goldsboro. For some reason, Compton did not send a detachment to the Lenoir County jail, yet he did transfer three of the prisoners to Fort Macon. On June 2, two weeks after Worth's letter to Bomford, a gang of Regulators freed the remaining prisoners. Lenoir County sheriff E. F. Cox appealed to bureau official Foster for assistance. "There is no protection here for life or property," the sheriff wrote, "and we look to you, Major, as an Officer of the Government, to see that we obtain relief." Foster enclosed Cox's letter with his own message to Compton. He noted that thirteen murders had been committed during the past eighteen months in a county with a population of barely ten thousand. "It must certainly show to you a most deplorable condition of society," Foster commented. In a postscript, he reported that Lenoir County's murder count had just increased by two. On June 6, three black men had murdered a white farmer named Miller and his wife.[26]

Compton immediately ordered a detachment of twenty men from the 40th U.S. Infantry to Kinston. On June 12, he instructed the commander, Lt. Sylvester Soper, to assure the citizens that the army would protect them but that their cooperation was needed "to bring to justice . . . the desperadoes who have inaugurated such a reign of terror in that section." Compton also ordered a company of the 5th U.S. Cavalry under Capt. Jeremiah C. Denney to Kinston and placed Denney in overall command. The major directed the infantry detachment to guard the jail and the cavalry "to ferret out and arrest all offenders that they be speedily brought to trial." Compton instructed Denney to "use all the means at your disposal" to capture the Millers' murderers. Should the outlaws resist, "they will be treated as Guerrillas and summarily punished."[27]

The outlaws meanwhile intercepted a letter bound for Raleigh with the intention of publicizing the Regulators' outrages in Greene County. They returned the missive to the sender, Sidney A. Busbee, along with a warning that he would soon receive "a coat of tar & feathers." An African American teacher at the local freedpeople's school, Busbee had written a friend in Raleigh about the Snow Hill lynching of the previous January. A few days after the letter came back, arsonists burned Busbee's school. Busbee hurried to Raleigh to request "*permanent* Military Protection" for freedpeople in Greene County. During his stay, he wrote a letter urging his friends back home to hold a mass meeting and appeal for federal troops. "Do not be afraid of the regulators," Busbee advised them. "If you let these men go now by not telling on them, they will murder you after awhile."[28]

A Freedmen's Bureau officer named Capt. Hannibal D. Norton delivered Busbee's message. Sent to Greene County to investigate conditions there, Norton reported that local citizens had taken up a collection to rebuild the school and that construction was already under way. He evidently frowned on Busbee's attempt to publicize the Snow Hill lynching, for he maintained that a teacher "who kept his own counsel and attended strictly to his duties *as* a teacher . . . would be supported by the respectable portion of the inhabitants of Snow Hill." He nevertheless echoed Busbee's appeal to send a troop detachment to Greene County for the freedpeople's protection.[29]

During the spring and summer of 1867, federal soldiers slowly began to restore order in eastern North Carolina. The military, however, only responded after the situation had reached critical proportions. Worth bears much of the blame for his stubborn refusal to concede the civil authorities' inability to bring the outlaws to justice. Even so, the army should have intervened once it had become apparent that civil law enforcement officials either could not or would not suppress the Regulators. By mid-1866, numerous Freedmen's Bureau officials had called attention to the crisis, and Sickles had responded by issuing General Orders No. 7. Yet the U.S. Army waited until February 1867 to take action and therefore must share equal blame with Worth for a costly and unnecessary lapse in law and order.[30]

Lawlessness also remained a problem in the western half of the state. "To the assertions of Gov. Worth and others, that justice in all cases, is administered by the courts, I firmly and emphatically deny it," declared Oscar Eastmond, the Freedmen's Bureau agent at Asheville. "If there is a place in North Carolina where Military power is needed, it is west of the Blue Ridge." From Trinity College in Randolph County, President Braxton Craven appealed to Capt. William S. Worth, the post commander at Greensboro, for a troop detachment to maintain order during the June commencement exercises. "In former times," Craven wrote, "the sheriff was always present, but at this time the civil law is without force in this section." A few months after Craven's letter, Captain Worth informed B. A. Sellars, the presiding judge of the Randolph County superior court, of numerous complaints made to his headquarters indicating "that many of the citizens" in Sellars's home county "refuse to obey the laws and openly defy the civil authorities." Worth warned the judge that a continuance of the problem would compel him "to interfere in behalf of law and order. Sheriffs, constables, and other [civil] officers will be protected and if necessary assisted in the proper performance of their duties."[31]

In Wilkesboro, the Wilkes County seat, a Fourth of July celebration came to an abrupt end when a mob of former Confederates assaulted and severely injured several blacks and white Unionists. The local authorities made no attempt to apprehend the perpetrators. In neighboring Iredell County, ex-Rebels wielding knives and clubs broke up a citizens' meeting called "to secure order and decorum" in their community. Several Unionists were ambushed while returning home after dark and were nearly stoned to death. One of the victims, William F. Gray, appealed to the post commandant at Salisbury for troops to protect the loyal citizens of Iredell County. The troops evidently could not be spared, for attacks against Unionists continued in Iredell County.[32]

Letters from Unionists in the western counties to the post commander at Salisbury complained of persecution by the local courts. A former
Union army scout stated that the Caldwell County superior court was
unjustly prosecuting him for crimes that, in fact, were legitimate acts of
war. A Burke County man alleged that he was indicted for sheltering escaped Union prisoners and harboring Confederate deserters and that the
county sheriff had threatened to auction off his property. In both cases,
the post commander informed the presiding judges "that prosecution for
alleged offenses which were in fact acts of war committed during hostilities, will not be permitted, and that costs upon indictments for such acts
already prosecuted must not be collected."[33]

Nervous civil officials sometimes called on post commanders to arrest outlaws hiding out in western North Carolina. The sheriff of Henderson County, W. D. Justus, informed Capt. Gustavus Urban, the post
commander at Morganton, that he was unable to apprehend several men
accused of murdering Unionists during the war. Urban promptly sent
a detachment commanded by Lt. Edward M. Hayes, who had served in
North Carolina under General Sherman in 1865. Hayes reported that all
but two of the accused had moved to Texas since the surrender. Despite
warnings that "there would be some difficulty" in arresting the remaining suspects, Hayes stated that they offered no resistance. The lieutenant
transported the two men to the county jail at Hendersonville, where they
awaited trial.[34]

During his journey through the western part of the state, Hayes noted
"a strong desire on the part of all to obey the Laws" and the presence
of "a strong Unionist element." He found that "the greatest harmony
and good feeling exists between Whites and Blacks" and received "only
one or two complaints." A subsequent report to district headquarters by
Maj. William B. Royall, the new post commander at Morganton, suggests
that Hayes's assessment was excessively optimistic about the strength
of Unionism in the region. "The Rebel portion of the population in
my post," Royall wrote, "are much more intelligent and powerful as a
class" than the Unionists. "Although the Rebels are much in the minor-
ity," Royall continued, "yet they manage to intimidate the Union men."
Royall noted that former Confederates' public denunciation of prominent Unionists "was subversive of good order," but that there were no
state laws prohibiting such misconduct unless accompanied by "some
improper act." He therefore recommended authorization to arrest the
wrongdoers "to prevent more serious consequences." Sickles, however,

instructed Royall to take no action against ex-Confederates unless they attempted to obstruct the Reconstruction Acts.[35]

Civilian law enforcement officials sometimes harassed large assemblages of freedpeople on the grounds of preserving law and order, but the gatherings invariably proved to be harmless political rallies. In one instance, a pair of county sheriffs managed to convince two post commanders that a peaceful assembly of freedmen in fact violated General Orders No. 7. The procession of a large body of freedmen from Wake County into Harnett County alarmed Harnett County sheriff J. R. Grady, who immediately notified Maj. Milton Cogswell, the commandant of the Post of Fayetteville. Cogswell directed Grady to investigate the "incursions," and he recommended that Colonel Bomford, the commander of the Post of Raleigh, do likewise. Bomford, in turn, ordered Wake County sheriff E. H. Ray to cooperate with Grady. The sheriffs reported that the freedmen were heavily armed and that they marched in military order. According to Sheriff Ray, the marchers threatened and disturbed the citizens along their route. The sheriffs' reports convinced the post commanders that the freedmen were violating General Orders No. 7. They therefore directed the sheriffs to "disperse" the marchers. Fearing resistance, Grady recommended that the army intervene instead.[36]

Although the sheriffs' reports persuaded Cogswell and Bomford, the acting provost marshal for the Second Military District, Maj. E. W. Dennis, remained skeptical. He therefore sent a civilian detective named W. H. Griffin to Harnett County to conduct his own investigation. Griffin found a far different situation from the one described by Grady and Ray. The freedmen were neither armed nor organized into companies, and Grady had confiscated their only drum while leading a large posse. The detective learned that the freedmen from Wake County were members of the Union League, a Republican political organization, and that they were attending a rally in Harnett County. "This charge against the freedmen all arises from the antipathy of the whites to the Union League," Griffin reported. After receiving Griffin's report, Dennis immediately notified Cogswell that the sheriffs' statements were "exaggerated" and that they should take no further action. Cogswell ordered Grady to restore the drum to its rightful owners.[37]

In 1865 and 1866, white North Carolinians had feared large assemblages of blacks because they portended bloody insurrections to seize whites' land and livestock. By 1867, white racial fears had shifted from violent uprisings to political mobilization. Complaints that blacks were forming paramilitary companies served as a pretext for denying them the right of public assembly. Conservatives had good reason to dread large numbers of freedmen becoming voters. The leader of the state's newly established Republican (or Union) Party, William W. Holden, was forming a broadly based coalition of blacks, "carpetbaggers" (northern Republicans), and "scalawags" (native white Republicans). Thanks to the solidarity of the black electorate under the auspices of the Union League, the Republicans seemed poised to unseat their Conservative rivals. The Union League had originated in the North during the war as a middle-class patriotic organization and had since spread to the South, where it mobilized Republican voters of both races. Although most Union League chapters were segregated, several in North Carolina were biracial.[38]

In a letter to Sickles, Governor Worth insinuated that Holden and the Republicans were up to no good. He informed the general that the state Republican Party was "operating chiefly through secret political societies . . . particularly among the blacks." Regardless of the Republicans' objectives, Worth could "conceive of no justification, at this time, for *any secret* political organization." In truth, it was no secret that the Republican Party and the Union League planned to end the Conservatives' political dominance by mobilizing as many black voters as possible. Worth grasped the threat posed by the opposition. "If our white men will not register and vote," Worth declared, "the domination of [the] negro party is enevitable." The political revolution that Worth had dreaded since the onset of Military Reconstruction appeared to be under way.[39]

In accordance with the Reconstruction Acts, Sickles began voter registration by asking Governor Worth to recommend registrars for the upcoming election of convention delegates. On April 26, meanwhile, the new state director of the Freedmen's Bureau, Col. Nelson A. Miles, provoked an immediate controversy with his first circular, which directed the state's bureau personnel to supply their own list of registrars. The controversy revolved around the circular's requirement of one black and two white registrars for each voting precinct. One of the white men had to be a native able to take the Ironclad Oath, while the other could be a bureau agent or a Union army veteran. In selecting the freedmen, "care will be taken to procure, as far as possible, those of sufficient intelligence and education." If qualified registrars could not be found for each precinct, the number could be reduced to two white men and one black man per county.[40]

Miles's circular appeared six days after Worth had sent his own circular to supporters in each county, soliciting their recommendations for registrars. Worth suspected that his archrival Holden had persuaded Sickles to adopt Miles's more radical plan. Miles's circular led most of Worth's advisors to defer their recommendations until they could be sure of Sickles's intentions. They had only a short time to wait. On May 8, Sickles issued General Orders No. 18, outlining the registration procedure for the Second Military District. The order called for registration boards "consisting of *three discreet and qualified persons* [italics added]." Sickles's order specified that the registrars be "persons of recognized consideration and worth, fairly representing the population"—a far cry from Miles's exacting specifications. For at least a week, Worth was unaware of Sickles's new order. On May 15, the governor informed Sickles that he planned to recommend few freedmen as registrars, for only a handful possessed "the requisite scholarship." Sickles replied that he had not authorized Miles's circular, but he suggested that the freedpeople would appreciate the appointment of some qualified blacks. Sickles's suggestion failed to sway Worth, however. The governor's final list of nominees bore the names of few freedmen. Anxious to expedite voter registration, Sickles appointed Worth's nominees without comment.[41]

In late May 1867, Worth learned that President Johnson had accepted an invitation to attend the dedication of a monument to his father in Raleigh, the president's birthplace. The ceremony was scheduled for June 4, followed by a trip to Chapel Hill the next day to attend the University of North Carolina's commencement exercises. Worth wired an invitation to General Sickles and received his acceptance the same day. The governor believed that his second opportunity to confer with the general could scarcely have come at a better time. Since his first meeting with Sickles in Charleston a few months earlier, Worth had begun to wonder if Sickles was losing faith in him, for the general seldom answered his letters. He feared that Holden had poisoned Sickles against him. Although his fears were groundless, Worth thought he had good reason to suspect Holden, for the governor had long wielded the poison pen against his political archrival. In a letter to South Carolina governor James L. Orr, Worth denounced Holden as "the most malignant, mean, unscrupulous Radical the Devil has raised up to afflict our people." In Worth's opinion, Holden's sudden transformation into a "Black Republican" betrayed his willingness to exploit ignorant freedmen to fulfill his political ambitions.[42]

President Andrew Johnson (Library of Congress)

Needless to say, Holden was not among the dignitaries who joined Worth at the Raleigh railroad depot on the afternoon of June 3 to welcome President Johnson and his entourage to the state capital. The U.S. Army was well represented, however. As he stepped off the train, Johnson was serenaded by the 40th U.S. Infantry band. General Sickles, Colonel Miles, and several other officers were present, as well as an escort of infantry and cavalry. After a brief ceremony at the depot, the president was taken to Yarborough House, Raleigh's finest hotel, where he received an "enthusiastic welcome" from what the *Raleigh Sentinel* described as "one of the largest crowds we have ever seen in the Capital of North Carolina." The president no doubt found his homecoming far more enjoyable than the ill-fated "Swing around the Circle."[43]

During his weeklong stay in North Carolina, Sickles apparently failed to dispel Worth's concerns regarding his status as governor, for the latter complained afterward that the opposition press was misrepresenting him as an obstructionist. On July 9, Worth assured Sickles, "I have deemed it my duty to co-operate with you in carrying out these [Reconstruction] acts fairly and honestly." Four days later, Worth wrote Sickles that an editorial in the *North Carolina Standard* unfairly accused the governor of "'covering up' and taking no steps to punish parties guilty of outrages on Union men" in the western counties. Worth noted that the joint commission he and General Robinson had appointed the previous year had failed to uncover any conspiracies to persecute Unionists. "I defy malevolence itself," Worth declared, "to specify any instances when I have not done all in my power to have justice impartially administered to all persons irrespective of party, color, or any thing else." Robinson, however, would have replied that the governor invariably dismissed Unionists' charges of persecution as groundless. Worth's anxiety to refute his detractors betrayed his awareness that his inaction might be construed as obstruction—which is precisely what it was.[44]

Thanks to a legal opinion drafted by Johnson's attorney general, Henry Stanbery, Sickles suddenly became as anxious about his position as Worth was about his. Before his trip to North Carolina, the president had directed Stanbery to draft an opinion defining the powers of the district commanders in the South under the First Reconstruction Act. Like Worth, Stanbery argued that the act merely granted district commanders the power to maintain law and order and punish criminals by means of civil courts or military tribunals. Although that was the extent of their power, Stanbery contended, some of the commanders acted on the incorrect assumption that the act endowed them with unlimited authority.[45]

Several of Stanbery's comments referred indirectly to Sickles. "The military commander is made a conservator of the peace, not a legislator," the attorney general wrote. "He has no authority to enact or declare a new code of laws for the people within his district under any idea that he can make a better code than the people have made for themselves." Stanbery then cited several of Sickles's orders and remarked that their author had assumed the combined legislative, executive, and judicial authority of the state, in effect placing himself above the president by declaring, "I am the State."[46]

Stanton persuaded Johnson not to issue Stanbery's opinion as an executive order to the district commanders, thereby allowing them to continue acting as they thought best. Sickles nevertheless believed that Stanbery's opinion rendered his position untenable, for it challenged his authority to remove recalcitrant civil officials. "The military force under my command is insufficient to meet the essential requirements of the Reconstructing Acts," Sickles warned, "unless by the exercise of control over all civil functionaries I can have their prompt and certain cooperation." On June 19, Sickles requested that he be relieved of his command, and he demanded a court of inquiry to answer Stanbery's accusations. For reasons known to him alone, Johnson passed up the opportunity to replace Sickles with a more acceptable general. The president instead directed the adjutant general to refuse Sickles's resignation and deny his request for a court of inquiry.[47]

Sickles, meanwhile, decided to delay voter registration in his district pending Congress's response to another Stanbery opinion concerning the First Reconstruction Act. In May, the attorney general had issued an opinion on voter registration, in which he severely restricted disfranchisement and ruled that registration boards could not challenge voters' qualifications. In a letter to Republican senator Lyman Trumbull, the chairman of the Senate Judiciary Committee, Sickles explained his dilemma. "If I proceed now and disregard the instructions of the President," he wrote, "my action would be regarded as insubordination. If I follow [his] instructions, many would probably be registered [who are] not eligible according to the true interpretation of the acts of Congress."[48]

To save time and effort, Sickles proposed a simple solution. He believed that the increase in the loyal vote resulting from the enfranchisement of the freedmen had eliminated the need for a disqualification clause. "The true solution" to the voter registration problem, he argued, "is to declare Universal Suffrage and Universal Amnesty." Sickles maintained that such a law would simplify voter registration and increase the number of qualified candidates for public office. "Now, more than ever," he wrote, "men of ability & experience in public business are needed for the State government[s] in the South." He contended that it was foolish for the government to expect the cooperation of the southern elite until it removed their disabilities.[49]

Congressional Republicans ignored Sickles's advice regarding universal male suffrage, but on July 19, 1867, they upheld his actions as district commander by passing the Third Reconstruction Act over Johnson's veto. The legislation overruled Stanbery's narrow interpretation of the first two Reconstruction Acts by specifying what the previous acts had merely implied. The Third Reconstruction Act declared the southern civil governments organized during Presidential Reconstruction illegal, yet it retained them on a provisional basis under the supervision of Congress and the district commanders. As agents of congressional authority, district commanders could remove civil officials and appoint replacements. The act enumerated a broad range of former officeholders who were ineligible to vote or serve in public office, and it authorized registrars to reject anyone suspected of perjuring himself under the oath specified in the Second Reconstruction Act. To preempt future legalistic assaults, the act also declared that neither the district commanders nor the registration boards were bound "by any opinion of any civil officer of the United States." Sickles could resume voter registration without fear of presidential interference.[50]

In their eagerness to emasculate Stanbery's legal opinions, the authors of the Third Reconstruction Act neglected to insert a clause that stripped the president of the power to remove district commanders. Keenly aware of their omission, Johnson sought to weaken the impact of the Third Reconstruction Act by suspending Secretary of War Stanton, the chief architect of the act, and by removing the district commanders most likely to use it. The first to go was Maj. Gen. Philip H. Sheridan, the truculent commander of the Fifth Military District. The consensus around Washington was that Sickles would be next.[51]

Sickles soon offered Johnson a golden opportunity to dismiss him. On July 27, Capt. Royal T. Frank, the post commander at Wilmington, prohibited a deputy U.S. marshal from enforcing a judgment issued by the U.S. Circuit Court for the District of North Carolina. The federal court enjoined a Wilmington business firm to pay off two wartime debts. In suspending the judgment, Frank cited the second clause of General Orders No. 10, which forbade the collection of debts incurred between December 19, 1860, and May 15, 1865. The court notified the U.S. marshal for North Carolina, Daniel R. Goodloe, of Frank's action. On July 30, Goodloe informed Sickles. "I feel assured that [Frank] is mistaken,"

Goodloe wrote, "since I cannot suppose that you would undertake to set aside any law of the Government to which you owe allegiance." On the thirty-first, Goodloe assured Stanbery that Sickles would declare General Orders No. 10 inoperative in cases involving the federal courts.[52]

Goodloe was mistaken: Sickles upheld Frank's action. Meanwhile, Grant directed Sickles to suspend the order but then reversed himself when the district commander accused the court of subverting the Reconstruction Acts. A few days later, Grant warned Sickles to intervene only if the federal court was clearly guilty of obstruction. By then, however, the headstrong Sickles's fate was already decided. On August 26, Johnson replaced Sickles with Brig. Gen. Edward R. S. Canby.[53]

The news of Sickles's dismissal elicited a mixed reaction among conservative North Carolinians. Some believed that his successor could only be an improvement. "Gen. Sickles has been removed and that is hopeful," wrote Beaufort attorney John M. Perry. Others seemed less certain. Although the *Raleigh Sentinel* could name "many things which [Sickles] has done, which meet our severest condemnation . . . , we seriously question, nevertheless, whether he has done worse . . . than any other person, in the same position, would have done." The *Sentinel* also applauded the conciliatory sentiments contained in Sickles's letter to Senator Trumbull, which had appeared in several Tar Heel newspapers. Although hardly a Sickles supporter, Worth praised the general's letter to Trumbull as "magnanimous and statesmanlike." The governor even came to regret Sickles's departure.[54]

On August 30, Sickles wrote a lengthy report to Grant justifying his course of action in the federal court case. Sickles also defended his tenure as commander of the Second Military District. "The work of reconstruction has all been done quietly," he maintained, "without violence, without the actual exercise of force." In a brief speech given during President Johnson's visit to Raleigh, Sickles had contended that "order, dignity, and quiet" prevailed in North Carolina. One statistic challenges that rosy assessment: during Sickles's five-month tenure, military commissions in the Second Military District had to try 280 citizens for crimes ranging from larceny to murder. Like Governor Worth, Sickles denied that lawlessness plagued the Tar Heel State, because he believed that acknowledging the fact was an admission of failure. Possessing Worth's talent for self-deception, Sickles claimed that he had nearly completed the task of Reconstruction in North Carolina. Sickles's replacement, General Canby, would soon discover that his predecessor had been unduly optimistic.[55]

Sickles's obliviousness to unrest in the Carolinas manifested itself in other ways. Amid the constant press of urgent business, he sometimes immersed himself in the minutiae of civil affairs. In one instance, Sickles felt compelled to take personal charge of bankruptcy proceedings against the Bank of Lexington, North Carolina, a routine task that he could have delegated to his judge advocate or even a civilian attorney.[56]

Sickles's flaws tended to obscure his finer qualities. As commander of the Second Military District, he provided the Carolinas with expanded civil rights, debtor relief, alcohol and gun control, racially integrated public transportation, and penal reform. Bolstered by the conviction that he was acting in accordance with the Reconstruction Acts, Sickles attempted to establish stability and justice in postwar North Carolina while overseeing its restoration to the Union. Yet nearly all of Sickles's reforms soon became a memory. From the standpoint of longevity, "Sickles's code" must be accounted a failure. Even so, the general had failed in a worthy enterprise.[57]

Chapter Seven

MILITARY RECONSTRUCTION UNDER CANBY

Unlike his predecessor General Sickles, Brig. Gen. Edward Richard Sprigg Canby was a professional soldier, having served in the army for twenty-eight of his forty-nine years. Canby was a graduate of West Point (class of 1839), and a veteran of the Second Seminole War, the Mexican War, and the Mormon Expedition. He was also one of the most underrated Union generals of the Civil War. In 1861, Canby was appointed colonel of the newly formed 19th U.S. Infantry and then placed in command of the Department of New Mexico. The following year, Canby frustrated an attempt by the Confederate Army of New Mexico under Brig. Gen. Henry H. Sibley to invade California.

Canby was then transferred to Washington, D.C., where he served in the army adjutant general's office. On March 31, 1862, he was promoted to brigadier general of volunteers. After the New York City draft riots of July 1863, Canby assumed command of the force sent in to restore order. On May 7, 1864, he was promoted to major general of volunteers and assigned to command the Military Division of West Mississippi. In April 1865, Canby captured Mobile, Alabama; the following month, he accepted the surrender of Confederate forces commanded by Lt. Gen. Richard Taylor and Gen. Edmund Kirby Smith. After the war, Canby commanded the Department of Louisiana and ran afoul of his superior, Maj. Gen. Philip H. Sheridan. Numerous complaints of widespread fraud and persecution of blacks and white loyalists led Sheridan to the mistaken

Brig. Gen. Edward R. S. Canby (Library of Congress)

conclusion that Canby was neglecting his duties. In February 1866, Sheridan recommended that Canby be mustered out of the army. Finding his position untenable, Canby requested a transfer on the grounds of failing health and was recalled to Washington.[1]

Former Confederate officer and Republican convert William Blount Rodman described Canby as tall and dignified, "rather sensible looking & good natured—dresses in plain clothes and a wig," which partially concealed a pair of large ears. Lacking his predecessor's charisma, Canby instead gave an air of calm self-possession. Governor Worth found Canby unfailingly courteous, despite their frequent disagreements.[2]

From the start, Canby and Worth clashed over "Sickles's code," the appointment or removal of judges and other civil officials, the military's intervention in the state's judicial process, and the civil courts' alleged persecution of blacks and white loyalists. Canby's correspondence with Worth consumed much of his time for, unlike Sickles, he felt compelled to answer Worth's complaints item by item. In addition, Canby had to oversee each step of the Reconstruction process: voter registration, the convention vote, the constitutional convention itself, and the state elections. His most challenging task was to ensure that citizens could register and vote without being threatened, harassed, or harmed. Maintaining law and order therefore remained a constant preoccupation.

On September 5, 1867, Canby officially assumed command of the Second Military District. Worth wasted no time in urging Canby to revoke or modify several of Sickles's orders. On September 10, Worth took issue with Sickles's jury and stay laws and his order establishing a provost court at Fayetteville. Canby did not bother to address Worth's opposition to the provost court or the jury law—they would remain in force—but instead focused on Sickles's stay law, which the general ably defended in an exhaustive analysis. Suffice it to say that Canby believed "the order has been productive of good" in the Carolinas, whereas its revocation "would be productive of evil." Much to Worth's dismay, Canby's letter revealed that he intended to uphold Sickles's orders. The general's candor merely strengthened Worth's conviction that he was an uncompromising radical—an accusation the governor had never leveled at Sickles. Worth even came to believe that Canby was "more tyrannical" than Sickles, whose orders had provoked the controversy in the first place.[3]

Thanks to an order of Canby, the jury issue refused to die. On September 13, Canby issued General Orders No. 89, reaffirming that all citizens who had paid taxes during the current year were eligible for jury duty.

The order stipulated that jurors must be registered voters, and it revoked the state property qualification. On October 25, Canby issued General Orders No. 109, requiring that each sheriff be issued a list of registered voters for his county to determine jurors' eligibility. Worth condemned the exclusion of citizens who had not registered, for the Reconstruction laws barred him and many other Conservative politicians from voting.[4]

The governor nevertheless derived some consolation from a subtle concession in General Orders No. 89. Canby modified Sickles's General Orders No. 32 by inserting the phrase "and who are qualified" into his own jury order, permitting judges to disqualify persons whose mental or physical disabilities rendered them unfit for jury duty. The governor wasted no time in notifying the judges. "You are not required to exclude from the list from which the jury is to be drawn *the unregistered voter*," Worth advised one county court judge, "and from the list of tax-payers you are authorized to purge . . . those clearly unfit to serve on account of want of intelligence. You are not to assume that *all* negroes are unfit," he cautioned, "but you may exclude those who are deficient in ordinary intelligence or degraded by moral obliquity."[5]

The jury order controversy resurfaced in late November, when superior court judge Daniel G. Fowle resigned in protest over Canby's requirement that jurors be admitted even if they failed to meet the property qualification. Fowle justified his resignation on the grounds that the "Military have heretofore been restraining the Courts from doing certain things which the law commanded[,] but this is the first order requiring the Courts to be participators in over riding the law of the State." Worth notified Canby, who, in turn, authorized the governor to summon the Council of State and choose Fowle's successor. Finding a replacement proved more difficult than anticipated. Worth offered the judgeship to three men, and each man turned it down. At this point, Worth suddenly fell ill, and the search for a judge ground to a halt. Only later did Canby learn the cause of the delay. Assuming that Worth and his advisory council were dragging their feet amid a mounting backlog of cases, Canby undertook his own search. He nominated a twenty-nine-year-old Union army veteran from Ohio named Albion W. Tourgée to fill the vacancy. In Worth's opinion, Canby could not have made a worse choice. Since settling in North Carolina in the fall of 1865, Tourgée had earned a reputation among white Tar Heels as a notorious carpetbagger through his outspoken advocacy of freedmen's rights. Canby unwisely invited Worth to submit references attesting to Tourgée's "bad character." The governor eagerly complied, sending him a letter of condemnation signed by three dozen prominent men from Greensboro, Tourgée's hometown. Worth's smear campaign against Tourgée induced Canby to withdraw his name and authorize the governor and the Council of State to submit yet another nomination. But the general warned that he would reject a devotee to "our holy and lost cause."[6]

Worth faced the challenge of finding a candidate not only acceptable to Canby and the Council of State but who would also accept the post. The list of potential candidates must have been short indeed. After conferring with the Council of State, the governor nominated Clinton A. Cilley, a former Union army officer and Freedmen's Bureau official from Massachusetts who was practicing law in Lenoir. Although a carpetbagger himself, Cilley managed to avoid the heated controversy that continually swirled around Tourgée. Instead, Cilley had opened a law firm with a former Confederate colonel and had married the daughter of a prominent Lenoir merchant and politician. Canby approved Worth's nomination, and Cilley donned the superior court judge's robes in February 1868, three months after Fowle's resignation.

During the autumn of 1867, Worth and Canby became embroiled in a dispute over the military's intervention in the state's judicial process. The case of Caswell County sheriff Jesse C. Griffith marked the culmination of their disagreement. Griffith's case originated in a wartime incident that involved a Confederate deserter-turned-Union scout named William Johnson. In early 1864, Johnson and two comrades deserted from the Confederate army and headed for Union-held east Tennessee. During their flight, the three men entered a house and stole about $20 worth of food and $5 in Confederate currency. Whereas Johnson succeeded in making his escape, his comrades were captured and tried for burglary. They received a pardon after agreeing to rejoin the Confederate army. Johnson, meanwhile, became a lieutenant in a federal regiment in east Tennessee and later served as a guide for Maj. Gen. George Stoneman's Union cavalry during its raid through western North Carolina. After the war, Johnson returned home to Rockingham County. He was arrested, tried for burglary in the Caswell County superior court, and sentenced to die. Johnson was then incarcerated in the county jail at Yanceyville under the watchful eye of Sheriff Griffith. Acting on the assumption that the military authorities would overturn the conviction, Worth pardoned Johnson but ordered him to pay the jail fees and court costs. Unable to pay, Johnson remained incarcerated in the Caswell County jail. In April

1867, Johnson's attorney, Albion W. Tourgée, informed General Sickles that he would post bond for his "penniless" client if the general secured his release.[7]

Sickles ordered an investigation of the Johnson case. The investigating officer, Lt. John O'Connell, reported that Griffith had already released Johnson, evidently to avoid military intervention. The lieutenant described Johnson's former cell as an iron cage nine feet square by six feet high, and he noted that the prisoner had been bound by a six-foot chain. According to O'Connell, Johnson "was punished chiefly because of his union sentiment" and his actions as a federal officer. In October, Canby's judge advocate, Maj. E. W. Dennis, recommended that Sheriff Griffith be arrested and tried by a military commission for cruel and inhumane treatment of Johnson.[8]

Acting on Dennis's recommendation, Canby had Griffith arrested and taken to Charleston, South Carolina, for trial by a military commission. Worth informed President Johnson that Griffith was arrested "on some unknown charge" preferred by Johnson and Tourgée, "both of them men of the most detestable moral character." The governor noted that this was but the latest in a series of arbitrary arrests by the military, in which the accused were "transported to distant places of confinement" and held for months without trial. The governor indicated that he had "earnestly remonstrated against the iniquity of such proceedings" in letters to Sickles and Canby, but to no avail. "No form of Military despotism can be more terrible to the orderly citizens than these summary arrests," Worth declared. The governor thus employed a stratagem he would use often in his disputes with Canby—accusing the military of injustice to deflect criticism of the civil judiciary.[9]

Johnson handed Worth's letter to General Grant, and Grant sent it to Canby for comment. On November 14, the district commander wrote a detailed report and enclosed over a dozen corroborating documents. Canby explained that he had ordered Griffith's arrest and trial because the evidence implicated him "as one of the agents of the injustice and oppression practiced on [William] Johnson." The general stated that Griffith was brought to Charleston—"not thirty-six hours from his home"— because a military tribunal was already in session there, offering the prospect of a speedier trial than anywhere else in the district. When it became apparent that the trial would be delayed, Canby explained, he released Griffith on his own recognizance and allowed him to return home pending his trial date.[10]

Canby blamed the ongoing persecution of loyal North Carolinians on a loophole in the state's Amnesty Act of 1866. The act shielded all persons who had been "in the civil or military service of the State [or] the late Confederate States or as officers & soldiers of the Armies of the United States." But the law did not protect native loyalists who had served the Union army as civilian scouts, spies, or guides, or who had committed acts of war while deserting from or resisting conscription into the Confederate army. "The case of Johnson is of this class," Canby noted. "[He] was tried not for the offense for which he was indicted and ostensibly tried, but . . . for deserting from the Rebel Army." According to Canby, the wartime indictment against Johnson had expired with the downfall of the Confederacy; had he been executed, it would have been murder.

The general next turned to Worth's allegations regarding the military's arbitrary arrest and confinement of civilians. He noted that before Griffith's arrest, the governor had made two complaints to him on that subject. The first concerned the arrest and imprisonment of six Perquimans County men charged with breaking an accused murderer out of the Chowan County jail at Edenton. Canby indicated that the sheriff, Miles C. Brinkley, had made no effort to apprehend either the prisoner or his rescuers, compelling the military to intervene. Federal troops arrested the "Perquimans Six" and jailed them pending their trial.

Worth's second complaint concerned the arrest and detention of Duncan G. McRae, the Fayetteville magistrate accused of complicity in the murder of Archibald Beebee. Canby reported that McRae had been acquitted and released from custody after several months' imprisonment. "It is always to be regretted that innocent persons should be arrested or subjected to any restraint . . . from false accusations or unfounded suspicion," Canby wrote, "but this is an incident of civil as well as of military arrests." Canby characterized Worth's complaints of "military despotism" as "disingenuous" and accused him of having them published "for political effect."[11]

Canby sent a copy of his report to both Worth and Grant. The governor could not resist writing a lengthy rebuttal. He denied having accused Canby of using his power "oppressively or unjustly," but then he described the army's treatment of Sheriff Griffith as "very oppressive." Worth next disputed Canby's report item by item. But the fact that a military tribunal had just acquitted Sheriff Griffith and that Duncan G. McRae and the Perquimans Six were already free weakened the governor's case for "military despotism."[12]

Not content with making a rebuttal to Canby, Worth traveled to Washington to give President Johnson a personal account of the dire situation in North Carolina. The president urged him to publicize the injustice of military government in the Old North State, but the governor demurred out of concern that Canby would remove him. Johnson then suggested that Worth send him a report detailing the instances of military oppression. The governor eagerly complied, amassing a thirty-page catalog of military outrages, despite an illness that kept him bedridden most of the time. Emulating Canby's heavily documented report to Grant, Worth solicited firsthand accounts from participants such as Sheriff Brinkley and Duncan G. McRae. The governor recited a litany of outrages: the arrests of Griffith, McRae, and the Perquimans Six; the provost court at Fayetteville; Canby's jury order; and several others. Worth believed that his letter to Johnson would result in either Canby's removal or his own. But aside from venting his anger, Worth's letter accomplished nothing. From the governor's standpoint, this was probably just as well, for Canby's replacement might have proved even more objectionable.[13]

Although Worth perceived Canby as "an extreme Radical," the general was no more a radical than Sickles had been. On the contrary, Canby demonstrated a willingness to bend the rules in certain situations. In one instance, the general permitted hunters to shoot game on the Outer Banks when informed that was how they earned their livelihood. He also permitted a large number of Wilkes County farmers to distill their surplus corn when informed that the shipping costs ate up their profits. At the end of the year, the general decided to revoke several of Sickles's more objectionable orders. On December 31, Canby issued General Orders No. 164, ending the ban on the distillation of grain and transferring authority over the sale of alcohol to the local officials. Canby also pleased North Carolina creditors by changing the effective date of judgment suspensions in the Old North State from December 20, 1860, the day South Carolina had seceded, to May 21, 1861, the day after North Carolina had seceded.[14]

Canby's order failed to mollify Worth, however. The governor's hostility to Canby arose from the fear that the Conservatives would be swept out of office in the coming election. As the district commander, Canby oversaw the execution of the Reconstruction Acts and thus served as a convenient scapegoat for what Worth viewed as the impending catastrophe.

However loudly Worth might rail against "military despotism," he could not drown white loyalists' complaints of injustice. In his November 14

report, Canby presented the governor with four cases. The first case involved the alleged wartime murder of four prisoners by a local Home
Guard unit, and the second case concerned a Union veteran indicted for
stealing horses in obedience to orders. The third case involved an indictment against seven Madison County Unionists for the shooting death of
Sheriff Ransom P. Merrill, a pro-Confederate who allegedly had shot one
of the Unionists without provocation. The man who had killed Merrill
pleaded self-defense. Canby's fourth case concerned a former Union army
recruiter named William Blalock, a Caldwell County resident indicted on
twenty charges ranging from forcible trespass to murder. According to
Blalock's attorney, a former Confederate colonel named George N. Folk,
the charges against Blalock stemmed from his wartime service as a recruiting agent. Folk requested that the post commander at Salisbury, Lt.
Col. John R. Edie, suspend "the ruinous bill of [court] costs" against
Blalock and grant his client a trial before a military tribunal. Lacking the
authority to grant Folk's requests, Edie sent the letter to district headquarters in Charleston. Canby's judge advocate, Maj. E. W. Dennis, declared that "prosecutions for alleged offenses, which were in fact acts of
war committed during hostilities, will not be permitted," and he further
ruled that "costs upon indictments for such acts already prosecuted must
not be collected." The military thus barred the civil judiciary from penal-
izing Blalock for his alleged "crimes."[15]

Canby noted that the members of the Home Guard who allegedly had
murdered their prisoners were protected by the Amnesty Act, whereas
Blalock, a Union recruiter who had acted under the orders of a superior
officer, was not. The four cases convinced Canby to close the loophole
in the state's Amnesty Act. On November 27, 1867, he issued General
Orders No. 134, absolving all civilian and military personnel of criminal
liability for acts of war committed while in the service of the state, the
Confederacy, or the United States. The order included "all private citizens" who had served in local defense units or who had resisted state or
Confederate authority.[16]

Worth also received reports of numerous outrages against blacks. The
most notorious such incident involved the murder of a Chowan County freedman named James Norcom by his employer, Thomas Pratt. On
June 24, 1867, the two men became embroiled in a dispute that ended
with Norcom brandishing an axe and Pratt seizing a shotgun. As Norcom began walking home, Pratt approached to within thirty yards of
the freedman and fired, severely wounding him in the hip and leg. That

evening, Norcom died, shortly after his leg was amputated. After learning of Norcom's death, Pratt turned himself in to the county sheriff, Miles C. Brinkley. On the night of July 29, a gang of masked desperadoes— allegedly the Perquimans Six—took the keys from the jailor and released Pratt. Brinkley learned of Pratt's escape soon afterward but concluded that he could not assemble a posse in time to overtake the outlaws. After reporting the jailbreak to the post commander at Plymouth, the district provost marshal general at Charleston, and Governor Worth, Brinkley took no further steps. Even Worth's offer of a $300 reward for Pratt's capture failed to spur the sheriff into action.[17]

When it became apparent that the civil authorities were making no effort to capture either Pratt or his liberators, the district provost marshal general, Lt. Col. Edward W. Hinks, sent a private detective named Edward Hoffman to investigate the Norcom-Pratt affair. Hoffman spent several weeks in Chowan and Perquimans counties questioning persons connected with the case, including Pratt's wife and Sheriff Brinkley. During the investigation, Hoffman learned that several of Pratt's friends from Perquimans County had visited him shortly before his escape. Hoffman also learned that Sheriff Brinkley had placed a guard of four men over Pratt but then dismissed them a few days before the jailbreak. The army arrested the Perquimans Six on the strength of Hoffman's findings, held them for two months, and then released them for lack of evidence. The Perquimans Six were never tried for breaking Pratt out of jail, and Pratt was never tried for Norcom's murder.[18]

During Military Reconstruction, criminal justice remained more oppressive for blacks than it was for whites. The arrest statistics for the Second Military District indicate that the civil authorities arrested a disproportionate number of blacks. From January 1, 1867, to June 30, 1868, the civil authorities in the Carolinas arrested 5,295 blacks and only 1,501 whites, yet blacks comprised less than one-half the total population of the two states. When the figures are compared with the proportion of blacks and whites arrested by the military authorities, the disparity becomes manifest. From March 2, 1867, to July 24, 1868, the army arrested 611 blacks and 526 whites. In short, the civil authorities arrested more than three blacks for every white, whereas blacks composed only one-half of those arrested by the military authorities. The most telling statistic involves the proportion of blacks and whites convicted by military tribunals. Of the army's 445 convictions, 303, or 68 percent, involved white defendants. Only 142 of the 611 blacks arrested, or 23 percent, were tried and convicted, compared with 58 percent of the whites. Although the military authorities dealt more justly with blacks than did their civilian counterparts, they were far more likely to arrest blacks than whites on flimsy evidence.[19]

Perhaps the most notorious military prisoner in the Carolinas was James A. Keith, a former Confederate officer who, in January 1863, had ordered the summary execution of thirteen Unionists—including several teenage boys—for plundering Marshall, the Madison County seat. It later came to light that few of the victims had taken part in the raid. The execution became known as the "Shelton Laurel Massacre," after the community in which the killings had occurred. Although he faced no criminal charges for his action, Keith had to resign his commission. As a civilian, he later led a gang of desperadoes allegedly responsible for numerous crimes, including several cold-blooded murders. In November 1867, Canby ordered Keith's arrest and imprisonment at Castle Pinckney in Charleston harbor. Canby then notified Sheriff S. G. Brigman of Madison County.[20]

Fearing that Keith's "rebel friends" would break him out of the county jail, Brigman requested that the prisoner be kept in military custody. He also suggested that a military commission try Keith for murdering native loyalists and federal soldiers. A local resident warned the provost marshal general that a civil trial involving Keith in western North Carolina would "seriously endanger the peace of the community. It would revive old feuds, which are [only] being forgotten." Lt. George F. Price, the district judge advocate, reported finding "abundant evidence" to convict Keith, but he argued that a military tribunal could not try him for wartime crimes because they would have occurred outside the federal occupation zone. To expedite the case against Keith, Price recommended that the prisoner be turned over to the civil authorities. Canby heeded Price's advice and handed Keith over to Sheriff Brigman. A lengthy civil trial ensued, but, as Brigman had feared, Keith's friends engineered his escape from the Buncombe County jail in February 1869.[21]

Canby's decision to turn Keith over to the civil authorities typified his judicial policy. The general intervened in civil court proceedings only when cases fell into one of three categories: if a person was prosecuted for acts of war committed under orders of either belligerent, if a civil court attempted to execute a judgment rendered by a southern court during the war, or if a civil court denied the right of appeal or removal to the federal courts. Canby noted that cases in the first category were "quite numerous," with about three-fourths being against Unionists and the remainder being against former Confederates. Whenever Canby uncovered evidence indicating that an indictment stemmed from wartime animosity, he ordered an immediate halt to the proceedings.[22]

Canby likewise removed civil officials only in cases of extreme incompetence or flagrant misconduct. When Canby assumed command, the state head of the Freedmen's Bureau, Col. Nelson A. Miles, had urged him to make a clean sweep of the state government. Conceding that the incumbent state officials "may not be in open hostility towards the [federal] Government," Miles nonetheless maintained that they were "by their influence and sympathies antagonistic to" Congressional Reconstruction. Even so, Canby agreed with Sickles that too few qualified replacements were available to make a wholesale change possible.[23]

During his tenure, Canby replaced about two-dozen civil officials. The largest such removal involved eighteen Jones County officials accused of negligence. In October 1867, a group of Jones County residents petitioned Governor Worth, complaining that the army had arbitrarily removed Sheriff Thomas Wilcox and seventeen magistrates "at a time of profound peace and quiet and harmony." Worth informed Canby that the former officials had no idea why they were dismissed and never had an opportunity to confront their accusers. The governor further alleged that the new sheriff, Orson R. Colgrove, could not be bonded because he owned no real estate in Jones County. Landholding qualifications aside, Worth's opposition to Colgrove stemmed from the sheriff's notoriety as one of the county's leading Republicans.[24]

Canby ordered his judge advocate, Lt. George F. Price, to investigate the Wilcox case. Price reported that the county court had rejected Colgrove's bond because he was a "military appointee" but that the local post commander, Capt. James J. Van Horn, had installed him anyway. As for the removal of Wilcox and the seventeen magistrates, Price noted that whenever crime victims appealed to the sheriff or one of the magistrates for help, the officials refused to act. Price indicated that many Jones County residents suspected Wilcox and the magistrates of colluding with the desperadoes. As a result, Price wrote, "bands of lawless men roamed over the County, defying law and order, doing as they pleased." Price also reported that Van Horn had informed Wilcox and the magistrates of the grounds for their removal. Price's report convinced Canby to uphold the removals, and the controversy ended there.[25]

In addition to removing civil officials, Canby postponed elections throughout the state. The general ordered the incumbents at Elizabeth City, Goldsboro, and Williamston to remain in office until the local post commander could submit a list of qualified men to fill the vacancies. Anticipating the end of Military Reconstruction and the resumption of civil government, Canby chose to fill the vacant offices with temporary appointees until the local governments could hold their own elections.[26]

One of Canby's most important tasks was to hold a statewide election in North Carolina to decide on a constitutional convention and to choose delegates should voters approve the convention. When Canby assumed command in early September, voter registration in the Tar Heel State was already under way, continuing to the end of the month. Some complaints of improprieties arose. The registration board for a Davidson County precinct allegedly refused to register citizens who had admitted to volunteering for the Confederate army, and a Forsyth County registration board reportedly asked several questions to determine ex-Confederates' current loyalties. Word of the infractions soon reached Capt. William S. Worth, the post commander at Greensboro. Worth ordered the registrars "to allow all such persons to register," provided they had held no public office in the state or federal government before the war and met all other legal qualifications.[27]

On October 18, Canby issued General Orders No. 101, announcing that the election would be held on November 19 and 20. The order warned that the use of intimidation or violence to prevent citizens from registering or voting would be severely punished. The order likewise threatened punishment for white employers who dismissed their black laborers for voting, but discharged workers would soon discover the difficulty of proving such allegations. Canby also prohibited post garrisons from interfering with elections unless they were summoned to restore order at the polls; individual soldiers, however, could enter polling places to vote. Sheriffs and other civil law enforcement officers would be responsible for maintaining order at the polls. The final tally indicated that 106,721 whites and 72,932 blacks had registered, for a total of 179,653 voters.[28]

Conservative elder statesman William A. Graham exhorted supporters to vote against a convention, while the leading Conservative daily, the *Raleigh Sentinel*, urged the election of Conservative delegates. Governor Worth advocated yet another course that meshed with his strategy of passive resistance to the Reconstruction Acts. Believing the Republicans outnumbered the Conservatives, Worth concluded that the Conservatives' best chance for defeating the convention was to refrain from voting on it. Under the Reconstruction Acts, a majority of registered voters had to cast their ballots in the affirmative for the convention measure to pass. Worth hedged his bets, however, counseling supporters to "vote for the best delegates" on the ballot. He refused to publicize his opposition to the convention for fear that Canby would remove him from office. "You may use these ideas as you please," Worth advised one supporter, "but *not as coming from me.*" Although Graham and several other Conservative leaders endorsed the no-vote stratagem at the last minute, the Republicans remained confident of a resounding victory at the polls.[29]

Election campaigning across the state was generally peaceful and orderly, but according to the *Wilmington Morning Star* (a Conservative paper), a Republican rally staged by blacks in Brunswick County got out of hand due to the inflammatory speech of "one Legg, the Radical candidate," and too much free whiskey. The *Star* reported that "a considerable riot" erupted and the mob stoned several white bystanders before they could escape. Led by several black soldiers, the rioters then "paraded about" the streets of Smithville "in triumph," occasionally stopping to stone the houses of the county sheriff and other prominent citizens. Local authorities never identified the uniformed ringleaders. In any event, the Brunswick County riot was an apparent anomaly. Thanks in large part to federal troops, the statewide election that followed a few days later was unmarred by disturbances.[30]

North Carolina voters overwhelmingly approved the convention initiative. Of the state's 179,653 registered voters, 93,006 voted for the convention and 32,961 voted against it. The white vote split, with 31,284 for and 32,961 against. The black vote was 61,722 for and 0 against. Canby nevertheless reported that blacks cast "a few" votes against the convention, but he regarded those votes with suspicion. Voter turnout among registered blacks was an impressive 85 percent. Of the 14,000 eligible freedmen who did not vote, only about 3,000 failed to register. The high black voter turnout indicated that the Union League had done its job of mobilizing African American voters for the Republican Party. The black vote ensured the success of the convention measure. Even if the roughly 33,000 whites who had voted against the convention had abstained instead, the Conservatives still would have fallen a few thousand votes shy of their objective. Of the 53,686 registered voters who failed to vote, 42,476 of them were white. Many of them had heeded Graham's counsel to refrain from voting, while a substantial number had refused to vote out of defiance, apathy, or despair. Conservative voters had followed two strategies in their futile effort to defeat the convention measure, with roughly one-half voting against the convention and the other one-half not voting at all. As a result, not only did the divided Conservatives suffer a lopsided defeat in the convention vote, but also they enabled the Republicans to gain 107 of the upcoming convention's 120 delegates. The lack of a unified campaign strategy betrayed a lack of cohesiveness in the Conservative ranks. This should have come as no surprise, for the Conservatives were united only by their opposition to Republican reforms.[31]

Now that the election was over, Canby decided that he no longer had to keep small troop detachments scattered across the Carolinas. When Sickles had assumed command of the Second Military District, he had divided North Carolina into eleven posts, each one embracing several counties. Canby believed that civil law enforcement could now fill the constabulary role formerly assigned the occupation troops. He also wished to simplify the logistical requirements of his command and to prevent the erosion of discipline and morale that often befell units on detached duty. On December 6, 1867, Canby issued General Orders No. 145, directing that the federal forces in the state be consolidated into five posts at Morganton, Raleigh, Goldsboro, Wilmington, and Fort Macon, the last-named remaining a military prison.[32]

Alarmed by the news that the occupation troops would soon be withdrawn from their communities, prominent citizens in Fayetteville, Greensboro, New Bern, and Smithville petitioned Canby to cancel the removal order. "In our opinion the presence of the troops here is absolutely necessary for the preservation of order and the enforcement of the laws," pleaded the mayor of Greensboro and eleven other town officials. The petition from Smithville probably marked the first time that white North Carolinians urged the retention of black troops in their community. Even more surprising, the Smithville petition came on the heels of the riot reportedly led by African American soldiers. Among the petitioners urging Canby to retain the garrison at Fayetteville was Duncan G. McRae, the magistrate who had spent several months in an army prison before being tried by a military commission for the murder of Archibald Beebee.[33]

A second group of petitioners from Greensboro sent their letter to Governor Worth for his endorsement, but it was a wasted effort. The petition arrived as Worth was compiling his catalog of military outrages for President Johnson, and the governor had no use for encomiums to federal troops. "The conduct of the officers and men has been exemplary," the petition stated, "and we believe every good citizen feels in their presence a greater security both in person and property. They are a powerful police force and a terror to evil doers." Worth sardonically commented that if this were so, "then the blessing of military government, in preference to civil government, should be greatly extended." But he hastened to add, "I am very far from concurring in this doctrine. I would gladly see every soldier removed from the State . . . , and therefore cannot endorse your petition." Even with Worth's cooperation, it is doubtful that the petition- ers could have swayed Canby, for the general maintained that the railroad placed the troops in Raleigh within easy reach of Greensboro.[34]

The eastern part of the state proved a different matter, as the region suffered yet another outbreak of violence and lawlessness. One group of petitioners from New Bern urged Canby to retain the current garrison of "white soldiers" in their community "to protect the citizens in their pres- ent helpless and unarmed condition" and prevent additional outrages. A second petition from New Bern signed by the mayor and dozens of other local officials requested that the troops be retained because "the civil officers of the Counties in this District have not been and will not be able to preserve peace and order." Along with the petitions, Canby received word that a former Confederate colonel named John H. Nethercutt had been murdered in his home near Trenton in Jones County. Canby sent his provost marshal general, Lt. Col. Edward W. Hinks, to New Bern to investigate the killing.[35]

On December 15, Hinks traveled to the crime scene, where he learned that Nethercutt was killed by a shotgun blast during a home invasion and that the four robbers were black men dressed in Union army overcoats. The gang had made off with $100 in cash and coin and some of Neth- ercutt's personal effects. After his return to New Bern, Hinks learned that a second home invasion and murder had just occurred about ten miles from the Nethercutt plantation. Hinks rushed to the crime scene, only to discover that both the assailant and his victim had died of gunshot wounds sustained during a desperate struggle inside the house. The colo- nel noted that the attacker matched the description of Nethercutt's killer. He also found several items in the pockets of the dead robber, which Nethercutt's widow identified as her husband's. Hinks found some tracks made by the dead robber's partners, who abandoned him after firing a few rounds into the house. No sooner had Hinks returned to New Bern than he learned of yet another killing, this time in Pitt County. "Murders and robberies are of almost daily occurrence in this vicinity," Hinks in- formed Canby. "I think that the public buildings at this Post should not be disposed of at present[,] for it will be necessary to retain troops here till greater security to life and property is obtained." Canby heeded Hinks's advice and held the company at New Bern. The general also placed a mounted detachment at the disposal of Jones County sheriff Orson R. Colgrove.[36]

In his report to Canby, Hinks enclosed a list of murder victims for the past nine months. Of the eighteen victims, fourteen were white and four were black. Eight of the murders had occurred in Jones County, five in Lenoir County, four in Craven County, and one in Pitt County. Before Hinks's report could reach Canby in Charleston, the murder count rose to nineteen. A gang of black robbers in Pitt County had killed a white man and severely wounded a freedman.[37]

While in Trenton, Hinks talked to a number of leading Jones County residents. They confessed that the outlaws had made them afraid of traveling alone on the highways. "I urged upon the citizens the importance of speedily organizing a police force of whites and blacks," Hinks informed Canby. A biracial group of Jones County residents had already reached that conclusion. On December 16, they appealed to Canby "for permission to organize an armed civil police," for Sickles's General Orders No. 10 prohibiting the possession of firearms had rendered law-abiding citizens helpless against the outlaws. The petitioners pledged "not to abuse the privalege if granted, and to see that the most sacred regard is observed for the rights of persons and property without regard to race or color." Ten days later, Pitt County citizens held a biracial community meeting to decide on a course of action. The citizens appointed a committee of five to draft a request that General Canby authorize a local police force commanded by a "competent millitary officer" to capture the bandits and bring them to justice. "The Civil Law is powerless or inoperative," the petition read, "the people are disarmed & disheartened, and are an easy prey to what would under other circumstances be only a contemptible band of criminals."[38]

Two salient points emerged from the above petitions. First, the white petitioners were so terrified of the outlaws that they reluctantly swallowed their racial pride and joined forces with their black neighbors. The whites did so assuming that the alliance would be brief. Had the past given any indication, there would have been no alliance had the bandits been white and the victims exclusively black. Second, the petitioners linked the boldness of the outlaws and the helplessness of their victims to Sickles's order banning firearms. In effect, the civilians blamed the army as well as the desperadoes for the current crime wave. But rather than point fingers, the citizens merely requested that they be allowed to defend themselves, their families, and their property.

Canby found the petitioners' appeal compelling. He realized that the crisis offered citizens in the eastern part of the state an opportunity to show their mettle. On New Year's Day 1868, Canby issued Special Orders No. 1, empowering the county courts of Craven, Jones, Lenoir, and Pitt counties to organize special police forces for the purpose of capturing the outlaw gangs. The order mandated that a portion of the forces consist of blacks. "I have adopted this course with some hesitation," Canby informed General Grant, "because there is still, in many parts of North Carolina, a feeling of bitterness" resulting from the war "that influences any party that may be in power to use that power against their former enemies, and their present political opponents." Canby assured Grant that he would watch his "experiment" closely and replace the local police with federal troops if the former began to misuse their power.[39]

On receiving Canby's order, three of the counties wasted no time in forming police companies and sending them after the outlaws. Craven County proved the exception, however. Local authorities complained that funding a police force for so large a county presented too great a financial burden for the impoverished taxpayers to bear. Colonel Hinks had no patience with the officials' excuses. He expressed the hope that they had "neither weighed the public peace against the mere pecuniary consideration involved nor been influenced by the fact that the measure proposed requires a due portion of the force to be constituted of loyal colored men." Craven County sheriff James E. Fleming took the hint. Fleming informed Hinks that he had sworn in twelve black men as deputy sheriffs to restore order in James City, an African American settlement across the Trent River from New Bern.[40]

Even before Canby granted the petitioners' request, citizens in Lenoir and Pitt counties had captured "15 or 20 of the criminals," reported the local solicitor, William T. Faircloth. On December 31, Faircloth informed Governor Worth that the prisoners were held in the two counties' jails and several had "confessed the whole matter." They stated that there were two large gangs, one ranging through Lenoir and Pitt and the other through Jones County. Faircloth reported that nearly all of the captured gang members were black and that two of the white men apparently had directed the gang's operations without participating in them. Anxious to prevent the prisoners' escape, Worth requested that the post commander at New Bern, Capt. James J. Van Horn, send a detachment to the Pitt County jail at Greenville. Given his antipathy for the occupation force, Worth must have found this a galling request to make. Van Horn responded by sending a detail of six men with orders to report "without delay" to Pitt County sheriff John Foley.[41]

Within a month of their formation, the county police companies captured or drove off most of the outlaws and quickly restored law and order in their communities. On February 3, 1868, Sheriff E. F. Cox of Lenoir County reported that since the formation of an "armed Police force" on January 11, "few crimes have been committed" in his county. "Several prisoners are confined in jail and the police are guarding them at night." Cox believed that "the force has had a good effect upon the community—[especially on] the lawless ones." On April 1, Cox informed the military authorities that he disbanded the county police force because "the necessity which called for this organization has passed away." The successful but all-too-brief experiment in biracial cooperation had ended.[42]

By early 1868, nearly all the Regulators who had terrorized the eastern counties of North Carolina for the past two years were either in jail or in hiding. The remnant of the Reddick Carney gang remained at large, however, and fresh reports of their outrages soon reached Colonel Hinks, the new post commander at Goldsboro. In December 1867, former Freedmen's Bureau agent Horace James accused Carney of assaulting him on a busy street. Since the unsuccessful storming of the Carney house by a detail of the 28th Michigan Infantry in January 1866, the gang had lived unmolested in Pitt County. Several gang members were wanted for numerous murders and other crimes; Carney alone reportedly had killed eight persons since 1865. In April 1868, Hinks sent Capt. Wyllys Lyman and a detachment of twenty men from the 40th U.S. Infantry to capture Carney and his gang.[43]

The second assault on the Carney house began in eerily similar fashion to the first. When Lyman and his troops arrived on the scene, Carney and his son George were ready and waiting for them. Carney's son-in-law, wife, and older daughter also remained inside. Once the soldiers had surrounded the house, Lyman demanded Carney's surrender. When Carney refused, Lyman ordered several men forward to batter down the front door. As soon as the soldiers made an opening, Lyman entered the house and was shot as he ascended the stairs. The storming party then withdrew to the porch carrying the wounded Lyman, closely followed by the Carney women and the son-in-law, who had been wounded twice.

After several more attacks failed to dislodge the defenders, the soldiers set fire to the house. George Carney then rushed downstairs and shot a private who had entered the burning structure. As the younger Carney headed toward the doorway, a sergeant appeared. The two men shot each other dead. Defiant to the last, Reddick Carney remained inside the house. Soldiers later found a few of his bones among the smoldering ruins. In addition to the two Carney men, the sergeant and the private were killed during the shootout; both Lyman and the son-in-law recovered from their wounds.[44]

Two local Conservative newspapers seized on the Carney incident and exploited it for political capital. The *Tarboro Southerner* portrayed Reddick Carney as a tragic hero who had "died, as he had lived, an utter stranger to fear or cowardice." In contrast, the *Southerner* depicted Captain Lyman and his "negro troops" as cowards guilty of "inhuman warfare." The *New Bern Journal of Commerce* pronounced the incident a "tragedy" that "illustrates most forcibly the unsettled condition of the country under Radical rule." The *Journal* called for "a prompt and rigid investigation" of the incident "to place the responsibility and affix the penalties where they belong." The two papers omitted any reference to the many crimes Carney had committed, transforming his violent death into a senseless atrocity and Carney himself into a brave martyr who refused to knuckle under to military rule.[45]

The death of Reddick Carney marked the demise of the Regulators, but violence and lawlessness in North Carolina were far from suppressed. Seizing stills and arresting illegal operators in the western counties remained a dangerous business, even with the aid of federal troops, as Deputy Collector E. R. Hampton of the Bureau of Internal Revenue discovered. In March 1868, Sgt. John Mulloy and five enlisted men of the 5th U.S. Cavalry assisted Hampton in Jackson and Macon counties. About midnight on March 12, a dozen or so armed men surrounded Mulloy's camp and opened fire on the sleeping cavalrymen. Mulloy and his dazed troopers returned fire until their ammunition was almost exhausted. At Hampton's suggestion, the cavalrymen destroyed the stills, emptied the liquor onto the ground, and then abandoned their camp.[46]

Beginning in late 1867, North Carolinians faced a new and diabolical threat: railroad sabotage. A train wreck that occurred on the Wilmington & Weldon Railroad was typical of the devastation saboteurs wrought. A northbound locomotive was approaching a trestle bridge about twenty-five miles south of Weldon when it suddenly left the tracks, plunged down a twenty-foot embankment, and crashed into a creek, dragging the rest of the train with it. Fortunately for the passengers, the sleeper car came to rest less than a foot from the end of the track. The investigating officer found it "beyond comprehension" how such a terrible crash had caused no fatalities. The removal of a single rail near the bridge caused the wreck. On November 17, 1867, Canby issued General Orders No. 120, specifying the punishment for sabotaging railroads. The fines ranged from $200 to $1,000 and the prison sentences from six months to seven years. In the event of fatalities, the order mandated the death penalty. Despite Canby's order, saboteurs continued to tamper with railroads in 1868, and most escaped punishment. Of the nine suspects tried by military commissions for obstructing railroads, only one was convicted.[47]

Aside from retaining the Post of New Bern, Canby proceeded with the consolidation of his forces in North Carolina. He also made some sweeping changes to the Freedmen's Bureau, which he outlined in General Orders No. 145. At Canby's request, bureau head Oliver O. Howard appointed him supervisory assistant commissioner for the Second Military District; in turn, Canby designated each post commander as a subassistant commissioner. As such, the post commanders would "exercise all functions of that Bureau, except so far as relates to the administration and control of the funds or property of the Bureau." Canby authorized the post commanders to employ their officers and men in bureau work, and he directed that all bureau employees report to their post commander and obey his orders "in all that relates to the protection of person and property." In administrative matters, bureau personnel would continue to report to the assistant commissioner, Col. Nelson A. Miles.[48]

No one was more dissatisfied with the new arrangement than Colonel Miles. Believing that Canby's order encouraged post commanders to defy his authority, Miles contended that several of the officers "are not in sympathy with the colored people" and should not be entrusted with their welfare. Miles soon clashed with the post commander at Wilmington, Capt. Royal T. Frank, who wanted to assume control of the local bureau office and remove the current chief, Capt. Allan Rutherford.[49]

The Rutherford controversy became a cause célèbre in Wilmington's African American community. The local black political leader, Abraham H. Galloway, a former runaway slave and Union spy, organized a mass meeting of several hundred blacks to declare their support for Rutherford. They also petitioned Howard to retain Rutherford rather than Frank.

Abraham H. Galloway (Courtesy of the North Carolina State Archives)

Galloway accused Frank of being "totally disinterested as to whether the negro gets justice or not," and he stated that Rutherford enjoyed "the respect and confidence of both white and black Loyalists." Frank dismissed Galloway's accusation as a malicious falsehood and charged Rutherford with failing to assist him in maintaining law and order. Miles nevertheless strongly objected to Frank. "I have no use for this Officer as a Bureau Agent," he wrote Canby, "and the Colored people . . . have no confidence in him." Despite Miles's strong opposition, Canby retained Frank as the new subassistant commissioner.[50]

During the holidays, Canby hosted Miles at his headquarters in

Charleston. Miles seized the opportunity to argue once more against the use of post commanders as bureau officials but failed to sway Canby, who was preoccupied with the upcoming state constitutional conventions in his district. On New Year's Eve 1867, Canby announced that the North Carolina convention would meet in Raleigh on January 14, 1868. Aside from a brief visit to the state capital in February to address the convention delegates, Canby did not involve himself in the proceedings.[51]

The convention worked quickly. After two months of deliberation, the Republican majority had drafted a new state constitution. The document made numerous changes to the state's laws and government. The governor's term doubled from two to four years, and, in addition to the pardoning power, he could now commute sentences. The new constitution added the elective office of lieutenant governor. State senate seats would be apportioned according to population rather than wealth, and senators would no longer elect their own president, for the lieutenant governor would occupy the office. Instead of receiving lifetime appointments, state supreme court justices would be elected to eight-year terms, and they would be increased from three to five persons. The constitution reduced the county courts' power, for the Republican delegates considered them responsible for much of the persecution that had befallen blacks and white loyalists. The voters rather than the county courts would choose sheriffs and other local officials, and the superior courts would assume more of the legal caseload. The new constitution also mandated a free public school system for black and white children alike. The revised state penal code would be less draconian than its predecessor, and the initiative for a state penitentiary indicated that the state law now linked rehabilitation to punishment. In response to the public outcry arising from the failure of the 1867 grain harvest and the precipitous drop in the price of cotton, the convention passed an ordinance suspending debt collection. The new state constitution afforded citizens a greater voice in their government and promised to benefit the people as never before.[52]

On March 17, 1868, the convention passed an ordinance submitting the new constitution to the registered voters for ratification. The ordinance also called for an election of senators and representatives for the General Assembly, state and county officials, and U.S. congressmen. Six days later, Canby announced that the election would be held on April 21–23, 1868. As he had done for the convention vote, Canby placed the sheriffs and their deputies in charge of peacekeeping at the polls while holding the military force in reserve. He also repeated his warning against the use of force to prevent persons from registering or voting.[53]

The ensuing campaign proved to be as boisterous as it was brief. In an effort to lure native whites from the Republican Party, the Conservatives—with William A. Graham as chief spokesman—espoused white supremacy over "negro equality." Despite Canby's warning, some Conservatives resorted to threats or violence to intimidate their political opponents. From Yanceyville in Caswell County, the Republican candidate for the county's state senate seat, John W. Stephens, complained that Conservatives in his community were intimidating voters and fomenting discord. Afraid to canvass the county without an escort, Stephens made a futile appeal to the military authorities for a troop detachment. Other petitioners enjoyed greater success. The mayor of Fayetteville and several other prominent citizens requested a company of federal soldiers after a recent campaign appearance by Republican gubernatorial candidate William W. Holden nearly triggered a riot. In response, Canby sent a troop detachment to Fayetteville to preserve order during the election.[54]

During the campaign, the most violent region of the state consisted of a half-dozen eastern counties within the Post of Goldsboro. At Clinton in Sampson County, knife-wielding Conservatives injured several freedmen while breaking up a Republican campaign rally. The post commandant, Lt. Col. Edward W. Hinks, sent a detachment to Clinton to arrest the perpetrators. Soon afterward, Hinks ordered a second detachment to Washington in Beaufort County to arrest several white men for assaulting blacks and white Republicans, and he replaced the local police chief. He also sent detachments to Elizabeth City to arrest a Conservative named William F. B. Ehringhaus for caning Republican candidate John R. French and to New Bern to arrest a Conservative election official for punching his Republican counterpart. From Edenton, Elizabeth City, and Kinston, Hinks received reports that a mysterious organization called the Ku Klux Klan was posting signs that bore an ominous message filled with "rattling bones" and "yawning graves" imagery. Bureau agent William H. Doherty reported that the posters had alarmed Elizabeth City's African American community. As a precaution, Hinks sent troops to each county within his command to keep the peace during the election.[55]

In response to the emergence of white supremacist organizations such as the White Man's Club and the Ku Klux Klan, Canby issued General Orders No. 61, warning that conspiracies to obstruct the execution of federal law or prevent voting would be severely punished. The general declared that he would order a new election for any precinct in which there was evidence of fraud or interference. As a precaution, Canby authorized post commanders to appoint army or Freedmen's Bureau officers as "military commissioners" to oversee elections in remote areas of their commands. The military commissioners were no mere figureheads, for their authority was equivalent to that of post commanders.[56]

The example of Alexander E. Drake, a retired U.S. Army officer, indicates the difference an active commissioner could make. Within an hour of assuming office, Drake learned that the Republican congressional candidate for his district, Calvin J. Cowles, was threatened with violence if he attempted to speak in Iredell County. Drake immediately traveled to Statesville, the county seat, to determine if the local law enforcement officers were equal to the task of securing a peaceful election. The mayor, the sheriff, and the local Freedmen's Bureau agent assured Drake that his visit was worth more in maintaining order at the polls than a company of troops because it demonstrated the vigilance of the military while leaving the people in doubt as to the strength and location of the available force. Satisfied that the local authorities at Statesville had the situation well in hand, Drake traveled to Salisbury to evaluate conditions there.[57]

On his arrival, Drake found posters all over town displaying a skull and crossbones symbol on a coffin with the caption: "The hour is arrived—the graves are opened, and Hell yawns." Drake soon learned that the posters were intended to summon the local White Man's Club and the "Fantastics"—or Ku Klux Klan—to take part in a procession just before the election. Although Drake found the posters ridiculous, he received several letters from local women begging him "to prohibit any night parades." A "lady of refinement" informed Drake that her servants were so frightened by the posters that they refused to go out after dark. To calm the locals' fears, Drake instructed the mayor of Salisbury to prohibit any nighttime demonstrations. When the leaders of the local White Man's Club protested Drake's infringement on their right of assembly, the commissioner warned that if the civil authorities failed to stop the parade, he would intervene at the head of federal troops. The leaders relented and then obtained Drake's permission to hold a daytime parade instead. To ensure a peaceful election, Drake ordered a troop detachment to Salisbury. At the close of his report, Drake described the situation as "a trifling matter, out of which molehill, for political effect, certain parties would erect a mountain."[58]

The commander of the temporary detachment at Charlotte, Capt. Henry M. Lazelle, noted a similar alarmist tendency among citizens within his command. Canby had ordered Lazelle and his company to Charlotte in response to a letter from the Reverend W. L. Miller, a local Presbyterian minister. Miller complained that a Unionist was threatened and insulted during a Conservative torchlight procession through town and a riot had erupted during a Republican rally in Union County. A few days after his arrival, Lazelle reported that the seriousness of the disturbances was exaggerated. He noted that "some mischievous and unprincipled persons, not connected with the political procession, dressed themselves fantastically and insulted by rude actions" the family of a local Republican politician. But Lazelle stated that the group stopped before the politician's house for just a few minutes and neither threatened nor assaulted him. As for the riot in Union County, Lazelle reported that "one man was stabbed and several [were] more or less injured. The fight was not general, serious, or of long duration." Perhaps Lazelle's combat experience led him to regard a brawl that had resulted in a stabbing and some broken bones as "not serious," but it is doubtful that the victims regarded their injuries in the same light. Lazelle probably also sought to convey the impression that he had the situation well in hand. In any event, he assured his superiors that when the election was over, there would be no more excitement "to alarm the proverbial timidity of any reverand gentlemen."[59]

Drake and Lazelle dismissed the alarm over the White Man's Club and the Ku Klux Klan as the needless fretting of timid parsons, overwrought women, and superstitious blacks. The officers' smugness is understandable, for the Klan in Charlotte and Statesville had confined their actions to parading in fantastic costumes and insulting a Republican politician. The Klan acted with comparative restraint in North Carolina, confident that their strategy of intimidation by nonviolent means would facilitate a sweeping Conservative victory at the polls.[60]

Instead, the state election resulted in an overwhelming triumph for the Republican Party. Republicans captured all the state offices and gained a substantial majority in both houses of the General Assembly. North Carolina voters also ratified the new state constitution, but the winning margin—93,084 to 74,015—was much narrower than the convention vote had been. The Fourth Reconstruction Act accounted for the sharp rise in Conservative voter turnout. Passed on March 11, 1868, the act declared a majority of the votes cast as sufficient for ratification, ending the Conservatives' no-vote stratagem. The Tar Heel State's 84 percent voter turnout indicated that the Klan had frightened away few citizens from the polls.[61]

Canby nevertheless received numerous reports of election fraud, intimidation, and disorder at the polls in North Carolina. While the general dismissed many allegations as "trivial," he also believed that some merited investigation. In Hyde County, citizens complained that violence had broken out in several voting places and that a man had tampered with a ballot box at the county courthouse. Canby removed the sheriff for negligence. In Camden County, white outlaws shot and killed a freedman named Albert Rogerson about a week before the election. Bureau agent William H. Doherty maintained that the killers sought "to terrify the Col[ore]d people, and thus prevent them from voting." Rogerson had voted Republican in the previous election. One freedman stated that Rogerson's murder and threatening Klan posters had induced many blacks to vote Conservative or not vote at all. Conservatives also employed less-violent means of persuasion. On election day, several white employers plied their black laborers with liquor, and at least one freedman accused his employer of bribery. Many blacks complained that their employers fired them for going to the polls.[62]

Despite the isolated disturbances, Canby could pronounce the election a success. It now remained for the General Assembly to convene and ratify the Fourteenth Amendment. Once the state legislature had surmounted that hurdle, Congress would determine if North Carolina could seat its U.S. senators and congressmen and thus rejoin the Union. In the meantime, Canby switched the white foot soldiers stationed in the Carolinas, transferring the 6th U.S. Infantry to North Carolina and the 8th U.S. Infantry to South Carolina. The move resulted in the transfer of two officers, Col. James V. Bomford and Capt. Royal T. Frank, who had become extremely popular with the white citizens in their commands. For over the past two years, Bomford had been stationed at Raleigh and Frank at Wilmington. Anticipating his transfer after Military Reconstruction, Canby wanted Bomford to command the troops in South Carolina and Colonel Miles to command those in North Carolina.

The news of Frank's transfer prompted Wilmington mayor John Dawson and the Board of Aldermen to petition Canby to retain the post commander and his garrison at Wilmington. The petitioners credited Frank with preserving "the peace, the quiet and good order which have characterized this city during the past two years." Canby received two similar petitions signed by several hundred white citizens who formed a cross-section of Wilmington's Conservative, scalawag, and carpetbagger factions. The general informed Dawson that he could not cancel the

Top row, left to right: Col. James V. Bomford and Capt. James J. Van Horn. *Seated,* Capt. Royal T. Frank (Zenas Randall Bliss Papers, Box 3S200c, Center for American History, University of Texas at Austin)

transfer of Frank and his company, for it was part of a larger redeployment that had already begun.[63]

The *Wilmington Journal*, a Conservative daily, expressed its "deep regret" that Frank was being transferred to South Carolina. The *Journal* described Frank as "firm and just, and withal perfectly impartial." The *Wilmington Morning Star* praised Frank's troops as "the best behaved ever at this post." On May 11, the day of Frank's departure, Mayor Dawson and several dozen other prominent citizens presented him with a $300 gold watch and chain.[64]

As commandant of the Post of Raleigh, Colonel Bomford likewise had earned the respect and gratitude of the area's white residents. Foremost among his conciliatory gestures, Bomford had participated in Raleigh's first Confederate Memorial Day service, laying flowers on the graves of several Confederate soldiers. In expressing regret at Bomford's departure, the Raleigh Board of Commissioners praised the colonel's "high soldierly qualities and gentlemanly bearing." The Conservative *Raleigh Daily Sentinel* commented that Bomford had "administered his delicate and responsible duties fairly, impartially and as a conscientious officer." During his tenure, Bomford had won over even Governor Worth, that vociferous opponent of Military Reconstruction. "I am pained to learn that you have been displaced as Commandant of this Post," Worth informed Bomford. The governor complimented the colonel on his skill in steering clear of partisan politics. On the day of departure, a delegation of prominent citizens bade farewell to Bomford and his family at the railroad station. Soon afterward, he sent a letter of appreciation to Kemp P. Battle, the state treasurer at Raleigh: "My stay in your city, I can truthfully say, was the most peaceful and happiest period of my military service—unalloyed by any regrets."[65]

The citizens' tributes to Bomford and Frank reveal the success of the officers' conciliatory policy despite the widespread unpopularity of Military Reconstruction. The December 1867 petitions from Fayetteville, Greensboro, New Bern, and Smithville urging the retention of federal troops in those communities likewise demonstrate that white North Carolinians regarded the soldiers as protectors rather than as oppressors. Most African Americans, however, remained silent amid all the accolades to the departing post commanders. Aside from two petitions calling for Frank's removal, blacks had made few public statements about the occupation troops. Collisions between white soldiers and freedmen continued to occur, and there were signs that the longstanding alliance of black soldiers and civilians was starting to unravel. It appeared that a gradual transformation was under way, in which native whites were supplanting blacks as the federal soldiers' southern friends.[66]

Former Confederate general D. H. Hill perhaps best expressed a sentiment shared by many white Tar Heels regarding the bluecoats in their midst. In his monthly *The Land We Love*, Hill praised the Charlotte garrison for being "the most active persons in extinguishing" a fire that had engulfed the local women's college. "We believe that the same spirit, to save and not destroy, actuates all who have been *fighting* soldiers," Hill wrote. The ex-Confederate favorably contrasted the federal soldiers' conduct with that of politicians, who seemed bent on perpetuating sectional animosities. Northern and southern veterans who had "tested each others' manhood in many a hard struggle," Hill contended, "will act fairly, squarely and honorably by each other. We would be ashamed of our American origin if we could believe otherwise." Hill thus implied that the veterans, if left to their own devices, would soon accomplish the task of sectional reconciliation.[67]

Yet the emergence of the Ku Klux Klan in North Carolina indicated that many former Confederates remained defiantly irreconcilable. The Republicans' sweeping victory at the polls had convinced Conservative leaders to adopt more ruthless methods to recover their political power. Sectional reconciliation remained a distant goal, for the ongoing struggle to determine the verdict of the war was about to escalate.[68]

Chapter Eight

North Carolina Rejoins the Union

In February 1868, as the first year of Congressional Reconstruction drew to a close, the Republicans sought to gain firm control of political affairs in Raleigh and Washington, D.C. As North Carolina's Republican-dominated constitutional convention laid the foundation for a biracial democracy, the U.S. House of Representatives voted to impeach President Andrew Johnson. Congressional Republicans had come to believe their Reconstruction policy remained in doubt as long as Johnson occupied the White House. The case against the president hinged on his violation of the Tenure of Office Act in his removal of Secretary of War Edwin M. Stanton without the Senate's approval.

The impeachment trial before the Senate began in March 1868. The Republicans' anxiety over Johnson meanwhile dissipated as North Carolina and several other southern states ratified new constitutions and elected Republican governments. Other factors further reduced the likelihood of Johnson's ouster, including the assurance of the president's chief counsel that his client, if acquitted, would cease to obstruct Congressional Reconstruction. The Senate voted on Johnson's fate in May 1868. Seven Republican senators broke party ranks and voted against removal. The conviction vote thus fell one short of the necessary two-thirds majority. Although the president was spared the humiliation of expulsion, he served out the remainder of his term as a political pariah, exerting no further influence on Reconstruction.[1]

While the Senate determined Johnson's fate, General Canby discovered that at least one more obstacle to the Reconstruction process loomed before him as commander of the Second Military District. He learned that many of the newly elected state officials in the district could not be sworn in until Congress removed their disabilities. In a letter to General Grant, Canby explained that in North Carolina, the governor, lieutenant governor, and many judges and legislators were disqualified under the Fourteenth Amendment, and still more incoming officials could not take the Ironclad Oath. Canby noted that the state could not be restored to the Union until the new legislature ratified the Fourteenth Amendment. He therefore recommended that Congress permit the men elected under the new state constitution to take the oath of office.[2]

At Grant's request, Stanton (who was back as secretary of war) sent Canby's letter to Congress. Canby's advice reinforced the congressional Republicans' determination to smooth the way for their allies in the South. On June 25, 1868, Congress removed the disabilities of seven hundred North Carolina Republicans, including Governor-elect Holden, and it declared that the congressional delegations of North Carolina and five other southern states would be admitted when their legislatures ratified the Fourteenth Amendment. Congress also approved North Carolina's new constitution and authorized Holden to convene the General Assembly, which the governor-elect had already announced for July 1.[3]

On June 30, Governor Worth received a copy of Canby's General Orders No. 120, indicating that Holden would replace him on July 1. Worth relinquished the governorship under protest, challenging the legality of the election and claiming that he was compelled to surrender his office under "military duress." As a parting gesture, Worth made some last-minute appointments, but Canby annulled them to enable Holden to name his own appointees. On July 3, Governor Holden informed Canby that the General Assembly had ratified the state constitution. In turn, Canby notified the new governor that he was ordering the post commanders to cease exercising their authority under the Reconstruction Acts and to intervene only if an attempt was made to obstruct the inauguration of the new state government. Much to Canby's satisfaction, no such crisis occurred. On the Fourth of July, Holden was inaugurated as governor of North Carolina. Two days later, Congress admitted three members of the state's congressional delegation. North Carolina had rejoined the Union.[4]

Ten days after Holden's inauguration, Raleigh became the scene of a violent confrontation when the new governor attempted to replace the Conservative mayor and town commissioners with Republican appointees. Refusing to surrender his office, incumbent Mayor William D. Haywood posted a cordon of police around city hall, resulting in several fights between Conservatives and Republicans. During the mêlée, a policeman fired on a freedman, and the police chief himself bludgeoned a Holden appointee. State attorney general William M. Coleman warned the post commander, Maj. George A. Williams, that there would be "a riot before night unless you send some men." Williams rushed two companies of the 6th U.S. Infantry into Raleigh to restore order. He then wired Canby, "Shall I eject the old Mayor or not?" Holden meanwhile appealed to the general for troops to install his appointees.[5]

Canby refused to act, however, until he had "a full understanding of the case." In the meantime, he ordered Williams to "use the troops only to keep the peace." The general also directed Williams to call on Mayor Haywood for an explanation of his actions and to ask Coleman for the article of the state constitution that authorized the governor to remove the Raleigh mayor and board of commissioners. The confusion rose from a vaguely worded clause that, according to Holden, granted him the authority to remove and appoint local officials. In fact, he had already replaced the directors of several railroad companies and the mayor and commissioners of Charlotte. The General Assembly later sustained Holden's action by declaring all municipal offices vacant and authorizing the governor to fill them pending statewide local elections in January 1869.[6]

Holden blamed Canby's refusal to intervene for the disturbance at the Raleigh city hall, but, in fact, the soldiers had restored order before the general was even informed of the situation. Canby probably did not savor the irony that the new governor desired the army's intervention in civil affairs as fervently as his predecessor had denigrated it. The general nevertheless complied with Holden's request to install several duly elected county sheriffs when the old sheriffs refused to vacate their offices.[7]

On July 22, Canby informed Holden that, as district commander, he no longer possessed legislative or judicial power. Two days later, Canby officially remitted his authority under the Reconstruction Acts to the civil governments of the two states within his command. With that, the Second Military District ceased to exist, and Military Reconstruction in North Carolina came to an end.[8]

On August 5, 1868, Canby relinquished command of the army in the

Carolinas. His tenure had lasted exactly eleven months. Unlike some of his more popular subordinates, Canby received no plaudits from grateful North Carolinians upon his departure. Lacking the charisma of his flamboyant predecessor Sickles, Canby made few friends during a brief visit to Raleigh in February 1868. Yet the general deserved credit for seeing his district through the tortuous process of Congressional Reconstruction. Although Canby refrained from using his considerable powers to suppress the Conservatives, he nevertheless attempted to protect Unionists and blacks from persecution. By closing the loophole in North Carolina's Amnesty Act, Canby shielded native loyalists in the west from unjust prosecution, and by authorizing biracial police units, he enabled citizens in the east to end the Regulators' crime spree. Canby performed a difficult and thankless task with his usual quiet competence, which explains why his achievement was largely overlooked.[9]

With Canby's departure, overall command of the troops in the Carolinas devolved to Maj. Gen. George G. Meade, the commander of the Department of the South. Meade's headquarters were in Atlanta, Georgia. The commander of the newly established District of North Carolina was Col. Nelson Appleton Miles, who also remained the state's assistant commissioner of the Freedmen's Bureau. Miles at last held the dual command he had so long coveted, but he did so as Congress began reducing the bureau's role after Military Reconstruction. On August 19, in response to orders from bureau headquarters in Washington, Miles instructed his agents to cease adjudicating disputes between blacks and whites and turn over their caseloads to the civil authorities. Several weeks later, Miles relinquished supervision of the state bureau to his adjutant, Maj. Jacob F. Chur. The Freedmen's Bureau closed its North Carolina offices in May 1869, though the bureau schools remained open for another year.[10]

The twenty-nine-year-old Miles had never attended West Point, but his brilliant war record earned him a promising career in the Regular Army. By peacetime standards, his rise was meteoric. When the Civil War began, Miles was a store clerk in Boston attending night school and studying military science with a former French army officer. During his four years with the Army of the Potomac, Miles rose from first lieutenant to brigadier general. He was wounded four times. After the war, Miles served as former Confederate president Jefferson Davis's jailor at Fort Monroe, Virginia. In September 1866, Miles accepted the colonelcy of the 40th U.S. Infantry, a new regiment of black regulars. On March 15,

Col. Nelson A. Miles (Library of Congress)

1867, Miles assumed command of the Post of Fort Johnston on the North Carolina coast. The following month, he received orders to report for duty at Raleigh as the assistant commissioner of the state Freedmen's Bureau. Under Miles's supervision, the bureau and the army distributed large quantities of food to thousands of North Carolinians who were suffering as a result of poor grain harvests in 1866 and 1867. Most of the food was donated by northern relief societies. In August 1868, Miles assumed command of the District of North Carolina.[11]

Shortly after Miles began his new duties, General Meade laid down the ground rules for his new department. In an August 25 circular, Meade informed Miles that any use of the military force in North Carolina must first be authorized by the department commander. Should an emergency "arise requiring instant action," Meade continued, the responsible officer "will be held to a strict accountability." The cautious Meade thus sought to curb any rashness on the part of his headstrong young subordinate, whom he had commanded in the Army of the Potomac.[12]

Meade also made several changes to the military force in North Carolina. Just before his departure, Canby had suggested that after the new state government was established, the number of posts could be reduced from six to four: Raleigh, Goldsboro, Fort Macon, and Fort Johnston. Meade followed Canby's advice in the belief that the end of Military Reconstruction had relegated federal forces in the South to a passive role. He stationed two companies of the 5th U.S. Cavalry and one company of the 40th U.S. Infantry at Raleigh, nine companies of the 40th at Goldsboro, and one company each of the 5th U.S. Artillery at Forts Macon and Johnston. Meade also transferred the six companies of the 6th U.S. Infantry at Raleigh to Charleston, South Carolina.[13]

The arrival of the 40th Infantry infuriated the white residents of Goldsboro. William T. Dortch, a former Confederate senator and a leading Conservative, urged President Johnson to order the black soldiers' removal on the grounds that the area's "colored voters are disposed to vote the Democratic ticket, but are overawed by the [black] troops." Dortch's rationale implied a sudden transformation in the black electorate, for only a short time earlier, white North Carolinians were accusing black soldiers and civilians of conspiring to massacre white property owners and seize their land. In any event, Johnson referred Dortch's appeal to the War Department. Meade replied that the black soldiers' "presence in any other state of the Department, would be equally objected to, by those opposed to their use." Much to the white residents' dismay, the black soldiers remained at Goldsboro.[14]

Since the 40th's arrival off the North Carolina coast in February 1867, the regiment had been dogged by misfortune. The ocean journey of six companies from their training camp in Virginia ended with a shipwreck near Fort Fisher. No soldiers were lost, but all regimental equipment and personal baggage sank with the vessel. The shipwreck was an omen of trouble to come. In March 1867, several companies passed through Wilmington and Goldsboro en route to their duty stations, and some soldiers evidently decided to replace their losses at the local shopkeepers' expense. The soldiers' alleged misconduct provoked an outcry from white residents. Merchants complained that black troops entered their stores and brazenly stole their goods in plain view; anyone who stood in the thieves' way met with a barrage of insults and threats. A farmer who lived near Fort Fisher claimed that four enlisted men of the 40th plundered his storehouses and insulted himself and his family. When the man complained to the soldiers' commanding officer, he reportedly was told that "it was impossible to keep the men in camp." The fact that the soldiers' personal possessions were lying at the bottom of the ocean indicates the accusations had some merit. Regardless of their accuracy, the reports appeared in several local newspapers, reinforcing many white Tar Heels' belief that black soldiers were incapable of discipline and good order.[15]

In addition to being despised by the local white populace, black regulars had to cope with racism inside the army. In March 1868, a squad of African American soldiers who traveled from Goldsboro to Raleigh on a guard detail discovered that they could not enter the post mess hall until the white soldiers had finished eating and they had to sleep on the wooden floor of the guardhouse because the white enlisted men's barracks were off-limits. The white troops also subjected them to a barrage of racial slurs. The commander of the detail, Sgt. John Sample, complained to his commanding officer in Goldsboro. "Now I ask not nor expect social equality with the white man," Sample wrote, "but I am a soldier in the service of the United States and ask for what is provided by law for troops." According to an anonymous group of soldiers in the 40th who petitioned the secretary of war, relations between the regiment's white officers and black enlisted men were no better. The soldiers complained that their officers treated them like brutes. "If this is to be the regulations," they commented, "I think that we better be slaves."[16]

An incident at the Post of Goldsboro suggested that the punishment for murdering a black enlisted man was negligible if the perpetrator was a white officer. On September 13, 1868, Lt. Charles E. Hargous shot and killed Pvt. George Robinson while the latter was locked inside the post stockade. Hargous was charged with manslaughter and then tried by a general court-martial. According to the court of inquiry that had recommended the court-martial, Hargous's action was "wholly unjustifiable" and "entirely unwarranted." The lieutenant testified that he had shot Robinson because the post commander had directed him to restore order in the stockade "at all hazards." Several inmates testified that Robinson was not involved in the disturbance, and one eyewitness even stated that the private was quietly eating his supper when Hargous shot him. Hargous was convicted, but the charge was mitigated from manslaughter to "conduct to the prejudice of good order and military discipline." The lieutenant was sentenced to one year's suspension of rank and pay and confinement to the Post of Goldsboro, which General Meade reduced to six months. Hargous served out his sentence and remained in the army until his retirement in 1891.[17]

These incidents exemplify the racism that pervaded the U.S. Army during the late 1860s. When considered alongside the haphazard training of the 40th's officers and enlisted men, it came as no surprise that their morale suffered. Dissatisfied with his regiment's discipline, Colonel Miles had sought permission to station several of his companies at Raleigh for additional training under his personal supervision, but Canby had denied his request. In the meantime, Miles reported that Company C alone had suffered thirty desertions during a recent six-month stretch. Miles blamed the company's sorry state on its commander, Capt. Frank M. Coxe, whom he described as "incompetent to command a company, owing to a want of knowledge in the management of men." Although Miles replaced Coxe with a more capable officer, a riot involving some of Company C's enlisted men indicated that the change had come too late to avert disaster.[18]

Company C of the 40th had been at New Bern since February 1868, when it replaced the white garrison from the 8th U.S. Infantry. As expected, the town's white citizens opposed the switch and urged Canby to retain the white troops. More surprising was the reaction of the residents of James City, the black settlement across the Trent River from New Bern, who came to share their white neighbors' aversion to the soldiers of Company C.[19]

On the evening of July 6, 1868, the enlisted men learned of a dance at James City. About fifteen to twenty of the soldiers crossed the railroad bridge spanning the river. They had been drinking and were heavily armed, indicating that they were looking for trouble. When told they were not welcome, the soldiers opened fire on the house where the dance was held. The guests inside scattered for cover. Among the black partygoers were some Union veterans who grabbed their weapons and returned fire. In doing so, they were obeying the instructions of Sheriff James E. Fleming to defend themselves if attacked. Other black veterans joined in, and the defenders soon heavily outgunned the soldiers. Forming a line of battle, the veterans drove the men of Company C back to the railroad bridge. As the soldiers withdrew across the bridge, Sheriff Fleming and the acting commander of Company C, Lt. Walter S. Long, arrived on the scene and persuaded the combatants to cease fire. To maintain order, Long posted troops on both sides of the river. During the brawl, the soldiers had suffered seven casualties, four of them severe. The most seriously wounded of the three civilian casualties was Frank Memminger, the white owner of a brickyard in James City and the brother of Henry J. Memminger, the secretary of state for North Carolina. A soldier had bayoneted Memminger as he attempted to stop the riot. The veterans helped the soldiers carry their severely wounded comrades across the bridge to New Bern, where they were treated by the post surgeon and a local doctor. Fortunately for all concerned, there were no fatalities. According to the reports of Sheriff Fleming and Lt. D. B. Wilson, the adjutant for the Post of Goldsboro, the riot was "premeditated and a result of a growing feud" between the black soldiers and civilians.[20]

On receiving word of the riot at James City, the commandant of the Post of Goldsboro, Maj. Charles E. Compton, directed Lieutenant Long to report the names of all soldiers absent from camp during the incident and to cancel all passes until further notice. Compton also informed the mayor of New Bern that he would turn over all suspects to the civil authorities for trial. Four days later, Compton changed his mind. He ordered Long to arrest all soldiers involved in the brawl and charge them with conduct to the prejudice of good order and military discipline.[21]

Contrary to orders, Long refused to hold any of his men responsible for the riot, believing that such a course would leave him open to charges of negligence. As a result, Long's account bore little resemblance to the reports of Sheriff Fleming, Lieutenant Wilson, and the New Bern papers. Instead, Long credited the soldiers' statement that a mob of black civilians in New Bern had attacked them without provocation. According to Long, the soldiers then drove the civilians across the railroad bridge toward James City until heavy reinforcements enabled the latter to hold the bridge. Long reported that only five soldiers were involved in the disturbance, four of them severely wounded and all unarmed when he found them. Long's tale, however, failed to explain the soldier's wounding of Frank Memminger outside his James City business. Although none of Long's men had to face a court-martial for their part in the riot, Long himself was cashiered the following year during a reduction of the army's officer corps.[22]

While the James City riot was the most serious collision between black soldiers and civilians in North Carolina during Reconstruction, it was by no means the only one that involved enlisted men of the 40th U.S. Infantry. Pvt. Richard Boston was dishonorably discharged for making an unprovoked assault on a local freedman at a dance hall in New Bern; Boston cut the man on the side of the head with a razor. Pvt. Thomas H. Smith was drummed out of the service for assaulting the black minister of the African Methodist Episcopal Church at Goldsboro. In Raleigh, Privates Alexander Willis and Anthony Jackson and a local freedman were charged with murdering a black civilian named Anderson Selby. The army arrested the two soldiers and then turned them over to the civil authorities for trial. A civilian jury found Willis guilty of murder, and the judge sentenced him to hang. The other two defendants were acquitted. Although Willis was dishonorably discharged from the army, Colonel Miles intervened on the condemned man's behalf and appealed to Governor Holden for clemency. On the eve of the execution, Holden commuted Willis's sentence to life imprisonment.[23]

Five days after the James City riot, the *Raleigh Sentinel* commented that the "ill-feelings existing there between the citizen and soldier negroes are the same which exist throughout the State." Alluding to Willis and Jackson's role in "the shameless murder" of Anderson Selby, the *Sentinel* indicated that the crime had "excited very great hostility to" black soldiers among the freedpeople of Raleigh. A Conservative daily, the *Sentinel* was no authority on African American opinion in North Carolina, yet the paper came near the mark in assessing the impact of Selby's murder and the James City riot. By 1868, the bond that once united black soldiers and civilians had dissolved. This was largely because the 40th U.S. Infantry, unlike the 37th USCT before it, had in its ranks few native sons or men who planned to settle in North Carolina after their military service. Unless their official duties compelled it, few enlisted men of the 40th evinced much interest in the local freedpeople's welfare. In North Carolina, the freedpeople could no longer look to black soldiers or the Freedmen's Bureau for support and guidance. Black Tar Heels either had to fend for themselves or rely on Governor Holden, local Republican authorities, and the Union League.[24]

With the end of Military Reconstruction, the army no longer oversaw civil affairs in North Carolina but could intervene only when the civil authorities proved unable to maintain law and order. After the reestablishment of civil government and North Carolina's return to the Union, the presidential election of 1868 loomed as the next crucial event in the Tar Heel State. The Republican presidential candidate was Gen. Ulysses S. Grant, the most popular man in the North. As general-in-chief of the army, Grant had demonstrated his support of Congressional Reconstruction, yet his campaign slogan—"Let Us Have Peace"—marked him as a moderate who favored conciliating former Confederates. Grant's running mate was House Speaker Schuyler Colfax of Indiana. The Democratic presidential candidate was former New York governor Horatio Seymour. A dedicated foe of Reconstruction, Seymour pledged to restore all southern states to the Union, terminate the Freedmen's Bureau, grant full amnesty to all ex-Confederates, and allow the states to determine their own suffrage laws. Seymour's running mate was Senator Francis P. Blair Jr. of Missouri, an ex-Union general and an outspoken advocate of white supremacy. A few Tar Heels may have known that Blair had briefly attended the University of North Carolina some thirty years earlier. Not surprisingly, the Seymour-Blair ticket proved extremely popular with North Carolina's Conservative voters, whereas Tar Heel Republicans supported Grant and Colfax. Partisans on either side of the political fence firmly believed that the election would decide the fate of the Republic.[25]

During the summer of 1868, Freedmen's Bureau officials throughout the state reported that Conservatives were expressing their dissatisfaction with the new political order in no uncertain terms. From Elizabeth City, bureau agent William H. Doherty reported that the Republicans' recent victory at the polls "has had the effect of exciting the rage & hatred of the old slave-holding aristocracy . . . to a degree that cannot be conceived by those who are not in daily intercourse with both races." Doherty noted that local Conservative stump speakers were "continually laboring to excite the evil passions of the whites, & to stir up strife & animosity between them & the col[ore]d people." According to several bureau agents, white employers were threatening their black laborers with dismissal for their political opinions. A Gates County farmer informed Governor Holden that several Conservatives in his neighborhood boasted that they would "go to Raleigh and take old Holden out and hang him to the first limb as they would another negro." Although much of the Conservatives' rhetoric could be dismissed as bluff and bravado, their actions often proved otherwise.[26]

As the campaign season shifted into high gear, some Conservatives resorted to violence in an effort to intimidate their political opponents. At Yanceyville in Caswell County, a Democratic rally and barbecue came to an abrupt end when a dozen whites led by a youth named Nat Johnson attacked a group of blacks in attendance. The local Freedmen's Bureau officer, Lt. William J. Dawes, credited the older whites and a large contingent of freedmen with preventing the disturbance from escalating into a full-blown riot. Two days later, Johnson provoked a second incident when he shot a black man for no apparent reason. A week later, Dawes reported that Johnson and the other perpetrators had been arrested and charged with several crimes, which appeared to satisfy Caswell's black community. "A better state of feeling has not existed in this county than at any time since I have been here than at present," Dawes maintained. The local white Republican leader, John W. Stephens, did not share Dawes's rosy view of the situation. Stephens informed Holden that the county's freedmen believed a detachment of federal troops was "indispencable here for the protection of themselves."[27]

Elsewhere in North Carolina, Conservatives disrupted several Republican campaign rallies. As state legislator Dixon Ingram addressed a crowd at Wadesboro in Anson County, an onlooker drew a revolver and threatened to shoot him. At another rally in Wadesboro, a second Republican politician beat a hasty retreat when Conservatives began hurling stones as well as insults at him. The man later received several anonymous death threats. At Clinton in Sampson County, a black politician from Wilmington named Duncan Holmes spoke outside the county courthouse and soon found himself in a perilous situation. During Holmes's speech, white men in the audience shouted at him to stop or they would drag him away. Holmes noted that many of the hecklers were armed. He also observed that the blacks in the audience appeared "completely subjected, and so great was their fear of death in Consequence of the threats made by the whites that none of them dared say a word." After the speech, several dozen freedmen urged Holmes to tell the governor "that in said County of Sampson there was no protection for the life or property of any union man either Black or White."[28]

From Fayetteville, Freedmen's Bureau official Richard Dillon reported three incidents in which unidentified whites fired into black churches, wounding parishioners each time. Black congregations in the area had since resorted to posting armed guards outside their churches. Dillon maintained that "if the well disposed whites would but frown down such rascally proceedings[,] they [would] soon stop." In a subsequent report, Dillon enclosed a local gunsmith's newspaper advertisement addressed "TO THE SPORTING PUBLC AND THE K. K. K." After receiving several death threats, the wife of the superior court judge at Fayetteville, Ralph P. Buxton, traveled to Raleigh and appealed to Holden for protection. In response to these and other reports from Fayetteville, Holden reminded Cumberland County sheriff John Reilly that it was his duty to preserve the peace "at all hazards." The governor promised to assist Reilly if he proved unable to restore law and order. "I am determined that 'life, liberty and property' shall be protected in the town of Fayetteville," Holden declared. In August, the General Assembly authorized Holden to organize the state militia during the presidential campaign, but he hesitated to adopt a measure so unpopular with North Carolinians, many of whom regarded the militia as the governor's private army. Instead, Holden turned to the U.S. Army for assistance. The governor requested that General Meade send federal troops to Clinton and Fayetteville, but Meade refused on the grounds that the civil authorities must first attempt to restore order there.[29]

Meanwhile, the Ku Klux Klan embarked on a campaign of terror in several eastern and central counties. In Halifax County, the Klan shot several prominent blacks, including a justice of the peace named John H. Everitt, who fled to Norfolk, Virginia, as soon as he could travel. In Granville County, the Klan raided an African American community, shooting a black woman and whipping several other residents. Holden urged the county sheriff to call out the militia to aid him in "ferreting out" the criminals. In a meeting with local Union League members, Lt. Robert Avery, the chief inspector for the state Freedmen's Bureau, offered to persuade the Klan to cease its outrages in exchange for the league's promise to disband. But neither the sheriff nor Lieutenant Avery could induce the Granville County Klan to suspend operations.[30]

As soon as he learned of the Klan outrages in Halifax County, Holden urged Meade to send a detachment there to assist the county sheriff in restoring order. The governor indicated that "the mere presence of troops" would act as "a salutary terror" to the county's "disaffected and disloyal" residents. Holden inexplicably omitted any mention of the shootings in Halifax. Once again, Meade denied Holden's request for federal soldiers, explaining that the civil authorities must first attempt to keep the peace.[31]

Miles likewise requested permission to station his soldiers throughout the state as a preventive measure, but Meade refused to act until the civil authorities proved unable to restore law and order. The general stated that the federal troops were "no longer available for police purposes or such duty as they performed under the reconstruction acts." While conceding that "the presence of troops has a salutary effect on repressing disorder," Meade nevertheless believed that "this advantage does not counterbalance the evil of scattering the troops, placing them in small bodies where they are inefficient in the event of such emergency" as would necessitate their use.[32]

Meade's refusal to intervene enabled the Klan in North Carolina to strike with impunity, as the outrages in Halifax and Granville counties demonstrated. In August, Meade had received instructions from the War Department to submit all requests for military aid from civil authorities to the president "if time permitted." If not, the senior officer on the scene would "alone assume the responsibility of action." The War Department also granted Meade discretion to send detachments to potential flash points to serve as peacekeepers: "by their passive interposition between hostile parties, danger of collision may be averted." Meade, however, had no intention of deploying his troops until the civil authorities proved incapable of suppressing lawlessness, and Holden had yet to convince him that such a situation existed. Meade's refusal to intervene on behalf of the civil authorities soon led to a conflict with Miles.[33]

On September 25, Miles sent Meade a report indicating that a Democratic club in Wilmington had received a large shipment of repeating rifles. Miles requested permission to seize the arms on the grounds that the owners had purchased them "for future use in resisting" the civil authorities. Four days later, Meade denied Miles's request because he had no evidence to support his allegation. The general also observed that the civil authorities had taken no action in the matter. Meade then commented that Miles did "not seem to properly conceive the [subordinate] position now occupied by the Military power."[34]

Miles could not resist the temptation to challenge Meade's admonition. On October 4, he informed Meade of several recently uncovered arms caches in Charlotte, Fayetteville, and New Bern, said to be the property of local "Seymour and Blair Clubs" and "K.K.K.'s." Miles described the owners of the rifles "as remnants of the rebel army, guerillas, bandits and rebels, soldiers violating their paroles and renewing the strife." He could see "no reason why the U.S. troops should not operate against them when they are to be found the same as when they were in stronger battalions." Miles's letter struck the short-tempered Meade as insubordinate. On the eighth, he fired off a letter to Grant, stating that Miles evidently found obeying his orders "in the highest degree unsatisfactory." Meade therefore requested a ruling on whether "myself or [Colonel] Miles be relieved from further command in this Department."[35]

Meade's temper soon cooled, however. A few days later, he traveled to North Carolina to give his young subordinate an opportunity to explain himself face to face. Miles hastened to assure the general that his "orders and instructions will always be cheerfully observed and enforced to the best of my ability." His ruffled feathers smoothed, Meade withdrew his request that Miles be relieved. The two men then discussed troop dispositions in North Carolina during the election. On September 24, Meade had directed Miles to provide him with a plan of deployment, but the order was briefly forgotten during the arms shipment controversy.[36]

Meade's sudden about-face regarding the use of troop detachments stemmed from the massacre at Camilla, Georgia. On September 19, 1868, armed whites broke up a Republican rally there, killing seven blacks and wounding at least thirty others. As department commander, Meade later justified the army's failure to intervene on the grounds that Camilla and the rest of southwestern Georgia had been so peaceful that he saw no reason to station troops there. The Camilla riot convinced Meade that using numerous small detachments to deter violence and lawlessness made far better sense than waiting for trouble to erupt. As authorization, Meade cited an 1865 act of Congress granting army officers discretion to use federal troops "to preserve the peace at the polls."[37]

In accordance with Miles's recommendation, Meade directed that one company each of the 40th U.S. Infantry be sent to Charlotte, Fayetteville, Greensboro, Plymouth, Salisbury, and Weldon, with two companies each held in reserve at Goldsboro and Raleigh. Meade also transferred a detachment of the 5th U.S. Artillery from Fort Johnston to Wilmington. As a further precaution, Meade authorized Miles to send smaller detachments of the 40th to ten potential trouble spots across the state. The general was confident that "the distribution of troops will tend greatly to allay existing excitements" arising from the presidential campaign and that their presence would "remove some existing delusions" regarding the federal government's commitment to ensuring a peaceful election. Meade reminded his subordinates that their sole objective was "to preserve the peace and uphold law and order."[38]

Miles issued similar orders three weeks later. "Under no circumstances will officers or soldiers fraternize with political parties," he wrote, "or in any manner interfere with the peaceable exercise, by all citizens, of their rights and privileges as such." Miles then claimed that "the political campaign has so far progressed with a degree of quietness and good order creditable to all concerned." Holden meanwhile issued a proclamation that stated, "North Carolina is at present as quiet and peaceable as any state in the Union." In describing North Carolina as "quiet and peaceable," Holden and Miles contradicted numerous reports of violence and intimidation, as well as their own private assessment of the situation. They probably sought to reassure anxious voters but stretched the truth in the process. Holden reminded county officials that they could call on the militia in case of an emergency, but the governor remained so unsure of the militia that he activated units in only two counties.[39]

Although certain areas of North Carolina could scarcely have been called peaceful before the election, the presence of federal soldiers across the state resulted in a quiet election day on November 3. Asheville proved to be a bloody exception, however, probably because Miles had stationed no soldiers there. On election day, a gang of Conservatives fired into a crowd of unarmed blacks near the Buncombe County courthouse, killing one and wounding eight. Acting mayor Oscar Eastmond, an ex-Freedmen's Bureau agent, requested a troop detachment to restore order but had to settle for an ad hoc police company. The Asheville riot underscored the necessity for federal soldiers to deter lawlessness in North Carolina.[40]

Thanks to the bluecoats, the Republican Party in North Carolina enjoyed another triumph at the polls. Grant carried the state with 96,939 votes to Seymour's 84,560, and Republicans won six of the state's seven Congressional seats. Conservative efforts to prevail through violence and intimidation had proved futile. Yet Grant's margin of victory was seven thousand votes narrower than Holden's had been six months earlier, enabling the Conservative Party to gain eleven counties. The results suggested that Conservatives were uniting behind the cause of white supremacy, but the victorious Republicans chose to ignore signs of the opposition's resurgence. In the euphoria over Grant's election, Holden even forgot his alarm over the Klan. "The Ku Klux—who is afraid of them now?" Holden gloated at a victory celebration in Raleigh. "The truth is, we were never afraid of them in North Carolina." The governor would soon regret those words.[41]

On November 9, Miles ordered the companies of the 40th on detached duty back to their permanent posts at Goldsboro and Raleigh. According to some white residents of Greensboro, the conduct of the black soldiers was superb. A committee of townspeople presented the commanding officer with a letter of thanks, and the *Greensboro Patriot and Times*, a Conservative paper, praised the "good behavior and soldier[l]y bearing of the troops" under his command. The tributes indicated that the discipline of the 40th had improved and that some Conservatives were beginning to judge black soldiers by their conduct rather than by their color.[42]

No sooner had Miles issued his recall order than Freedmen's Bureau agents across the state urged that the detachments be retained. Bureau official Richard Dillon believed that the company at Fayetteville "was the principal cause of the order and law abiding conduct of the people during the election." From Charlotte, Agent T. D. McAlpine warned that "the state of feeling in this city, is such that it would be unwise and dangerous to remove the troops now stationed here." McAlpine noted that the Conservatives had been "growing more bitter . . . everyday since the election." Lt. F. W. Liedtke, the bureau agent for Alamance County, reported that "unreconstructed rebels" were throwing hundreds of black laborers out of work because they had voted Republican. According to Liedtke, only "the prompt measures taken by" Miles before the election had discouraged the Conservatives from resorting to violence. Despite the agents' warnings, Miles recalled the detachments, doubtless with the intention of avoiding another conflict with Meade.[43]

If the civil and military authorities in North Carolina had an opportunity to curtail the Ku Klux Klan's lawless activities, it came during the winter of 1869. Up to then, Klan atrocities had been isolated and sporadic. Just after the 1868 presidential election, the Klan's future in the Tar Heel State appeared uncertain. Had Meade and Miles heeded bureau officials' warnings and held the detachments of the 40th U.S. Infantry at their temporary posts, Klansmen would have found their opportunities for mayhem severely restricted. The federal troops' presence might even have emboldened prominent Republicans and some Conservatives to unite in denouncing the Klan, as Republican state supreme court justice Thomas Settle and Democratic ex-governor David S. Reid later did in their home county of Rockingham. Their outspoken opposition convinced the local Klan to disband before it could do much harm. Most politicians, however, refused to condemn the Klan publicly, either for fear of reprisal or because they supported the Klan's efforts to restore the Conservatives to power.

Even without the civil authorities' cooperation, the army probably could have suppressed the Klan in North Carolina. The quiet 1868 presidential election had proved that. As one Klan victim observed, "the sight of U.S. Muskets and [shoulder] *Straps* is sufficient to bring these rebs. to terms at once, without any trial." Yet the army left law enforcement to the civil authorities, much as it had done during the Regulator crisis. The bluecoats thus squandered their best opportunity to prevent the Klan insurgency from spreading across the state.[44]

The opportunity quickly slipped away. On March 3, 1869, Congress passed an army manpower reduction act. Since law enforcement was once again a civil affair, the budget-minded Congress decided to cut the federal occupation force in the South. The War Department accordingly transferred the 40th U.S. Infantry to Louisiana and replaced it with five companies of the 8th U.S. Infantry from South Carolina. The number of federal troops in North Carolina thus fell from one thousand to about three hundred. The message from Congress was clear. In keeping the peace, the civil authorities in North Carolina would have to rely on their own resources.[45]

In the meantime, Miles was ordered to Kansas to assume command of the 5th U.S. Infantry, a white regiment. As Freedmen's Bureau director and military commander in North Carolina, Miles had championed the freedpeople and Holden's Republican administration. Whereas the Republicans regretted the loss of a valuable ally, the Conservatives rejoiced at Miles's departure. No one, however, was more delighted that Miles was leaving the Old North State than Miles's wife, Mary. As the niece of Gen. William T. Sherman, Mary Miles had to bear far more than the usual quota of slights and snubs aimed at the wives of occupation commanders. Miles's former superior Meade also was transferred elsewhere. Command of the Department of the South devolved to a former department commander in North Carolina, Col. Thomas H. Ruger.[46]

In December 1868, about one month after the election, the Klan's late-night raids began in deadly earnest. In Alamance and Stokes counties, Klansmen dragged freedmen from their homes and whipped or beat them severely; the infant of one victim died from injuries sustained during an attack. On January 24, 1869, heavily armed nightriders abducted five prisoners—four of them black—from the Lenoir County jail in Kinston. The outlaws took their captives to a bridge outside town, shot them to death, and then dumped their bodies into the Neuse River. The execution of the five prisoners at Kinston recalled the lynching of seven men at Snow Hill in January 1867, suggesting a link between the Regulators and the Klan.[47]

As ruthless as these attacks were, one Klan atrocity became notorious for its savagery. In late January, Klansmen burst into the home of Moore County resident Daniel Blue and began firing randomly, wounding Blue and killing his pregnant wife and one daughter. During the shooting spree, several Klansmen set fire to the house, and flames soon engulfed the wooden structure. Although Blue and three of his daughters managed to escape through an opening in the floor, four children became trapped and burned to death. Blue became a target of Klan violence because he was a prosecution witness in an arson trial involving several Klansmen. In the meantime, the Klan also struck in the counties of Caswell, Chatham, Orange, and Rockingham.[48]

Determined to overturn the Republicans' recent electoral triumph, the Ku Klux Klan embarked on a campaign of terror to facilitate the Conservatives' political resurgence. In effect, the Klan functioned as the terrorist wing of the Conservative Party. Many prominent Conservatives helped to organize the Klan, and some numbered among the leaders. The Klan attempted to secure Conservative majorities by threatening, intimidating, beating, or murdering their Republican opponents. Blacks bore the brunt of Klan atrocities, but many whites also became victims. The objective was to discourage the freedmen from voting and to coerce racial solidarity on the part of the whites. Klansmen also fancied themselves vigilantes or "regulators" who punished black criminals and violators of community mores, particularly white women who cohabited with black men. But above all, the Klan sought to restore the Conservatives to political dominance.[49]

To circumvent criminal prosecution, Klansmen employed several effective stratagems. At their initiation, Klansmen swore an oath to aid comrades in distress. This aid included obstructing justice, or "getting in the way of the sheriff," as they called it. A Klansman might finagle a place on a jury to secure a comrade's acquittal or commit perjury in the form of false alibis. Sometimes nightriders resorted to more extreme measures. In Lenoir County, Klansmen broke two accomplices out of jail after their arrest. Even the names of Klan organizations served to shield members from prosecution. The general public regarded the Ku Klux Klan as a monolithic entity, but the Klan actually consisted of many small local cells that bore different names depending on the region. Initiates knew the Klan as the Constitutional Union Guard (CUG) in the east, the White Brotherhood in the piedmont (with the CUG coexisting beside it in Alamance County), and the Invisible Empire in the west. When asked under oath if he belonged to the "Ku Klux Klan," a CUG member could truthfully answer that he did not. But this was a mere contrivance, for few Klansmen harbored any qualms about committing perjury. Because of the Klan's systematic obstruction of justice, obtaining indictments proved difficult and securing convictions next to impossible.[50]

Albion W. Tourgée indicated that victims who experienced the frustration of identifying their assailants, only to see them escape punishment through subterfuge, sometimes employed their own brand of justice when the courts failed them. Tourgée had recently become the superior court judge for a judicial district in which Klan atrocities were frequent. He noted that freedpeople sometimes avenged "*masked* violence" with "hidden destruction." Although vengeful blacks burned barns, stables, and mills of suspected nightriders, Klan outrages far outnumbered retaliatory arson cases. When under attack, freedpeople struck back at their assailants if possible, as in the case of an Alamance County woman who nearly killed a Klansman with an ax blow to the head. But nightriders usually struck at night in overwhelming numbers, seldom giving victims an opportunity to defend themselves. To avoid such an attack, many potential targets hid out in the woods or fled to large towns such as Raleigh, while some terrified refugees left the state altogether.[51]

Confident that their crimes would go unpunished, Klansmen became ever bolder, their numbers swelled, and their crimes multiplied. By March 1869, the White Brotherhood in Alamance County numbered about seven hundred members, slightly more than one-half of the county's white voters. The membership included the county sheriff and eleven deputies. In reprisal for the mayor's formation of a biracial night watch, about eighty of the White Brotherhood paraded en regalia through the streets of Graham, the county seat, and fired into the homes of several blacks. The nightriders then formed a line in front of a prominent Republican's house and warned him they would be out for blood on their next visit. On March 22, six Alamance County magistrates informed Holden that

Albion W. Tourgée (Courtesy of the North Carolina State Archives)

they were "unable to maintain the peace of the county" and urged him to send the militia at once. A few days later, the governor dispatched a white militia company under Capt. Royal T. Bosher to Graham. While working in Alamance as an undercover detective, Bosher had amassed considerable evidence against suspected Klansmen. On his return to Graham, Bosher arrested several men accused of committing outrages. Justice was swift: the defendants were freed after some friends stepped forward with airtight alibis. Bosher's militia returned to Raleigh after about a month, having failed to secure the conviction of one Klansman. Judge Tourgée described Alamance as "decidedly the worst county in the district. The juries are all Ku Klux," he wrote. "There is no crime [that] can be committed by a white conservative."[52]

The General Assembly's first attempt to counteract Klan atrocities proved largely ineffectual. In April 1869, the state legislature passed a law that sentenced persons convicted of committing crimes while disguised to imprisonment at hard labor for a year or more. While the law may have given some Klansmen pause for thought, it punished few if any nightriders. Tourgée could cite "many indictments" under the new law, but he knew of only two convictions, and they happened to be black men convicted in his own court.[53]

In May 1869, the Constitutional Union Guard added political assassination to its repertoire of terror. The Jones County CUG targeted carpetbagger Sheriff Orson R. Colgrove, a local Republican leader who arrested CUG members. The Jones County organization called on the CUG in neighboring Lenoir County to do the job. This was customary whenever murder was involved, for strangers were difficult to identify. But, as Klansmen everywhere realized, perjury and intimidation proved far more effective in obstructing justice than disguises and costumes.[54]

On May 29, the Lenoir County CUG ambushed Colgrove, killing the sheriff and mortally wounding a black man who was with him. CUG members reportedly celebrated their triumph with "one of the biggest barbecues ever given in Jones County." The Lenoir County CUG also murdered two freedmen around this time. Responding to appeals from local Republicans such as state senator David D. Colgrove, the slain sheriff's brother, Holden sent a company of white militia to Jones County, where it remained for six weeks. Satisfied that the militia had restored order, Holden summoned the company back to Raleigh. Soon afterward, the CUG struck again, gunning down a second Jones County carpetbagger, county vommissioner M. L. Shepard, and two black men who worked for him. The CUG assassinated Shepard because he had formed a local black militia company. When Holden sent detectives into Jones and Lenoir to investigate the murders, the CUG marked them for assassination. One of the detectives, Lewis H. Mowers, not only eluded death but also persuaded three suspects to turn state's evidence. Of the two dozen detectives Holden employed to hunt Klansmen across the state, the fearless and resourceful Mowers proved by far the most successful. Armed with a list of CUG members, Mowers and the sheriff of Lenoir County arrested twenty-five suspects and prudently locked them away in the Craven County jail at New Bern. The accused faced charges of murder, as well as numerous lesser crimes.[55]

Holden used the carrot-and-stick technique with the CUG. On October 20, 1869, the governor issued a proclamation warning that he would declare Jones and Lenoir in a state of insurrection if the crime wave continued. After the indictments and the proclamation, peace returned to the two counties. As a conciliatory gesture, Holden freed the prisoners. No suspects were tried for their alleged crimes.[56]

Holden also included Chatham and Orange counties in his October 20 proclamation. In August, Alamance County Klansmen broke into the Orange County jail at Hillsborough and abducted two black men arrested for barn burning. They shot both men several times at close range, but one victim somehow survived. He was later tried and acquitted. The same Klansmen then hanged the uncle and brother of the slain man, for they, too, were arson suspects. Nightriders murdered yet another Orange County freedman for being "too intimate with white women." The victim was found with his throat cut and his tongue torn out. On several autumn evenings, about one hundred Klansmen paraded through the streets of Chapel Hill, abducting and beating Republicans of both races.[57]

Alarmed at the impunity with which the Klan operated in Orange County, Holden urged Brig. Gen. Alfred H. Terry to order a company of troops to Chapel Hill. Terry had commanded the Department of the South since May 31, 1869. Holden justified his request on the grounds that he had only black militia to combat the Klan, and he feared their presence in Chapel Hill would aggravate the situation. On November 2, Terry dispatched a company of the 8th U.S. Infantry. For some reason, the soldiers did not leave Raleigh until the sixth, arriving at Chapel Hill the next day. The deployment marked the first use of federal troops as peacekeepers in North Carolina since the presidential election one year earlier.[58]

In his November 16 message to the General Assembly, an exasperated Holden blasted Congress for reducing the army and thereby depriving North Carolina of an adequate garrison. Recalling the federal troops' crucial role in the peaceful election of November 1868, Holden maintained that a regiment of infantry and four companies of cavalry stationed at various points in the state "would have a most salutary effect in repressing these outrages and maintaining the peace." After stressing the need for a larger garrison, Holden then contradicted himself, declaring that President Grant could be relied on to send reinforcements if they became necessary.[59]

Meanwhile, conditions in the piedmont deteriorated. On the night of November 26, 1869, Alamance County Klansmen assaulted a Freedmen's Bureau teacher named Alonzo B. Corliss and his wife, who lived at Company Shops (present-day Burlington). The nightriders gave Corliss a severe beating and then warned him to leave the state. As soon as he learned of the incident, Holden obtained a seven-man federal guard for Corliss, but the detail arrived just in time to escort the teacher to Greensboro en route to Danville, Virginia. Before his departure, Corliss identified four of his assailants. The civil authorities in Alamance arrested them but did not prosecute due to insufficient evidence.[60]

Widely reported, the Corliss atrocity called national attention to Klan outrages in North Carolina. The notoriety failed to impress the Grant administration, however, and the state's Freedmen's Bureau schools remained conspicuous targets. In 1869, the Klan burned down several schools, including one near Company Shops. H. C. Vogell, the Freedmen's Bureau supervisor of education for North Carolina, informed Commissioner Howard that the Klan had compelled many of his schools to close. Even so, a few brave souls refused to knuckle under. Despite repeated demands that she abandon her "Nigger school," a bureau teacher in Orange County defiantly remained at her post while applying to Vogell for three pistols. "I hope something may be done to protect our schools," Vogell wrote Howard. "It requires all my efforts and influence to keep them going."[61]

In December 1869, Alamance and Caswell counties tottered on the brink of anarchy. Klansmen were rampaging through the two counties on a nightly basis, and their raids were becoming more lethal. The shooting of Caswell Holt, an Alamance County freedman, was a case in point. Nightriders had already assaulted Holt the preceding December for voting Republican. Despite the beating, Holt remained loyal to the party of Lincoln and even brought charges against his attackers. During the second raid, Holt's assailants shot him six times in the chest and arms. He barely escaped with his life.[62]

The two counties became a vortex of Klan violence because the Republicans' success in mobilizing the black vote spurred local Klan chieftains to a comparable level of activity. Although Conservatives held most of the local offices, the state senators for the two counties—T. M. Shoffner of Alamance and John W. Stephens of Caswell—were homegrown white Republicans with a strong black following. During the holidays, Senator Shoffner became the Klan's primary target in Alamance County. Shoffner recently had sponsored a bill intended to strengthen Holden's hand in combating the Klan. Although an unconstitutional provision authorizing the governor to suspend the writ of habeas corpus had to be cut, the bill nevertheless reiterated the governor's authority to declare a state of insurrection, call out the militia, and request presidential aid. The Shoffner Act passed on January 29, 1870. The bill's sponsor was fortunate to be alive for the occasion.[63]

During the General Assembly's holiday recess, the Klan conspired to assassinate Shoffner at his Alamance County home. The White Brotherhood of Alamance asked their Orange County comrades to return the favor for lynching the alleged barnburners at Hillsborough. The leader of the Orange County nightriders sent to kill Shoffner was Frederick N. Strudwick, a lawyer and future state legislator. While on the road to Shoffner's house, Strudwick and his men encountered Dr. John A. Moore, a fellow Klansman and state representative from Alamance. Moore's appearance was no accident, for he was on an errand to prevent Shoffner's murder. To that end, Moore told Strudwick that the senator was in Greensboro. After a brief discussion, a disappointed Strudwick and his men wheeled their horses about and headed back to Orange County. But Shoffner remained a marked man and thereafter received numerous warnings to leave the state. At the next legislative recess, the senator returned home to his wife and small child, loaded his family's belongings into a wagon, and moved to Indiana.[64]

Republican mayor William R. Albright of Graham met with Holden several times in 1869 and appealed to him for a company of federal troops to restore order. Each time Holden said there were no soldiers to spare, but he promised to send them as soon as they became available. In the meantime, bluecoats in Goldsboro posed a greater threat to freedpeople than to Klansmen.[65]

On the evening of October 23, a race riot pitting white troops against black civilians erupted in Goldsboro. The riot was the culmination of several smaller collisions. On October 21, a group of white enlisted men beat a black man unconscious as he and his wife were leaving night school. According to the *Goldsboro Messenger*, the incident was but the latest in a series of outrages against local blacks by the garrison. The following night, a mob of black men out for revenge assaulted several bluecoats and beat one of them severely. As darkness fell on the twenty-third, squads of heavily armed freedmen patrolled the streets in expectation of a show-down with the troops. About 8 P.M., a phalanx of bluecoats armed with rifle-muskets confronted the blacks in the center of town. The two sides opened a furious, yet mostly inaccurate, fire. One soldier was shot in the thigh and had to be carried back to the post by several comrades. The soldiers told their commanding officer, Capt. John F. Ritter, that a gang of black ruffians had fired on them without provocation. Ritter directed Lt. A. W. Corliss to lead a patrol into town and request Mayor J. B. Whitaker to arrest the perpetrators. As Corliss prepared to leave, several shots whizzed past from the direction of town. The gunfire remained intense for sev-eral minutes and then gradually diminished until it ceased altogether around 10 P.M. In addition to the soldier with the thigh wound, several bluecoats and at least one freedman were slightly wounded. Although the nighttime shootout resulted in few casualties, the townspeople had found it a terrifying ordeal. In any event, the editor of the Army and Navy Journal—who was not present—made light of the incident. Expressing surprise that the expenditure of so much ammunition had caused so little bloodshed, the editor quipped, "if these statements be correct, [then] the garrison should be instructed in target practice forthwith."[66]

In truth, the riot revealed poor marksmanship as the least of the garrison's shortcomings. On that night, military discipline in Goldsboro was nonexistent. The failure of Ritter and Corliss to take charge of their men indicates that they either approved of the soldiers' actions or could not control them. The officers credited the statements of their men that armed black civilians had provoked the riot, thereby absolving themselves and their men of all blame for the incident, much as Lt. Walter S. Long had done regarding the James City riot of July 1868. Acting on the soldiers' statements, the Goldsboro police arrested several blacks but no bluecoats. The conduct of the soldiers at Goldsboro suggests that the difference be-tween their racial attitudes and those of the Klansmen was negligible.

Goldsboro resident H. L. Stevens Jr. blamed the disturbance on the garrison's large Irish contingent, likening their racist fury to that of the Irish street toughs during the July 1863 New York City draft riots. "Now we can't walk through Town to school for fear of losing our lives," Ste-vens complained to Governor Holden. "What shall we do?" The question assumed even greater urgency when, a few days after the riot, eight soldiers reportedly forced their way into a black couple's home on the outskirts of town, abducted the woman, and gang-raped her in a nearby field.[67]

Blacks were not the only residents of Goldsboro to encounter trouble with the bluecoats. About one month before the riot, a white citizen named J. M. Hollowell complained to both Captain Ritter and Mayor Whitaker that drunken federal soldiers had repeatedly shot at his dogs and had once fired a round at him, striking the house about a foot from where he stood. But Ritter took no action in the matter. Hollowell's complaint indicates that Ritter knew of the disciplinary problem but either could not or would not take control of the situation.[68]

In October 1869, the garrison at Goldsboro was Company B of the 8th U.S. Infantry. Two years earlier, Company B had earned an excellent reputation while stationed at Greensboro. Before the company's departure, the townspeople had petitioned General Canby to retain the troops because of their effectiveness in preserving order. What accounted for the contrast in Company B's conduct in Greensboro and in Goldsboro? The probable culprit was the consolidation in May 1869 of the 33rd U.S. Infantry and the 8th U.S. Infantry, resulting in the absorption of Company H of the 33rd into Company B of the 8th. The garrison's outrages against black citizens began after the consolidation, suggesting that the perpetrators numbered among the company's recent additions. On October 31, Company B departed for Raleigh, much to the relief of Goldsboro's residents. One week later, the company was sent to Chapel Hill to restore order there, an ironic assignment given the soldiers' flagrant misconduct at their previous post.[69]

In Goldsboro in October 1869, freedpeople once again had to defend themselves against their purported guardians—the U.S. Army—as they were compelled to do at James City in July 1868. The Goldsboro riot marked the army's most conspicuous action in North Carolina for the year 1869, but this lamentable record was not entirely the troops' fault. In March, Congress had drastically reduced the number of soldiers in North Carolina and elsewhere in the South, and the Grant administration refused to send reinforcements unless a state of open rebellion existed. The post commanders in the Tar Heel State had orders to intervene in civil affairs only if absolutely necessary, as in the Chapel Hill deployment. The national government's hands-off policy enabled the Ku Klux Klan's reign of terror to spread unchecked across much of the state. Whatever opportunity the army may have had to suppress the Klan in 1869 was lost. As 1870 opened, the terrible consequences of federal inaction unfolded.

Chapter Nine

FIGHTING TERRORISM

The Army and the Klan

The years 1870 and 1871 marked the height of the Klan terror in North Carolina. The army refused at first to step in, believing it a disturbance the civil authorities were equipped to handle. Only after the assassination of two county Republican leaders, numerous other Klan-related atrocities, the Conservative electoral triumph of 1870, and the impeachment of Governor Holden did the president and Congress decide to intervene. Ignoring Conservative accusations of "bayonet rule," the army assisted federal law enforcement agents in arresting Klansmen and moonshiners. Although the army helped to subdue the Klan, it failed to corner the Lowry band, half a dozen outlaws who had terrorized Robeson County since the Civil War. The bluecoats continued to preserve order at the polls on election day, facilitating the Republican resurgence of 1871.

At 1 A.M. on Saturday, February 26, 1870, a column of one hundred horsemen clad in white robes and hooded masks rode south down Graham's Main Street toward the Alamance County courthouse. The night was dark and cold and the air still damp after a late-night drizzle, but the column shone with the bright light of numerous pine torches. The procession was greeted by a chorus of barking dogs, followed by the flickering of lights in several bedroom windows.[1]

The nightriders halted before the home of Wyatt Outlaw, a fifty-year-old woodworker, Union army veteran, town commissioner, and Union

League leader. Outlaw was the foremost African American in Alamance County and a voice of restraint in unsettled times. When local blacks met to decide on a response to mounting Klan violence, Outlaw answered the cries for vengeance by urging his hearers to obey the law. Since the meeting, most blacks in the county had followed Outlaw's counsel, but the outrages continued to multiply.[2]

Twenty nightriders dismounted, forced open Outlaw's front door, and burst into the four-room house. In addition to torches, many men carried swords or revolvers. They first entered the bedroom occupied by Outlaw's mother, Jemima Phillips, and threw off her covers. "Where is Wyatt?" they demanded, threatening to kill her if she refused to talk. Before Phillips could answer, the men left the room. By the time she reached her son's bedroom, they had surrounded him. Phillips grabbed a stick and "laid away as hard as I could" into them. Several men knocked her down and then stamped on her head, chest, and arms. The nightriders found Phillips so difficult to subdue that they had to knock her down two more times. Outlaw meanwhile pulled on his pants. As he was led barefoot into the night, his youngest son cried, "Oh daddy, oh daddy!" A few men entered the house of Outlaw's neighbor, Henry Holt, with the intention of carrying him off, but they did not find him there. They settled for a five-foot length of cord. Outlaw was pushed and prodded down Main Street toward the courthouse by three men, one of them dressed in black, conspicuous amid a sea of white. Shrieking the rebel yell, several horsemen thundered ahead to the courthouse square, a few buggies clattering along close behind.[3]

The procession briefly halted as several men at the head of the column surveyed the square for a sturdy tree from which to hang Outlaw. They chose a tall elm near the center of town. The cord was swung over a branch that pointed toward the courthouse just thirty yards away. Outlaw's body was left hanging from the tree. He was found with a paper pinned to his coat that read, "Beware, you guilty, both white and black." His hanging in the shadow of the county courthouse served notice that Klan justice reigned supreme in Alamance. At 11 A.M., Sheriff Albert Murray, a former Klansman, finally cut him down. The coroner ruled that Outlaw had died at the hands of persons unknown. Sheriff Murray made no attempt to track down the perpetrators. As far as the local Conservatives were concerned, the Wyatt Outlaw lynching case was closed.[4]

The Klan's campaign of terror appeared to be an unqualified success, for many Republicans were fleeing Alamance and the leaderless county

Union League soon dissolved. But the atrocity also galvanized Governor Holden into action. On February 28, five Graham Republicans notified Holden of Outlaw's lynching. "The Civil Authorities are powerless to bring these Offenders against law and humanity to justice," they wrote. "Out of the numberless cases occurring in the County[,] not one has yet been indicted[,] much less punished; and we know of no way in which these bands of lawless men can be put down and punished except by the strong arm of the military." The next day, Holden relayed the news of Outlaw's murder to the post commander at Raleigh, Lt. Col. Samuel B. Hayman, and urged him to send a detachment to Graham. Hayman dispatched a forty-man force to the town two days later.[5]

Several weeks before Outlaw's lynching, North Carolina was transferred to the Department of Virginia under General Canby. The five companies of the 8th U.S. Infantry in the Tar Heel State were sent to South Carolina and replaced by two companies of the 17th U.S. Infantry. Colonel Hayman warned his superiors that neither company was ready for detached duty; one was understrength while the other was filled with untrained recruits. He therefore requested reinforcements. In the meantime, Hayman had to rely on the troops already stationed at Raleigh.[6]

Lt. Calvin P. McTaggart commanded the detachment of the 17th Infantry sent to Graham. McTaggart's orders were to aid the civil authorities if they met with resistance and otherwise serve as a passive deterrent to lawlessness. The day after his arrival, McTaggart reported finding "the loyal people of this place in a high state of excitement" over the Klan's lynching of Outlaw and the subsequent murder of a freedman who claimed to know the perpetrators' identities. McTaggart noted that the Klan had threatened the lives of several other Alamance County Republicans, including the postmaster at Company Shops. He sent the postmaster a guard of eleven soldiers. The lieutenant reported that persons of both races had been beaten, but he was unable to determine the exact number, for many victims were too frightened to come forward. McTaggart recommended that "a large number of troops" be sent "to protect the loyal citizens from this band of outlaws." In his report to Canby, Colonel Hayman echoed McTaggart, requesting "an additional force of at least two hundred men" for Alamance and recommending that the writ of habeas corpus be suspended there "until the insurrection is suppressed."[7]

McTaggart's detachment arrived at Graham the day before a town meeting called by local Conservative leaders, who hoped to forestall military intervention by publicly condemning the Outlaw lynching. The organizers therefore canceled the meeting immediately after the soldiers' arrival. Soon afterward, a local Klan chieftain named Adolphus G. Moore confronted Republican leader Henry A. Badham, a coauthor of the February 28 letter to Holden. Moore cursed Badham and his associates for bringing "the d—d blue-coated sons of bitches" to Graham. The Klansman then assaulted the scalawag and succeeded in breaking his leg.[8]

Moore and his henchmen soon found that they had little to fear from the federal detachment. According to a local Conservative named James A. Graham, the soldiers posed a greater threat to blacks than to Klansmen. In a letter to his father, William Alexander Graham—in whose honor the town was named—James commented that the soldiers "get drunk pretty often and have beaten several negroes. They do not interfere with anyone else, and behave very well while they are sober." The younger Graham noted that the troops sought to curry favor with the whites by professing to be "good democrats."[9]

On March 5, several Republicans went to McTaggart's camp on the edge of town and warned the lieutenant that the Klan reportedly planned to attack his camp that night. "We were up and under arms all night, praying that they might come," McTaggart later informed Colonel Hayman, "but morning came and no Ku-Klux." Although McTaggart felt confident that his foot soldiers could defend the town, he knew that he lacked both the mobility and the manpower to pacify the countryside. There was little the lieutenant could do anyway, for until the civil authorities took action, his detachment had to remain on the sidelines.[10]

On March 7, Holden took the first crucial step, declaring Alamance County in a state of insurrection. One week later, he urged North Carolina's congressional delegation to press for a bill authorizing President Grant to suspend the writ of habeas corpus in Alamance. Holden also asked Grant to send federal troops, explaining that the local militia could not be trusted. He assured the president that if a few nightriders were "tried before military tribunals and shot, we should soon have peace and order." For all their urgency, Holden's appeals to Grant and the North Carolina congressmen went unanswered. On the seventeenth, Holden telegraphed North Carolina senator Joseph C. Abbott, a New Hampshire-born carpetbagger and former Union general. "What is being done to protect good citizens in Alamance County?" Holden asked. "We have Federal troops, but we want power to act. Is it possible the government will abandon its loyal people to be whipped and hanged" by the Klan?[11]

Holden also appealed to General Canby and Canby's superior, General

Meade, who commanded the Military Division of the Atlantic. On March 7, Holden sent his adjutant general, A. W. Fisher, to Canby's headquarters in Richmond, Virginia, to describe conditions in Alamance County and request more federal troops. After Fisher pleaded the governor's case, Canby replied that only the president could grant Holden's request. In any event, Canby remained unconvinced that an insurrection existed in Alamance County. While crediting reports that the Klan in Alamance was "formidable" and their outrages were "horrible," Canby believed the federal troops at Graham "ought to restore confidence, and inspire the civil authorities with some degree of energy and activity." Meade agreed with Canby that no reinforcements in Alamance were necessary. Disregarding the generals' advice, Secretary of War William W. Belknap directed that "a few companies be sent to the district in insurrection." Canby sent two companies of the 17th U.S. Infantry as ordered.[12]

Given the overwhelming evidence of a crisis in central North Carolina, the complacency of Canby and Meade appears callous, to say the least. As many other federal officers had already done, the two generals downplayed the violence and lawlessness that gripped much of the state. They did so for three reasons. First, Canby and Meade wished to convey the impression that they had the situation under control. Second, they did not want state and local officials to regard the army as a federal police force that could be called on in preference to civil law enforcement. Third, the two generals considered the so-called insurrection in Alamance County a minor affair. The generals were unaware that the list of known Klan victims in Alamance had topped fifty and the actual casualty figure was much higher. In any event, Canby soon received confirmation of the crisis from a source he deemed reliable.[13]

Distrusting the reports of Holden and Fisher, Canby sent a staff officer named Lt. Paul R. Hambrick to investigate the situation in Alamance County. A Virginia native, Hambrick had lived in Alamance before the war and thus knew many of the residents. After a weeklong investigation, Hambrick submitted his report to Canby. The lieutenant confirmed the governor's bleak account. Hambrick described the Klan in Alamance as "a formidable body of men . . . under thorough discipline and training." He reported that the nightriders had committed at least six murders and a series of assaults "too numerous to mention." Hambrick recommended that Canby send a company of cavalry with authority to arrest suspected Klansmen and that the general establish a military tribunal, for it was "impossible . . . to bring them to justice before the civil authorities."

Thanks to Hambrick's report, Canby now realized the gravity of the situation in Alamance County, but he could do little to alleviate the crisis. Canby had no cavalry at his disposal, and even if he had, the troopers would have needed Grant's authorization to arrest nightriders. Military tribunals likewise required presidential approval to try civilians. Canby and Meade probably also knew that Grant would not intervene until he was sure Holden had exhausted his options.[14]

In early 1870, Alamance County was one of more than a dozen North Carolina counties plagued by Klan violence, ranging from Wayne County in the east to Rutherford County in the west. Holden prodded local law enforcement and judicial officers to do their duty, but they proved even less effective than the state detectives. The governor also enlisted the aid of prominent Conservatives N. A. Ramsey of Chatham and Pride Jones of Orange to end Klan violence in their home counties, and their efforts achieved some success. Without the governor's knowledge, the two men offered amnesty to local Klansmen if they pledged to disband, warning that the alternative was military intervention. While maintaining that he could not grant amnesty to nightriders, Holden ordered no arrests of suspected Klansmen. As a result, atrocities in the two counties decreased sharply.[15]

On May 1, Colonel Hayman and his four companies of the 17th U.S. Infantry were transferred from North Carolina. Their withdrawal uncovered Graham. One week later, Holden urged Brig. Gen. Irvin McDowell, the commander of the Department of the East, which included North Carolina, to send a company of the 8th U.S. Infantry to Graham and a detachment to Yanceyville, the Caswell County seat. McDowell issued the necessary orders, and a company of the 8th Infantry arrived at Graham on May 14, with the usual admonition to act not "as a police force but to act solely . . . in subordination to the civil authorities." McDowell, however, sent no troops to Yanceyville. Meanwhile, Holden engaged in a futile search for a Conservative in Caswell County to act as his agent. Even if the governor had found someone, such a mission probably would have failed, for nightriders in Caswell had become as brazen as their counterparts in Alamance. That spring, the Caswell Klan passed a death sentence on the county's leading Republican, state senator John W. Stephens.[16]

Accustomed to threats on his life, Stephens traveled heavily armed, rendering an attack problematic. On May 21, Stephens obliged his would-be assassins by entering the lions' den—the Democratic county convention inside the courthouse at Yanceyville. During the rally, a conspirator lured Stephens into the basement, where several Klansmen disarmed and then murdered the senator. The authorities in Caswell made a show of investigating Stephens's death but failed to indict any suspects. A few days after the Stephens slaying, Wilson Carey, the black state representative for Caswell, fled the county. On May 25, Holden offered a reward of $500 for the arrest and conviction of Stephens's assassins. Two weeks later, he issued yet another proclamation offering a $500 reward for the murderers of Outlaw and other Klan victims. Believing that retaliation against suspected Klansmen only provoked further violence, Holden offered a $400 reward for the capture of arsonists in Caswell County.[17]

On May 31, Congress passed the Enforcement Act to provide southern civil authorities with federal assistance in suppressing the Klan. Paraphrasing the recently ratified Fifteenth Amendment, it stipulated that no citizen could be denied the right to vote because of "race, color, or previous condition of servitude." The act made it a felony for two or more persons "to band or conspire together, or go in disguise upon the public highway, or upon the premises of another" with criminal intent. Congress authorized the president, as well as federal marshals and commissioners, to call on the army or the militia for aid in bringing the perpetrators to justice, and it assigned jurisdiction over such cases to the federal courts. For all the lawmakers' good intentions, the Enforcement Act benefited few people because Grant refused to employ it. Left with no alternative, Holden called up the state militia.[18]

Until now Holden had refused to mobilize the militia because of fears that white militiamen might also be Klan members and that armed blacks would heighten racial tensions. Without the prospect of federal intervention, the governor concluded that he had no choice. On June 8, Holden conferred with U.S. senator John Pool and other state Republican leaders. All agreed on the need to call up the militia, but they divided over the question of trying suspects in the civil courts or before a military tribunal. After listening to his advisors, Holden chose a military commission in the belief that it would prove more reliable than the civil courts. The governor also decided that, if necessary, he would ignore writs of habeas corpus, despite his awareness that such a course would open him to impeachment charges.[19]

Holden next chose his two militia commanders, Colonels William J. Clarke and George W. Kirk. A former Confederate colonel, Clarke commanded a regiment of white and black troops from the eastern part of the state. Kirk was a Tennessee native and an ex-Union colonel notorious for several destructive raids into western North Carolina. Kirk's regiment consisted of white soldiers from the wartime Unionist stronghold of east Tennessee and western North Carolina. Like their commander, many were Union veterans. Lacking funds to outfit his militia, Holden sent Clarke to Washington to request President Grant's assistance. Accompanied by Senators Abbott and Pool, Clarke met with Grant at the White House and received the president's word that the federal government would arm and equip the militia. Grant also promised to send four companies of federal troops to North Carolina. The governor's decision to mobilize the militia had convinced Grant that Holden meant business. When Holden paid a visit to the White House two weeks later, the president repeated his pledge of assistance. Thanks to Grant, militia recruits received the same uniforms, rations, and pay as federal soldiers. As a result, the militia regiments soon met their enlistment quotas.[20]

While the state militia was recruiting and organizing, two companies of the 4th U.S. Artillery—the men armed and equipped as infantry—traveled to Yanceyville in Caswell County, and one company headed to Roxboro in Person County. They arrived during the second week of July. A fourth company of the 4th Artillery was sent to Ruffin in Rockingham County a few weeks later. On reaching Yanceyville, Capt. George B. Rodney reported that the town was peaceful and that, as far as he could tell, "there is no danger of any outbreak, or resistance to authorities." Rodney also noted that Caswell County sheriff Jesse C. Griffith "has had no trouble with anyone, & does not apprehend any." But Griffith was unlikely to encounter much difficulty with the Klan, for he reputedly belonged to the organization.[21]

In addition to stationing troops in the northern piedmont, Capt. Royal T. Frank, the commandant of the Post of Raleigh and the senior army officer in North Carolina, sent an eleven-man detachment of the 8th U.S. Infantry into Chatham County to apprehend a dozen Klansmen accused of shooting a freedman named Wyatt Prince. Local Republicans maintained that Prince was shot to intimidate the county's black voters. On July 6, U.S. marshal Samuel T. Carrow requested a detachment of federal soldiers to assist him in arresting the nightriders for violating the Enforcement Act. Frank granted Carrow's request in the belief that he was obeying General McDowell's instructions to "comply with all requisitions of United States marshal and district attorney for troops to enforce United States laws." Frank cautioned the commander of the detachment, Lt. James W. Powell, to "abstain as far as practicable from extreme measures or bloodshed." Powell left Raleigh on July 8 and returned two days later with nine of the suspects, the other three having fled Chatham County before the bluecoats' arrival. Four of the prisoners were indicted. Frank informed McDowell of the mission's success. Despite Carrow's contention that an attempt to make the arrests with a civilian posse would have resulted in bloodshed, Frank concluded that the troop detachment was probably unnecessary because the suspects had offered no resistance. Perhaps, as Carrow believed, this merely indicated that the bluecoats had served their purpose. McDowell approved Frank's action but instructed him to first notify department headquarters if he had time to do so.[22]

The apprehension of the Chatham County nightriders proved to be the army's sole operation against the Klan in North Carolina for 1870. A few days after Powell's return, Carrow applied to Frank for a second detachment to arrest ten Klansmen accused of savagely beating a white Republican. Frank requested instructions from McDowell and instead received a message from General Meade, McDowell's superior. Meade refused to consider Frank's request until the captain reported the circumstances and gave his opinion regarding the necessity of the detachment. He then directed that federal troops "should only be employed when their services are imperatively necessary, and after the civil authorities have exhausted all other measures." As for the present case, Meade continued, the U.S. marshal had made no effort to arrest the suspects. The general directed Frank to inform the marshal that he must provide evidence of such an attempt when requesting federal troops.[23]

Meade's instructions left Frank no choice but to deny the marshal's request. Carrow replied that "it was difficult, if not impossible, to get a posse large enough to arrest so many under less difficult circumstances." He warned that a botched attempt to capture the Klansmen would likely scatter them, rendering futile any later pursuit by federal troops. Frank found Carrow's argument compelling enough to suggest to his superiors that a military escort for the marshal would serve a useful peacekeeping function. But Frank's suggestion fell on deaf ears. Both Meade and Mc-Dowell refused to intervene under the Enforcement Act, leaving federal authorities in North Carolina no better equipped to combat the Klan than before.[24]

In mid-July, Kirk's regiment of state militia began to assemble at Company Shops. Kirk himself traveled to Raleigh to confer with Holden. Having just declared Caswell County in a state of insurrection, the governor instructed Kirk to occupy Yanceyville and presented him with a list of suspects to arrest. On the way to Yanceyville, Kirk arrested several men in Alamance County, including Sheriff Albert Murray and reputed Klan leader Adolphus G. Moore. When Kirk reached Yanceyville on July 18, he learned that congressional candidates William L. Scott and James M. Leach were in the middle of a debate at the Caswell County courthouse. Seizing the opportunity, Kirk directed his second-in-command, Lt. Col. George B. Bergen, to surround the courthouse and permit no one to leave. Kirk then entered the building and arrested two dozen men, including Leach, the Conservative candidate. Only the intervention of Republican candidate Scott saved Leach from being jailed. As the militia moved through the crowd, a man struck one of Kirk's officers, prompting the soldiers to fix bayonets. Among those arrested were Sheriff Jesse C. Griffith, former U.S. congressman John Kerr, and onetime Freedmen's Bureau agent William B. Bowe. Kirk then ordered Bergen to return to Company Shops and assume command of the state militia in Alamance County. Bergen proved to be an unreliable commander. Reports soon reached Holden that Bergen had threatened to hang a prisoner who refused to confess. "Evidence obtained in this way is worthless," Holden admonished Kirk. "All prisoners . . . should be treated humanely."[25]

A few weeks after the Caswell County courthouse arrests, *Raleigh Sentinel* editor Josiah Turner Jr. was incarcerated in the basement room where John W. Stephens was murdered. On August 5, the vitriolic Turner was arrested near his Hillsborough home by order of Colonel Bergen. Although dubbed the "King of the Ku Klux" by detractors, Turner probably never became a formal member of the Klan. Even so, his sympathies clearly lay with the nightriders, and it would scarcely be an exaggeration to label him the Klan's self-appointed minister of propaganda. Regardless of his organizational status, Turner was a dangerous political adversary, as Holden knew only too well. In fact, Bergen had arrested Turner without orders from either Holden or Kirk. The Conservatives nevertheless exploited Turner's arrest for maximum political advantage, depicting the *Sentinel* editor as a martyr and Holden as a cruel despot. In the meantime, Turner, his fellow prisoners, and Kirk's militia remained at Yanceyville for about one month.[26]

No sooner had Kirk made his arrests than he began to fear an attempt by the Klan to free the prisoners at Yanceyville. Kirk conveyed his misgivings to Holden. On July 20, the governor appealed to President Grant for a regiment of federal soldiers, explaining that the Klan heavily outnumbered the state militia in the insurrectionary counties. Grant telegraphed that he would rush more federal troops to North Carolina, and he directed the secretary of war to send six companies at once. [27]

The army took additional steps to aid Holden in his campaign against the Klan. On July 27, General Meade established the temporary District of North Carolina and placed Col. Henry J. Hunt in command. From all appearances, the fifty-year-old Hunt made an excellent choice. He was a West Pointer (class of 1839), Mexican War veteran, and Union brigadier during the Civil War. The former chief of artillery for the Army of the Potomac and a coauthor of the U.S. Army's light artillery manual, Hunt was widely regarded as the foremost authority on his branch of service. But he received his present command because of his coolness and discretion rather than his technical expertise. Hunt's orders were the same as those issued to Captain Frank: he was to commit his troops only if the civil authorities met with open resistance. When Hunt assumed command on August 1, two companies of the 8th U.S. Infantry, one company of the 1st U.S. Artillery, one company of the 2nd U.S. Artillery, and six companies of the 4th U.S. Artillery—about seven hundred soldiers in all—were stationed at Raleigh, Graham, Yanceyville, Roxboro, and Ruffin. [28]

The federal troops and the state militia in North Carolina comprised a substantial force. The militia numbered roughly six hundred officers and men. Fewer than four hundred white troops under Kirk were stationed at Yanceyville and Company Shops, with a sixty-man detachment in Gaston County. Clarke had one hundred white and sixty black soldiers at Raleigh and another sixty white troops at Hillsborough. In late July, Holden ordered Clarke to send detachments to Carthage in Moore County and Chapel Hill, while Kirk sent thirty men to Shelby in Cleveland County. By posting state militia units in known Klan strongholds left unoccupied by federal detachments, Holden hoped to secure a peaceful election on August 4. [29]

As election day approached, Kirk became increasingly alarmed about conditions in Caswell County. On July 24, Kirk informed Holden that two companies of the Klan were within a few miles of town and that he had arrested one of the supposed leaders, Capt. Pink Graves. Kirk assured Holden that he could hold out for several days if attacked, but he requested two pieces of artillery with which he could "beat off 5000." Captain Rodney scoffed at Kirk's view of the situation. Rodney informed Captain Frank that "there is no fear of any disturbance between the citizens and military unless Kirk provokes them to it." Nevertheless, Rodney

Col. Henry J. Hunt (Library of Congress)

continued, Kirk had made "great preparations for defense by barricading the court-house, doubling his guard, and posting a strong force of pickets." Rodney dismissed the "whole cause for alarm" as "some foolish reports given by negroes." Among the victims of the false reports was Captain Graves, the alleged Klan leader, who stated that he had traveled from Danville, Virginia, to look after a relative during Kirk's occupation. Kirk ordered Graves's release after his accuser fled town.[30]

Rodney's distrust of Kirk led him to doubt the Klan's very existence. "In regard to Ku-Kluxism I know very little," Rodney declared, "save that I have not been able to find any one, black or white, that has ever seen one, but only heard of them." Although Kirk claimed to have "plenty of evidence" that linked the Klan to numerous crimes, Rodney remained skeptical. "What the outrages are," he wrote, "or when they have been committed, is a mystery to me." Unknown to Rodney, abundant documentary evidence of the Klan's crimes was available at the Alamance County court-house. The clerk of court, William A. Albright, was receiving signed confessions from dozens of frightened Klansmen seeking amnesty. The defectors included a state legislator, as well as doctors, lawyers, and merchants.[31]

Given that Klan outrages in Alamance and Caswell had ceased by the time of his arrival at Yanceyville, Rodney could hardly be blamed for questioning the nightriders' shadowy existence. Indeed, the onset of military occupation and wholesale arrests—along with the prospect of military tribunals—intimidated the local Klan into disbanding, with some Klansmen fleeing the state. Yet eyewitnesses still refused to come forward, either because they sympathized with the Klan or feared retaliation. In contrast, Republican refugees such as state legislator Wilson Carey felt secure enough to return home. Federal commanders in the insurrectionary counties reported that election day passed uneventfully at their stations. In Caswell County, however, Colonel Kirk received numerous complaints that white farmers were discharging and refusing to pay black laborers because they had voted.[32]

The Klan's baleful influence was most evident in the statewide election returns, which indicated a resounding triumph for the Conservative Party. Thanks to a thirteen-thousand-vote drop-off in the Republican total from the presidential election of 1868, the Conservatives managed to elect their candidate for state attorney general with just a three-thousand-vote increase. The Conservatives also gained six of the state's seven congressional seats and almost a two-to-one majority in the state legislature. Of the fifteen counties added to the Conservative column, ten had experienced considerable Klan activity. While the Republicans remained strong in the east and in other counties where the army or militia was present, the rest of the state belonged to the Conservatives. The Klan's campaign of terror was by no means the sole reason for the Conservatives' electoral victory. Critics accused Holden of using the state militia to silence his political opponents. The failure of a multimillion-dollar state railroad bond initiative fueled charges of fraud and corruption against Republican incumbents, the critics conveniently forgetting that the bond had once enjoyed bipartisan support. Suffice it to say that the Klan's intimidation of Republican voters, combined with accusations of corruption and oppression against Holden and his administration, enabled the Conservatives to prevail at the polls.[33]

The citizens who most feared the consequences of the Conservatives' electoral triumph were the freedpeople. After the election, Colonel Hunt noted "a general feeling of uneasiness" among blacks in Raleigh. Fearing that a Conservative-dominated state legislature might undertake mass persecutions or even a return to slavery, many freedmen begged army officers for permanent jobs that would enable them to relocate. Rumors of a Conservative pogrom of freedpeople in the Tar Heel State spread to South Carolina, prompting concerned African Americans in Newberry to send a delegation to meet with the military commander in Raleigh. The members submitted a list of questions to Hunt: Were North Carolina blacks now required to carry passes? Were they publicly whipped? Were public schools closed to them? Were whites violating their constitutional and legal rights? Hunt attempted to reassure the delegation that their fears were groundless. He answered each question in the negative, yet noted that the state's public schools remained segregated. The delegation returned to Newberry with the answers they had sought, but it is doubtful their fears were put to rest.[34]

Another source of anxiety was the state militia, particularly among the white citizens of Raleigh, who found the presence of sixty black militiamen more than they could bear. The federal troops also became antagonized when a black militiaman shot a white soldier in the 4th U.S. Artillery. About 1 A.M. on August 8, a drunken bluecoat became confused and wandered toward the camp of the 1st North Carolina State Troops. A militia sentry twice ordered the soldier to halt and then fired once, wounding him in both legs.[35]

Capt. Royal T. Frank, the post commander, found it "incredible" that "troops so utterly wanting in discretion and intelligence" should be entrusted with loaded weapons on the outskirts of Raleigh. He directed the wounded soldier's commanding officer to ensure that the sentry was appropriately punished. Frank was soon disappointed, however. On August 9, the mayor of Raleigh held a hearing in which the sentry's superiors sustained his conduct. The officers' testimony satisfied the mayor, who ordered the sentry's release. Frank and his men were furious that neither the sentry nor his commanding officer was punished. Thereafter the federal and state troops at Raleigh maintained an uneasy truce, taking care not to stray too near the others' camp. The sensible solution would have been for one of the two forces to relocate. But Hunt would not move because his men occupied permanent barracks, and Colonel Clarke, the militia commander, claimed there were no other good camp sites near Raleigh.[36]

The situation at Yanceyville appeared equally bad. While no shootings occurred, the federal and state troops often traded insults and sometimes threw rocks at each other. Captain Rodney dismissed Kirk's militia as "nothing more than an armed mob." He warned that Kirk's men had threatened to burn the town and maintained that "nothing but a strong force of United States troops" could prevent them from carrying out their threat. For Rodney and many other federal soldiers in North Carolina, the enemy was not the Ku Klux Klan but the state militia.[37]

Despite Rodney's opinion to the contrary, the state militia was more than just an "armed mob." The true source of the difficulty between the army and the militia was the absence of a unified command structure. With two distinct forces operating in such close proximity under different orders, conflicts were bound to arise. An experienced officer such as Colonel Hunt entrusted with overall command of the army and the state militia might have averted the difficulties that arose at Raleigh and Yanceyville, but the best solution would have been to deploy the state and federal troops at separate posts. Such a disposition would have made maximum use of the available force. Although Captain Frank correctly observed that the army's "presence did much to allay excitement and inspire confidence and a sense of security," the mere presence of federal soldiers was not enough to end the Klan's reign of terror. In truth, the state militia broke up the Klan in Alamance and Caswell while the army watched on the sidelines.[38]

A week after the election, the army found itself on the verge of a confrontation with the governor and the state militia over writs of habeas corpus issued by U.S. district judge George W. Brooks. In mid-July, Holden had refused to honor several writs issued by state supreme court chief justice Richmond M. Pearson for the delivery of Kirk's prisoners. After Pearson declared his inability to enforce the writs, the prisoners' attorneys petitioned Brooks. Basing his action on the Habeas Corpus Act of 1867 and the due process clause of the Fourteenth Amendment, the district judge issued writs for Kirk's prisoners to be brought before him. The two measures Brooks cited were meant to protect supporters of Reconstruction but now served its enemies, an irony that Holden failed to appreciate. In an August 7 telegram to Grant, the governor argued that the federal courts had no jurisdiction in state murder cases, and he declared his intention to hold the prisoners "unless the army of the United States, under your orders, should demand them." Holden sent this message under the assumption that the president would uphold his course of action.[39]

While Holden awaited the president's reply, Brooks instructed U.S. marshal Samuel T. Carrow to serve Kirk the writs. Certain that Kirk would resist, Carrow requested Captain Frank to provide him with a detachment of federal troops. Colonel Hunt was present when Carrow's request arrived at Frank's headquarters. He suggested that they pay the marshal a visit. Carrow told the two officers that he needed federal soldiers because he could not assemble a posse large enough to intimidate Kirk, who had thus far managed to evade him. Hunt suggested that Carrow ask the governor to suspend Kirk or have Kirk's second-in-command arrest him. Should Holden or Kirk refuse to cooperate, Hunt told Carrow, he would intervene with federal soldiers. Hunt's intervention proved unnecessary, however, for Carrow soon learned that he no longer had to serve the writs.[40]

On August 8, Holden was shocked to learn that Grant's attorney general, Amos T. Akerman, had ruled against him. In truth, Akerman privately sympathized with his fellow scalawag. Although a longtime resident of Georgia and a Confederate veteran, the New Hampshire-born and Dartmouth-educated Akerman was as zealous a foe of the Klan as Holden was. But Akerman saw no alternative. "I do not see how [Brooks] can refuse to issue the writ, if the petition makes out a case for it," he wrote. "I advise that the State authorities yield to the U.S. Judiciary." Unwilling to challenge the president, Holden directed Kirk to deliver the prisoners to Pearson in Raleigh and Brooks in Salisbury. Having assumed that a military tribunal would try the defendants, Holden and other state officials were unprepared for this contingency. Brooks had to release the prisoners before him because the state attorney general failed to present evidence to justify their detention. In Raleigh, the state prosecutors managed to convince Pearson to arraign forty-nine prisoners, yet not one had to stand trial. Although the guilty went unpunished, Holden had succeeded in breaking the power of the Klan in the insurrectionary counties.[41]

On September 13, General Meade discontinued the temporary District of North Carolina in the belief that the emergency was over. Colonel Hunt returned to his permanent post, as did four companies of artillery sent to aid in suppressing the Klan. One company each of the 4th remained at Fort Macon, Fort Johnston, Raleigh, and Yanceyville. In October, Captain Frank and the two companies of the 8th U.S. Infantry at Raleigh and Graham were transferred to New York City. By then, Alamance County had become so peaceful that a company of the 4th Artillery sent to Graham remained there just a few weeks before it received orders to move elsewhere.[42]

In September, Holden disbanded the militia. Two months later, he rescinded the insurrection proclamations for Alamance and Caswell. In his last annual message to the General Assembly, Holden declared that "peace and good order have been restored to all parts of the State." Holden's declaration proved premature, for he continued to receive reports of Klan outrages from across the state.[43]

In December, Holden himself became the target of a Klan attack launched from within the Conservative-dominated General Assembly. Spearheading the assault was Frederick N. Strudwick, a freshman representative from Orange County and the would-be chief assassin of state senator T. M. Shoffner. On December 9, Strudwick introduced a resolution to impeach Holden. Ten days later, the house passed the resolution, as well as eight articles of impeachment. The first two articles accused Holden of violating the state constitution by using the militia to oppress the people on the pretext of quelling a nonexistent insurrection. The remaining six articles cited more specific charges, including the governor's unlawful suspension of the writ of habeas corpus. The trial lasted from December 23, 1870, to March 22, 1871. More than one hundred defense witnesses testified, including many victims of Klan raids. Their chilling testimony failed to alter the fact that the Conservatives possessed enough votes to secure Holden's conviction. A straight party vote ensured that the first two articles fell short of the necessary two-thirds majority, yet enough Republicans believed that Holden had overreached his authority to convict him of the other six charges. The senate then voted to expel him from office. Holden thus earned the dubious distinction of being the first state governor ousted by impeachment. A victim of political assassination, he was both the last and the highest-ranking casualty of the so-called Kirk-Holden War. Barred from state office for life and hounded by lawsuits, Holden moved to Washington, D.C., where he briefly resumed his career as a newspaperman. He later returned to Raleigh and served as the state capital's postmaster.[44]

Although Holden's successor, Lieutenant Governor Tod R. Caldwell, was a likeminded Republican, he had to labor under political handicaps engineered by the Conservative majority. Unlike his predecessor, Caldwell lacked the veto power and therefore could not block the Conservatives' legislative agenda. Indeed, the opposition wasted no time in divesting Caldwell of his emergency powers. During the impeachment trial, the General Assembly repealed the Shoffner Act and most of the 1868 militia law, ensuring that Caldwell could not mobilize the state troops. As if Caldwell needed reminding, Holden's downfall served notice that the new governor would meet the same fate if he proved obnoxious to the Conservative-dominated legislature. One development that gave Caldwell cause for hope was a new statute outlawing secret organizations such as the Klan and the Union League, even though the latter had already ceased to exist in North Carolina. But he was soon disappointed by the lawmakers' reluctance to enforce the new law, despite the nightriders' ongoing activity. Powerless to combat the Klan, Caldwell had to turn to the U.S. Army for assistance. Thanks to the efforts of Congress, the new governor would find the army far more cooperative than Holden had.[45]

During the impeachment proceedings against Holden, Congress had undertaken an investigation of Klan outrages in North Carolina. On December 16, the U.S. Senate passed a resolution requesting Grant to submit all the information in his possession regarding politically motivated crimes committed by "organized bodies of disloyal and evil-disposed persons." The president, in turn, sent an order down the army's chain of command directing Col. Henry J. Hunt and all post commanders in North Carolina to furnish reports on the subject. Their written responses betrayed little or no knowledge of the Klan, but that did not prevent Hunt and a former subordinate, Capt. Royal T. Frank, from venturing opinions as to the nightriders' intentions. The two officers arrived at very different conclusions. During the habeas corpus hearings in August, Hunt had sat at the judges' bench beside Chief Justice Pearson and had heard testimony regarding the assassination of state senator John W. Stephens. The prosecution failed to convince Hunt that Stephens's murder was politi-

Governor Tod R. Caldwell (Courtesy of the North Carolina State Archives)

cally motivated or that the accused belonged to a secret political organization. Rather, Hunt believed that, in fact, Klansmen were vigilantes
"used to punish theft, burglaries, insults to women, and other offenses
in no way connected with politics." He further concluded that their sup-

posed crimes "were greatly exaggerated and misrepresented" for political advantage. Frank, on the other hand, had a far better understanding of the Ku Klux conspiracy. He believed that in addition to causing the Union League to disband, the Klan summarily punished crimes committed by blacks against whites and that it served the interests of the Conservative Party. As for the murder of Senator Stephens, Frank could find "no other assignable reason" than political partisanship.[46]

The officers' reports comprised only a small portion of the relevant documents in President Grant's possession. On New Year's Day 1871, Holden sent Grant a sheaf of papers that included official state acts and proclamations, outrage casualty lists, trial transcripts, victims' affidavits, and Klansmen's confessions. Grant sent the documents to Congress along with a stack of army reports and official correspondence. On January 19, 1871, the Senate appointed a committee to continue the investigation. Because the Forty-first Congress was about to adjourn and most of the information provided by the president dealt with North Carolina, the committee decided to focus on the Tar Heel State. The investigation centered on the two insurrectionary counties, Alamance and Caswell. Fifty-two witnesses testified before the committee, including Conservatives and Republicans, blacks and whites, civil officials and army officers, Klansmen and Klan victims. On March 10, the committee released its report as the Forty-second Congress began a special session to deal with the Klan crisis. The majority report found that the many organizations known as the Ku Klux Klan were indeed political in nature and they employed intimidation, whipping, and murder to benefit the Conservative Party. The report further stated that the organizations routinely ordered members to break the law and then shielded them from criminal prosecution. As a result, not one member had been convicted of a crime. Although the committee made no recommendations, their report brought to light the extent of the Klan's campaign of terror in North Carolina. It now remained for the Forty-second Congress to act on this information.[47]

On February 28, 1871, Congress passed the Second Enforcement Act, a set of tough regulations aimed more at ending Democratic election fraud in northern cities than at suppressing nightriders. The Klan, however, was clearly the target of the Third Enforcement Act, which passed on April 20, after the House had rejected a more stringent version of the bill. The law answered Grant's request for legislation to "secure life[,] liberty[,] and property" in the South. Aptly dubbed the "Ku Klux Act," the measure targeted secret organizations that used intimidation and violence to achieve their objectives. Whenever Klan conspiracies proved too powerful for the civil authorities to suppress, the Ku Klux Act authorized the president to call in the military and suspend the writ of habeas corpus in the insurrectionary district. To silence critics eager to accuse him of establishing a military dictatorship, Grant suggested that Congress limit the habeas corpus clause to one year. Attorney General Amos T. Akerman thought the Ku Klux Act at last put the federal government's efforts to suppress the Klan on the right footing. "Really these combinations amount to war," Akerman wrote, "and [they] cannot be effectually crushed on any other theory."[48]

Although the original Enforcement Act authorized Grant to employ the military to suppress the Klan, he had steadfastly refused to invoke it. Holden's downfall convinced the president that he—like so many military commanders in the South—had underestimated the Klan insurgency in North Carolina and other southern states. Two additional considerations had discouraged Grant from playing an active role against the Klan in 1870. The former general did not wish to give the Democratic opposition a pretext to brand him an American Caesar, nor did he wish to encourage Republican governors in the South to regard the bluecoats as a federal police force. By early 1871, the president concluded that his policy of executive restraint had failed. When Governor Robert K. Scott of South Carolina appealed to Grant for help in suppressing the Klan, the president proved far more cooperative than he had been with Holden. On March 24, Grant issued a proclamation commanding the insurgents in South Carolina "to disperse and retire peaceably" within twenty days or face the consequences. He also sent three companies of the 7th U.S. Cavalry to the Palmetto State.[49]

In North Carolina, the Ku Klux Klan continued to terrorize counties in the piedmont and the foothills. In the west, Cleveland and Rutherford were hardest hit. The two counties were remote and sparsely populated, and wartime animosities remained strong. Conservatives held most of the political offices in Cleveland County, while a biracial coalition of Republicans predominated in Rutherford. During the war, Unionists had joined the Heroes of America and later formed Union League chapters with local blacks. Ex-Confederates countered by forming ad hoc militia companies that evolved into Ku Klux Klan units. Bordering the most Klan-infested region of South Carolina, Klansmen in Cleveland and Rutherford counties belonged to the same order—the Invisible Empire—as their comrades to the south. They sometimes combined for large-scale raids on either side of the state line.[50]

On December 27, 1870, superior court judge George W. Logan, writing from Rutherford County, warned Governor Caldwell that the local Klan had renewed its outrages after a brief hiatus. The leading Republican in Rutherford, Logan had been appointed to the Ninth District bench despite the opposition of thirty-two Conservative lawyers, who had unsuccessfully petitioned for his removal on the grounds of incompetence and bias. "I have no confidence in County officers nor in *any state Militia*," Logan told Caldwell, "& I think the only force to be effectual must be *blue coats*." Caldwell promised to do all in his power to assist Logan in bringing the Klan to justice but stopped short of pledging assistance from the army.[51]

On April 9, Logan informed the governor that the Klan had committed numerous outrages in Cleveland and Rutherford since his last letter. Thus far, he wrote, the victims had refused to identify their assailants for fear of retaliation. Logan noted that the most recent casualties, Aaron V. Biggerstaff and his daughter, Mary Ann Norville, had been assaulted by forty Klansmen the previous night. The sixty-year-old Biggerstaff was an outspoken Republican, a former Union League member, and a "tory" who had aided escaped federal prisoners during the war. He was also embroiled in a longstanding feud with his half-brother Samuel, a former Confederate and an alleged Klansman. After the Biggerstaff raid, the nightriders warned Logan not to enter Cleveland County. He wisely postponed the upcoming term there and then urged Caldwell to call for federal troops. Referring Logan's letter to President Grant, the governor expressed no confidence in the civil authorities' ability to suppress the Klan. Caldwell therefore asked Grant to dispatch a company of U.S. cavalry to the troubled region.[52]

The president seemed in no hurry to respond to Caldwell's appeal, however. Three weeks later, J. B. Carpenter, the Ninth District clerk of court and the editor of the pro-Republican *Rutherford Star*, wrote Grant. "We have anxiously waited to hear from you," Carpenter began, "as our Country is in a deplorable condition. Murder, arson & midnight outrages on peaceable citizens is rampant. There is scarcely a night, but that some person is whipped or scourged by the Ku Klux." Carpenter then repeated Caldwell's plea for federal soldiers. Grant sent the letter to the War Department with orders for the commander in North Carolina to investigate Carpenter's allegations. After a leisurely journey down the chain of com-

Maj. Charles H. Morgan
(U.S. Army Military
History Institute)

mand, Carpenter's letter landed on the post commander's desk in Raleigh in early June. By then, Carpenter was insisting that U.S. troops were no longer needed at Rutherfordton, an action he would soon regret.[53]

While the governor waited in vain for word from Grant, Biggerstaff brought charges against a number of his assailants, including his half-brother Samuel and several of his nephews. In May, deputy U.S. marshal Joseph G. Hester arrested fifteen of the suspects and handed them over to J. L. Moore, the U.S. commissioner for Cleveland County. Maj. Charles H. Morgan of the 4th U.S. Artillery had provided Hester with a detachment of ten federal soldiers to assist him in making the arrests. Since February 1, Morgan had been the commandant of the Post of Raleigh and the senior army officer in North Carolina. A graduate of West Point (class of 1857), the thirty-seven-year-old Morgan had served as a staff officer in the Army of the Potomac during the Civil War.[54]

Moore ordered a hearing for the following Monday and then placed the prisoners in the custody of Sheriff B. F. Logan. Unknown to Moore, Logan also happened to be a local Klan leader. The sheriff immediately released his prisoners after they swore to appear before the U.S. commissioner as scheduled. They decided to make the most of their freedom by ensuring that Aaron Biggerstaff would not testify against them.[55]

In the meantime, Biggerstaff and his family were en route from Rutherford County to the Cleveland County courthouse at Shelby. Due to a late start, the Biggerstaff party had to stop for the night at a deserted house about ten miles from town. A few hours later, the nightriders struck. The outlaws broke Biggerstaff's arm as they dragged him from the wagon in which he was sleeping, and then hanged him by the neck until he swore not to testify against them. During the attack, Biggerstaff's nephew received a severe head wound. The other family members managed to escape into the night. Early the next morning, the Biggerstaff party headed back to Rutherford. On Monday, the accused appeared before Commissioner Moore as ordered, but the witnesses of course failed to materialize. Moore had to release the suspects for lack of evidence. Thus far, the Klan in Rutherford and Cleveland had succeeded in preventing the civil judiciary from prosecuting them.[56]

On May 17, Caldwell received several reports of the second Biggerstaff assault and showed them to Morgan. The major immediately ordered Company A of the 4th U.S. Artillery to Shelby. The troops arrived on the twenty-seventh. In reporting the deployment to department headquarters, Morgan noted that he needed to send "more than one company to meet the demands made upon the Governor." Morgan, however, had no more troops to spare, for he had only three companies of the 4th Artillery at his disposal. Two companies that served as the Fort Macon prison guard were unavailable for detached duty. Morgan also bore in mind that the Klan remained active in several piedmont counties. In Chatham County, a railroad contractor and Republican activist named William R. Howle had to abandon a construction project because repeated Klan raids had terrified his crew and disrupted his schedule. At least a half-dozen men and women were whipped, and one man was shot. Howle told Morgan that the outlaws sought to intimidate Republican voters and therefore violated the Ku Klux Act. Suspecting that the attackers might be vigilantes out to punish disreputable persons, Morgan asked if any of the victims fit that description. Howle assured him they did not.[57]

On May 4, Morgan sent a detachment of nine men under Lt. Harry C. Cushing to Chatham County to assist the newly deputized Howle in making arrests. Determined to bring his tormentors to justice, Howle had obtained an appointment as a deputy U.S. marshal. After a thirty-mile train ride from Raleigh, the detachment arrived at Haywood and then set out on foot. Howle arrested three suspects, but the remainder were warned of the bluecoats' approach and made their escape on horseback. Arriving at the site of the worst outrage, Cushing noted that the house bore unmistakable evidence of a Klan raid. The door was riddled with shot, and the furniture and walls inside were pocked with bullet holes. The three white women who lived there were covered with cuts and bruises, the result of knotted hickory clubs, bird shot, and flying debris. Too terrified by their ordeal to sleep in their own beds, the women now spent their nights in the woods.[58]

Concluding that the alarm was sounded and that his foot soldiers stood no chance of overtaking fugitives on horseback, Cushing returned to Raleigh that evening with his three prisoners. Morgan accused Howle of "making a false statement" after learning that the white "women involved are degraded characters, two of them having one or more black children each." The major doubted that "politics had any thing to do with the affair, or that it came fairly under the [Third] enforcement act." The U.S. commissioner handling the case thought otherwise, indicting all three prisoners under the Ku Klux Act. Even if they were tried, Morgan asserted, the prisoners would escape conviction, for each had an alibi. The major proved correct.[59]

In early June, Morgan received a copy of *Rutherford Star* editor J. B. Carpenter's May 10 letter to Grant, along with orders to investigate conditions in Cleveland and Rutherford. Morgan therefore arranged to travel to Shelby on June 12. Just before his departure, Morgan met with Carpenter, who was en route to Washington to testify before a congressional committee investigating Klan atrocities. Contradicting his letter to Grant, Carpenter stated that Rutherford no longer needed federal troops. He argued that the local Republicans enjoyed a comfortable majority and could therefore take care of themselves. Carpenter and many other Rutherford Republicans had lowered their guard after a public meeting called in response to the Biggerstaff raids. During the meeting, several prominent Conservatives had denounced the outrages and passed resolutions calling for an end to Klan violence. Before the meeting, the scalawags had posted a night watch over Rutherfordton, but they discontinued the practice in the belief that they no longer needed the guard. The Republicans discovered too late that they had been lulled into a false sense of security.[60]

Reassured by Carpenter's assessment, Morgan was shocked to learn a few days later that on Sunday night, June 11, the Ku Klux Klan had raided Rutherfordton. Morgan was at Shelby when he received the news, and he hurried to Rutherfordton to investigate. Eyewitnesses indicated that about one hundred nightriders stole into town in three groups amid a heavy downpour. The first group wrecked the office and presses of the

Rutherford Star; the second made a futile search for Aaron Biggerstaff and Mayor Robert Logan, the judge's son; and the third abducted Republican state legislator James M. Justice. The leaders threatened to kill Justice if he participated in the upcoming political campaign and then released him. Morgan summoned a ten-man detachment from Shelby to Rutherford-ton, ordering the rest of the company to follow a week later.[61]

The Rutherfordton raid convinced Morgan that Klansmen were political terrorists, as well as vigilantes. During his investigation of the nightriders in Cleveland and Rutherford, Morgan interviewed both Conservatives and Republicans in the belief that he stood to learn as much from the Klan's supporters as from the victims. At Rutherfordton, he saw firsthand the physical and psychological devastation of a Klan raid. Morgan thus gained a keener understanding of the Klan than his predecessors had. They had relied mostly on rumors and secondhand reports for their intelligence, seldom venturing beyond the confines of their posts. The knowledge derived from personal investigation, coupled with the discretion allowed under Grant's May 3 proclamation, enabled Morgan to make effective use of his force against the Klan.[62]

As soon as the troop detachment from Shelby arrived at Rutherfordton, deputy U.S. marshal Royal T. Bosher requested the bluecoats' assistance in arresting thirty-five suspects in Cleveland and Rutherford counties linked to the Biggerstaff assaults. A former state detective and militia captain, Bosher was a veteran of anti-Klan campaigns dating back to 1869. With the aid of the federal troops, Bosher arrested thirty men, including Aaron Biggerstaff's half-brother Samuel. The commander of the detachment, Lt. Francis V. Greene, reported that the prisoners offered no resistance, a few suspects even turning themselves in. "They all protested their innocence," a skeptical Greene commented, "some men before they were told there was a warrant for them." Using witnesses as guards, Bosher escorted his prisoners to Raleigh, while Greene and his detachment returned to Rutherfordton.[63]

Anticipating many more arrests and mindful that his foot soldiers were ill equipped for such duty, Morgan requested a company of cavalry. On June 28, Company C of the 7th U.S. Cavalry was transferred from South Carolina to Rutherfordton. From July 7 to September 4, detachments of Company C made over forty arrests, some with the aid of civilian posses. The prisoners included Rutherford County Klan leader Randolph A. Shotwell, who maintained that his bluecoat guards openly sympathized with his plight and had once chided him for failing to escape when given

Randolph A. Shotwell (Courtesy of the North Carolina State Archives)

the chance. Shotwell noted that they also smuggled whiskey into his cell. Many prisoners were freed on bond, but Shotwell and other suspected ringleaders had to remain in the county jail. In the meantime, U.S. commissioner Nathan Scoggins conducted preliminary hearings, assisted by several local Republicans. Morgan thought the participation of so many Klan victims lent the proceedings a vindictive tone. For that reason, he rejected a proposal to form a Republican militia company armed with Spencer carbines sent by the secretary of war.[64]

During the hearings, about sixty Klansmen voluntarily surrendered, while Cleveland County sheriff B. F. Logan and many others fled the state. Morgan believed the defectors thus hoped "to avoid the jurisdiction of the U.S. Courts," reflecting the nightriders' intent to avoid a direct confrontation with the federal government. He thought that two to three hundred persons would be implicated in the Cleveland-Rutherford Klan conspiracy, an estimate that ultimately fell short of the mark. To aid Morgan, General McDowell made available the three companies of the 4th U.S. Artillery at Forts Macon and Johnston. He also transferred to Raleigh one company each of the 2nd and the 4th from Fort Monroe, Virginia, and two companies of the 4th from Fort McHenry, Maryland. "Exercise your own judgment as to posting the troops," McDowell instructed Morgan. Although he would have preferred another company of cavalry, Morgan was nonetheless grateful for the reinforcements.[65]

Company C of the 7th Cavalry proved so successful in making arrests that the county jail in Rutherfordton soon became overcrowded. Some of the prisoners were transferred to the McDowell County jail in Marion, where their comrades promptly liberated them. Judge Logan and Commissioner Scoggins understandably credited rumors that a Klan jailbreak at Rutherfordton appeared imminent. On August 7, they appealed to Morgan for another company of soldiers, but he was convinced the troops already there were sufficient to deter the Klan. Morgan, however, promised to transfer the prisoners to Raleigh as soon as he received authorization to do so. The federals later learned that members of a South Carolina den had sought to free Shotwell by posing as U.S. soldiers. They apparently had obtained some blue uniforms from deserters of the 7th U.S. Cavalry. An officer of the 7th in South Carolina, Maj. Lewis Merrill, believed that the Klan had enticed some of his men to desert by offering them sanctuary. In any event, the blue-clad nightriders withdrew from Rutherfordton when they discovered that real federal troops guarded the jail.[66]

Morgan proved more obliging when federal judges Hugh L. Bond and George W. Brooks requested escorts for fifty-six suspected Klansmen being transferred from Marion and Rutherfordton to Raleigh for trial. On August 17, Morgan transferred Company K of the 4th Artillery from Fort Macon to Rutherfordton; a week later, he dispatched Company C of the 4th to Marion the day after its arrival from Fort McHenry. A federal grand jury indicted the fifty-six defendants under the Ku Klux Act. The defendants stood trial in the U.S. Circuit Court in Raleigh. Morgan noted that the Klan trial was causing "more uneasiness and disturbance among the people [of Raleigh] than at any time since I have been here." He attributed the unrest to "very industriously spread" rumors that "the prosecution is a political one against innocent parties."[67]

While en route to South Carolina in mid-September, Attorney General Amos T. Akerman made a brief stop in Raleigh to oversee the prosecution. Akerman knew that the Raleigh trials would establish a precedent, for they were among the first Klan trials in a federal court. The outcome pleased him immensely. Of the forty-three defendants tried for the Biggerstaff and Rutherfordton raids, twenty-five were convicted, including Randolph Shotwell, who received a $5,000 fine and six years at hard labor. Shotwell and several other ringleaders were incarcerated in the federal penitentiary in Albany, New York. As Akerman had hoped, the successful prosecution of Klansmen in Raleigh established a solid precedent, but after the departure in October of the energetic Judge Bond, the docket soon became backlogged. The mounting caseload failed to discourage Commissioner Scoggins, who continued to issue arrest warrants and hold preliminary hearings in Rutherfordton and Shelby.[68]

In October 1871, Randolph Shotwell turned state's evidence in a bid for clemency but had to wait two years for a presidential pardon. The former Klan leader nevertheless advised his onetime followers and fellow inmates to confess their crimes, declaring that the Klan's oath of secrecy no longer bound them. The numerous arrests, combined with Shotwell's announcement, triggered a deluge of confessions and accusations by Klansmen seeking immunity from prosecution. As a result, the Klan in southwestern North Carolina soon collapsed. During the autumn of 1871, federal troops in Cleveland, Rutherford, and Gaston counties devoted most of their energies to apprehending fugitive nightriders from South Carolina, who had fled the state in response to Grant's suspension of the writ of habeas corpus in nine counties of the Palmetto State. Although the Klan in North Carolina appeared to have disbanded, in March

1872, Judge Logan contended that his district was "still infested" with nightriders. The U.S. attorney for North Carolina, D. H. Starbuck, disputed Logan's assertion, stating that he had received no reports of outrages within his jurisdiction since the September Klan trials in Raleigh.[69]

Even so, former Klansmen in Cleveland County attempted to revive the order after several Ku Klux defendants returned from Raleigh with news that the judge had dismissed their cases without trial. On Christmas Day 1871, a procession of mounted men in disguises began to form on Shelby's main street. The masked riders attracted the attention of the commanding officer at Shelby, Lt. Albion Howe of the 4th U.S. Artillery, who also noticed a large crowd gathering in the center of town. Many of the onlookers were drunk, and the mood soon turned ugly. Preparing for the worst, Howe summoned his men and deployed them for riot control. The riders told Howe that they were merely forming for a parade, but the lieutenant declared the horsemen in violation of the Ku Klux Act and ordered them to disperse. Although the riders obeyed Howe's order, many in the crowd drew their revolvers and threatened to fire on Howe's detachment. Howe stood his ground and, as tempers cooled, the crowd drifted away. Despite some tense moments, the last—and shortest—ride of the Cleveland County Klan ended peacefully.[70]

On the eve of the 1871 state election, Morgan attempted to end the nightriders' intimidation of Republican voters in central North Carolina, a perennial Klan stronghold. At Governor Caldwell's request, he stationed a detachment of the 4th U.S. Artillery in Robeson County and Company K of the 2nd Artillery in Chatham, Moore, and Harnett counties. Meanwhile, General McDowell recommended that Morgan send a troop detachment to Yanceyville in Caswell County. Despite Morgan's assurance that he had received no reports of disturbances in Caswell, McDowell thought it a worthwhile precaution. Should the detachment prove necessary, it "will be well to have sent it," the general advised. "If not needed[,] no harm will be done." McDowell's telegram indicates that he had come to appreciate the benefits of preventive measures against the Klan—a practice he and Meade should have adopted one year earlier.[71]

The commander of Company K, Capt. Samuel N. Benjamin, reported that the August 3 election "passed off very quietly" in Chatham, Moore, and Harnett. He noted that the Klan had been inactive the past six months after committing a series of outrages the previous winter. Despite the recent lull, residents believed that the reign of terror was far from over.

A Klansman, circa 1870 (Courtesy of the North Carolina State Archives)

"The negroes, and many whites are very much afraid of the Ku Klux," Benjamin noted, "and are also afraid to come into camp and give information for fear of being whipped" in retaliation. Benjamin therefore traveled to the homes of Klan victims and compiled a list of atrocities that he sent to Morgan. The blacks Benjamin interviewed admitted to being too frightened to vote in 1870, but they found the current election a different matter, thanks to the presence of federal troops and the recent arrests of Klansmen by U.S. marshals and Secret Service detectives. Company K stayed about a week and then returned to Raleigh on August 9.[72]

The 1871 election returns indicated that 181,359 North Carolina voters cast their ballots, the state's largest turnout to date. The fact that it was an off-year election made the record even more impressive. In 1871, eleven thousand more Republican voters went to the polls than had done so the year before, just two thousand fewer than in the presidential election of 1868. The increased turnout—combined with a three-thousand-vote drop-off in the Conservative column—gave the Republicans a nine-thousand-vote majority, which defeated a Conservative-sponsored referendum for a state constitutional convention. The result shocked the Conservatives, who had become overconfident after the previous year's electoral triumph. The Republican resurgence of 1871 was misleading, however. Republicans comprised more than two-thirds of the thirty-six thousand registered voters who did not go to the polls, suggesting that many still feared the consequences of doing so.[73]

By the fall of 1871, the Klan in North Carolina appeared to be in full retreat, albeit with the notable exception of Sampson County. At Kinyons Point, about thirty nightriders broke into every cabin in the all-black community, confiscating firearms and making a futile search for two freedmen, Gabriel Rialls and Menus Herring. The Klansmen had to content themselves with raping several women, burning a cabin, and threatening to kill everyone who was not gone within two weeks. Thanks to careless or nonexistent disguises, the victims recognized eight of their assailants. After his return home, Rialls obtained a warrant for the men from the local justice of the peace and presented it to Judge Daniel L. Russell Jr. of the superior court at Wilmington. In the hearing that followed, Russell granted the defendants a continuance and a change of venue to Brunswick County. In the meantime, they conspired to silence their accusers.[74]

On September 23, Herring, Rialls, and two friends were lured into an ambush near Clinton, the Sampson County seat. The bushwhackers killed

Herring with a shotgun blast. They severely wounded Rialls and another man, but the two somehow escaped. The fourth man fled unharmed. Several days later, Rialls went to U.S. commissioner Edgar H. McQuigg and swore out a warrant for a bushwhacker he recognized, as well as a second warrant for the eight defendants awaiting trial. The incident soon came to the attention of Governor Caldwell, who immediately notified Morgan. At the request of the U.S. marshal, Morgan sent a ten-man detachment of the 4th U.S. Artillery to Sampson County to make the arrests.[75]

During their mission to apprehend the Klan suspects, the federal troops encountered numerous obstacles. At the railroad depot, the detachment needed more than an hour to obtain transportation to Clinton. During the delay, the deputy U.S. marshal handling the case informed the commander, Lt. Edward Field, that he had seen a rider gallop off toward Clinton, apparently to warn the suspects of the soldiers' arrival. The detachment reached Clinton after nightfall, compelling Field to wait until daybreak to begin making arrests. The next morning, Field had to undergo another long delay in finding transportation. As a result, the deputy marshal made only two arrests, the remaining suspects having fled. Field assumed that the delays were intended to buy time for the fugitives' escape. He found blacks and whites equally uncooperative. Local freedpeople told him they had heard whites express the wish "that the damned Yankees would get a bullet through them." The blacks Field met seemed friendly and supportive, yet they were "afraid to tell what they know, or to point out parties against whom there are warrants." Even the intrepid Gabriel Rialls, who served as Field's guide, told the lieutenant that he intended to leave Sampson County as soon as the army no longer needed his services. Field learned that many other blacks had already left. Believing that he could do nothing more, a disappointed Field led his detachment back to Raleigh. The two prisoners meanwhile appeared before Commissioner McQuigg, who had to release them for lack of evidence.[76]

In his report, Field held his commanding officer to account for the suspects' escape. "I would respectfully call Major Morgan's attention to the impossibility of making any important arrests with Infantry, and without transportation." Field noted that citizens had assisted him "most reluctantly and grudgingly," placing "every possible delay" in his path. In future operations against the Klan, the lieutenant recommended "a small force of cavalry, avoiding Rail Roads and not requiring 3 or 4 telegraphic messages [from headquarters] to set them in motion (which messages are generally seen by outside parties)." Morgan heeded his subordinate's frank advice but resisted the temptation to send in another detachment at once. Instead, he decided to give the fugitives an opportunity to return to their homes. He also requested thirty cavalry horses with appropriate arms and equipment for his special detachments. The hardware arrived on schedule, but the horses were delayed until the end of the year. Morgan therefore had to scramble to provide mounts for the next detachment bound for Sampson.[77]

On November 17, Morgan sent Company H of the 4th U.S. Artillery to Fayetteville. Two days later, a detachment commanded by Lt. John S. McEwan traveled to Sampson County to assist the U.S. commissioner and the deputy marshal in arresting suspects. McEwan's encounter with the Klan could scarcely have differed more than Field's. As he entered the Klan-infested district north of Clinton, his force was beset by over forty nightriders eager to confess. Reports of the Ku Klux trials in Raleigh evidently had convinced many Klansmen in Sampson County to make a clean breast. "From present appearances," McEwan informed Attorney General Akerman, "we will not have anything to do for the next ten days but hear confessions." By November 28, McEwan had taken more than one hundred confessions, many from young men who claimed they were threatened or deceived into joining a secret organization they knew nothing about. Regardless of the truth of their claims, the defectors were sincere in their desire to distance themselves from the order.[78]

The main body of Company H meanwhile marched from Fayetteville to Clinton, where it remained until December 9. By then, the Klan in Sampson had collapsed. As a precaution, Morgan established a temporary post at Clinton and left a detachment of fifteen men under Lt. Samuel R. Jones. The federal troops remained until April 1, 1872, occasionally assisting the U.S. marshal in arresting Klan suspects. Morgan was proud of the army's accomplishment in suppressing the Klan in North Carolina. "I think it has been clearly demonstrated by events in this State," he asserted, "that nothing makes any impression on the order except the presence of US Troops." Morgan, of course, was mistaken. In 1870, the state militia had suppressed the Klan in Alamance and Caswell, but he was not present to witness it.[79]

The federal government had waited two full years to act against the Klan. In 1871, Congress passed the Ku Klux Act, President Grant authorized the army to assist federal law enforcement agents in arresting nightriders, and the Justice Department prosecuted its first Klan cases. Once committed, the army, U.S. marshals, Secret Service detectives, and federal prosecutors went about their work with a will. By the end of 1871, federal officers had made twelve hundred arrests in North Carolina under the Enforcement Acts. The federal judiciary found 763 indictments that resulted in 23 guilty pleas, 24 convictions, 13 acquittals, and 9 dropped cases. But as the case backlog mounted, the Justice Department lost interest in tackling Ku Klux cases. In 1873, Attorney General George H. Williams instructed federal attorneys in North Carolina to prosecute only new cases. By the close of 1874, Williams ordered all remaining Klan cases dismissed from the docket, in effect, granting clemency to hundreds of former Klansmen.[80]

The initial success of the federal prosecutions inspired superior court judge Albion W. Tourgée to reopen the Wyatt Outlaw case and several others in December 1871. The grand jury indicted sixty-three persons, but the Conservative-dominated legislature blocked the indictments by repealing the law that supported them. To ensure that no Klansmen would go to trial, Conservatives introduced another bill to extend amnesty to all members of secret organizations. Republicans regarded the inclusion of the Heroes of America and the Union League as devious, for none of their members faced criminal charges. The General Assembly passed the new Amnesty Act in 1873, absolving Klansmen of all crimes committed while in disguise.[81]

The Klan had ceased to exist in North Carolina, but the organization had served its purpose. The Conservatives—or Democrats, as they increasingly called themselves in the 1870s—had the Klan's three-year reign of terror to thank for their political resurgence. Yet state Democratic leaders had found the Klan too volatile to control. Although grateful for the Klan's support, the Democratic elite was no less thankful for its demise.

In addition to suppressing the Klan, the army attempted to subdue the Lowry band, an elusive outlaw gang that had terrorized central Robeson County since the Civil War. Most of the gang members were Lumbee Indians who lived in a swampy and densely wooded district known as Scuffletown. The state government had classified the Lumbees as "free persons of color," which prohibited them from bearing arms. During the war, the state conscripted military-age Lumbee males into labor battalions and put them to work on the coastal fortifications south of Wilmington. Fearful of wasting away on the yellow fever–ridden coast, many Scuffletonian laborers deserted and hid in the swamps back home, a practice that Unionists called "lying out." The Lumbee deserters soon discovered that they were sharing their hiding places with escaped Union prisoners from the Confederate stockade near Florence, South Carolina. To obtain provisions, the Lowry band united with the bluecoats and preyed on the area's prosperous white planters. The bandits shared their bounty with starving neighbors, a practice that ensured them early warning of approaching danger. In the meantime, the Lowry band killed two Confederate officials, including a conscription officer who had dispatched three of their young relatives. On March 4, 1865, the local Home Guard retaliated by executing two more Lowry relations.[82]

The blood feud between the Lowry band and the local white authorities did not end with Johnston's surrender—if anything, it intensified. The outlaws continued to rob, and sometimes kill, their wealthier neighbors, the civil authorities proving unable to stop them. Led by the shrewd and fearless Henry Berry Lowry, the gang of six to eight men had little difficulty in eluding the county militia and Sheriff Roderick McMillan's posses. In November 1870, Governor Caldwell requested the army to assist the civil authorities in subduing the Lowry band. On the twenty-second, Company A of the 4th U.S. Artillery arrived at Lumberton, the Robeson County seat. The commander, Capt. Evan Thomas, headed at once for Scuffletown, determined to capture the Lowry band. After scouting "the whole country for thirty miles," he returned to headquarters empty-handed.[83]

A frustrated Thomas decided that drastic measures were in order. In a letter to General McDowell, the captain requested authorization to declare martial law in order to arrest several Lowry family members. Thomas noted that "a great many of the citizens have asked me to take matters in my hands." McDowell replied that "there is no warrant under our Government . . . in time of peace for any one to give you the power to arrest whom you please on suspicion." The general directed Thomas to act "under the direction of the civil authority, and as a part of its posse."[84]

Denied permission to declare martial law, Thomas had to settle for deploying troop detachments at several stations on the Wilmington, Charlotte, & Rutherfordton Railroad. At first, the presence of federal soldiers seemed to awe the Lowry band. The *Lumberton Robesonian* commented that the county had been "unusually quiet" since the bluecoats' arrival, whereas the *Wilmington Morning Star* warned that "the present quietude is only the calm that precedes the storm." On January 14, 1871, gunfire shattered the morning stillness at the federals' camp near Mossy Neck Station. Just a few hundred yards off, Henry Berry Lowry shot and killed a wealthy planter named John Taylor for ordering the execution of a relative. A sergeant and several enlisted men immediately set out in pursuit of Lowry but soon lost his trail. Thomas's entire detachment, accompanied by Sheriff McMillan and a large posse, resumed the search but could find no trace of Lowry.[85]

As commandant of the Post of Raleigh, Major Morgan's command responsibilities included Captain Thomas's detachment in Robeson County. After a brief investigation of the Taylor shooting, Morgan decided that the army's top priority was to protect the family and friends of the Lowry band from vengeful posses. He instructed Thomas to deploy his command at Scuffletown whenever the sheriff formed a posse and to remain there until the posse had disbanded. Morgan also ordered a ten-man detachment to Harper's Ferry near the outlaws' homes. The orders provoked an outcry from Lowry hunters, who regarded the bluecoats as an obstruction. But Morgan refused to withdraw the troops as long as he perceived the posses as a threat to Scuffletown's residents.[86]

Morgan's orders to protect the Scuffletonians convinced Sheriff McMillan that he would be better off without federal troops. Thereafter, McMillan's pursuit of the Lowry band became sporadic. Thomas's men spent the next few months performing their routine duties and little else. On May 10, 1871, the monotony ended. Shortly after midnight, the Lowry band stole into Lumberton and rescued two comrades from the county jail, within earshot of the federal camp. The next morning, Thomas conducted a futile search for the Lowry band and the liberated prisoners. The jailbreak culminated six months of frustrating inactivity for Thomas and his command. Believing that the soldiers stationed in Robeson would be more useful elsewhere, on May 17, Morgan ordered Thomas's company to Cleveland County.[87]

Two months after the transfer, Sheriff McMillan decided that he needed federal troops after all. The county militia had just attempted to lure the Lowry band into an ambush by using the outlaws' wives as bait, but the plan had backfired. McMillan urged Governor Caldwell to appeal to the president for "a strong detachment" of bluecoats. In a message to McDowell, Morgan argued against granting McMillan's request. "There would be more propriety in sending troops there if the civil authorities would improve the occasion to hunt out Lowery," Morgan wrote. "But the effect hitherto has been the reverse, the civil authorities expecting the troops to take the initiative, perform all the labor, and encounter all the dangers." Morgan explained that he had tried to convince the civil authorities that the search for the Lowry band should be made by detachments of twenty men in continuous shifts. Instead, Morgan commented, the usual procedure was for the entire county militia to turn out for three days and then go home, enabling the Lowry band to resurface after hiding out for a brief stretch. Morgan thought the three-day forays betrayed a lack of resolve on the part of the militia and the civil authorities.[88]

In answer to Caldwell's request that a detachment be posted at Lumberton for the 1871 election, Morgan sent a lieutenant and twelve enlisted men to maintain order at the polls and ensure that the county militia committed no more murders. On two recent occasions, Morgan noted, the militia had assuaged their bloodlust by lynching innocent black men. Having no orders to assist the civil authorities in capturing the Lowry band, the troop detachment returned to Raleigh on August 9, about a week after the election. No sooner had the soldiers returned than Caldwell requested a fifty-man force "to assist the civil authorities" in capturing the Lowry band. McDowell granted Caldwell's request, leaving Morgan no choice. On August 24, he sent two companies of the 4th U.S. Artillery to Robeson County. The federal soldiers remained there for six weeks, assisting the militia in its hunt for the Lowry band. As Morgan expected, the militiamen soon tired of the chase and dwindled to a mere handful. Just before the bluecoats' departure, a new recruit in the 4th was charged with murdering a black man and then jailed at Lumberton. The incident prompted the Lumberton Robesonian to grumble that the bluecoats were leaving "without effecting anything beyond the destruction of a good deal of mean whiskey, and the murder of an innocent negro." Alluding to the mass arrests of Klansmen, the Wilmington Journal complained that "white men are arrested by the hundred, but it is impossible to secure a dozen mulatto outlaws."[89]

On May 13, 1872, Caldwell requested another detachment of federal troops for Robeson County. Morgan appeared in no hurry to oblige him, waiting until July 5 to transfer a company of the 4th Artillery from Fort Johnston. The company remained in Robeson until the end of July. During that time, the local authorities made no calls for assistance, so Morgan ordered the company back to Fort Johnston. This proved to be the fourth and final federal detachment sent to Robeson. "There can be no question," Morgan wrote, "that in every instance harm rather than good has been done, the presence of the troops causing the citizens to relax their efforts, by which alone the capture or extermination of this band of out-laws can be accomplished."[90]

Morgan's exasperation with civil law enforcement was nothing new, for army officers had expressed a similar frustration with the state militia during the Kirk-Holden War. On the other hand, the civil authorities in Robeson became just as frustrated with the federals. If the army officers condemned the civilian authorities' lack of resolve, the civilians complained that the officers fretted too much over the rights of outlaws and their accomplices. Morgan probably could have ended the Lowrys' rampage had he adopted the ruthless tactics used against Indians on the western frontier, but he knew that such a course might well have provoked a bloodbath involving many innocent victims. Instead, the army played no part in the demise of the Lowry band. Shortly after the gang's final heist, Henry Berry Lowry disappeared, a second member received immunity under the Amnesty Act of 1873, and bounty hunters made short work of the rest.[91]

During the 1870s, U.S. troops in North Carolina often received orders to enforce the federal liquor tax. Before the Civil War, there had been no alcohol tax. In 1862, Congress levied a wartime duty on liquor, tobacco, and other "luxury" goods, establishing the Bureau of Internal Revenue to collect the tax. Although intended as a war measure, the tax proved too lucrative to revoke when the fighting ceased. Many North Carolina distillers refused to pay the federal liquor tax, deeming it unjust and oppressive. Worst of all, the $0.50 per gallon tax cut deeply into their profits. Anger over the tax revived wartime animosities. Many illegal distillers were ex-Confederates who regarded revenue agents as Yankee hirelings sent to subjugate them—in fact, some revenuers had been wartime Unionists. Moonshiners such as Amos Owens of Rutherford County joined the Ku Klux Klan to protect their illegal businesses.[92]

Federal soldiers in North Carolina had been chasing bootleggers since 1867, when General Sickles issued General Orders No. 25, prohibiting the manufacture of alcohol. Angry moonshiners sometimes fought back, bushwhacking bluecoats and revenue agents alike. The army nonetheless played only a minor role in enforcing the liquor tax in the Tar Heel State—that is, until the Ku Klux Act.

By 1871, the Klan systematically protected illegal distillers, including some Republican bootleggers who had joined the order as a security measure. Revenuers seeking information about the moonshiners found most local residents sullen and uncooperative, because they either feared the nightriders or applauded their actions. Thanks to the Klan, illegal distilling in western North Carolina flourished in 1871. C. C. Vest, the revenuer for the North Carolina counties bordering Georgia, counted "at least one hundred illicit distilleries" in his district alone. Vest's superior, Pinkney Rollins, had been sending an escort of two deputy marshals with his collectors, but he no longer deemed this sufficient protection. About this time, fifty Klansmen rode into Cherryville in Gaston County and seized several barrels of confiscated whiskey while the terrified revenuers huddled inside their hotel room.[93]

On June 21, 1871, Rollins's supervisor, P. W. Perry, appealed to Internal Revenue Commissioner Alfred Pleasanton for "a force of U.S. Cavalry. [The moonshiners] would fight a police force," Perry maintained, "but would hardly care to resist U.S. troops." About a week later, Company C of the 7th Cavalry arrived in Rutherford County to assist the U.S. marshal in arresting Klansmen. The prisoners included moonshiners such as Amos Owens, who was later tried and convicted for participating in the Biggerstaff and Rutherfordton raids. Like Rutherford Klan chieftain Randolph Shotwell, Owens received a sentence of six years in federal prison and a $5,000 fine.[94]

Company A of the 4th U.S. Artillery also participated in raids on illegal distillers. Securing good mounts for the foot soldiers remained a problem until the arrival of fifteen cavalry horses in May 1872. Moonshine production in North Carolina did not cease with the demise of the Klan in 1872, nor was it confined to the western part of the state. In March 1873, a detachment of the 2nd U.S. Artillery assisted a revenuer in a raid through Cumberland and several other southern counties. In July, General McDowell, the commander of the Department of the South, sent a detachment of the 2nd to Buncombe County at the request of Supervisor P. W. Perry. "More illicit distilling is done in this District than in any others in this State," Perry informed McDowell. The revenue official reported that his agents "are almost powerless to protect the interests of the Government against the armed resistance" of the moonshiners.[95]

General of the Army William T. Sherman personally authorized the detachment sent to Buncombe, but he did so against his better judgment. Sherman disliked using small detachments because of their tendency to erode discipline and morale. He also hesitated to place troops in situations that could lead to civil murder or assault charges, followed by trials before juries composed of the very persons the soldiers were trying to put out of business. Therefore, Sherman directed McDowell to send a small force from Raleigh to Asheville for thirty days only. Despite Sherman's injunction, the detachment remained in western North Carolina for two months, arresting moonshiners and destroying illegal stills. The expedition was hardly routine. During a raid in Burke County, moonshiners fired on the bluecoats in a vain attempt to protect their equipment and inventory. In McDowell County, a soldier shot and wounded a prisoner who attempted to escape. The local authorities' response confirmed Sherman's reservations. Both the revenue agent and the troop commander, Lt. James L. Mast, were arrested and indicted for assault with intent to kill. The federal judiciary intervened, however, and ordered the case transferred to district court, where the two men were acquitted.[96]

During the mid-1870s, federal troops had to assist Internal Revenue agents so often that the army established permanent posts at Marion in McDowell County and Morganton in Burke County. On January 10, 1877, a mounted detachment of the 2nd Artillery commanded by Lt. William T. Howard, a South Carolinian fresh out of West Point, left Morganton on a major raid. Howard reported that his detachment captured thirty illegal distilleries, destroyed two hundred tubs, twenty-five thousand gallons of beer, two hundred gallons of whiskey, and eight copper stills. Howard's raid proved to be one of the army's last such expeditions, for Congress attached a rider to the army appropriation bill of 1878 that prohibited the use of soldiers as a posse under civil officials. The Posse Comitatus Act of 1879 made the prohibition permanent.[97]

A reluctant partner in state and local authorities' efforts to subdue the Ku Klux Klan and the Lowry band, the U.S. Army enjoyed far more success in assisting federal law enforcement officials in breaking up the Klan and illegal distillers. Army officers found that cooperating with civil authorities often meant having to violate their own orders and regulations, whereas few such conflicts arose when assisting federal officials. The bluecoats seldom encountered resistance when pursuing outlaws, because few Klansmen or moonshiners dared provoke the federal government into taking more decisive action. Officers such as Evan Thomas and Albion Howe of the 4th Artillery and James Calhoun of the 7th Cavalry found battling hostile Indians west of the Mississippi far more lethal than pursuing outlaws in the mountains and hollows of western North Carolina. Thomas and Howe were killed by Modoc Indians in California, and Calhoun fell at the Little Big Horn while serving under his brother-in-law George Armstrong Custer.[98]

In contrast to the rugged, and sometimes perilous, existence of the frontier soldier, life for the several hundred troops stationed in North Carolina during the mid-1870s seemed quiet and dull. Aside from the occasional detail to arrest moonshiners or preserve order on election day, their service was routine. But the soldiers' role in the Tar Heel State proved more significant than appearances suggested, for they also fostered sectional reconciliation. The bluecoats proffered their conciliatory gestures in public rituals and on social occasions; white Tar Heels responded favorably to their overtures. To appease ex-Confederates, the federals pointedly excluded African Americans from the rites of national reunion. Blacks protested that their wartime contributions and sacrifices were too readily forgotten for the sake of blue-gray rapprochement. But white soldiers and civilians from the North deemed the assumption of collective amnesia in such matters a necessary step in the transition from war to peace.

Epilogue

RECONCILIATION
WITH A VENGEANCE

By 1872, the widespread, organized violence that had plagued North
Carolina since the war had ceased. Even so, the army still had to contend
with moonshiners and a few disturbances that stemmed from election-
year campaigning. Perhaps the worst such incident involved a drunken
brawl between soldiers and civilians that erupted in Lincolnton during
a Democratic political rally. Several citizens and one soldier were slightly
wounded during a brief exchange of gunfire. The mayor of Lincolnton
and the local post commander, Capt. V. K. Hart of the 7th U.S. Cavalry,
happened to be nearby and prevented further bloodshed. In an interview with the *Richmond Dispatch*, Hart stated that this was "the first conflict
between soldiers and citizens" that had come to his attention since his
arrival in the Carolinas nearly two years before. Whereas Hart praised
"the peaceful disposition of the people" within his command, he also
complained that the locals ignored his wife and himself.[1]

The state election occurred on August 1, 1872, a few days after the
brawl at Lincolnton. The returns indicated that neither party could claim
a complete victory: the Democrats retained control of the legislature,
while the Republicans held onto the governor's office. Governor Caldwell
was elected to a second term over his Democratic opponent, Augustus S.
Merrimon, but just barely. Of the nearly two hundred thousand ballots
cast, Caldwell's margin of victory was a scant nineteen hundred. In the
state senate, the Democrats maintained a two-to-one majority, yet their

advantage in the house shrank from twenty-two seats to twelve. Three months later, the presidential election returns in North Carolina revealed widespread demoralization in the Democratic ranks. Grant soundly defeated his Liberal Republican-Democratic opponent, *New York Tribune* editor Horace Greeley. Although Grant's twenty-five-thousand-vote margin exceeded even his staunchest supporters' expectations, the president polled about four thousand fewer votes than Caldwell had in August. The Democrats' poor showing betrayed a lack of enthusiasm for Greeley, indicating that his notoriety as a former free soiler and antislavery proponent continued to haunt him, despite his conciliation of southern whites. Grant also undercut Greeley's conciliatory overtures by endorsing an amnesty bill intended to remove the Fourteenth Amendment's office-holding prohibition from all but a few ex-Confederates. The Amnesty Act passed in May 1872, shortly after Greeley's nomination.[2]

Election day was quiet in most North Carolina communities, including several that had witnessed some of the previous year's worst Klan outrages. In fact, Rutherford County had become so peaceful that the local post commander, Capt. Harry C. Cushing, saw no reason to keep troops in that part of the state. Cushing reported that the only justification for doing so was the possible resumption of violence and lawlessness after the soldiers' departure. "If such is the case," Cushing argued, "our stay might be indefinite." He noted that the officers at his post "have associated freely with citizens of all political parties" but studiously avoided discussing politics. The officers' diplomacy paid ample dividends. "We have been treated with courtesy by all," Cushing indicated, "and in fact from experience in other parts of the state with marked courtesy."[3]

Cushing's experience with white North Carolinians indicated a significant improvement on the calculated snubs and outright hostility that his predecessors often encountered. As Democrats regained political power, they became more willing to reciprocate the conciliatory gestures of their "conquerors." The year 1875 stood as a watershed in this respect. Several years earlier, the Democrats had abandoned violence and intimidation to achieve their political ends because they had found those methods too volatile. In 1871, they had turned to a legal remedy—a state constitutional convention. While their first attempt at calling a convention had failed, the Democrats succeeded in marshalling enough votes in 1875 to get both a convention and a slim majority of the delegates. The Democrats passed amendments that outlawed secret political organizations, prohibited racially integrated schools and interracial marriages, and authorized the legislature to change the operating rules of county governments. The Democratic elite in the state capital thus consolidated their authority and promoted white supremacy. Several years earlier, the amendment legalizing racial discrimination would have provoked a stern response from Washington, but much had changed since then.

With the ratification in 1870 of the Fifteenth Amendment, intended to protect southern blacks' voting rights, most northern Republicans considered their Reconstruction work finished. Although reports of Klan violence continued to rouse the dwindling radical faction led by Massachusetts senator Charles Sumner, other northern party members began to lose patience with the apparent inability of southern Republicans to manage their affairs. The Panic of 1873 and the resulting nationwide depression spurred the ascendancy of conservative Republicans, who sought to link the party to sound fiscal management and economic recovery rather than to the rights of southern blacks. Indeed, the ill-fated Civil Rights Act of 1875 marked the Republicans' final Reconstruction initiative. Offered as a tribute to the late Sumner, the bill had to be watered down to ensure passage. The act mandated equal access to public transportation, hotels, and theaters but omitted churches and schools; the absence of an enforcement clause rendered the bill more a guideline than a law. Eight years later, the Supreme Court struck down the 1875 Civil Rights Act as unconstitutional.[4]

In 1875, conciliation became the byword. Two public ceremonies in Raleigh—a Memorial Day service and a state funeral—doubled as rites of sectional reconciliation. On May 31, U.S. soldiers and Confederate veterans jointly observed federal Memorial Day for the first time. In the procession to the National Cemetery, a battalion of the 2nd U.S. Artillery marched beside the Raleigh "Grays" militia. The ceremony featured the recital of a poem titled "The Blue and the Gray" and an oration by Albion W. Tourgée, an outspoken radical Republican who ranked as one of the state's most controversial political figures. At first, ex-Confederates at the National Cemetery were wary of the carpetbagger, but Tourgée's conciliatory tone soon disarmed them. The Raleigh News reported that Tourgée "referred in touching language to the memory of Lee and Jackson." The paper pronounced the speech "unobjectionable to either North or South."[5]

Conspicuously absent from Raleigh's first blue and gray Decoration Day was the African American contingent that had participated every year until then. In a letter to the Raleigh Elevator, a young black teacher named

Osborne Hunter noted "a spirit of reconciliation pervading the political atmosphere of both the Republican and Democratic parties of this State," which Hunter attributed to the trouncing the Democrats had given the Republicans in the election of 1874. Hunter maintained that Tar Heel Republicans blamed their defeat at the polls on the controversial Civil Rights bill, which they repudiated, and now seemed eager to court the Democrats. He cited the participation of the Raleigh Grays in the Memorial Day procession as proof that the Republicans sought to conciliate their former enemies at the blacks' expense. In deference to the Grays, Hunter commented, two black fire companies that had participated in years past were not invited, nor were blacks encouraged to pay homage at the cemetery. The headline above Hunter's letter read, "Reconciliation with [a] Vengeance."[6]

In August 1875, soldiers of the 2nd U.S. Artillery once again marched with the Raleigh Grays. On this occasion they escorted the remains of North Carolina's elder statesman, William A. Graham, from the railroad depot to the state capitol. The bluecoats were invited to participate because "of the distinguished Federal positions formerly held by the deceased." Before the war, Graham had been a U.S. senator and a secretary of the navy, but the invitation was notably silent about Graham's more recent public career. In all likelihood, the federal troops remained blissfully unaware that Graham had been a Confederate senator, the Conservative Party's chief spokesman for white supremacy, and a defense attorney for suspected Klansmen in the Ku Klux hearings of 1870.[7]

In promoting sectional reconciliation, federal soldiers in North Carolina not only served as symbols in public rituals but also were gaining acceptance in the social realm. On January 6, 1876, the enlisted men of Company F, 2nd Artillery, gave a ball in Morganton. They rented a large hall and decorated it with evergreens, flags, and lights. The refreshments included turkey, ham, apples, grapes, cakes, jellies, candies, and nonalcoholic beverages. About two hundred invitations were sent out, and nearly every invitee attended. The guests included seventy-five women from the town's most prominent families. "Not an intoxicated person was seen," noted one participant, "and not a cross word spoken the whole time." The party did not break up until dawn. Far more than time separated the bluecoats' social triumph at Morganton from the fiasco at Goldsboro eleven years earlier, when federal officers had rented the town hall and hand-delivered one hundred party invitations, only to have one local woman respond.[8]

The stage provided bluecoats with another opportunity for conciliating white North Carolinians. In May 1877, the garrison at Fort Johnston in Smithville scored a theatrical triumph while aiding some local civilians in desperate circumstances. The officers, enlisted men, and wives of Company M of the 2nd Artillery joined with several citizens in staging plays to raise money for a local church. During rehearsals, a pilot ship sank in a severe storm and all hands were lost. The bluecoat thespians therefore added a special benefit performance for the families of the deceased sailors. Large and appreciative audiences attended the amateur theatricals, earning the Fort Johnston troupe an invitation to perform in the opera house at Wilmington. Not only did the encore performance raise additional money for the widows and orphans, but also the drama critic for the *Wilmington Morning Star* pronounced it an artistic success. The experiences of the federal soldiers at Morganton and Smithville revealed that they had become an accepted part of the North Carolina communities in which they were stationed.[9]

After the election of 1876, the Democrats could afford to be magnanimous to the handful of federal soldiers in North Carolina. Using white supremacy as their rallying cry, the Democrats secured a stranglehold on both houses of the General Assembly and won seven of eight congressional seats. The Democratic gubernatorial candidate, Zebulon B. Vance, likewise defeated his able Republican opponent, superior court judge Thomas Settle. The election marked Vance's triumphant return to the governorship. Although barred from public office for a decade after the war, Vance had long been the leading Democrat in North Carolina, thanks in part to his heroic status as the state's war governor from 1862 to 1865.[10]

In contrast to the Democrats' decisive victory in North Carolina, the presidential election between Republican Rutherford B. Hayes and Democrat Samuel J. Tilden was deadlocked, with rival election boards in three southern states—South Carolina, Florida, and Louisiana—declaring for their party's candidate. To secure the election, Hayes in effect abandoned blacks and white Republicans in the South, though he persuaded himself that such was not the case. In backroom negotiations between his representatives and southern Democrats, Hayes pledged to withdraw U.S. troops from the southern states. In return, the Southerners promised to respect the rights of blacks. The agreement became known as the Compromise of 1877. A few months after the inauguration, Hayes fulfilled his end of the bargain. In April 1877, the Post of Raleigh concluded a

dozen years of continuous operation begun with Sherman's entry into
the state capital on April 13, 1865. In November, the Post of Morganton
also closed, ending the use of federal troops to arrest illegal distillers
in the western part of the state. That left a garrison of two officers and
fifteen enlisted men at Fort Johnston and one ordnance sergeant each at
Forts Caswell and Macon. As part of the army's coastal defense network,
the three forts had been garrisoned before the war. Reconstruction was
over in North Carolina. The Tar Heel State was "redeemed."[11]

For their part, the southern Democrats—or "Redeemers"—halfheartedly
honored their promise to Hayes. In North Carolina, the Redeemers paid
lip service to protecting blacks' rights and giving them an equal opportunity for education while proclaiming the restoration of "home rule"—a
euphemism for government by ex-Confederates. The Republican Party
nonetheless remained a viable force in North Carolina politics. Although
the Democrats retained control of the governorship and the state legislature for the next two decades, the Republicans presented a serious challenge at each election. Blacks continued to vote and hold political office,
especially in eastern counties where they formed majorities, mindful that
Democrats would respond to challenges to their dominance with summary reprisal. Democrats, in contrast, stopped short of proscribing black
political activity to avoid federal intervention.[12]

Southern Democrats also sought to attract northern customers and
investors in hopes of fueling the South's postwar economic recovery. In
the 1880s, southern men who had come of age during the Civil War
and Reconstruction preached the New South gospel of industrialization,
agricultural modernization, and reconciliation with the North. Tar Heel
businessmen and their northern counterparts had strong economic mo-
tivations to build on the conciliatory foundation established by the army
during Reconstruction.[13]

Sectional reconciliation began in April 1865 with William T. Sherman's generous surrender terms. His successor, John M. Schofield, continued the conciliatory policy by ordering the formation and arming of
county police companies. Schofield thus placed substantial power in the
ex-Confederates' hands less than one month after the Bennett Place surrender. He also distributed thousands of rations to needy civilians of both
races. The next commander in North Carolina, Thomas H. Ruger, soothed
the racist sensibilities of white Tar Heels by transferring black soldiers to
isolated coastal forts. Ruger's military courts also dealt far more leniently
with white criminals than with their black counterparts. Although the

commanders who followed Ruger—John C. Robinson, Daniel E. Sickles, Edward R. S. Canby, and Nelson A. Miles—struck many Conservatives as uncompromising "radicals," post commanders such as James V. Bomford and Royal T. Frank earned the Tar Heels' confidence and respect by exercising discretion and impartiality. Proof of this can be found in the numerous community petitions requesting the officers' retention and in the public tributes on their departure. During the height of the Ku Klux terror, white Tar Heels accused the army of "bayonet rule," but they also favorably contrasted the bluecoats' restraint with the excesses of Governor Holden's state militia. By the mid-1870s, federal troops were marching beside Confederate veterans in memorial rituals that doubled as rites of national reunion. Before their departure in 1877, bluecoats were once more welcome in polite society, much as they had been in the antebellum South.

Federal troops and white Southerners also discovered that their racial attitudes were not very different. A substantial number of enlisted men were Irish immigrants or native Southerners whose dislike of blacks verged on open hostility; most other bluecoats were only somewhat less racist. According to Maj. Lewis Merrill of the 7th U.S. Cavalry and Klan chieftain Randolph Shotwell, many enlisted men sympathized with the Klan, and some even deserted to the Invisible Empire. With alarming frequency, bluecoats robbed, beat, raped, and murdered African Americans; black soldiers also numbered among the perpetrators. From time to time, bluecoats and black civilians clashed in full-blown riots. Freedpeople nevertheless continued to rely on the army to protect them from Regulators, Klansmen, and other outlaws—at least until sectional reconciliation came with a vengeance in the mid-1870s.[14]

During the 1890s, the postwar rapprochement between bluecoats and white Tar Heels vanished beneath an avalanche of Lost Cause propaganda that demonized the U.S. Army during Reconstruction. In North Carolina, the demonization was an outgrowth of the state's political turmoil at the turn of the twentieth century. In the early 1890s, the "Bourbon" Democrats—so-called by their opponents in mocking reference to the Bourbon kings of France—faced their most serious challenge in almost two decades. As the "ancien régime"of North Carolina politics, the Democratic Party had become identified with big business, industry, and the political status quo. Their intransigence led to the rise of the third-party Populist movement, which won over many Democratic converts, especially among disgruntled farmers. In 1894, the Republicans and the

Populists formed the Fusionist coalition and won a stunning victory over the Democrats. The Fusionist majority in the General Assembly included five blacks among the Republican legislators.

After a second Fusionist victory in 1896, the Democrats struck back with white supremacy campaigns in 1898 and 1900, pledging to end "negro rule" in state politics. In 1900, the Democrats' frankly racist appeals were accompanied by an embroidered account of Raleigh's first Confederate Memorial Day on May 10, 1867. The author, Mrs. Garland Jones, was the president of the Ladies Memorial Association (LMA) of Wake County. Founded in 1866, the Wake County LMA led local efforts to commemorate the Confederate dead, including the establishment of Raleigh's Oakwood Cemetery.[15]

In Jones's version of the tale, honoring fallen Confederates took a back seat to depicting Yankee officers' villainy. With poetic license, she transformed that sunny afternoon in May 1867 into a rainy one and noted that Raleigh was then occupied by "Sherman's bummers," even though Sherman and his hated "bummers" had left the state two years before. According to Jones, several federal officers followed the faithful to the cemetery to ensure that the army's stricture against processions was obeyed. In Jones's narrative, the officers had warned that if the LMA formed a procession, the women and children "would be fired on without further warning." She indicated that there was no graveside ceremony, "not even a prayer, and it demanded some courage and some independence from those who walked under the dripping skies through the ankle-deep mud of the country . . . to fulfill this poor duty to the dead." Jones's account became the official version of the LMA's first Memorial Day and was reissued by the United Daughters of the Confederacy in 1938. A recent monograph on Civil War memorializing takes Jones's story at face value, quoting it without comment.[16]

A much earlier eyewitness account of Raleigh's first Confederate Memorial Day stands in sharp contrast to Jones's rendition. A leader of the Wake County LMA named Peter Pescud penned the recollection around 1882. Pescud's chief protagonist was Col. James V. Bomford, the commandant of the Post of Raleigh in 1867. During the Civil War, Bomford had been a Confederate prisoner for almost a year. Six months after his release, he was severely wounded in the Battle of Perryville. Even so, the colonel bore no grudges against former Confederates. According to Pescud, Bomford permitted the LMA to stage a procession from the state capitol to the cemetery, even though similar Memorial Day processions had been prohibited in New Bern and Wilmington. Bomford did accompany the LMA to the cemetery, but only as a participant with his wife and daughter at his side. The *Raleigh Sentinel* reported that the service consisted of a prayer, a hymn, and a brief oration, during which Bomford stood with his head uncovered. At the conclusion, he placed "a large quantity of rare flowers" on the graves of several Confederate dead.[17]

Although Pescud's narrative accorded with efforts of New South proponents to foster sectional reconciliation, it portrayed federal officers in too favorable a light to suit Mrs. Garland Jones and other shapers of Lost Cause ideology. For them, proclaiming the Confederate cause just and noble fell short—the enemy had to be demonized as well. They often portrayed blacks and bluecoats as coconspirators in the South's subjugation, despite the grim reality that the latter often victimized the former. "The presence of the Federal soldiers in every community encouraged the negroes . . . to acts of violence," North Carolina educator John T. Alderman wrote in 1914, "and if the sufferers complained[, they] were answered with a sneer or [an] oath." Alderman maintained that the U.S. Army was "being deliberately used to suppress the good and protect the vile." Just as it appeared that "negro insolence" had prevailed, Alderman continued, "the Ku Klux Klan came to our relief," restoring southern whites to their rightful preeminence in the racial hierarchy.[18]

Alderman was but one of many white North Carolinians who characterized the bluecoats as an oppressive, omnipresent force. Shelby native Thomas Dixon Jr. was a small boy when the federals came to neighboring Rutherford County in 1871. "In the town of Rutherfordton there were a thousand U.S. troops," Dixon recalled, "a company of cavalry, a unit of artillery and eight hundred infantry." Contrary to Dixon's recollection, barely one-half that many bluecoats occupied the entire state in 1871. Dixon further recalled that the soldiers at Shelby often paraded "to overawe the timid and create the proper atmosphere in which to force confessions from the venal and the treacherous." Three decades later, Dixon wrote *The Clansman*, a novel loosely based on the life of his uncle, Klan chieftain Leroy McAfee, and the inspiration for the motion picture *The Birth of a Nation*. Extremely popular in their day, the book and the film romanticize Klansmen as knightly defenders of southern civilization and stereotype blacks as ignorant savages bent on destroying whites and their world.[19]

Around the turn of the twentieth century, Professor William A. Dunning of Columbia University and his circle stamped Lost Cause ideology with academic legitimacy. The Dunning school condemned Reconstruction as a conspiracy by vindictive radical Republicans to subjugate southern whites at bayonet point, using federal troops to prop up corrupt state regimes led by an unholy trinity of carpetbaggers, scalawags, and freedmen. Despite the occasional appearance of revisionist works such as W. E. B. DuBois's *Black Reconstruction in America,* the Dunning school paradigm remained the dominant interpretive framework for over half a century. During the 1920s and 1930s, the Lost Cause mythos received compelling treatment in such popular works as Claude Bowers's *The Tragic Era* and Margaret Mitchell's *Gone with the Wind*—both the best-selling novel and the blockbuster film.

By the 1960s, a thoroughgoing reappraisal of Reconstruction scholarship took hold. Inspired by the civil rights movement, neo-abolitionist historians such as John Hope Franklin, Kenneth M. Stampp, and Eric Foner took their cue from DuBois and placed blacks front and center in their Reconstruction narratives. Although the neo-abolitionists regarded Reconstruction as a failed or an unfinished experiment, they also characterized the freedpeople's futile quest for civil and political equality as a noble endeavor.

For all the far-reaching changes in Reconstruction historiography since the 1960s, the U.S. Army's complex role remains as misunderstood today as it was during the heyday of the Dunning school. In emphasizing the conservative aspects of Reconstruction, present-day historians have swung the analytical pendulum to the opposite extreme. They portray the U.S. Army as "working hand in glove with former slaveowners to thwart the freedmen's aspirations and force them to return to plantation labor," comments Eric Foner, today's foremost Reconstruction scholar. While this depiction contains some truth, it is also a vast oversimplification, for it neglects the army's pivotal role in Military Reconstruction, as well as its ongoing efforts to protect freedpeople from their former masters. Likewise, the assumption among scholars such as John Hope Franklin that the federal occupation force in the South was too small to affect southern affairs after Military Reconstruction has led them to overlook the army's subsequent efforts to suppress the Klan and foster sectional reconciliation. As historian James E. Sefton observed, "power, influence, and activity are functions of much more than mere numbers."[20]

The army's complex role in North Carolina suggests that a similar process occurred in other southern states, indicating that a reappraisal of civil-military relations in the South during Reconstruction is long overdue. After the publication of Foner's magisterial *Reconstruction* two decades ago, the historiography has flourished, yet the army's role remains sadly neglected. The standard work, Sefton's *The United States Army and Reconstruction*, dates from 1967. Since then, just two state-level monographs have been published: Joseph G. Dawson's *Army Generals and Reconstruction: Louisiana* (1982), and William L. Richter's *The Army in Texas during Reconstruction* (1987). Although *Bluecoats and Tar Heels* is the fifth study to examine the U.S. Army in North Carolina during Reconstruction, it is the first published work. Three of the earlier monographs appeared between 1964 and 1973, and the most recent is a 1991 master's thesis. Much work remains to be done. Reconstruction scholars with an interest in civil-military relations can still choose from eight southern states.[21]

In summarizing the often contentious interaction of bluecoats and Tar Heels, this much is certain. The U.S. Army held the respect—if not always the affection—of North Carolinians throughout its dozen-year tenure in the Tar Heel State. All but a handful of the most diehard ex-Confederates avoided violent confrontations with federal soldiers, expressing their hostility to the U.S. government by refusing to pay the liquor tax or by victimizing blacks and white loyalists. During North Carolina's lengthy transition from war to peace, the army protected those most in need of it when the civil authorities proved unwilling or unable to do so. But the federal government ultimately abandoned African Americans for the sake of national reunion. In doing this, it bequeathed to later generations the task of securing full citizenship for blacks.

APPENDIX

Regional and Ethnic Origins of Federal Troops in North Carolina, 1868–1870

40TH U.S. INFANTRY

1. The 40th U.S. Infantry consisted of white officers and black enlisted men. The recruits were mustered in and trained at Camp Distribution, Virginia. Roughly one-half the enlisted men hailed from Maryland, Virginia, and Washington, D.C.

2. The regiment was stationed in the Carolinas for two years, yet only 11 percent of the enlisted men were native North Carolinians.

3. Some 12 percent of the enlisted men were natives of New York and Pennsylvania. Many were literate men from New York City and Philadelphia recruited to perform administrative and clerical duties.

Native-Born Enlisted Men

Alabama 6	Maine 5
California 1	Maryland 196
Connecticut 9	Massachusetts 13
Delaware 17	Michigan 1
District of Columbia 81	Mississippi 4
Florida 4	Missouri 2
Georgia 19	New Jersey 24
Illinois 1	New York 67
Indiana 3	North Carolina 121
Iowa 1	Ohio 10
Kentucky 21	Pennsylvania 60
Louisiana 7	Rhode Island 4

(continued on next page)

(continued from previous page)

South Carolina   114

Tennessee   7

Virginia   243

West Virginia   1

Subtotal   1,042

Foreign-Born Enlisted Men

Canada   5

Germany   1

India   1

Jamaica   3

South America   1

West Indies   2

Subtotal   13

Unknown Place of Birth   4

Total Enlisted Men 40th Infantry   1,059

8TH U.S. INFANTRY

The only relevant Descriptive Book for the 8th U.S. Infantry, an all-white regiment, dates from 1866. The 1870 U.S. Census provides the most current information on the soldiers of the 8th who served in the Carolinas from 1866 to 1870.

1. Some 54 percent of the enlisted men in the 8th Infantry were foreign-born: 21 percent were Irish immigrants and 20 percent were German.

2. The Eastern Seaboard (DC, DE, MD, NJ, NY, PA) furnished 21 percent of the enlisted men, the Midwest (IL, IN, IA, KY, MI, MO, OH, WI) 11 percent, the former Confederate states (GA, LA, NC, SC, TN, TX, VA) 9 percent, and New England (CT, MA, ME, NH, RI, VT) 4 percent.

3. Nineteen enlisted men were native North Carolinians. According to the *North Carolina Daily Standard*, at least some of the Tar Heel bluecoats were Confederate veterans. "We are personally acquainted with the soldiers of this garrison (Co. K, 8th Infantry) who served in North Carolina regiments during the Confederacy, and who are now proudly wearing the blue," wrote a correspondent for the *Standard* (Raleigh, November 3, 1869).

Native-Born Enlisted Men

California   1

Connecticut   4

Delaware   2

District of Columbia   2

Georgia   12

Illinois   13

Indiana 15	New York 66
Indian Territory 1	North Carolina 19
Iowa 1	Ohio 22
Kentucky 1	Pennsylvania 28
Louisiana 2	Rhode Island 2
Maine 5	South Carolina 5
Maryland 7	Tennessee 3
Massachusetts 7	Texas 1
Michigan 1	Vermont 2
Missouri 1	Virginia 6
New Hampshire 2	Washington 1
New Jersey 7	Wisconsin 2

Subtotal   241

Unknown Place of Birth   10

The census taker listed the place of birth of these soldiers as "SC," but it appears that he arbitrarily inserted this information on discovering that he had left the spaces blank.

Foreign-Born Enlisted Men

Austria 1	Germany 105
Belgium 3	Holland 1
Bohemia 1	Ireland 113
Canada 13	Scotland 5
Denmark 2	Spain 2
England 26	Sweden 1
France 3	Switzerland 8

Subtotal   284

Total Enlisted Men 8th Infantry   535

Sources   Data about the 40th U.S. Infantry was compiled from "Where Born" in Descriptive Book, 1866–1868, E1995, 40th U.S. Infantry, RG 391, NA. Data for the 8th U.S. Infantry was compiled from the 1870 Federal Census, M593, Reels 1121, 1127, 1162, 1163, 1487, 1507, and 1508, all in Federal Population Census, NA.

NOTES

Abbreviations

ACHM	Alamance County Historical Museum
ACNC	Assistant Commissioner of North Carolina (Freedmen's Bureau)
AGO	Adjutant General's Office, Washington, D. C.
BBSHS	Bentonville Battlefield State Historic Site
BC	Bowdoin College: Hawthorne-Longfellow Library
BRFAL	Bureau of Refugees, Freedmen, and Abandoned Lands
CHS	Chicago Historical Society
CWMC	Civil War Miscellaneous Collection
CWTIC	*Civil War Times Illustrated* Collection
Dept East	Department of the East
Dept NC	Department of North Carolina
Dept South	Department of the South
Dist NC	District of North Carolina
Dist WNC	District of Western North Carolina
DU	Duke University: Perkins Library
ECU	East Carolina University: J. Y. Joyner Library
FPC	Federal Population Census
GFO	General Field Orders (in OR)
GO	General Orders
GOC	General Orders and Circulars
GLB	Governor's Letterbooks
GP	Governor's Papers
HCWRTC	Harrisburg Civil War Round Table Collection
HSPA	Historical Society of Pennsylvania
ILHS	Illinois State Historical Library
INHS	Indiana Historical Society
KMNP	Kennesaw Mountain National Park
LB	Letterbook
LC	Library of Congress

LR	Letters Received
LS	Letters Sent
M	Microcopy
MHI	Military History Institute, U.S. Army
NA	National Archives, Washington, D.C.
NAII	National Archives, College Park, Maryland
NCC-GPL	North Carolina Collection, Greensboro Public Library
NCC-UNC	North Carolina Collection, University of North Carolina at Chapel Hill
NCSA	North Carolina State Archives
NHHS	New Hampshire Historical Society
NYHS	New-York Historical Society
NYPL	New York Public Library
OR	[Official Records] The War of the Rebellion: A Compilation of the Official Records of the Union and Confederate Armies, U.S. War Department
PC	Private Collections
PGLB	Provisional Governor's Letterbook
PGP	Provisional Governor's Papers
RG	Record Group
2MD	Second Military District
SCF	Source-Chronological File
SHC-UNC	Southern Historical Collection, University of North Carolina at Chapel Hill
SFO	Special Field Orders (in OR)
SO	Special Orders
UMI	University of Michigan: Bentley Historical Library
UND	University of Notre Dame: Archives
UVA	University of Virginia: Alderman Library
UWA	University of Washington Libraries
VHS	Virginia Historical Society

Prologue

A word about the book's title. "Bluecoats" denotes the blue-uniformed federal soldiers stationed in North Carolina from 1865 to 1877. "Tar Heels"—a nickname coined during the Civil War—refers to North Carolinians, whether they were male or female, soldier or civilian, black or red or white.

1. Tourgée, Fool's Errand, 152–53.

2. U.S. Bureau of the Census, Eighth Census, xvii; Yearns and Barrett, N. C. Civil War Documentary, 125, 247.

3. U.S. Bureau of the Census, Eighth Census, 357.

4. Miles, Serving the Republic, 111.

5. Hogue, *Uncivil War*; Hollandsworth, *Absolute Massacre*; Lemann, *Redemption*; Zuczek, *State of Rebellion*.

1. The Warrior as Peacemaker

1. Zebulon B. Vance to Joseph E. Brown, January 18, 1865, in McKinney and McMurry, *Papers of Vance*, reel 13; W. T. Sherman to James M. Calhoun et al., September 12, 1864, in Simpson and Berlin, *Sherman's Civil War*, 708; Charles Manly to "My Dear Gov.," March 29, 1865, David Lowry Swain Papers, SHC-UNC. For a thorough account of the devastating impact of Union and Confederate forces on North Carolina in March and April 1865, see Angley et al., *Sherman's March through North Carolina*.

2. Henry Hitchcock to Mary Hitchcock, April 14, 1865, in Howe, *Marching with Sherman*, 295–96; T. S. Bowers to Major General Sherman, April 9, 1865 (enclosing copies of U. S. Grant to R. E. Lee, April 9, 1865, and R. E. Lee to U. S. Grant, April 9, 1865), and W. T. Sherman to U. S. Grant, April 12, 1865, both in OR 47(3): 140, 177 (all citations are for series 1 unless otherwise indicated); Sherman, *Memoirs*, 2: 344.

3. Z. B. Vance to W. T. Sherman, April 12, 1865, and W. T. Sherman to Z. B. Vance, April 12, 1865, both in OR 47(3): 178; Sherman, *Memoirs*, 2: 137–40; U.S. Congress, "Sherman-Johnston," 3: 6, 14; Bradley, *Astounding Close*, 127.

4. Henry Hitchcock to Mary Hitchcock, April 14, 1865, in Howe, *Marching with Sherman*, 295–96, 298; Johnston, *Narrative of Military Operations*, 398–400; J. E. Johnston to W. T. Sherman, April 14 [13], 1865, in OR 47(3): 206–7; Bradley, "'I Rely upon Your Good Judgment,'" 163.

5. W. T. Sherman to J. E. Johnston, April 14 [15], 1865, and W. T. Sherman to U. S. Grant and Secretary of War, April 15, 1865, both in OR 47(3): 207; Henry Hitchcock to Mary Hitchcock, April 15, 1865, in Howe, *Marching with Sherman*, 299; Nichols, *Story of the Great March*, 309; Bradley, *Astounding Close*, 148, 333n45.

6. J. Kilpatrick to Major General Sherman, April 16, 1865 (2 A.M.), J. Kilpatrick to Major General Sherman, April 16, 1865 (8:30 A.M.), W. T. Sherman to General Kilpatrick, April 16, 1865, and J. Kilpatrick to Major General Sherman, April 16, 1865 (enclosing dispatch from Wade Hampton to J. Kilpatrick [n.d.]), all in OR 47(3): 233–34; Henry Hitchcock to Mary Hitchcock, April 16, 1865, in Howe, *Marching with Sherman*, 302.

7. Sherman, *Memoirs*, 2: 347–50; Johnston, *Narrative of Military Operations*, 402–4; Bradley, *Astounding Close*, 157–60.

8. Manning F. Force Letter Book-Journal, April 17, 1865, and Manning F. Force to Mr. Kebler, April 18, 1865, Manning Ferguson Force Papers, UWA; Wills, *Army Life*, 371; W. T. Sherman to Mary Miles, September 18, 1868, Nelson Appleton Miles Family Papers, LC; Marszalek, *Sherman*, 344; Bradley, *Astounding Close*, 163–64.

9. Sherman, *Memoirs*, 2: 351–52; W. T. Sherman to James M. Calhoun et al., September 12, 1864, in Simpson and Berlin, *Sherman's Civil War*, 709; W. T. Sherman to I. N. Arnold, November 28, 1872, Isaac Newton Arnold Papers, CHS.

10. Johnston, *Narrative of Military Operations*, 404; John H. Reagan, "A Basis of Pacification," OR 47(3): 244–45, 806–7 (two copies); Bradley, *Astounding Close*, 171–72.

11. Johnston, *Narrative of Military Operations*, 404–5; Sherman, *Memoirs*, 2: 352; U.S. Congress, "Sherman-Johnston," 3: 4; Report of William T. Sherman, May 9, 1865, in OR 47(1): 32–33; W. T. Sherman to John W. Draper, November 6, 1868, John William Draper Papers, LC.

12. Johnston, *Narrative of Military Operations*, 405; Sherman, *Memoirs*, 2: 353.

13. William T. Sherman, "Memorandum or basis of agreement," April 18, 1865, and John H. Reagan to Jefferson Davis, April 22, 1865, both in OR 47(3): 243–44, 824; J. E. Johnston to A. H. Stephens, April 29, 1868, Alexander Hamilton Stephens Papers, LC; U.S. Congress, "Sherman-Johnston," 3: 14.

14. W. T. Sherman to Thomas Ewing, March 31, 1865, in Howe, *Home Letters of Sherman*, 338.

15. U. S. Congress, "Sherman-Johnston," 3: 4, 13, 15; Report of William T. Sherman, May 9, 1865, in OR 47(1): 32–33; W. T. Sherman to U. S. Grant, April 25, 1865, and April 28, 1865, both in Simpson and Berlin, *Sherman's Civil War*, 876–77, 880–82; W. T. Sherman to John W. Draper, November 6, 1868, John William Draper Papers, LC; Sherman, *Memoirs*, 2: 353.

16. W. T. Sherman to William M. McPherson, March 24, 1865, W. T. Sherman to Ellen [Sherman], May 10, 1865, and W. T. Sherman to S. P. Chase (both letters), May 6, 1865, all in Simpson and Berlin, *Sherman's Civil War*, 833, 888–90, 897.

17. Sherman, "Memorandum or basis of agreement," April 18, 1865, in OR 47(3): 244; W. T. Sherman to Ellen Sherman, April 18, 1865, in Simpson and Berlin, *Sherman's Civil War*, 867; Bradley, *Astounding Close*, 206.

18. GO No. 8, Army of Georgia, March 7, 1865, in OR 47(2): 719; *Raleigh Daily Progress*, April 19, 1865.

19. GFO No. 15, Army of the Tennessee, April 19, 1865, Circular, Office of the Inspector General, Fifteenth Army Corps, April 22, 1865, SFO No. 97, Army of the Tennessee, April 22, 1865, and A. M. Van Dyke to John A. Logan, April 23, 1865, all in OR 47(3): 251, 280–81, 288; King, *Anna Fuller's Journal*, 44; *Raleigh Daily Progress*, April 22, 1865.

20. Endorsement of W. T. Sherman on Willard Warner to John Walker, April 16, 1865, LR, Dept NC, box 2, RG 393, NA; David L. Swain to W. T. Sherman, April 18, 1865, and W. T. Sherman to D. L. Swain, April 22, 1865, both in OR 47(3): 247–48, 279–80.

21. W. T. Sherman to generals Johnston and Hardee, April 23, 1865, in OR 47(3): 287.

22. Report of William T. Sherman, May 9, 1865, in OR 47(1): 34; Edwin M.

Stanton to Lieutenant-General Grant, March 3, 1865, and April 21, 1865, both in OR 47(3): 263; Sherman, *Memoirs*, 2: 358–60; Grant, *Personal Memoirs*, 570.

23. W. T. Sherman to General Johnston (two dispatches), April 24, 1865, and J. E. Johnston to W. T. Sherman, April 25, 1865, all in OR 47(3): 293–94, 304; Johnston, *Narrative of Military Operations*, 410–11.

24. Report of William T. Sherman, May 9, 1865, in OR 47(1): 34; "Terms of a Military Convention," in OR 47(3): 313; John M. Schofield, "Narrative Part V: The Army of the Ohio. Closing Events of the War in North Carolina," 5–6, John McAllister Schofield Papers, LC; Schofield, *Forty-Six Years*, 351; Simpson, *Let Us Have Peace*, 106–9; Raphael Semmes to U. S. Grant, December 17, 1865, and W. T. Sherman to J. E. Johnston, January 2, 1866, both in OR 8, series 2: 836–37, 842.

25. W. T. Sherman to General Johnston, April 27, 1865, J. E. Johnston to W. T. Sherman, April 28, 1865, and "Military Convention of April 26, 1865: Supplemental Terms," all in OR 47(3): 320, 336–37, 482; Bradley, *Astounding Close*, 239.

26. Edwin M. Stanton quoted in *New York Times*, April 23, 1865; Ellen [Sherman] to Cump, April 26, 1865, William T. Sherman Family Papers, UND; Bradley, *Astounding Close*, 228–30.

27. W. T. Sherman to John A. Rawlins, May 19, 1865, in OR 47(3): 531; W. T. Sherman to John Sherman, September 21, 1865, and November 4, 1865, both in William Tecumseh Sherman Papers, LC; W. T. Sherman to H. W. Walter, October 19, 1874, Harvey Washington Walter Papers, SHC-UNC; Bradley, *Astounding Close*, 255.

28. Quoted in Crow and Barden, *Live Your Own Life*, 210.

29. Spencer, *Last Ninety Days*, 181–82.

30. Clipping from *Wilmington Weekly Dispatch*, March 15, 1867, Reconstruction Scrapbook, 24, NCC-UNC.

31. SFO No. 65 and SFO No. 66, Military Division of the Mississippi, April 27, 1865, both in OR 47(3): 322–23.

2. Military Rule by Default

1. Carbone, *Civil War in Coastal North Carolina*, 83, 86, 98; J. M. Schofield to Major-General Sherman, May 5, 1865, in OR 47(3): 405.

2. Connelly, *Schofield*, passim; Powell, *Powell's Records*, 529–30; Heitman, *Historical Record*, 1: 865; Warner, *Generals in Blue*, 425–26; Boatner, *Civil War Dictionary*, 726–27.

3. GO No. 31, Dept NC, April 27, 1865, in OR 47(3): 330–31; W. C. Hackett to "Dear Companion," May 8, 1865, W. C. Hackett Letters, CWMC, MHI; Hayes, *One Hundred and Third Ohio*, 141–42.

4. GO No. 32, Dept NC, April 27, 1865, in OR 47(3): 331. See also Circular, Dept NC, May 4, 1865, in ibid., 397.

5. J. M. Schofield to W. T. Sherman, April 29, 1865, J. M. Schofield to J. E.

Johnston, April 29, 1865, J. M. Schofield to J. E. Johnston, April 30, 1865, and Circular, Army of the Tennessee, May 1, 1865, all in OR 47(3): 349, 350, 354–55, 358.

6. Jacob Dolson Cox Diary, May 1 [2], 1865, KMNP; Cox, "Surrender of Johnston's Army," 2: 248–59; Z. B. Vance to C. P. Spencer, April 7, [1866], Cornelia Phillips Spencer Papers, SHC-UNC; William A. Graham to David L. Swain, May 11, 1865, in Hamilton et al., *Graham Papers*, 6: 310.

7. Jacob Dolson Cox Diary, May 2 [3], 1865, KNMP; Pinney, *104th Ohio*, 86; William Hartsuff to Major-General Schofield, May 2, 1865, J. D. Cox to Major Cox, May 2, 1865, and J. D. Cox to Theodore Cox, May 2, 1865, all in OR 47(3): 376.

8. Archer Anderson to Brigadier-General Kennedy, May 2, 1865, in OR 47(3): 866; Pinney, *104th Ohio*, 85–86; L. F. Becker, "Campaigning with a Grand Army," W. O. Myers, "In North Carolina," and W. A. Johnson, "Closing Days with Johnston," all in *National Tribune*, November 23, 1899, March 30, 1916, May 29, and June 5, 1902; Gaskill, *Footprints through Dixie*, 179–82.

9. Everts, *Ninth Regiment New Jersey*, 176–77; Drake, *Ninth New Jersey*, 299–301; Runyan, *Eight Days*, 8–14; Theodore Cox to David Kille, May 8, 1865, and M. C. Runyan to E. W. Welsted, May 13, 1865, both in OR 47(3): 442, 490.

10. Drake, *Ninth New Jersey*, 301–2; Runyan, *Eight Days*, 14–20; M. C. Runyan to E. W. Welsted, May 13, 1865, in OR 47(3): 490.

11. Runyan, *Eight Days*, 20–25; M. C. Runyan to E. W. Welsted, May 13, 1865, in OR 47(3): 490–91.

12. Runyan, *Eight Days*, 28–30, 35; M. C. Runyan to E. W. Welsted, May 13, 1865, in OR 47(3): 491; Drake, *Ninth New Jersey*, 303; J. E. Johnston to Major-General Schofield, May 8, 1865, and J. M. Schofield to J. E. Johnston, May 12, 1865, both in OR 47(3): 443, 483.

13. "At a meeting of a portion of the citizens of Granville [County], held in the Court House at Oxford," April 20, 1865, LR, Dept NC, box 1, RG 393, NA; "Island Creek District Duplin County NC. At a meeting of the citizens of this District," April 25, 1865, "At a meeting of citizens of Carvers Creek district [Bladen County] held on Thursday 27th inst.," April 27, 1865, and James F. Oliver to Brig. Gen. Hawley, May 15, 1865, all in Joseph Roswell Hawley Papers, LC; Edmund J. Cleveland Diary, May 4, 1865, SHC-UNC; Everts, *Ninth Regiment New Jersey*, 175–76; Pinney, *104th Ohio*, 86; J. Kilpatrick to J. A. Campbell, April 30, 1865, J. A. Cooper quoted in Theodore Cox to J. Kilpatrick, May 15, 1865, and Thomas T. Heath to Major Carleton, May 20, 1865, all in OR 47(3): 354, 502, 545. See also Mary T. Brown to John Evans Brown, June 20, 1865, William J. Brown Correspondence, W. Vance Brown Collection, PC, NCSA; Samuel F. Patterson to Son, May 15, 1865, Patterson Papers, NCSA; William E. Ardrey Diary, May 1865, p. 2, William E. Ardrey Papers, DU; Williamson D. Ward Diary, May 17, June 3, 1865, INHS.

14. Abstract from the returns of the Dept NC for April 30, 1865, GO No. 35, Dept NC, May 4, 1865, in OR 47(3): 361, 396.

15. Marching Orders, 3rd Division, 10th Army Corps, April 28, 1865, in OR 47(3): 342. The only other black unit in Schofield's command, the 14th U.S. Colored Heavy Artillery, was assigned to Paine's division on June 1, 1865. See SO No. 77, Dept NC, June 1, 1865, in OR 47(3): 609.

16. Chaplain Turner Letter, *Christian Recorder* (Philadelphia), May 27, 1865; Blight, *Race and Reunion*, 147–49.

17. Leonard A. Boyd to Family, n.d., John S. Miles Papers, MHI.

18. Francis E. Wolcott to Thomas H. Ruger, August 19, 1865, LR, Dept NC, box 2, RG 393, NA; Henry Brown to Chief of Police, May 7, 1865, J. M. Schofield to J. Kilpatrick, May 16, 1865, J. M. Schofield to Major-General Kilpatrick, May 17, 1865, J. M. Schofield to T. W. Sanderson, May 17, 1865, and J. Kilpatrick to Major-General Schofield, June 6, 1865, all in OR 47(3): 431, 512, 521, 522, 632.

19. George F. Towle Diary, May 11–15, 24, 1865, NHHS.

20. Harrison Nesbitt to Wife, May 24, 1865, Harrison Nesbitt Letters, CWMC, MHI; Kittinger, *Diary, 1861–1865*, 208; W. H. W. to Sister, May 27, 1865, William Henry Walling Letters, CWMC, MHI; James McCartney quoted in Thompson, *112th Regiment of Illinois*, 321; Joseph R. Hawley to J. A. Campbell, May 11, 1865, in OR 47(3): 472. See also Cox, "Surrender of Johnston's Army," 2: 272; Leonard A. Boyd to Family, n.d., John S. Miles Papers, MHI; Benjamin W. Todd to Martha Todd, May 23, 1865, Benjamin W. Todd Letters, CWMC, 3rd series, MHI; Edmund J. Cleveland Diary, May 30, 1865, SHC-UNC; Harrison M. Shuey to C. A. Cilley, June 10, 1865, in OR 47(3): 642–43.

21. Thomas T. Heath to J. A. Campbell, May 16, 1865, LR, Dept NC, box 2, RG 393, NA; Thomas J. Henderson to Wife, May 21, 1865, June 4, 1865, Thomas J. Henderson Papers, ILHS. For a similar assessment by a northern civilian, see Andrew, *South after the War*, 111.

22. H. P. Thompson to George Allen, May 20, 1865, and Joseph R. Hawley to J. A. Campbell, May 21, 1865, both in OR 47(3): 544, 550; David Gore to Gen. Hawley, May 15, 1865, Joseph Roswell Hawley Papers, LC; Testimony of George O. Sanderson, in U.S. Congress, *Report of the Joint Committee*, 179.

23. J. M. Schofield to Major-General Sherman, May 5, 1865, in OR 47(3): 405. In his reply to Schofield, Sherman wrote, "Any thing positive would be infinitely better than the present doubting halting, nothing to do policy of our poor bewildered government." Sherman's disgust at the federal government's apparent inaction is hardly surprising, given his outrage at Stanton and the northern press regarding his April 18 surrender agreement. See W. T. Sherman to Genl. Schofield, May 5, 1865, in Simpson and Berlin, *Sherman's Civil War*, 887.

24. GO No. 46, Dept NC, May 15, 1865, in OR 47(3): 503.

25. Ibid.

26. Circular, Dept NC, May 4, 1865, in ibid., 397–98.

27. Allan Rutherford to J. F. Chur, September 25, 1867, M843, reel 22, Reports, and E. Whittlesey to O. O. Howard, October 15, 1865, M843, reel 1, LS, ACNC, RG 105, NA. The War Department stipulated the following food items and quantities as the daily ration for adult refugees: fresh beef (16 oz.), pork or bacon (10 oz., in lieu of beef), flour or soft bread (16 oz., twice a week), hard bread (12 oz., in lieu of flour or soft bread), corn meal (16 oz., five times a week). The following items were issued per 100 rations: beans, peas, or hominy (10 lbs.), sugar (8 lbs.), vinegar (2 qts.), candles (8 oz.), soap (2 lbs.), salt (2 lbs.), pepper (2 oz.). Women and children were also issued rye coffee at the rate of 10 pounds or tea at the rate of 15 ounces per 100 rations. Children under fourteen received half rations. See Circular No. 8, U.S. War Department, June 20, 1865, M843, reel 20, GOC, ACNC, RG 105, NA.

28. S. P. Chase to Major-General Schofield, May 7, 1865, and J. M. Schofield to U. S. Grant, May 10, 1865, both in OR 47(3): 427, 461–63.

29. J. M. Schofield to U. S. Grant, May 10, 1865, in OR 47(3): 462; Simpson, *Let Us Have Peace*, 114–15; Sefton, *Army and Reconstruction*, 15.

30. J. M. Schofield to U. S. Grant, May 10, 1865, and U. S. Grant to J. M. Schofield, May 18, 1865, both in OR 47(3): 463, 529.

31. GO No. 36, Dept NC, May 4, 1865, GO No. 45, Dept NC, May 12, 1865, J. D. Cox to Major-General Schofield, May 16, 1865, J. M. Schofield to Major-General Cox, May 16, 1865, Tristram T. Dow to J. A. Cooper, May 17, 1865, Thomas H. Ruger to Theodore Cox, May 21, 1865, Henry A. Hale to John S. Jones, May 26, 1865, Henry A. Hale to W. W. Wheeler, May 28, 1865, and GO No. 68, Dept NC, May 30, 1865, all in OR 47(3): 397, 484, 511, 524, 549, 575, 587, 602; J. M. Schofield to Genl. Hawley, May 16, 1865, Joseph Roswell Hawley Papers, LC.

32. T. S. Bowers to John M. Schofield, May 20, 1865, in OR 47(3): 542.

33. J. M. Schofield to J. S. [J. L.] Pennington, May 10, 1865, in OR 47(3): 458; *Raleigh Daily Progress*, May 10, 11, 1865.

34. J. M. Schofield to Major-General Halleck, May 6, 1865, U. S. Grant to J. M. Schofield, May 8, 1865, J. M. Schofield to Lieutenant-General Grant, May 9, 1865, J. M. Schofield to Major-General Cox, May 9, 1865, and J. Kilpatrick to J. A. Campbell, May 15, 1865, all in OR 47(3): 416, 440, 450, 451, 502; C. Schurz to Charles Sumner, May 9, 1865, Carl Schurz Papers, LC; Jacob Dolson Cox Diary, May 12, 1865, KMNP; Z. B. Vance to C. P. Spencer, April 7, [1866], Cornelia Phillips Spencer Papers, SHC-UNC; Bradley, *Astounding Close*, 260–61.

35. J. R. Hawley to J. A. Campbell, April 28, 1865, J. A. Campbell to Joseph R. Hawley, April 28, 1865, J. A. Campbell to A. Ames, May 23, 1865, Henry A. Hale to John S. Jones, May 26, 1865, J. A. Campbell to J. Kilpatrick, June 1, 1865, J. A. Campbell to J. R. Hawley, June 1, 1865, and J. M. Schofield to A. Ames, June 2, 1865, all in OR 47(3): 343, 565, 575, 612, 615–16; Archibald McLean to J. R. Hawley, May 1, 1865, and Major Genl. Schofield to J. R. Hawley, May 10, 1865, both in Joseph Roswell Hawley Papers, LC;

S. H. Stilson to Commanding Officer, Fayetteville, N.C., June 18, 1865, William Woods Holden PGLB, NCSA.

36. Diary, Redmond F. Laswell Papers, May 6–7, 9–10, 1865, ACHM; Kittinger, *Diary*, 208; Everts, *Ninth Regiment New Jersey*, 176; Pinney, *104th Ohio*, 86.

37. Jacob Dolson Cox Diary, May 2 [3], 1865, KMNP; Jacob Henry Smith Diary, May 5, 1865, box 15, H. Richardson Smith Papers, SHC-UNC; Cox, "Surrender of Johnston's Army," 265–66, 272; Kirwan and Splaine, *Seventeenth Regiment Massachusetts*, 391; GO No. 6, Post of Greensboro, July 19, 1865, reprinted in *Greensboro Patriot*, July 22, 1865; Circular, Post of Raleigh, April 23, 1865, and GO No. 2, Post of Raleigh, April 23, 1865, both in *North Carolina Daily Standard* (Raleigh), May 4, 1865.

38. David Schenck, "The Fall of the Confederacy" [ca. May 1865], David Schenck Papers, SHC-UNC; Mary T. Brown to John Evans Brown, June 20, 1865, W. Vance Brown Collection, NCSA; A. C. Cowles, "To the Citizens of Yadkin County" [ca. May 1865], and Calvin J. Cowles to Andrew C. Cowles, May 5, 1865, both in Calvin J. Cowles Papers, PC, NCSA; R. L. Patterson to W. W. Holden, June 8, 1865, in Raper and Mitchell, *Holden Papers*, 181–82; Inscoe and McKinney, *Heart of Confederate Appalachia*, 269. See also Clark, *Histories*, 4: 376, 5: 292–95; Samuel F. Patterson to Son, June 2, 1865, Patterson Papers, PC, NCSA.

39. J. D. Cox to Maj. Genl. Kilpatrick, May 28, 1865, L. G. Estes to Bvt. Brig. Gen. Atkins, May 28, 1865, and Bvt. Brig. Gen. Atkins to William C. Stevens, May 30, 1865, all in William C. Stevens Correspondence, UMI.

40. William C. Stevens to Father, June 7, 20 1865, and William C. Stevens to Sister, June 20, 1865, all in William C. Stevens Correspondence, UMI.

41. Thomas J. Henderson to Wife, June 4, 1865, Thomas J. Henderson Papers, ILHS; Tom to Jane, May 13, 1865, Thomas J. Jordan Letters, HSPA; Benjamin W. Todd to Martha Todd, May 23, 1865, Benjamin W. Todd Letters, CWMC, 3rd series, MHI; William A. Ketcham, "A Part of His Story of War," 53, William A. Ketcham Papers, John Lewis Ketcham Collection, INHS; Edmund J. Cleveland Diary, June 11, 1865, SHC-UNC. See also Thomas T. Heath to J. A. Campbell, October 9, 1865, LR, Dept NC, box 1, RG 393, NA; Abner Eisenhower Diary, May 16–20, 1865, CWMC, 3rd series, MHI; Charles A. Tournier Diary, May 23, 1865, CWMC, MHI; Eldredge, *Third New Hampshire*, 669.

42. Will Ketcham to Aunt Kate, May 6, 1865, and W. A. Ketcham, "Story of War," 53, both in John Lewis Ketcham Collection, INHS; Dwight Fraser to Lizzie, May 18, 1865, Dwight Fraser Papers, INHS. See also William Wade to "Brother Soldiers," May 9, 1865, reprinted in *Raleigh Daily Progress*, May 10, 1865; George F. Towle Diary, May 24, 1865, NHHS; Isaiah Hutchison to Cindrilla Hutchison, November 26, 1865, Isaiah Hutchison Papers, INHS.

43. John A. Stanly et al. to Andrew Johnson, April 29, 1865, and Innis N. Palmer to Andrew Johnson, May 30, 1865, both in Andrew Johnson Papers, LC; Alfred H. Terry to "Dear General," May 6, 1865, Joseph Roswell Hawley Papers,

LC. See also I. N. Palmer to "Dear General," May 13, 1865, box 7, John McAllister Schofield Papers, LC.

44. E. D. Townsend to Major-General Schofield, May 9, 1865, and GO No. 73, Dept NC, June 2, 1865, both in OR 47(3): 451, 614–15; Sefton, *Army and Reconstruction*, 261.

45. N. B. Sterrett Letter, *Christian Recorder* (Philadelphia), August 26, 1865; Sefton, *Army and Reconstruction*, 261.

46. Joseph R. Hawley to J. A. Campbell, May 21, 1865, SO No. 77, Dept NC, June 1, 1865, J. M. Schofield to Brigadier-General Hawley, June 4, 1865, and J. M. Schofield to U. S. Grant, June 1, 1865, all in OR 47(3): 551, 609–10, 621.

47. Charles A. Tournier Diary, May 8–19, 1865, CWMC, MHI.

48. Anonymous soldier quoted in Longacre, *Regiment of Slaves*, 169.

49. Simpson, *Let Us Have Peace*, 113–14; Glatthaar, *Forged in Battle*, 210.

50. *North Carolina Daily Standard* (Raleigh), April 27, May 9, 1865.

51. Richardson, *Messages and Papers*, 6: 312–14. See also GO No. 74, Dept NC, June 5, 1865, in OR 47(3): 625.

52. Richardson, *Messages and Papers*, 6: 313.

53. Schofield, *Forty-Six Years*, 376; J. M. Schofield to U. S. Grant, June 4, 1865, J. M. Schofield to General Halleck, June 20, 1865, and GO No. 85, Dept NC, June 20, 1865, all in OR 47(3): 621, 659, 660.

3. An Uncertain Relationship

1. Johnston, *Narrative of Military Operations*, 419; Elizabeth Collier Diary, April 25, 1865, SHC-UNC; Emily Tillinghast to Brother, October 1, 1865, Tillinghast Family Papers, DU. See also Mary Ann S. M. Buie to Cousin, June 27, 1865, Mary Ann S. M. Buie Papers, DU.

2. Manning F. Force Letter Book-Journal, April 22, 1865, Manning Ferguson Force Papers, UWA; Will to Sister, April 22, 24, 1865, both in William C. Stevens Correspondence, UMI; Bradley, *Astounding Close*, 189, 193; Wiley, *Billy Yank*, 354–57. See also Hiram M. Austin to "father and mother," April 28, 1865, Hiram M. Austin Letters, BBSHS.

3. Nicholas J. De Graff Diary, June 19, 1865, CWTIC, MHI; Conyngham, *Sherman's March*, 365; John Johnson Diary, April 17–18, 1865, DU; Henry Hitchcock to Mary Hitchcock, April 25, 1865, in Howe, *Marching with Sherman*, 311.

4. Dwight Fraser to Lizzie, July 16, 1865, Dwight Fraser Papers, INHS; G. P. Collins to Anne Collins, May 26, June 5, July 4, July 16, 1865, all in George P. Collins Letters, Anne Cameron Collins Papers, SHC-UNC.

5. Quoted in Crow and Barden, *Live Your Own Life*, 212; Mary Ann S. M. Buie to Cousin, June 27, 1865, Mary Ann S. M. Buie Papers, DU; Orville T. Chamberlain Diary, April 20, 1865, and O. T. to Father, April 21, 1865, both in Joseph W. and Orville T. Chamberlain Papers, INHS.

6. Transcript of Clarke, "Gen. Sherman's Officers," 1, Mary Moulton Barden Collection; GO No. 106, July 15, 1865, Dept NC, Joseph F. Boyd Papers, DU; Trial of John B. Gilbert, Case No. MM-2526, RG 153, NA.

7. Transcript of Clarke, "Gen. Sherman's Officers," 1–2, Mary Moulton Barden Collection; Frances Miller to Mary Bayard Clarke [ca. June 1865], in Crow and Barden, *Live Your Own Life*, 182–83.

8. *Charlotte Western Democrat*, August 6, 1872; Charlie to Mother, June 9, 1865, Charles F. Barnes Correspondence, Barnes Family Papers, UVA. For the argument that the intransigence of southern white women was exaggerated, see Foster, *Ghosts of the Confederacy*, 29–30; Silber, *Romance of Reunion*, 28. For the contention that the animosity of white North Carolina women was genuine and persistent, see McKitrick, *Andrew Johnson*, 40. The evidence in Campbell, *When Sherman Marched*, indicates that the defiance of elite white women in the face of defeat persisted into the postwar years, manifesting itself in their ongoing hostility to Union soldiers. For additional evidence, see Anne Ruffin to "my darling Child," May 21, 1865, box 8, Ruffin, Roulhac, and Hamilton Family Papers, SHC-UNC; M. to Brother, August 11, 1865, Pettigrew Family Papers, SHC-UNC; Maria De Rosset to Lou, July 18 [1865], box 3, folder 65, De Rosset Family Papers, SHC-UNC; Laura Craven to Em, May 5 [1865], Craven-Pegram Family Papers, DU; King, *Anna Fuller's Journal*, 47.

9. McMurray, *Recollections*, 88.

10. Laura Craven to Em, November 19, 1866, Craven-Pegram Family Papers, DU.

11. Leander S. Gash to Wife, February 4, 1866, Leander S. Gash Papers, PC, NCSA; Fred C. Foard Reminiscences, 28, Fred C. Foard Papers, PC, NCSA; George to Fannie, May 16, 1865, George Shuman Letters, HCWRTC, MHI. See also Dwight Fraser to Lizzie, January 26, April 9, 1866, both in Dwight Fraser Papers, INHS.

12. Crabtree and Patton, "*Journal of a Secesh Lady*," 711; Mary C. R. to Sister, July 17, 1865, Tod Robinson Caldwell Papers, SHC-UNC.

13. William to Sister, June 20, 1865, William C. Stevens Correspondence, UMI; Mary T. Brown to John Evans Brown, June 20, 1865, W. Vance Brown Collection, PC, NCSA; William F. King to Wife, April 17, 1865, William F. King Papers, INHS. See also Maria De Rosset to Cousin, May 18, 1865, box 3, folder 65, De Rosset Family Papers, SHC-UNC.

14. Cornelia Phillips Spencer Journal, August 23, 28, 1865, and "The Decline of the University: The Cause of the Decline," 67, all in Cornelia Phillips Spencer Papers, SHC-UNC; E. J. Thompson to B. S. Hedrick, August 17–September 24, 1865, Benjamin S. Hedrick Papers, DU; Chamberlain, *Old Days in Chapel Hill*, 98–99; Fred C. Foard Reminiscences, 28, Fred C. Foard Papers, PC, NCSA. For a North-South romance that ended tragically, see Sherwood, *Memories of the War*, 192–95.

15. Escott, "Clinton A. Cilley," 404–26; "Cilley, Clinton A.," North Carolina Collection Clipping File, 26: 456, NCC-UNC.

16. [Walker], *Surrender in Greensboro*, 4–5; Jacob Henry Smith Diary, May 4–5, 1865, box 15, H. Richardson Smith Papers, SHC-UNC; Mrs. Jacob H. Smith, "The Women of Greensboro," North Carolina Biography File, NCC-GPL.

17. Deposition of R[ichard] Blacknall, August 8, 1872; deposition of Leddy Garrett, August 9, 1872; deposition of Mrs. Jane Dick, August 10, 1872; deposition of Eugene Eckels [n.d.]; deposition of Edmund Hill, August 9, 1872, all in Records Concerning the Conduct and Loyalty of Certain Union Army Officers, Civilian Employees of the War Department, and Other U.S. Citizens during the Civil War, 1861–1872, under file heading: "Statements dated 1872 concerning H. Judson Kilpatrick's affair with a woman during the Civil War," box 2, RG 107, NA; George F. Towle Diary, May 3, August 10–11, 1865, NHHS; George to Fannie, June 6, 1865, George Shuman Letters, HCWRTC, MHI; Arnett, *Confederate Guns*, 85.

18. W. H. Boney to "My Dear Gov," June 8, 1865, and W. H. Boney to "My Dear Sir," December 7, 1865, both in McKinney and McMurry, *Vance Papers*, reel 4; A. McLean et al. to M. Kerwin, July 5, 1865, reprinted in *North Carolina Daily Standard* (Raleigh), July 19, 1865. See also *Raleigh Daily Record*, June 19, 1865.

19. Tod R. Caldwell to Gov. Holden, September 18, 1865, LR, Dept NC, box 1, RG 393, NA; W. G. MacRae to Donald MacRae, July 13, 1865, MacRae Family Papers, DU. See also Jacob Henry Smith Diary, May 2, 6, 1865, H. Richardson Smith Papers, SHC-UNC; Edmund J. Cleveland Diary, May 11, 1865, SHC-UNC; John Wilkes to Father, May 28, 1865, Wilkes Family Papers, DU; GO No. 65, May 29, 1865, and GO No. 101, July 14, 1865, Dept NC, Joseph F. Boyd Papers, DU.

20. Will to Father, May 13, 1865, William C. Stevens Correspondence, UMI; Tom to Jane, May 13, 1865, Thomas J. Jordan Papers, HSPA; Abner Eisenhower Diary, May 13, 1865, CWMA, 3rd series, MHI; GO No. 100, July 14, 1865, Dept NC, Joseph F. Boyd Papers, DU.

21. GO No. 97, July 9, 1865, Dept NC, and GO No. 157, John S. Bowles, November 14, 1865, Dept NC, both in Joseph F. Boyd Papers, DU. See also Trial of John S. Bowles, Case No. MM-3114, RG 153, NA.

22. GO No. 170, December 9, 1865; GO No. 161, November 23, 1865; GO No. 165, Isaac Cramer and Joseph Harrison, November 29, 1865; GO No. 181, David Lions, December 26, 1865; GO No. 182, George Pursley and Richard Welch, December 26, 1865, Dept NC, all in Joseph F. Boyd Papers, DU; Stephen S. Burrill Diary, June 22, 1865, PC, NCSA; Trial of Charles F. Brown, Case No. MM-3226, RG 153, NA. For other officers who were cashiered by an army court-martial, see Augustus S. Boernstein to Clinton A. Cilley, July 28, 1865, and Thomas T. Heath to J. A. Campbell, October 9, 1865, both in LR, Dept NC, box 1, RG 393, NA; GO No. 103, July 14, 1865, Dept NC, Joseph F. Boyd Papers, DU; General Court Martial Orders No. 31, March 8, 1866, Dept NC, and Trial of Edward E. Sherridan, both in Case No. MM-3721, RG 153, NA.

23. Augustus S. Boernstein to John T. Hough, July 23, 1865, LR, Dept NC, box 1, RG 393, NA; GO No. 8, July 20, 1865, Post of Greensboro, GO No. 9, August 15, 1865, Post of Greensboro, William Lafayette Scott Papers, DU; *Wilmington Herald*, April 8, June 7, July 11, 1865; *North Carolina Daily Standard* (Raleigh), June 8, August 5, 1865. See also GO No. 11, Post of Wilmington, July 17, 1865, LS, Post of Wilmington, RG 393, NA. At the request of the mayor of Wilmington, the post commander suspended the prohibition order two weeks later and permitted dealers to renew their liquor licenses. See GO No. 15, Post of Wilmington, August 16, 1865, reprinted in *Wilmington Herald*, August 17, 1865.

24. Everts, *Ninth Regiment New Jersey*, 176–77; Morris to Sister, May 30, 1865, Morris W. Chalmers Letters, CWMC, MHI; Stark, "History of the 103rd Ohio," 452; Crow and Barden, *Live Your Own Life*, 180; Dwight Fraser to Lizzie, March 19, 1866, Dwight Fraser Papers, INHS; David Schenck Diary, July 24, 1865, David Schenck Papers, SHC-UNC; GO Nos. 34–35, July 18, 1865, District of Raleigh, both in Case No. OO-1232, RG 153, NA; William A. Ketcham, "A Part of His Story of War," 53–54, John Lewis Ketcham Collection, INHS; John D. Kidd to Father and Mother, June 9, 1865, and John D. Kidd to Father, June 16, 1865, both in Kidd Family Papers, INHS; Charles A. Carleton to G. F. Towle, July 1, 1865, Charles A. Carleton to Alonzo Alden, July 1, 1865, and Charles A. Carleton to John Wainwright, July 17, 1865, all in LS, Post of Raleigh, RG 393, NA.

25. *Raleigh Daily Progress*, May 16, 1865; *Wilmington Herald*, June 12, 1865. The editor of the *Progress* was John L. Pennington, a supporter of North Carolina's wartime peace movement and a violent opponent of the proposal to arm and emancipate the slaves. The editor of the *Herald* was Thomas M. Cook, a former *New York Herald* reporter who had accompanied the Union army to North Carolina in early 1865.

26. John MacRae to Donald MacRae, June 22, 1865, MacRae Family Papers, DU; John Tillinghast to Will, July 31, 1865, Tillinghast Family Papers, DU; Thomas Ruffin to David L. Swain, August 31, 1865, Letter Book, vol. 4, Walter Clark Papers, PC, NCSA.

27. General Paine, the commander of the black troops in North Carolina, advised black soldiers and civilians to "stir up" the black suffrage issue. See Charles J. Paine to Father, September 8, 1865, Charles Jackson Paine Papers, VHS. See also Zalimas, "Black Union Soldiers," 4–7.

28. U.S. Congress, *Report of the Joint Committee*, 178; N. B. Sterrett Letters, *Christian Recorder* (Philadelphia), April 1, July 8, 1865; Stein, *Thirty-Seventh Regt.*, 80, 129; Reid, "USCT Veterans," 392.

29. A. M. Waddell to W. W. Holden, June 18, 1865, in Raper and Mitchell, *Holden Papers*, 1: 195–97. About the time Waddell wrote Holden, presidential advisor Harvey M. Watterson was offering President Johnson a similar assessment from New Bern. Watterson reported that the townspeople believed "they deserve no such punishment as Gen. Payne [Paine] and his negro troops. That it is wholly

unnecessary and very bad policy, there can be no question." See H. M. Watterson to Andrew Johnson, June 20, 1865, in Simpson et al., *Advice after Appomattox*, 50.

30. For accounts of the alleged December 1864 insurrection plot, see James T. Leak et al. to Zebulon B. Vance, December 9, 1864, and H. Nutt to Zebulon B. Vance, December 1864, both in McKinney and McMurry, *Vance Papers*, reel 25. Citizens in western North Carolina were terrorized by a squad of black soldiers from Tennessee who claimed to be pursuing deserters. Col. Thomas T. Heath reported that the lieutenant in command of the soldiers allowed them to roam unsupervised. They robbed citizens rumored to have large amounts of gold in their possession. Heath described the soldiers as "the most vicious and insubordinate men I have ever seen in the Army." See Thomas T. Heath to L. G. Estes, August 18, 1865, LR, Dept NC, box 1, RG 393, NA.

31. W. W. Holden to J. D. Cox, June 22, 1865, and J. D. Cox to W. W. Holden, June 23, 1865, in Raper and Mitchell, *Holden Papers*, 1: 200–201; W. W. Holden to J. D. Cox, June 24, 1865, William Woods Holden PGLB, NCSA.

32. Soon after his transfer, Cox was elected Republican governor of Ohio. E. D. Townsend to J. D. Cox, June 25, 1865, J. D. Cox to E. D. Townsend, June 26, 1865, and J. D. Cox to T. H. Ruger, June 26, 1865, all in OR 47(3): 663–65; *Wilmington Herald*, July 10, 1865; J. W. Ames to J. R. Hawley, July 17, 1865, Joseph Roswell Hawley Papers, LC.

33. John Dawson et al. to W. W. Holden, July 12, 1865, with enclosed memorandum of C. C. Emerson, June 3, 1865, and W. W. Holden to Major General Ruger, July 15, 1865, both in Raper and Mitchell, *Holden Papers*, 1: 212–15, 217.

34. Samuel A. Duncan to C. A. Cilley, July 26, 1865, LR, Dept NC, box 2, RG 393, NA.

35. John Dawson et al. to W. W. Holden, August 3, 1865, with enclosed memorandum of L. W. Harmon [n.d.], and John M. Davies to Augustus S. Boernstein, July 26, 1865, both in LR, Dept NC, box 1, RG 393, NA; W. W. Holden to Andrew Johnson, August 10, 1865, and Andrew Johnson to W. W. Holden, August 10, 1865, both in Raper and Mitchell, *Holden Papers*, 1: 224–26, 231–32, 236; Samuel T. Bond et al. to Andrew Johnson, August 7, 1865, and Samuel Bond to Andrew Johnson, August 10, 1865, both in Andrew Johnson Papers, LC. Soon after Johnson received the Edenton petition, a resident of the town reported that the presence of black troops at Edenton and Elizabeth City "has been very annoying to the people, and has produced some hard feeling towards the government—though generally these troops have conducted themselves well." *Raleigh Daily Sentinel*, September 25, 1865. The letter to Holden from the mayor of New Bern was likewise forwarded to Johnson. See James Osgood, John M. Davies, and T. B. James to President Johnson, July 27, 1865, in Graf et al., *Johnson Papers*, 8: 486–87.

36. One of the policemen was sentenced to a year at hard labor and the other to six months, but Paine reduced their sentences because the sergeant was only

slightly injured. See trials of various citizens and police of New Bern, and GO No. 37, O. G. Sempler and F. N. Cook, August 30, 1865, District of New Bern, both in Case No. OO-1520, RG 153, NA; Charles J. Paine to Father, August 16, 26, 1865, Charles Jackson Paine Papers, VHS; *Wilmington Herald*, August 3–5, 11, 1865, *North Carolina Daily Times* (New Bern), July 20–22, August 16, 1865; Charlie to Mother, Charles F. Barnes Correspondence, June 9, 1865, Barnes Family Papers, UVA. At least two clashes between black soldiers and white police occurred in Beaufort and Wilmington as late as December 1865. See Phillipp Weinmann to Hiram R. Ellis, December 26, 1865, in LR, Post of New Bern, N.C., RG 393, NA; *Wilmington Herald*, December 25, 1865. For Goff's order, see n. 23 of this chapter.

37. *Wilmington Herald*, July 13, 15, 1865; *North Carolina Daily Times* (New Bern), June 24, 26, July 20, 21, 1865; Henry M. Turner Letter, *Christian Recorder* (Philadelphia), June 10, 1865; A. S. Gear to J. F. Boyd, June 24, 1865, Railroad Papers, Joseph F. Boyd Papers, DU; W. W. Holden to Andrew Johnson, June 26, 1865, in Graf et al., *Johnson Papers*, 8: 293–94. In Charleston, South Carolina, where both white and black soldiers served in the city's provost guard, continual interracial brawling culminated in a bloody race riot on July 8–10, 1865. See Zalimas, "Disturbance in the City," 374–76.

38. James L. Smythe to Jasper Myers, October 5, 1866, reel 12, LR, ACNC, RG 105, NA.

39. A. G. Gear to J. F. Boyd, June 24, 1865, Railroad Papers, Joseph F. Boyd Papers, DU; J. M. Schofield to U. S. Grant, June 1, 1865, in OR 47(3): 609; Trial of Robert Stewart, Case No. MM-3226, RG 153, NA; General Court Martial Orders No. 18, Pompey Harkell, Providence James, Aaron Benjamin, and Oretus Miller, February 20, 1866, Dept NC, and Trial of Pompey Harkell, Providence James, Aaron Benjamin, and Oretus Miller, both in Case No. MM-3643, RG 153, NA; Trial of Aaron Johnson, Case No. MM-3721, RG 153, NA; *Wilmington Daily Journal*, quoted in *Raleigh Daily Sentinel*, January 18, 1866; *Charlotte Western Democrat*, January 16, 1866; *Wilmington Herald*, August 11, 17, 1865; *North Carolina Daily Times* (New Bern), July 22, 1865; Trial of George Josey, Washington Flood, Jerry Pruden, and Edward Newson, Case No. MM-3615, RG 153, NA.

40. Trial of Manuel Davis, Samuel Alderman, George Smallwood, and Isaac Moore, MM-3979, RG 153, NA; Thomas H. Ruger to George D. Ruggles, October 4, 1865, LS, Dept NC, RG 393, NA. See also GO No. 169, December 6, 1865, Dept NC, Joseph F. Boyd Papers; *Wilmington Herald*, July 29, 1865; *North Carolina Daily Standard* (Raleigh), September 28, 1865; Trial of Joseph Yokeley, Case No. MM-3226, RG 153, NA; Stein, *Thirty-Seventh Regt.*, 93.

41. Thanks to the intervention of Maj. R. M. Taylor of the 12th New York Cavalry, President Johnson remitted the sentences of the regiment's mutineers, ending their imprisonment and restoring their pay and bounties to them. *Raleigh Daily Sentinel*, November 10, 1865; *Army and Navy Journal* (New York), November 11, 1865; Trial of Edward Burns and thirty others in M Troop, 12th New York

Cavalry, GO No. 30, July 23, 1865, and GO No. 45, July 25, 1865, District of Raleigh, and SO No. 588, November 7, 1865, War Department, all in Case No. OO-1232, RG 153, NA. See also GO No. 107, Edward C. Stewart, July 17, 1865, Dept NC, Joseph F. Boyd Papers, DU.

42. John D. Kidd to Mother and Father, June 9, 1865, Kidd Family Papers, INHS. See also William A. Ketcham, "A Part of His Story of War," 54–56, John Lewis Ketcham Collection, INHS.

43. GO No. 9, Post of Wilmington, July 3, 1865, reprinted in *Wilmington Herald*, July 8, 1865; ibid., July 10, 1865; Glatthaar, *Forged in Battle*, 209.

44. *Wilmington Herald*, August 12, 16, 1865.

45. Daniel T. Wells to W. A. Cutler, August 27, 1866, LS, Dept NC, RG 393, NA; James L. Gant to Edwin M. Stanton, July 31, 1865, Edwin McMasters Stanton Papers, LC; Trial of Dock Leech and Trial of Henry Bird, both in Case No. MM-3226, RG 153, NA. For a discussion of punishment in the USCT, see Glatthaar, *Forged in Battle*, 109–11.

46. Testimony of J. A. Campbell, in U.S. Congress, *Report of the Joint Committee*, 260; Reid, "USCT Veterans," 411–12.

47. Chaplain Turner Letter, *Christian Recorder* (Philadelphia), June 10, 1865; "Sallie" Letters, ibid., June 10, July 1, 1865.

48. Escott, "Clinton A. Cilley," 409; Richard Etheridge and William Benson to Genl. Howard, [n.d.], Francis George Shaw to O. O. Howard, June 7, 1865, Charles J. Paine to Captain McMurray, June 8, 1865, John McMurray to C. J. Paine, June 11, 1865, John H. Holman to Solon A. Carter, June 14, 1865, and John H. Holman to O. O. Howard, June 15, 1865, all in M843, reel 11, LR, ACNC, RG 105, NA; H. C. Thompson to B. S. Hedrick, June 14, 1865, Benjamin S. Hedrick Papers, DU; GO No. 28, Holland Streeter, July 24, 1865, District of New Bern, and Trial of Holland Streeter, both in Case No. MM-2836, RG 153, NA.

49. Dexter E. Clapp to Fred H. Beecher, August 7, 1865, M843, reel 22, Reports, ACNC, RG 105, NA. As late as July 1868, a Freedmen's Bureau official in Elizabeth City reported that "a great many" claimants appealed to him for assistance in obtaining the money that army officers had promised them but had never paid. See Report of William H. Doherty for July 1868, ibid.

50. Escott, "Clinton A. Cilley," 409; Charles A. Carleton to John S. Littell, July 13, 1865, LS, Post of Raleigh, RG 393, NA; Thomas T. Heath to J. A. Campbell, June 14, 1865, LS, Dist WNC, RG 393, NA.

51. *Wilmington Herald*, August 10, 15, 1865; J. W. Ames to Clinton A. Cilley, August 29, 1865, LR, Dept NC, box 1, RG 393, NA.

52. Samuel C. Oliver to E. C. Latimer, August 26, 1865, Clinton A. Cilley to J. W. Ames, August 14, 1865, J. C. Williams to Maj. Oliver [August 30, 1865], all in William Woods Holden PGP, NCSA; W. W. Holden to T. H. Ruger, August 14, 1865, William Woods Holden PGLB, NCSA.

53. Joseph C. Abbott to Clinton A. Cilley, July 8, 1865, LS, Post of Goldsboro,

RG 393, NA; Charlie to Mother, June 9, 1865, Charles F. Barnes Correspondence, Barnes Family Papers, UVA; M. C. Meigs to J. F. Boyd, August 19, 1865, Miscellaneous Letters, Joseph F. Boyd Papers, DU.

54. L. S. Burkhead, "History of the Front Street Methodist Church, Wilmington, for the Year 1865," 22–23, 73, box 6, Methodist Church Papers, DU. Ruger later ruled that the white congregation had clear title to the church. See Thomas H. Ruger to E. D. Townsend, May 31, 1866, and J. A. Campbell to R. T. Frank, June 6, 1866, LS, Dept NC, RG 393, NA.

55. Alexander, *North Carolina Faces the Freedmen*, 138.

4. The Return of Civil Government

1. Powell, *Powell's Records*, 516; Warner, *Generals in Blue*, 415–16; Boatner, *Civil War Dictionary*, 712; Howard, *Autobiography*, 1: 431–32; Pfanz, *Culp's Hill and Cemetery Hill*, 229–30.

2. GO No. 93, Dept NC, July 5, 1865, and Circular, Dept NC, July 11, 1865, both in U.S. Army, Department of North Carolina Papers, DU; GO No. 95, Dept NC, July 6, 1865, in OR 47(3): 675; Samuel A. Duncan to C. A. Cilley, July 24, 1865, LR, Dept NC, box 2, RG 393, NA; Armand De Rosset to Lou, August 9, 1865, De Rosset Family Papers, SHC-UNC.

3. GO No. 98, Dept NC, July 10, 1865, U.S. Army, Department of North Carolina Papers, DU; Charlotte Grimes Reminiscences, 24, Bryan Grimes Papers, SHC-UNC; Thomas T. Heath to J. A. Campbell, October 9, 1865, LR, Dept NC, box 1, RG 393, NA; Hamilton, *Recollections of a Cavalryman*, 219–20; *North Carolina Daily Standard* (Raleigh) quoted in *Army and Navy Journal* (New York), October 7, 1865.

4. R. C. Kise to W. L. Scott, July 15, 1865, William L. Scott to Gov. Holden, July 25, 1865, and C. A. Cilley to Commanding Officer, Greensboro, N.C., August 10, 1865, all in William Lafayette Scott Papers, DU; Daniel R. Goodloe to B. S. Hedrick, September 29, 1865, Benjamin S. Hedrick Papers, DU.

5. Clinton A. Cilley to Governor Holden, July 27, 1865, William Woods Holden PGLB, NCSA.

6. A. S. Boernstein to John T. Hough, July 23, 1865, John M. Davies to Augustus S. Boernstein, July 26, 1865, and Augustus S. Boernstein to Clinton A. Cilley, July 28, 1865, all in LR, Dept NC, box 1, RG 393, NA. See also James Osgood, John M. Davies, and T. B. James to President Johnson, July 27, 1865, in Graf et al., *Johnson Papers*, 8: 486–87.

7. Thomas H. Ruger to George G. Meade, September 19, 1865, M619, reel 331, LR, AGO, RG 94, NA.

8. A. Ames to W. W. Holden, July 24, 1865, William Woods Holden PGLB, NCSA; W. W. Holden to Brevet Maj. Gen. Ruger, July 27, 1865, in Raper and Mitchell, *Holden Papers*, 1: 221–22.

9. Thomas H. Ruger to W. W. Holden, August 1, 1865, in Raper and Mitchell, *Holden Papers,* 1: 222–24; Perman, *Reunion without Compromise,* 132–33.

10. W. W. Holden to T. H. Ruger, August 8, 1865, and Thomas H. Ruger to W. W. Holden, August 11, 1865, both in William Woods Holden PGLB, NCSA; W. W. Holden to George G. Meade, September 12, 1865, and Thomas H. Ruger to George G. Meade, September 19, 1865, both in M619, reel 331, LR, AGO, RG 94, NA; George G. Meade to W. W. Holden, September 22, 1865, in Raper and Mitchell, *Holden Papers,* 1: 245.

11. "Report of Known Outrages committed by Whites against Blacks in the Department of North Carolina since the surrender of the rebel army," in Thomas H. Ruger to T. S. Bowers, January 9, 1866, M619, reel 505, LR, AGO, RG 94, NA; GO No. 110, July 19, 1865, Dept NC, Joseph F. Boyd Papers, DU. The name of the executed freedman was Alfred Locke. See E. D. Townsend to Thomas H. Ruger, August 10, 1865, M565, reel 27, LS, AGO, RG 94, NA.

12. "Report of Known Outrages," in Thomas H. Ruger to T. S. Bowers, January 9, 1866, M619, reel 505, LR, AGO, RG 94, NA; Trial of Archibald Baynes, Case No. OO-1433, RG 153, NA; GO No. 134, August 30, 1865, Dept NC, Joseph F. Boyd Papers, DU; Trial of Temperance Neely, Case No. MM-2968, RG 153, NA; Testimony of J. A. Campbell in U.S. Congress, *Report of the Joint Committee,* 213; J. Kilpatrick to O. O. Howard, August 13, 1865, M843, reel 16, LR, ACNC, RG 105, NA.

13. Thomas T. Heath to C. A. Cilley, August 28, 1865, LR, Dept NC, box 1, RG 393, NA; E. Whittlesey to Charles A. Carleton, July 20, 1865, and E. Whittlesey to O. O. Howard, October 15, 1865, both in M843, reel 1, LS, ACNC, RG 105, NA. See also E. Whittlesey to C. A. Cilley, August 3, 1865, LR, Dept NC, box 1, RG 393, NA.

14. J. Holt to Andrew Johnson, December 19, 1865, in Trial of Archibald Baynes, Case No. OO-1433, RG 153, NA.

15. Thomas T. Heath to C. A. Cilley, July 15, 1865, LS, Dist WNC, RG 393, NA; Trial of Archibald Baynes, Case No. OO-1433, RG 153, NA; Bogue "Violence and Oppression," 42–43. See also George L. Dailey to F. H. Beecher, July 10, 1865, and H. D. Grant to B. N. Smith, July 17, 1865, with endorsements of Clinton A. Cilley, July 25, 1865, and A. Ames, July 25, 1865, both in LR, Dept NC, box 1, RG 393, NA.

16. In the 1860 Federal Census, Cherry is listed as a "Slave Trader" with a net worth of $32,550. See "T. R. Cherry," 1860 Federal Population Census, M653, reel 910, Pitt County, N.C., Greenville, p. 8. Edward M. Fuller to Clinton A. Cilley, July 31, 1865, LR, Dept NC, box 1, RG 393, NA; GO No. 90, July 1, 1865, Dept NC, Joseph F. Boyd Papers, DU; Bogue, "Violence and Oppression," 49–50.

17. W. W. Holden to Thomas H. Ruger, August 30, 1865, in Raper and Mitchell, *Holden Papers,* 1: 237; GO No. 141, September 12, 1865, Dept NC, Joseph F. Boyd Papers, DU.

18. Trial of George A. Pitts et al., Case No. OO-1514, RG 153, NA; Thomas T. Heath to J. A. Campbell, September 22, 23, 24, 1865, all in LS, Dist WNC, RG 393, NA.

19. GO No. 177 and GO No. 180, December 26, 1865, Dept NC, Joseph F. Boyd Papers, DU; J. A. Campbell to R. P. Harris, L. S. Brigham, and V. O. Barringer, January 27, 1866, LS, Dept NC, RG 393, NA. For a similar riot in Chapel Hill, see H. C. Thompson to B. S. Hedrick, September 14, 21, 1865, Benjamin S. Hedrick Papers, DU; Charles Phillips to Kemp P. Battle, September 20, 1865, Battle Family Papers, SHC-UNC; Cornelia Phillips Spencer Journal, September 17, 1865, Cornelia Phillips Spencer Papers, SHC-UNC.

20. In early November, an officer was sent to Cherokee County to organize a local police force there. R. K. Miller to A. S. Paul, November 28, 1865, LR, Dept NC, box 1, RG 393, NA; W. H. Herbert to W. W. Holden, October 14, 1865, with endorsement of Thomas H. Ruger, October 20, 1865, LR, Dept NC, box 2, RG 393, NA; Thomas T. Heath to Reverend Mr. Stewart, September 14, 1865, LS, Dist WNC, RG 393, NA; Thomas T. Heath to Clinton A. Cilley, August 28, September 7, 1865, and Thomas T. Heath to J. A. Campbell, September 11, September 19, October 16, 1865, all in LR, Dept NC, box 1, RG 393, NA; Thomas H. Ruger to George D. Ruggles, October 4, 1865, LS, Dept NC, RG 393, NA; W. W. Holden to the Sheriff and Justices of the Peace of Randolph County, September 16, 1865, and J. M. Pierce to W. W. Holden, September 17, 1865, both in William Woods Holden PGP, NCSA; W. L. Love to Jonathan Worth, May 19, 1865[6], Worth GP, NCSA; A. S. Merrimon to Jonathan Worth, June 7, 1866, in Hamilton, *Worth Correspondence*, 1: 601–2. See also Jordan Vollavey to "Col. commanding at Roanoke Island," September 25, 1865, Jordan Vollavey Letter, DU.

21. Thomas T. Heath to Clinton A. Cilley, August 28, 1865, LR, Dept NC, box 1, RG 393, NA.

22. Thomas T. Heath to J. A. Campbell, September 11, October 16, 1865, and R. K. Miller to A. S. Paul, December 13, 1865, all in LR, Dept NC, box 1, RG 393, NA; W. H. Herbert to W. W. Holden, October 14, 1865, with endorsement of J. A. Campbell, October 20, 1865, LR, Dept NC, box 2, RG 393, NA; GO No. 2, August 1, 1865, Dist WNC, reprinted in *North Carolina Daily Standard* (Raleigh), August 10, 1865; *Army and Navy Journal* (New York), September 30, 1865; Calvin J. Cowles to Capt. Hoke, June 15, 1865, Calvin J. Cowles to Capt. Baker, June 15, 1865, Calvin J. Cowles to G. E. Dunbar, July 13, 1865, and Calvin J. Cowles to Gen. Kilpatrick, September 7, 1865, all in Letterpress Books, Calvin J. Cowles Papers, PC, NCSA; John D. Kidd to Father, July 23, 1865, Kidd Family Papers, INHS.

23. D. Furches to Jonathan Worth, January 15, 1866, Frank C. Robbins to Gov. Worth, January 19, 1866, J. A. Campbell to Jonathan Worth, January 22, 1866, J. D. Hamlin to Gov. Worth, March 31, 1866, and Thomas H. Ruger to Jonathan Worth, April 5, 1866 (re. Helsebeck), all in Jonathan Worth GP, NCSA; Jonathan

Worth to Andrew Johnson, January 15, 1866, Jonathan Worth GLB, NCSA. Army quartermasters reportedly collected more than $650,000 from the sale of livestock in North Carolina. See *Army and Navy Journal* (New York), December 2, 1865.

24. GO No. 111, July 21, 1865, Dept NC, Joseph F. Boyd Papers, DU.

25. J. J. Bruner to Gen. Ruger, July 28, 1865, LR, Dept NC, box 2, RG 393, NA; GO No. 118, July 31, 1865, Dept NC, Joseph F. Boyd Papers, DU. See also *North Carolina Daily Standard* (Raleigh), August 5, 1865.

26. General Court Martial Orders No. 1, January 17, 1866, Dept NC, Joseph F. Boyd Papers, DU; *Army and Navy Journal* (New York), December 30, 1865; *North Carolina Daily Standard* (Raleigh), December 18, 1865, January 11, 1866; *Raleigh Daily Sentinel*, February 22, 1866; T. S. Bowers to Thomas H. Ruger, February 11, 1866, LR, Dept NC, box 2, RG 393, NA; Benjamin Robinson to Andrew Johnson, May 10, 1866, in Graf et al., *Johnson Papers*, 10: 488–89. The *Charlotte Western Democrat* condemned Waring's arrest as "tyrannical and unauthorized," earning the editor, W. J. Yates, a stern rebuke and a warning from Ruger. See J. A. Campbell to W. J. Yates, December 27, 1865, LS, Dept NC, RG 393, NA.

27. Harris, *Holden*, 187–89.

28. R. K. Miller to A. S. Paul, November 28, 1865, LR, Dept NC, box 1, RG 393, NA.

29. Jonathan Worth to William C. Smith, August 25, 1865, in Hamilton, *Worth Correspondence*, 1: 402; Harris, *Holden*, 195–98.

30. E. Whittlesey to "My dear General," June 24, 1865, Oliver Otis Howard Papers, BC; E. Whittlesey to O. O. Howard, October 15, 1865, M843, reel 1, Reports, ACNC, RG 105, NA; GO No. 102, June 20, 1865, War Department, M843, reel 20, GOC, ACNC, RG 105, NA.

31. E. Whittlesey to O. O. Howard, October 15, 1865, M843, reel 1, Reports, ACNC, RG 105, NA; *New York Tribune*, February 3, 1866, quoted in U.S. Congress, *Report of the Joint Committee*, 194–95.

32. E. Whittlesey to O. O Howard, October 15, 1865, M843, reel 1, Reports, ACNC, RG 105, NA; William B. Bowe to E. Whittlesey, January 27, 1866, M843, reel 16, LR, ACNC, RG 105, NA. See also E. Whittlesey to J. A. Campbell, March 24, 1866, M843, reel 1, LS, ACNC, RG 105, NA.

33. E. Whittlesey to General Howard, August 21, 1865, E. Whittlesey to C. A. Cilley, August 21, 1865, and Frederick H. Beecher to Horace James, September 13, 1865, all in M843, reel 1, LS, ACNC, RG 105, NA; Thomas H. Ruger to Major General Howard, October 6, 1865, M843, reel 8, LR, ACNC, RG 105, NA; Circular No. 44, September 9, 1865, War Department, AGO, OR 5 series 3: 108; *North Carolina Daily Standard* (Raleigh), September 16, 1865; Charles J. Paine to Father, September 12, 26, 1865, Charles Jackson Paine Papers, VHS.

34. Thomas H. Ruger to George G. Meade, September 19, 1865, M619, reel 331, LR, AGO, RG 94, NA. Ruger anticipated by several weeks the War Depart-

ment's GO No. 144, which directed occupation commanders to transfer black soldiers to coastal forts and to muster out all those no longer needed for garrison duty. See Zalimas, "Black Union Soldiers," 58.

35. W. W. Holden to Brevet Maj. Gen. Ruger, September 23, 1865, and J. A. Campbell to W. W. Holden, September 30, 1865, both in William Woods Holden PGP, NCSA; W. W. Holden to George Meade, September 12, 1865, M619, reel 331, LR, AGO, RG 94, NA.

36. Thomas H. Ruger to George G. Meade, September 19, 1865, M619, reel 331, LR, AGO, RG 94, NA. Ruger's concern regarding a race riot between black soldiers and white civilians was borne out in Memphis, Tennessee, the following May. But white officers, aided by the firepower of white soldiers, managed to prevent a large force of black troops from attacking Irish police and other armed whites during their murderous and destructive rampage through the black district of Memphis. The army did not intervene until the worst was over. The one-sided nature of the violence is reflected in the death toll of forty-two blacks and only two whites. See Rable, *There Was No Peace*, 38–39; Zalimas, "Black Union Soldiers," 143–44.

37. E. Whittlesey to O. O. Howard, December 1, 1865, Oliver Otis Howard Papers, BC,

38. Crabtree and Patton, *"Journal of a Secesh Lady,"* 718; E. Whittlesey to O. O. Howard, October 15, 1865, January 15, 1866, M843, reel 1, Reports, ACNC, RG 105, NA; Fred H. Beecher to C. W. Mills, September 14, 1865, and E. Whittlesey to William A. White, November 22, 1865, both in M843, reel 1, LS, ACNC, RG 105, NA; *New York Tribune*, February 3, 1866; David Schenck Diary, June 7, 1865, David Schenck Papers, SHC-UNC.

39. M. S. Sherwood to Nephew, March 31, 1866, Benjamin S. Hedrick Papers, DU; Report of F. D. Sewall, May 14, 1866, in U.S. Congress, "Message from the President of the United States," 36; E. Whittlesey to Asa Teal, July 19, 1865, and E. Whittlesey to General Howard, August 21, 1865, both in M843, reel 1, and William L. Scott to E. Whittlesey, August 21, 1865, in M843, reel 16, LS, ACNC, RG 105, NA. Whittlesey described Teal as "a good man and *essential* to the Bureau in his District." See ibid. Upon learning that their Freedmen's Bureau agents were to be removed, a group of citizens from Oxford sent a petition to Whittlesey requesting that they be retained. The petitioners noted that the agents "had been uniformly polite and respectful to all classes of persons, that they have been attentive and diligent in the business committed to them, and that their influence here, has been extremely salutary upon society, without distinction of color." See Petition from citizens of Oxford, N.C., to Eliphalet Whittlesey, October 19, 1865, in ibid., reel 16.

40. Circular No. 3, ACNC, BRFAL, August 15, 1865, William Lafayette Scott Papers, DU. Whittlesey's statement was incorrect. At the time of his first annual report, the bureau in North Carolina held 112 pieces of town property and

36,342 acres of farmland, 4,868 of which were under cultivation. See Howard, *Autobiography*, 2: 233.

41. Crabtree and Patton, *"Journal of a Secesh Lady,"* 714–15; Dexter E. Clapp to Frederick H. Beecher, August 7, 1865, and Dexter E. Clapp to Lieut. Beecher, September 13, 1865, both in M843, reel 22, Reports, ACNC, RG 105, NA; O. O. Howard to E. Whittlesey, September 16, 1865, M843, reel 16, LR, ACNC, RG 105, NA; Thomas H. Ruger to George D. Ruggles, December 20, 1865, LS, Dept NC, RG 393, NA. See also Samuel A. Duncan to C. A. Cilley, July 26, 1865, LR, Dept NC, box 2, RG 393, NA; John C. Barnett to Frederick Beecher, September 18, 1865, M843, reel 7, LR, ACNC, RG 105, NA; Carter, "Anatomy of Fear," 345–64.

42. Circular Letter, November 11, 1865, BRFAL, M843, reel 20, GOC, ACNC, RG 105, NA; *Hillsborough Recorder* and *Wilmington Herald* quoted in Bogue, "Violence and Oppression," 67–68.

43. R. W. Best to General [Ruger], December 13, 1865, LR, Dept NC, box 1, RG 393, NA; George D. Pool to W. W. Holden, December 16, 1865, William Woods Holden PGLB, NCSA.

44. Thomas H. Ruger to George D. Ruggles, December 20, 1865, LS, Dept NC, RG 393, NA; Thomas H. Ruger to D. D. Ferebee, December 13, 1865, reprinted in *North Carolina Daily Standard* (Raleigh), December 16, 1865; *Wilmington Daily Dispatch*, December 25, 1865. In truth, a detachment of the 37th USCT remained at Morehead City until January 1866, when it was replaced by a company of the 28th Michigan. See J. A. Campbell to W. W. Wheeler, January 2, 1866, LS, Dept NC, RG 393, NA.

45. Emancipation Day commemorated the enactment of Lincoln's Emancipation Proclamation on January 1, 1863. SO No. 270, December 18, 1865, Dept NC, General Court-Martial Orders Issued, 1865–1866, Dept NC, RG 393, NA; *Wilmington Herald*, January 2, 1866; E. Whittlesey to O. O. Howard, January 15, 1866, M843, reel 1, Reports, ACNC, RG 105, NA; Alexander, *North Carolina Faces the Freedmen*, 78.

46. Sefton, *Army and Reconstruction*, 261; GO No. 173, December 19, 1865, Dept NC, Joseph F. Boyd Papers, DU.

47. Tod R. Caldwell to Gov. Holden, September 18, 1865, Thomas T. Heath to J. A. Campbell, September 19, 1865, and R. K. Miller to A. S. Paul, December 13, 1865, all in LR, Dept NC, box 1, RG 393, NA; General Orders No. 157, November 14, 1865, Dept NC, Joseph F. Boyd Papers, DU.

48. Statements of W. J. Weatherly and three others, October 25–26, 1865, Statements of S. M. Sloan and three others, October 28, 1865, W. A. Casewell et al. to Maj. Genl. Ruger, n.d., and Frank M. Hinton to J. A. Campbell, October 29, 1865, all in LR, Dept NC, box 1, RG 393, NA.

49. N. J. Frink to J. A. Campbell, October 28, 1865, with endorsement of J. A. Campbell, November 2, 1865, LR, Dept NC, box 1, RG 393, NA; Thomas H. Ruger to George D. Ruggles, November 3, 1865, LS, Dept NC, RG 393, NA; General

Court Martial Orders No. 13, February 7, 1866, Dept NC, and Trial of William N. Mott and Owen Martin, both in Case No. MM-3632, RG 153, NA.

50. J. M. Blair et al. to J. Worth, January 27, 1866, and Jonathan Worth to Major Genl. Ruger, February 7, 1866, both in LR, Dept NC, box 3, RG 393, NA; James H. Anderson to Captain Bliss, February 19, 1866, and J. A. Campbell to George H. Granger, April 5, 1866, both in LS, Dept NC, RG 393, NA; Trial of George Josey, Washington Flood, Edward Newson, and Jerry Pruden, Case No. MM-3615, RG 153, NA.

51. Company E of the 3rd U.S. (Light) Artillery remained in North Carolina in 1866. *Raleigh Daily Sentinel*, January 18, 1866; *Army and Navy Journal* (New York), January 6, 13, 1866, and January 19, 1867; Price, *Across the Continent*, 127; Wilhelm, *Eighth U.S. Infantry*, 118–19; Thomas H. Ruger to S. F. Barstow, April 12, 1866, LS, Dept NC, RG 393, NA. During the winter and spring of 1866, General Grant sought to replace the remaining volunteer regiments with regular units. Congress meanwhile passed the Army Reorganization bill, making Grant's policy official. See Zalimas, "Black Union Soldiers," 67, 74.

52. Foner, *Reconstruction*, 224–27; Franklin, *Reconstruction*, 57–58; McKitrick, *Andrew Johnson*, 253–60. For a radical's view of conditions in the South, see the letters of former Union general Carl Schurz reprinted in Simpson et al., *Advice after Appomattox*, 78–150.

5. The Struggle for Civilian Supremacy

1. Citizens of —— County to Z. B. Vance, February 1864, and Governor Worth to the People of North Carolina, [June 1866], both in Hamilton, *Worth Correspondence*, 1: 287, 510, 613–14; Zuber, *Jonathan Worth*, 15–26, 109–23, 138, 179–83.

2. Zuber, *Jonathan Worth*, 192, 204–8; Escott, *Many Excellent People*, 96–100.

3. Zuber, *Jonathan Worth*, 207–8.

4. Stay laws suspend the collection of debt. Their purpose is to relieve debtors during times of economic hardship. Jonathan Worth, Address to the North Carolina General Assembly, January 18, 1865, Jonathan Worth Papers, SHC-UNC; Escott, *Many Excellent People*, 100–103; Alexander, *North Carolina Faces the Freedmen*, 158.

5. Jonathan Worth to George R. Ricketts, March 17, 1866, in Hamilton, *Worth Correspondence*, 614. Worth's aversion to radicalism was shared by most white North Carolinians. See Lancaster, "Scalawags of North Carolina," 189.

6. Jonathan Worth to T. H. Ruger, January 4, 1866, J. L. Rhodes to Sheriff of New Hanover County, December 25, 1865, and William H. Bagley to Sheriff of New Hanover County, January 4, 1866, all in Jonathan Worth GLB, NCSA.

7. Thomas H. Ruger to Jonathan Worth, January 4, 1866, Jonathan Worth to T. H. Ruger, January 26, 1866, J. A. Campbell to Jonathan Worth, January 26,

1866, and James H. Anderson to Jonathan Worth, January 26, 1866, all in Jonathan Worth GLB, NCSA; J. A. Campbell to George Crook, January 6, 1866, and Thomas H. Ruger to Jonathan Worth, February 6, 1866, both in Jonathan Worth GP, NCSA; Jonathan Worth to General Ruger; January 30, 1866, in Hamilton, *Worth Correspondence*, 1: 489–91; SO No. 21, District of New Bern, January 25, 1866, quoted in *North Carolina Daily Standard* (Raleigh), January 29, 1866.

8. General Court Martial Orders No. 18, Pompey Harkell, Providence James, Aaron Benjamin, and Oretus Miller, February 20, 1866, Dept NC, and Trial of Pompey Harkell, Providence James, Aaron Benjamin, and Oretus Miller, both in Case No. MM-3643, RG 153, NA; Jonathan Worth to Andrew Johnson, January 12, 1866, Jonathan Worth GLB, NCSA; J. A. Campbell to W. W. Wheeler, January 2, 1866, LS, Dept NC, RG 393, NA. For newspaper accounts of the alleged outrages, see *North Carolina Daily Standard* (Raleigh) and *Raleigh Daily Progress* quoted in *Charlotte Western Democrat*, January 16, 1866.

9. Three companies of the 37th USCT were transferred to South Carolina in 1866. The remaining seven companies were stationed on the North Carolina coast at Fort Hatteras, Fort Macon, Fort Fisher, Fort Caswell, and Fort Johnston. Jonathan Worth to Andrew Johnson, January 12, 1866, Jonathan Worth GLB, NCSA; *Army and Navy Journal* (New York), January 19, 1867. For an account of the 37th USCT's origins, see Reid, "Raising the African Brigade," 266–97.

10. Jonathan Worth to Maj. Genl. Ruger, January 15, 1866, Jonathan Worth to John Ives, January 15, 1866, and Jonathan Worth to T. H. Ruger, March 21, 1866, all in Jonathan Worth GLB, NCSA; Thomas H. Ruger to Jonathan Worth, January 15, 1866, and April 5, 1866, both in Jonathan Worth GP, NCSA.

11. William Foy to Jonathan Worth, January 20, 1866, and J. A. Campbell to Jonathan Worth, January 24, 1866, both in Jonathan Worth GP, NCSA.

12. E. Whittlesey to J. A. Campbell, January 8, 1866, M843, reel 1, LS, ACNC, RG105, NA; Testimony of Eliphalet Whittlesey in U.S. Congress, *Report of the Joint Committee*, 184–85; Hugo Hillebrandt to William H. Wiegel, June 18, 1866, LR, Dept NC, box 2, RG 393, NA; Annual Report of A. C. Bready, Superintendent Central District, October 30, 1866, M843, reel 9, LR, ACNC, RG 105, NA.

13. Clipping from *Wilmington Daily Journal*, February 9, 1867, enclosed in Allan Rutherford to J. F. Chur, February 12, 1867, M843, reel 10, LR, ACNC, RG 105, NA; *Wilson Carolinian* quoted in *Tarboro Weekly Southerner*, February 7, 1867; Barrett, *Civil War in North Carolina*, 174–77; Escott, *Many Excellent People*, 128; Bogue, "Violence and Oppression," 83–85.

14. "Semi-Monthly Report of Outrages by Whites against Blacks in the State of North Carolina for the Fifteen Days Ending February 15, 1867," M843, reel 33, Reports of Outrages and Arrests, ACNC, RG 105, NA; J. Thurston to Hon. H. Wilson, January 10, 1866, M843, reel 9, and Allan Rutherford to J. F. Chur, February 12, 27, 1867, M843, reel 17, all in LR, ACNC, RG 105, NA; Alexander, *North Carolina Faces the Freedmen*, 132.

15. Circular, District of Wilmington, December 11, 1865, and Charles J. Wickersham to E. Whittlesey, January 23, 1866, both in M843, reel 9, LR, ACNC, RG 105, NA.

16. E. Whittlesey to Major Genl. Ruger, February 20, 1866, M843, reel 1, LS, ACNC, RG 105, NA.

17. "We the undersigned citizens of Trenton," July 19, 1866, and William H. Bryan to Jonathan Worth, July 21, 1866, both in Jonathan Worth GP, NCSA; W. H. Bagley to William H. Bryan, July 26, 1866, in Hamilton, *Worth Correspondence*, 2: 698.

18. E. Whittlesey to J. A. Campbell, April 6, 1866, M843, reel 1, LS, ACNC, RG 105, NA; George Newcomb to E. Whittlesey, January 13, 1866, M843, reel 17, George S. Hawley to Stephen Moore, October 30, 1866, T. D. McAlpine to J. V. Bomford, December 20, 1866, and A. C. Bready to J. V. Bomford, December 18, 1866, M843, reel 11, all in LR, ACNC, RG 105, NA; SO No. 35, Post of Wilmington, July 17, 1867, in Case No. OO-2443, RG 153, NA; Bogue, "Violence and Oppression," 86, 126–27; Reid, "USCT Veterans," 392.

19. Fred H. Beecher to W. H. H. Beadle, February 28, 1866, M843, reel 1, LS, ACNC, RG 105, NA. See also Thomas H. Ruger to O. O. Howard, June 20, 1866, ibid.

20. Thomas H. Ruger to George D. Ruggles, February 15, 1866, LS, Dept NC, RG 393, NA; Testimony of Dexter H. Clapp, in U.S. Congress, *Report of the Joint Committee*, 208–9.

21. F. A. Seely to E. Whittlesey, May 13, 1866, and Hugo Hillebrandt to E. Whittlesey, May 15, 1866, both in M843, reel 8, LR, ACNC, RG 105, NA; Thomas H. Ruger to S. F. Barstow, May 22, 1866, LS, Dept NC, RG 393, NA; W. T. Faircloth to Governor [Worth], July 20, 1866, Worth GP, NCSA. For the army's efforts to track down Roberts, see James H. Anderson to Commanding Officer, Post of Charlotte, May 18, 1866, Justin Hodge to James H. Anderson, May 25, 1866, and George R. Bell to H. M. Lazelle, June 4, 1866, all in LR, Post of Charlotte, RG 393, NA; Thomas H. Ruger to A. H. Terry, June 7, 1866, LS, Dept NC, RG 393, NA; John C. Robinson to Jonathan Worth, July 3, 1866, Jonathan Worth GP NCSA; Jonathan Worth to J. C. Robinson, July 6, 1866, in Hamilton, *Worth Correspondence*, 2: 671–72.

22. Thomas H. Ruger to George D. Ruggles, February 15, 1866, in LS, Dept NC, RG 393, NA; Report of the Commissioner of the Bureau of Refugees, Freedmen, and Abandoned Lands, in U.S. Congress, "Report of the Secretary of War," 39th Congress, 2nd Session, 735.

23. In March 1866, the General Assembly penalized blacks and whites alike when it voted to abolish the state's common school system. Jonathan Worth to the General Assembly of North Carolina, January 18, 1866, Jonathan Worth Papers, SHC-UNC; Alexander, *North Carolina Faces the Freedmen*, 40–49, 157; Escott, *Many Excellent People*, 130–31; Foner, *Reconstruction*, 199–202; Walker, "Blacks in North Carolina," 175–76.

24. GO No. 3, U.S. War Department, January 12, 1866, and Thomas H. Ruger to Jonathan Worth, January 15, 1866, both in Jonathan Worth GP, NCSA; Perman, *Reunion without Compromise*, 78–79; Foner, *Reconstruction*, 200–201, 208–9, 243–44; Simpson, *Let Us Have Peace*, 127–28; Sefton, *Army and Reconstruction*, 67–71; McKitrick, *Andrew Johnson*, 277–79.

25. Thomas H. Ruger to Jonathan Worth, January 15, 1866, Jonathan Worth GP, NCSA; Circular No. 1, ACNC, February 16, 1866, M843, reel 20, GOC, ACNC, and E. Whittlesey to Thomas A. Montgomery, April 3, 1866, M843, reel 1, LS, ACNC, both in RG 105, NA.

26. Jonathan Worth to William A. Graham, January 12, 1866, Jonathan Worth to David L. Swain, March 16, 1866, and Jonathan Worth to W. H. Seward, May 4, 1866, all in Hamilton, *Worth Correspondence*, 1: 467, 509, 571; Zuber, *Jonathan Worth*, 216–17.

27. E. Whittlesey to O. O. Howard, March 23, 1866, M843, reel 1, LS, ACNC, RG 105, NA; Thomas H. Ruger to F. S. Barstow, April 26, 1866, LS, Dept NC, RG 393, NA; E. Whittlesey to O. O. Howard, February 27, 1866, Oliver Otis Howard Papers, BC; E. Whittlesey to O. O. Howard, April 10, 1866, in U.S. Congress, "Message from the President of the United States," 5; Jonathan Worth to W. H. Seward, May 4, 1866, Hamilton, *Worth Correspondence*, 1: 571; Zuber, *Jonathan Worth*, 217.

28. Testimony of Eliphalet Whittlesey, in U.S. Congress, *Report of the Joint Committee*, 184; G. F. Granger to Thaddeus Stevens, January 11, 1865[6], in Padgett, "Reconstruction Letters from North Carolina," 177; Franklin, *Reconstruction*, 58; Sefton, *Army and Reconstruction*, 60–64.

29. E. Whittlesey to O. O. Howard, February 27, 1866, and E. W. to Col. Woodhull, [February 28, 1866], both in Oliver Otis Howard Papers, BC; *Charlotte Western Democrat* quoted in *North Carolina Daily Standard* (Raleigh), March 9, 1866; McKitrick, *Andrew Johnson*, 288, 292–95, 314–16; Foner, *Reconstruction*, 247–51. For a more guarded southern response to Johnson's actions, see Perman, *Reunion without Compromise*, 185–88.

30. Trial of John H. Gee, Case No. MM-3972, RG 153, NA; Ford, *Prisoner: Major Gee*, 11–14; Marvel, *Andersonville*, 243–47; Sanders, *While in the Hands of the Enemy*, 271–72; Barrett, *Civil War in North Carolina*, 356–57.

31. Ford, *Prisoner: Major Gee*, 11–16, 19–22; Hamilton, *Reconstruction*, 163–64.

32. *Raleigh Daily Sentinel*, April 6, 1866; Sefton, *Army and Reconstruction*, 74–75; Perman, *Reunion without Compromise*, 190.

33. The Supreme Court did not issue its formal written opinions on *Ex parte Milligan* until December 1866. E. D. Townsend to J. M. Brannan and thirteen other generals (including Ruger), April 9, 1866, M565, reel 29, LS, AGO, RG 94, NA; Sefton, *Army and Reconstruction*, 75, 78–79; Simpson, *Let Us Have Peace*, 133, 135–36.

34. D. P. Holland to Daniel G. Fowle, April 10, 1866, Daniel G. Fowle to

Thomas H. Ruger, April 11, 1866, and Thomas H. Ruger to Daniel G. Fowle, April 13, 1866, all in Trial of John H. Gee, MM-3972, RG 153, NA; Daniel G. Fowle to Jonathan Worth, April 14, 1866, and Jonathan Worth to Andrew Johnson, April 17, 1866, both in Jonathan Worth GLB, NCSA; Thomas H. Ruger to S. F. Barstow, April 26, 1866, LS, Dept NC, RG 393, NA; Hamilton, *Reconstruction*, 164.

35. E. D. Townsend to Thomas H. Ruger, April 18, 1866, M619, reel 29, LS, AGO, RG 94, NA; Edward Cooper to Governor Worth, April 27, 1866, Jonathan Worth GLB, NCSA; *Raleigh Daily Sentinel*, April 30, 1866.

36. Trial of John H. Gee, Case No. MM-3972, RG 153, NA; *Semi-Weekly Floridian*, June 19, 1866, quoted in Ford, *Prisoner: Major Gee*, 592; *Raleigh Daily Sentinel*, June 19, 1866.

37. Findings of military commission for Gee trial and endorsement of John C. Robinson quoted in Ford, *Prisoner: Major Gee*, 569, 571.

38. Endorsement of E. A. Carr, June 28, 1866, on J. A. Campbell to E. A. Carr, June 27, 1866, LS, Post of Raleigh, RG 393, NA; E. D. Townsend to J. C. Robinson, July 5, 1866, M565, reel 30, LS, AGO, RG 94, NA.

39. The executed men had joined local defense battalions with the understanding that their units would not leave the state. When faced with conscription into the Confederate army, they deserted in the belief that their original agreement had been violated. They later enlisted in the 2nd North Carolina (Union) Infantry and were captured by Pickett's men in February 1864. W. H. Doherty to Brevet Major General Ruger, September 13, 1865, and J. Holt to Secretary of War, December 30, 1865, both in U. S. Congress, "Murder of Union Soldiers in North Carolina," 49–50, 53–55; W. H. Doherty to J. A. Campbell, November 8, 1865, LR, Dept NC, box 1, RG 393, NA. See also Collins, "War Crime or Justice?" 50–83; Gordon, *Pickett in Life and Legend*, 158–59.

40. Endorsement of U. S. Grant, March 16, 1866, on George E. Pickett to U. S. Grant, March 12, 1866, in Simon, *Grant Papers*, 16: 120–22; Gordon, *Pickett in Life and Legend*, 160–61.

41. H. R. Ellis to George McKnight, January 13, 1866, quoted in *North Carolina Daily Standard* (Raleigh), January 19, 1866.

42. E. Whittlesey to O. O. Howard, April 4, 1866, E. Whittlesey to Thomas A. Montgomery, April 3, 1866, and E. Whittlesey to John E. Brown, April 5, 1866, all in M843, reel 1, LS, ACNC, RG 105, NA; Allan Rutherford to O. O. Howard, June 17, 1866, Oliver Otis Howard Papers, BC .

43. Charles J. Wickersham to W. H. H. Beadle, March 19, 1866, M843, reel 17, LR, ACNC, RG 105, NA; E. Whittlesey to O. O. Howard, April 4, 1866, M843, reel 1, LS, ACNC, RG 105, NA.

44. E. Whittlesey to D. G. Fowle, April 4, 1866, in U.S. Congress, "Message from the President of the United States," 6. The Whittlesey-Fowle letters were initially reprinted in the *Raleigh Daily Sentinel*, April 10, 1866.

45. Daniel G. Fowle to E. Whittlesey, April 4, 1866, Daniel G. Fowle to Ma-

jor General Ruger, April 4, 1866, and Daniel G. Fowle to E. Whittlesey, April 5, 1866, all in U.S. Congress, "Message from the President of the United States," 6–8.

46. O. O. Howard to T. H. Ruger, April 7, 1866, M843, reel 9, LR, ACNC, RG 105, NA; E. D. Townsend to T. H. Ruger, April 9, 1866, LS, AGO, reel 29, RG 94, NA.

47. Report of F. D. Sewall, May 14, 1866, in U.S. Congress, "Message from the President of the United States," 38.

48. E. D. Townsend to O. O. Howard, May 15, 1866, M565, reel 29, LS, AGO, RG 94, NA; Report of James B. Steedman and J. S. Fullerton, May 8, 1866, in U.S. Congress, "Message from the President of the United States," 66–72; McFeely, *Yankee Stepfather*, 249–50, 252.

49. Report of James B. Steedman and J. S. Fullerton, May 8, 1866, in U.S. Congress, "Message from the President of the United States," 69–71; Trial of Eliphalet Whittlesey, Case No. OO-1682, Trial of Isaac A. Rosekrans, Case No. OO-1679, Trial of George O. Glavis, Case No. OO-1705, and Trial of Horace James, Case No. OO-1788, all in RG 153, NA; E. Whittlesey to "Dear General," July 13, 30, August 1, September 8, 1866, all in Oliver Otis Howard Papers, BC; McFeely, *Yankee Stepfather*, 253.

50. Report of U. S. Grant, December 18, 1865, in Simpson et al., *Advice after Appomattox*, 214; Report of James B. Steedman and J. S. Fullerton, in U.S. Congress, "Message from the President of the United States," 65, 71–72; Oliver O. Howard quoted in McFeely, *Yankee Stepfather*, 254.

51. To further confuse matters, Sickles's command was subsequently renamed the Department of the South. Circular No. 5, ACNC, May 21, 1866, Freedmen's Bureau Orders and Circulars, Nelson Appleton Miles Papers, MHI; W. E. Strong to "Dear Genl, May 28, 1866, Oliver Otis Howard Papers, BC; Thomas H. Ruger to S. F. Barstow, May 22, 1866, LS, Dept NC, RG 393, NA; E. D. Townsend to T. H. Ruger, May 16, 1866 (two letters), M565, reel 29, LS, AGO, RG 94, NA; *Army and Navy Journal* (New York), June 2, 1866.

52. *Raleigh Daily Sentinel*, August 13, 1866; Thomas H. Ruger to "Dear Howard," June 4, 1866, Oliver Otis Howard Papers, BC.

53. Powell, *Powell's Records*, 503–5; Boatner, *Civil War Dictionary*, 704, 870; Warner, *Generals in Blue*, 407–8; Heitman, *Historical Register*, 1: 838–39; Rhea, *Battles for Spotsylvania Courthouse*, 54, 56, 58.

54. John C. Robinson to Jonathan Worth, July 3, 1866, Jonathan Worth GLB, NCSA.

55. Jonathan Worth to Brevet Major Genl. Robinson, July 11, 1866, and Jonathan Worth to Andrew Johnson, July 11, 1866, both in Jonathan Worth GLB, NCSA; E. D. Townsend to J. C. Robinson, July 18, 1866, M565, reel 30, LS, AGO, RG 94, NA.

56. Jonathan Worth to Brevet Major Genl. Robinson, July 12, 1866, and John C. Robinson to Jonathan Worth, July 13, 1866, both in Jonathan Worth GLB,

NCSA; GO No. 3, ACNC, July 13, 1866, in Jonathan Worth GP, NCSA; GO No. 44, Headquarters of the Army, July 6, 1866, enclosed in H. E. Hazen to Asst. Adjt. Genl. Mil. Command of N.C., October 28, 1866, LR, Post of New Bern, RG 393, NA; Sefton, *Army and Reconstruction*, 73; Simpson, *Let Us Have Peace*, 135–36, 138–39; Alexander, *North Carolina Faces the Freedmen*, 50–51.

57. Barney, *Battleground for the Union*, 245–46.

58. Jonathan Worth to B. S. Hedrick, July 4, 1866, in Hamilton, *Worth Correspondence*, 2: 667; Zuber, *Jonathan Worth*, 242.

59. Foner, *Reconstruction*, 264–67.

60. John C. Robinson to Jonathan Worth, July 21, 1866, Jonathan Worth GP, NCSA.

61. E. A. Carr to J. A. Campbell, June 22, 1866, and Frank Wolcott to J. A. Campbell, July 18, 1866, both in Jonathan Worth GP, NCSA. See also H. E. Noble to Major Gen. Ruger, May 20, 1866, LR, Dept NC, box 3, RG 393, NA; Jonathan Worth to Nereus Mendenhall, September 10, 1866, in Hamilton, *Worth Correspondence*, 2: 773–74.

62. John C. Robinson to Jonathan Worth, July 21, 1866, Jonathan Worth GP, NCSA; Jonathan Worth to Andrew Johnson, July 27, 1866, Jonathan Worth GLB, NCSA; Jonathan Worth to B. S. Hedrick, July 25, 1866, in Hamilton, *Worth Correspondence*, 2: 693–94; Jonathan Worth to David A. Barnes, August 22, 1866, David A. Barnes Papers, SHC-UNC; Memorial to the President and Congress, enclosed in Benjamin S. Hedrick to Andrew Johnson, July 25, 1866, in McPherson, "Letters from North Carolina to Andrew Johnson," 28: 231–35.

63. W. P. Bynum to Jonathan Worth, August 3, 1866, and W. T. Caldwell to Jonathan Worth, July 31, 1866, both in Hamilton, *Worth Correspondence*, 2: 725–30; Jonathan Worth to David A. Barnes, August 22, 1866, David A. Barnes Papers, SHC-UNC; Bogue, "Violence and Oppression," 135, 200.

64. Jonathan Worth to William S. Mason, July 26, 1866, Jonathan Worth GLB, NCSA; Francis E. Wolcott to J. A. Campbell, August 16, 1866, Jonathan Worth GP, NCSA.

65. W. S. Mason to Jonathan Worth, August 17, 1866, Jonathan Worth GP, NCSA.

66. John C. Robinson to Jonathan Worth, August 24, 1866, Jonathan Worth GP, NCSA; Jonathan Worth to Bvt. Major Genl. Robinson, August 22, 27, 1866, and J. C. Robinson to Jonathan Worth, August 31, 1866, all in Jonathan Worth GLB, NCSA.

67. *Salisbury Old North State* quoted in *Wilmington Daily Journal*, May 10, 1866; Charles H. Whitney to Acting Assistant Adjutant General Military Command of N.C., January 25, February 4, 1867, Regimental Letters and Endorsements, 37th U.S. Colored Troops, RG 391, NA.

68. U.S. Congress, "Proceedings of a Military Commission Convened at Wilmington, North Carolina," 150–51, 224, 228–31, 242; Bogue, "Violence and Oppression," 193–94.

69. Edward R. S. Canby to Chief of Staff, Headquarters of the Army, November 14, 1867, Jonathan Worth GLB, NCSA; Bogue, "Violence and Oppression," 201–2.

70. Edward B. Northrup to Allan Rutherford, August 10, 1866, John C. Robinson to Jonathan Worth, August 18, 1866, and Jonathan Worth to Bvt. Maj. Genl. Robinson, August 21, 1866, all in Jonathan Worth GLB, NCSA.

71. Jonathan Worth to Andrew Johnson, August 27, 1866, Jonathan Worth GLB, NCSA; Zuber, *Jonathan Worth*, 225.

72. Alexander, *North Carolina Faces the Freedmen*, 114.

73. Testimony of W. H. H. Beadle in U.S. Congress, *Report of the Joint Committee*, 270–71; Alexander, *North Carolina Faces the Freedmen*, 116.

74. Daniel L. Russell to Governor Worth, October 23, 1866, Jonathan Worth GP, NCSA; Jonathan Worth to Bt. Maj. Genl. Robinson, October 29, 1866, and John C. Robinson to Jonathan Worth, October 30, 1866, both in Jonathan Worth GLB, NCSA.

75. Jonathan Worth to Bt. Maj. Genl. Robinson, November 1, 1866, and John C. Robinson to Jonathan Worth, November 3, 1866, both in Jonathan Worth GLB, NCSA; John C. Robinson to J. V. Bomford, December 20, 1866, M843, reel 13, LR, ACNC, RG 105, NA; Alexander, *North Carolina Faces the Freedmen*, 114–15.

76. Jonathan Worth to J. V. Bomford, November 26, 1866, J. V. Bomford to Jonathan Worth, November 27, 1866, and Jonathan Worth to Andrew Johnson, November 30, 1866, all in Jonathan Worth GLB, NCSA; GO No. 15, Department of the South, October 1, 1866, quoted in *Raleigh Weekly Progress*, December 20, 1866.

77. Robinson was transferred to Charleston to serve as acting department commander while General Sickles was on leave. J. V. Bomford to Jonathan Worth, December 7, 1866, Jonathan Worth GP, NCSA; *Raleigh Daily Progress*, December 20, 1866; *Army and Navy Journal* (New York), January 5, 1867.

78. E. D. Townsend to D. E. Sickles, December 19, 1866, and J. V. Bomford to Jonathan Worth, December 20, 1866, both in Jonathan Worth GP, NCSA; *Army and Navy Journal* (New York), January 5, 1867.

79. Abner S. Williams to Jonathan Worth, September 8, December 3, 1866, and John F. Bellamy to Jonathan Worth, November 29, 1866, all in Jonathan Worth GP, NCSA; Alexander, *North Carolina Faces the Freedmen*, 29–30.

80. Jonathan Worth to J. V. Bomford, December 3, 5, 1866, January 3, 1867, and C. W. Dodge to Colonel, January 15, 1867, all in M843, reel 12, LR, ACNC, RG 105, NA; C. W. Dodge to ?, September 20, 1866, Jonathan Worth GP, NCSA; Jonathan Worth to J. V. Bomford, February 8, 1867, Jonathan Worth GLB, NCSA.

81. *Army and Navy Journal* (New York), September 15, 1866.

82. Companies A and I of the 5th U.S. Cavalry were stationed at Raleigh and Morganton. The former post embraced seven piedmont counties, and the latter fifteen western counties. John G. Colgrove to Commanding Officer U.S. Troops at Newbern, October 27, 1866, H. E. Hazen to Asst. Adjt. Genl. Mil. Command

of N.C., October 28, 1866, and Charles Hull to Lieut. Wilhelm, November 18, 1866, all in LR, Post of New Bern, RG 393, NA.

83. Robert Avery to Jacob F. Chur, November 1, 1867, M843, reel 10, and Hannibal D. Norton to M. Cogswell, April 1, 1867, M843, reel 9, both in LR, ACNC, RG 105, NA.

84. *Tarboro Southerner* quoted in *Wilmington Daily Journal*, January 12, 1867; Hearne and Biggs to Jonathan Worth, January 14, 1866 [1867], Jonathan Worth GP, NCSA; Jonathan Worth to W. A. Hearne and William Biggs, January 19, 1867, Jonathan Worth to Editors of the *Wilmington Journal*, January 13, 1867, Jonathan Worth to A. W. Ingold, January 19, 1867, and Jonathan Worth to C. C. Clark, January 13, 1867, all in Hamilton, *Worth Correspondence*, 2: 869–70, 879–80; Bogue, "Violence and Oppression," 92–93, 101–4.

85. Allan Rutherford to Jacob F. Chur, February 12, 1867, and J. V. Bomford to Jonathan Worth, February 18, 1867, both in Jonathan Worth GLB, NCSA.

86. Jonathan Worth to J. V. Bomford, February 18, 1867, Jonathan Worth GLB, NCSA.

87. GO No. 17, Dept South, February 20, 1867, *Army and Navy Journal* (New York), March 2, 1867; Bogue, "Violence and Oppression," 103.

88. R. T. Frank to D. T. Wells, February 19, 1867, LS, Post of Wilmington, RG 393, NA. At least one white citizen offered to join Frank's detail and provide it with forage. See Allan Rutherford to R. T. Frank, February 19, 1867, LR, Post of Wilmington, RG 393, NA.

89. U. S. Congress, "Act to Provide for the More Efficient Government of the Rebel States," 3–4; Barney, *Battleground for the Union*, 247–49; Franklin, *Reconstruction*, 70–72.

90. Sefton, *Army and Reconstruction*, 113; Simpson, *Let Us Have Peace*, 179.

91. Jonathan Worth to Worth and Daniel, March 7, 1867, in Hamilton, *Worth Correspondence*, 2: 914–15; R. J. Powell to Bedford Brown, March 16, 1867, Bedford Brown Papers, DU; *Raleigh Daily Sentinel*, March 28, 1867; *Wilmington Daily Journal*, March 12, 1867; Hamilton, *Reconstruction*, 201–2.

92. *Land We Love* (Charlotte) 3 (May–June 1867): 86, 177; clipping of *Charlotte Western Democrat* editorial, Reconstruction Scrapbook, 251, NCC-UNC.

6. Military Reconstruction under Sickles

1. Warner, *Generals in Blue*, 446–47; Boatner, *Civil War Dictionary*, 760; Keneally, *American Scoundrel*, 279–80, 287–88, 290–91, 308–9; Pfanz, *Gettysburg: Second Day*, 46–48, 103, 333–34, 435–37; Robertson, "Peach Orchard Revisited," 33–56.

2. GO No. 1, 2MD, March 21, 1867, in U.S. Congress, "General Orders: Reconstruction," 35–36; D. E. Sickles to E. M. Stanton, June 16, 1867, Edwin McMasters Stanton Papers, LC; D. E. Sickles to Lyman Trumbull, July 1, 1867, LS, 2MD, RG 393, NA.

3. Jonathan Worth to R. M. Stafford, March 28, 1867, in Hamilton, *Worth Correspondence*, 2: 922; Morrill, "Administration of Sickles," 295.

4. GO No. 3, 2MD, March 27, 1867, and GO No. 25, 2MD, May 20, 1867, in U.S. Congress, "General Orders: Reconstruction," 36–37, 45–46; J. B. Weaver to Major General Sickles, March 30, 1867, and J. B. Weaver to J. W. Clous, May 23, 1867, both in LR, 2MD, RG 393, NA; J. W. Clous to J. B. Weaver, April 8, 1867, LS, 2MD, RG 393, NA.

5. GO No. 12, 2MD, April 20, 1867, in U.S. Congress, "General Orders: Reconstruction," 41; SO No. 26, Post of New Bern, May 24, 1867, reprinted in *Wilmington Daily Journal*, May 29, 1867; Trial of Jonas Reidel, John W. Dey, Frederick D. Schlachter, and Charles Sinkland, and SO No. 77, 2MD, June 20, 1867, both in Case No. OO-2419, RG 153, NA.

6. GO No. 10, 2MD, April 11, 1867, and Circular, 2MD, April 27, 1867, both in U.S. Congress, "General Orders: Reconstruction," 39–40, 42; D. E. Sickles to Henry J. Raymond, June 10, 1867, Daniel Edgar Sickles Papers, DU; Jonathan Worth to James L. Orr, May 3, 1867, in Hamilton, *Worth Correspondence*, 2: 943; Morrill, "Administration of Sickles," 296; Zuber, *Jonathan Worth*, 78.

7. GO No. 10, 2MD, April 11, 1867, Circular, 2MD, April 27, 1867, and Circular, 2MD, May 15, 1867, all in U.S. Congress, "General Orders: Reconstruction," 39–40, 44; Louis V. Caziarc to N. A. Miles, October 11, 1867, M843, reel 12, LR, ACNC, RG 105, NA; Jonathan Worth to H. T. Clark, August 24, 1867, in Hamilton, *Worth Correspondence*, 2: 1043. For Robinson's order prohibiting corporal punishment, see GO No. 26, Dept South, March 8, 1867, M843, reel 20, GOC, ACNC, RG 105, NA.

8. GO No. 32, 2MD, May 30, 1867, in U.S. Congress, "General Orders: Reconstruction," 46; Jonathan Worth to Andrew Johnson, June 8, 1867, Jonathan Worth GLB, NCSA; Zuber, *Jonathan Worth*, 264.

9. GO No. 32, 2MD, May 30, 1867, and Circular, 2MD, June 17, 1867, in U.S. Congress, "General Orders: Reconstruction," 46, 48; J. J. Van Horn to Assistant Adjutant General, 2MD, June 18, 1867, LS, Post of New Bern, RG 393, NA; Case No. OO-2443, RG 153, NA; John Brady to D. E. Sickles, August 1, 1867, LR, 2MD, RG 393, NA.

10. GO No. 10, 2MD, April 11, 1867, in U.S. Congress, "General Orders: Reconstruction," 40; John M. Perry to Della Barlow, July 18, 1867, Della Barlow Papers, Collection No. 107, ECU; "Perry, John Merritt," in Grant, *Alumni History of UNC*, 488.

11. The governor's Council of State was a seven-member advisory board appointed by the General Assembly. A. S. Merrimon to Jonathan Worth, July 22, 1867, Jonathan Worth GP, NCSA; Jonathan Worth to D. E. Sickles, July 23, 1867, LR, 2MD, RG 393, NA; D. E. Sickles to Jonathan Worth, August 6, 1867, quoted in Jonathan Worth to David A. Barnes, August 7, 1867, David A. Barnes Papers,

SHC-UNC; Jonathan Worth to W. P. Bynum, August 1, 1867, in Hamilton, *Worth Correspondence*, 2: 1012; Zuber, *Jonathan Worth*, 263.

12. Jonathan Worth to B. S. Hedrick, May 11, 1868, in Hamilton, *Worth Correspondence*, 2: 1201; Jonathan Worth to Andrew Johnson, June 8, 1867, Jonathan Worth GLB, NCSA; D. E. Sickles to Henry J. Raymond, June 10, 1867, Daniel E. Sickles Papers, DU.

13. *Proceedings in the Case of the United States against Duncan G. McRae*, passim; GO No. 118, 2MD, November 15, 1867, M843, reel 20, GOC, ACNC, RG 105, NA; Report of Isham Blake, Coroner's Inquest, February 12, 1867 (appearing under affidavit of Neill W. Ray, June 1, 1867), Jonathan Worth GP, NCSA; Jonathan Worth to Andrew Johnson, December 31, 1867, in Hamilton et al., *Graham Papers*, 7: 425; Bogue, "Violence and Oppression," 110–12.

14. J. W. Clous to Commanding Officer, Fayetteville, N.C., May 11, 1867 (first letter), LS, 2MD, RG 393, NA; J. W. Clous to N. A. Miles, May 11, 1867, M843, reel 10, and Jonathan Worth to Genl. Miles, May 18, 1867, M843, reel 11, both in LR, ACNC, RG 105, NA; D. G. McRae to Gov. Worth, May 17, 1867, Jonathan Worth GP, NCSA; Endorsement of M. Cogswell on Affidavit of C. P. Kingsbury, January [February?] 16, 1867, LS, Post of Fayetteville, RG 393, NA; *Proceedings in the Case of the United States against Duncan G. McRae*, 42; D. G. McRae to Seaton Gales, July 6, 1867, in Hamilton, *Worth Correspondence*, 2: 994–95; Duncan G. McRae to Jonathan Worth, December 20, 1867, and Joseph A. Worth to Bro Jonathan, June 28, 1867, both in Jonathan Worth GP, NCSA.

15. *Proceedings in the Case of the United States against Duncan G. McRae*, passim; Bogue, "Violence and Oppression," 109–10.

16. *Proceedings in the Case of the United States against Duncan G. McRae*, 16; GO No. 118, 2MD, November 15, 1867, M843, reel 20, GOC, ACNC, RG 105, NA.

17. Bogue, "Violence and Oppression," 106–9, 117–19. Governor Worth was one of the petitioners. See Jonathan Worth to Andrew Johnson, October 24, 1867, in Hamilton, *Worth Correspondence*, 2: 1056–57.

18. Thomas J. Curtis quoted in *Wilmington Dispatch*, Reconstruction Scrapbook, 149–50, NCC-UNC; SO No. 55, 2MD, May 27, 1867, in U.S. Congress, "Act to Provide for the More Efficient Government of the Rebel States," 84–86; J. W. Clous to Commanding Officer, Fayetteville, N.C., May 11, 27, 1867, both in LR, Post of Fayetteville, N.C., RG 393, NA.

19. SO No. 55, 2MD, May 27, 1867, in U.S. Congress, "Act to Provide for the More Efficient Government of the Rebel States," 84–86; Jonathan Worth to Andrew Johnson, December 31, 1867, in Hamilton et al., *Graham Papers*, 7: 428–29; Jonathan Worth to D. E. Sickles, May 25, 1867, Jonathan Worth GLB, NCSA.

20. GO No. 5, 2MD, April 1, 1867, M843, reel 20, GOC, ACNC, RG 105, NA; R. T. Frank to J. W. Clous, April 3, 1867, SO No. 45, 2MD, May 16, 1867, and SO No. 71, 2MD, June 14, 1867, all in U.S. Congress, "Act to Provide for the More Efficient Government of the Rebel States," 50, 79–80, 89; SO No. 6, 2MD March

29, 1867, SO No. 15, 2MD, April 10, 1867, and SO No. 28, 2MD, April 27, 1867, all in U.S. Congress, "General Orders: Reconstruction," 85–86, 87–88; J. J. Van Horn to Act. Asst. Adjt. General, 2MD, April 15, 1867, LS, Post of New Bern, RG 393, NA; Charles A. Snyder to J. W. Clous, April 1, 1867, LS, Post of Goldsboro, N.C., vol. 1, RG 393, NA; J. J. Van Horn to Assistant Adjutant General, 2MD, June 4, 1867, and SO No. 30, Post of New Bern, both in LR, 2MD, RG 393, NA; Thomas Wilhelm to Sheriff of Carteret Co., N.C., July 6, 1867, J. Henry Davis to Jonathan Worth, July 6, 1867, and Jonathan Worth to D. E. Sickles, July 9, 1867, all in Jonathan Worth GLB, NCSA; SO No. 16, Post of Wilmington, April 12, 1867, reprinted in *Wilmington Daily Journal*, April 16, 1867; GO No. 12, 2MD, April 20, 1867, and GO No. 34, 2MD, June 3, 1867, both in U.S. Congress, "General Orders: Reconstruction," 41, 47–48; R. T. Frank to Mayor of Wilmington, May 29, 1866, L. W. Means to Mayor of Wilmington, February 25, 1867, and R. T. Frank to John Dawson, February 26, 1867, all in LS, Post of Wilmington, RG 393, NA.

21. The order for the removals and appointments was issued by Sickles's successor, Brig. Gen. Edward R. S. Canby, on September 23, 1867. SO No. 163, 2MD, September 23, 1867, quoted in Jonathan Worth to Andrew Johnson, December 31, 1867, in Hamilton et al., *Graham Papers*, 7: 431; Endorsements of J. J. Van Horn, June 15, September 2, 1867, Endorsement of J. W. Clous, August 3, 1867, and Endorsement of E. W. Dennis, August 6, 1867, all attached to Petition of Citizens of Jones County to Daniel E. Sickles, April 26, 1867, LR, 2MD, RG 393, NA.

22. Jonathan Worth to Major Genl. Sickles, May 10, 1867, with Endorsement of J. W. Clous, May 19, 1867, and J. W. Clous to Jonathan Worth, August 23, 1867, both in Jonathan Worth GP, NCSA; Zuber, *Jonathan Worth*, 257; Morrill, "Administration of Sickles," 298–99. See also Jonathan Worth to James L. Orr, July 22, 1867, in Hamilton, *Worth Correspondence*, 2: 1007.

23. Petition of Citizens of Lenoir County to Jonathan Worth, May 14, 1867, Jonathan Worth GP, NCSA.

24. H. H. Foster to N. A. Miles, May 16, 1867, enclosed in Nelson A. Miles to Jonathan Worth, May 24, 1867, Jonathan Worth Papers, SHC-UNC.

25. Jonathan Worth to J. V. Bomford, May 18, 1867, Jonathan Worth GLB, NCSA; Jonathan Worth to Nelson A. Miles, May 25, 1867, in Hamilton, *Worth Correspondence*, 2: 968.

26. On May 20, Compton reported that he was sending a detachment of twelve mounted men to Lenoir County. See Endorsement of C. E. Compton, May 20, 1867, attached to Jonathan Worth to J. V. Bomford, May 18, 1867, Jonathan Worth GP, NCSA; E. F. Cox to H. H. Foster, June 3, 1867, and H. H. Foster to C. E. Compton, June 6, 1867, both in LR, 2MD, RG 393, NA. For information on the Miller murders, see H. H. Foster to C. E. Compton, June 9, 1867, Delia M. H. Miller to Gen. Sickles, June 10, 1867, Sylvester Soper to D. B. Wilson, June 11, 1867, Report of Crimes Committed in Lenoir County, June 1867, Affidavit of Jo-

seph Warters, May 15, 1868, Affidavit of Sylvester Soper, May, 15, 1868, Sylvester Soper to D. B. Wilson, May 16, 1868, and William H. Bagley to C. E. Compton, May 26, 1868, all in LR, Post of Goldsboro, RG 393, NA.

27. Soon afterward, Compton sent an entire company of the 40th to Kinston. C. E. Compton to Louis V. Caziarc, October 29, 1867, LR, 2MD, RG 393, NA; C. E. Compton to J. W. Broatch, June 8, 1867, C. E. Compton to S. Soper, June 12, 1867, and D. B. Wilson to J. C. Denney, June 12, 28, 1867, all in LS, Post of Goldsboro, vol. 1, RG 393, NA.

28. Sidney A. Busbee to F. A. Fiske, April 8, 1867, Busbee to Luke Shepherd, Edmund Harper, John Hall, Hardy Speirs, and others, April 11, 1867, and Sidney A. Busbee to M. Cogswell, April 11, 1867, all in M843, reel 9, LR, ACNC, RG 105, NA. In his annual report for 1867, Freedmen's Bureau Commissioner Oliver O. Howard noted that a schoolhouse in Chatham County was also burned, and that a schoolteacher in New Hanover County was assaulted. See U.S. Congress, "Report of the Secretary of War," 40th Congress, 2nd Session, 668.

29. Hannibal D. Norton to M. Cogswell, April 16, 1867, M843, reel 9, LR, ACNC, RG 105, NA.

30. In a special report to Commissioner Howard, Freedmen's Bureau inspector William J. Armstrong commented that "the military are decidedly slow in getting these [Regulator-plagued] counties under control." See William J. Armstrong to General, June 18, 1867, Oliver Otis Howard Papers, BC.

31. Oscar Eastmond to Jacob F. Chur, August 27, 1867, LR, 2MD, RG 393, NA; Braxton Craven to W. S. Worth, May 27, 1867, LR, Post of Greensboro, RG 393, NA; W. S. Worth to Dr. Sellars, August 4, 1867, LS, Post of Greensboro, RG 393, NA; North Carolina Tri-Weekly Standard (Raleigh), September 19, 1867.

32. Theo Campbell et al. to Colonel Eddie [Edie], October 7, 1867, and W. F. Gray to "Dear Colonel," October 17, 1867, both in LR, Post of Salisbury, RG 393, NA.

33. Louis V. Caziarc to Commanding Officer Salisbury, N.C., November 1, 1867, LS-2nd Mil. Dist., RG 393, NA; W. S. Worth to D. T. Wells, December 16, 1866, and John T. Deweese to J. W. Naylor, May 30, 1867, both in LS, Post of Salisbury, RG 393, NA.

34. G. Urban to W. D. Justus, April 27, 1867, LS, Post of Morganton, RG 393, NA; E. M. Hayes to Gustavus Urban, May 18, 1867, LR, 2MD, RG 393, NA; Heitman, Historical Register, 1: 515.

35. E. M. Hayes to Gustavus Urban, May 18, 1867, W. B. Royall to L. V. Caziarc, April 1, 1868, and L. V. C[aziarc] to Col. Royall, April 9, 1868, all in LR, 2MD, RG 393, NA.

36. J. R. Grady to Colonel, August 27, 1867, LR, ACNC, reel 9, RG 105, NA; M. Cogswell to Louis V. Caziarc, September 28, 1867, J. R. Grady to Col. Cogswell, September 27, 1867, J. V. Bomford to Louis V. Caziarc, October 26, 1867, and E. H. Ray to J. V. Bomford, October 19, 20, 1867, all in LR, 2MD, RG 393, NA.

37. W. H. Griffin to E. W. Dennis, October 24, 1867, and E. W. Dennis to Louis V. Caziarc, October 26, 1867, both in LR, 2MD, RG 393, NA; J. R. Grady to Col. Cogswell, September 2, 1867, and Louis V. Caziarc to Commanding Officer, Post of Fayetteville, October 29, 1867, both in LR, Post of Fayetteville, RG 393, NA; Hugo Hillebrandt to Milton Cogswell, September 5, 1867, and Jacob F. Chur to Milton Cogswell, September 18, 1867, both in M843, reel 2, LS, ACNC, RG 105, NA; M. Cogswell to Colonel, September 7, 1867, LR, ACNC, reel 9, RG 105, NA.

38. Harris, *Holden*, 219–23; Foner, *Reconstruction*, 283–86. Even in 1867, some white citizens still feared that blacks were conspiring to seize land belonging to their former masters. See John A. Richardson to J. W. Clous, August 10, 1867, LR, Post of Wilmington, RG 393, NA.

39. Jonathan Worth to D. E. Sickles, April 29, 1867, LR, 2MD, RG 393, NA; Jonathan Worth to P. T. Henry, July 11, 1867, in Hamilton, *Worth Correspondence*, 2: 1004.

40. Circular, ACNC, April 26, 1867, Freedmen's Bureau Orders and Circulars, Nelson Appleton Miles Papers, MHI.

41. Jonathan Worth to D. E. Sickles, April 29, 1867, LR, 2MD, RG 393, NA; Jonathan Worth to George Howard, May 11, 1867, in Hamilton, *Worth Correspondence*, 2: 950–51; GO No. 18, 2MD, May 8, 1867, in U.S. Congress, "General Orders: Reconstruction," 42–43; Jonathan Worth to D. E. Sickles, May 15, 1867, and endorsement on same, May 26, 1867, both in Jonathan Worth GLB, NCSA; Wooster, *Miles and the Frontier Army*, 48; Zuber, *Jonathan Worth*, 265–66.

42. Jonathan Worth to James L. Orr, May 3, 1867, in Hamilton, *Worth Correspondence*, 2: 943.

43. *Raleigh Daily Sentinel*, June 4, 1867; Murray, *Wake: Capital County*, 590–93. See chapter 5 for more discussion of Johnson's "Swing around the Circle."

44. Jonathan Worth to D. E. Sickles, July 9, 1867, LR, 2MD, RG 393, NA; Jonathan Worth to Maj. Genl. Sickles, July 13, 1867, Jonathan Worth GLB, NCSA.

45. *Opinion of Attorney General Stanbery under the Reconstruction Laws*, 5–6, in Edwin McMasters Stanton Papers, LC.

46. Ibid., 9–11.

47. D. E. Sickles to Adjutant General, U.S.A., June 14, 19, 1867, both in Edwin McMasters Stanton Papers, LC; Simpson, *Let Us Have Peace*, 182; Sefton, *Army and Reconstruction*, 158.

48. D. E. Sickles to Lyman Trumbull, July 1, 1867, LS, 2MD, RG 393, NA.

49. Ibid; Perman, *Reunion without Compromise*, 304–5.

50. Simpson, *Let Us Have Peace*, 186–87; Sefton, *Army and Reconstruction*, 135–36.

51. Simpson, *Let Us Have Peace*, 186, 191–94.

52. R. T. Frank to Joseph H. Neff, July 27, 1867, and Daniel R. Goodloe to Henry Stanbery, July 31, 1867, both in Daniel R. Goodloe, "Reconstruction," 478, 480, Daniel R. Goodloe Papers, SHC-UNC; Daniel R. Goodloe to Daniel E. Sickles, July 30, 1867, in "Major-General D. E. Sickles' report," 15, Daniel Edgar Sickles Papers, LC.

53. R. T. Frank to J. H. Neff, August 17, 1867, LR, 2MD, RG 393, NA; U.S. War Department, *Annual Report of the Secretary of War*, 23; Simpson, *Let Us Have Peace*, 194–95, 198.

54. John M. Perry to Della Barlow, August 30, 1867, Della Barlow Papers, Collection No. 107, ECU; *Raleigh Daily Sentinel*, August 30, 1867; "General Sickles," clipping from *Raleigh Sentinel*, Reconstruction Scrapbook, 304, NCC-UNC; Jonathan Worth to B. G. Worth, October 25, 1867, Jonathan Worth to John H. Wheeler, October 31, 1867, and Jonathan Worth to R. P. Dick, December 13, 1867, all in Hamilton, *Worth Correspondence*, 2: 1061, 1071, 1085.

55. D. E. Sickles to U. S. Grant, August 30, 1867, in "Major-General D. E. Sickles' report," 13–14, Daniel Edgar Sickles Papers, LC; Endorsement on Jacob F. Chur to L. V. Caziarc, November 20, 1867, LR, 2MD, RG 393, NA; *Raleigh Daily Sentinel*, June 4, 1867.

56. SO No. 121, 2MD, August 9, 1867, in U.S. Congress, "General Orders: Reconstruction," 91–92.

57. One reform proposal of Sickles that came to fruition was the state prison in Raleigh, constructed and eventually completed during the 1870s. See Murray, *Wake: Capital County*, 598.

7. Military Reconstruction under Canby

1. Warner, *Generals in Blue*, 67–68; Boatner, *Civil War Dictionary*, 118, Dawson, *Army Generals and Reconstruction*, 26, 34–35.

2. W. B. R. to Wife, February 16, 1868, William Blount Rodman Papers, Collection No. 329, ECU.

3. GO No. 85, 2MD, September 5, 1867, in U.S. Congress, "General Orders: Reconstruction," 60; Edward R. S. Canby to Governor of North Carolina, September 12, 1867, Jonathan Worth GP, NCSA; Jonathan Worth to E. R. S. Canby, September 10, 1867, LR, 2MD, RG 393, NA; Edward R. S. Canby to Jonathan Worth, October 12, 1867, Jonathan Worth GLB, NCSA; Jonathan Worth to R. P. Dick, December 13, 1867, in Hamilton, *Worth Correspondence*, 2: 1085. For a detailed discussion of Canby's letter, see Zuber, *Jonathan Worth*, 269.

4. GO No. 89, 2MD, September 13, 1867, and GO No. 109, 2MD, October 25, 1867, both in U.S. Congress, "General Orders: Reconstruction," 61, 68; Jonathan Worth to E. R. S. Canby, September 30, October 18, 1867, Jonathan Worth GLB, NCSA.

5. Jonathan Worth to John H. Wheeler, October 31, 1867, Jonathan Worth to Henry T. Clark, November 2, 1867, and Jonathan Worth to R. C. Holmes, November 27, 1867, all in Hamilton, *Worth Correspondence*, 2: 1070, 1072–73, 1082; Edward R. S. Canby to Jonathan Worth, November 9, 1867, in U.S. Congress, "Report of the Secretary of War," 40th Congress, 3rd Session, 346.

6. Daniel G. Fowle to Jonathan Worth, November 28, 1867, Jonathan Worth

GLB, NCSA; Jonathan Worth to John Kerr, January 1, 6, 1868, Jonathan Worth to B. S. Hedrick, January 8, 1868, and Jonathan Worth to General Canby, January 9, 1868, all in Hamilton, *Worth Correspondence,* 2: 1102, 1115–16, 1122–23, 1124–27; Edward R. S. Canby to Jonathan Worth, January 19, 1868, Jonathan Worth GLB, NCSA; Heyman, "'Great Reconstructor,'" 67. For an excellent biography of Tourgée, see Olsen, *Carpetbagger's Crusade.*

7. Edward W. Hinks to J. W. Clous, August 10, 1867, in McPherson, "Letters from North Carolina," 29: 104–5; Edward R. S. Canby to Chief of Staff, Headquarters of the Army, November 14, 1867, LS, 2MD, RG 393, NA; Albion W. Tourgée to Daniel E. Sickles, April 11, 1867, in McPherson, "Letters from North Carolina," 28: 486–87. See also Charles Wolff to M. Cogswell, April 17, 1867, Jonathan Worth GP, NCSA.

8. John O'Connell to Joseph K. Wilson, May 20, 1867, in McPherson, "Letters from North Carolina," 28: 493; Edward W. Hinks to J. W. Clous, August 10, 1867, and Edgar W. Dennis to Louis V. Caziarc, October 4, 1867, both in McPherson, "Letters from North Carolina," 29: 104–5, 259–60.

9. Jonathan Worth to Andrew Johnson, October 23, 1867, Jonathan Worth GLB, NCSA.

10. Edward R. S. Canby to Chief of Staff Headquarters of the Army, November 14, 1867, LS, 2MD, RG 393, NA.

11. Ibid.

12. Jonathan Worth to E. R. S. Canby, November 30, 1867, Jonathan Worth GLB, NCSA; Edward R. S. Canby to Chief of Staff, Headquarters of the Army, August 31, 1868, in U.S. Congress, "Report of the Secretary of War," 40th Congress, 3rd Session, 367; Bogue, "Violence and Oppression," 195.

13. Jonathan Worth to Andrew Johnson, December 31, 1867, in Hamilton et al., *Graham Papers,* 7: 414–34; Jonathan Worth to John Kerr, January 1, 1868, in Hamilton, *Worth Correspondence,* 2: 1100–1102; M. C. Brinkley to W. H. Bagley, December 9, 1867, and D. G. McRae to Gov. Worth, December 20, 1867, both in Jonathan Worth GP, NCSA.

14. Jonathan Worth to John H. Wheeler, October 31, 1867, in Hamilton, *Worth Correspondence,* 2: 1071; Thomas C. Allen et al. to Edward R. S. Canby, October 2, 1867, with Endorsements of L. V. Caziarc, October 7, 1867, and James P. Roy, October 9, 1867, A. L. Hackett et al. to Edward R. S. Canby, [n.d.], James Risly et al. to Edward R. S. Canby, [n.d.], with Endorsement of John R. Edie, November 25, 1867, and W. D. Haywood et al. to Edward R. S. Canby, December 27, 1867, with Endorsement of J. V. Bomford, December 29, 1867, all in LR, 2MD, RG 393, NA; GO No. 164, 2MD, December 31, 1867, in U.S. Congress, "General Orders: Reconstruction," 82–83.

15. J. J. Gudger and six others, July 20, 1867, in McPherson, "Letters from North Carolina," 28: 504–6; Clinton A. Cilley to Col. Edie, October 12, 1867, and G. N. Folk to John R. Edie, October 12, 1867, with endorsements of John

R. Edie, October 23, 1867, L. V. Caziarc, October 26, 1867, and E. W. Dennis, October 29, 1867, both in LR, 2MD, RG 393, NA; Clinton A. Cilley to Jonathan Worth, February 1, 1868, Jonathan Worth GP, NCSA.

16. GO No. 134, 2MD, November 27, 1867, in U.S. Congress, "General Orders: Reconstruction," 75–76.

17. M. C. Brinkley to Post Commander, Plymouth, N.C., June 25, July 29, 1867, and Affidavits of Thomas K. Feagan and Margaret Feagan, July 29, 1867, all in LR, Post of Plymouth, RG 393, NA; Frederick L. Roberts to J. Worth, December 10, 1867, M. C. Brinkley to Governor Worth, July 29, 1867, and M. C. Brinkley to Edward W. Hinks, July 29, 1867, all in Jonathan Worth GP, NCSA.

18. Edward Hoffman to Edward W. Hinks, August 9, 21, 1867, Jonathan Worth GP, NCSA.

19. Edward R. S. Canby to Chief of Staff, Headquarters of the Army, August 31, 1868, in U.S. Congress, "Report of the Secretary of War," 40th Congress, 3rd Session, 350–53.

20. A. S. Merrimon to Z. B. Vance, February 16, 24, 1863, both in OR 18: 881, 893; Newspaper clipping, Provost Marshal General's Office, 2MD, December 12, 1867, Edward W. Hinks to Louis V. Caziarc, January 3, 1868, and George F. Price to Louis V. Caziarc, April 1, 1868, all in Jonathan Worth GP, NCSA; Barrett, *Civil War in North Carolina*, 197–98.

21. S. G. Brigman to Major Genl. Canby, November 19, 1867, and George F. Price to Louis V. Caziarc, April 1, 1868, both in Jonathan Worth GP, NCSA; Paludan, *Victims*, 109–15.

22. Edward R. S. Canby to Chief of Staff, Headquarters of the Army, August 31, 1868, in U.S. Congress, "Report of the Secretary of War," 40th Congress, 3rd Session, 339.

23. Nelson A. Miles to Louis V. Caziarc, September 18, 1867, Nelson Appleton Miles Papers, MHI.

24. J. C. Bryan et al. to Jonathan Worth, October 15, 1867, enclosed in Jonathan Worth to Maj. Genl. Canby, October 31, 1867, and George F. Price to Louis V. Caziarc, April 8, 1868, both in Jonathan Worth GLB, NCSA; Jonathan Worth to Andrew Johnson, December 31, 1867, in Hamilton et al., *Graham Papers*, 7: 431–32.

25. George F. Price to Louis V. Caziarc, April 8, 1868, Jonathan Worth GP, NCSA; E. R. S. Canby to Jonathan Worth, May 1, 1868, and Jonathan Worth to E. R. S. Canby, May 5, 1868, both in Jonathan Worth GLB, NCSA.

26. C. E. Compton to Louis V. Caziarc, November 16, 1867, with Endorsement of A. J. Willard, November 21, 1867, LR, 2MD, RG 393, NA; Louis V. Caziarc to Commanding Officer Plymouth, N.C., December 7, 9, 1867, and Louis V. Caziarc to Commanding Officer Goldsboro, N.C., December 10, 1867, all in LS, 2MD, RG 393, NA; Heyman, "'Great Reconstructor,'" 67.

27. Edward R. S. Canby to Assistant Adjutant General, Headquarters of the Army, October 24, 1867, LS, 2MD, RG 393, NA; Joseph K. Wilson to Isaac Ken-

ney, August 19, 1867, and Joseph K. Wilson to I. V. Post, September 17, 1867, both in LS, Post of Greensboro, RG 393, NA.

28. GO No. 101, 2MD, October 18, 1867, GO No. 106, 2MD, October 22, 1867, and Circular, 2MD, October 31, 1867, all in U.S. Congress, "General Orders: Reconstruction," 65–67, 69–72; Edward R. S. Canby to Adjutant General of the Army, February 19, 1868, LS, 2MD, RG 393, NA; GO No. 119, 2MD, November 15, 1867, M843, reel 20, GOC, ACNC, RG 105, NA.

29. Jonathan Worth to J. C. Pass, October 25, 1867, James C. Pass Correspondence, Elizabeth Fearrington Croom Collection, Collection No. 58, ECU; Jonathan Worth to William A. Graham, October 28, 1867, and Jonathan Worth to James W. Osborn, October 29, 1867, both in Hamilton, *Worth Correspondence*, 2: 1066–68; Perman, *Reunion without Compromise*, 327–29.

30. *Wilmington Morning Star*, November 23, 1867.

31. Edward R. S. Canby to Adjutant General of the Army, February 19, 1868, LS, 2MD, RG 393, NA; Harris, *Holden*, 232–33; McKinney, *Zeb Vance*, 271, 273–74.

32. Canby also eliminated the Military Command of North Carolina, placing the former commander, Col. James V. Bomford, in command of the Post of Raleigh. GO No. 145, 2MD, December 6, 1867, M843, reel 20, GOC, ACNC, RG 105, NA.

33. The garrison at Smithville (Fort Johnston) was Company A of the 40th U.S. Infantry, which, like the rest of the regiment, consisted of white officers and black enlisted men. Petition of A. P. Eckel et al. to General Canby, [n.d.], Petition of R. G. Curtis et al. to Commanding General of Department of North and South Carolina, [n.d.], Petition of James R. Lee et al. to Bvt. Maj. Genl. Canby, [n.d.], all in LR, 2MD, RG 393, NA.

34. Jonathan Worth to C. P. Mendenhall, R. P. Dick, J. A. Gilmer, Thomas Settle, and H. C. Worth, December 14, 1867, and Jonathan Worth to J. A. Gilmer, December 15, 1867, both in Hamilton, *Worth Correspondence*, 2: 1085–86, 1087–88; Endorsement of L. V. C[aziarc], [n.d.], on Petition of A. P. Eckel et al., [n.d.], LR, 2MD, RG 393, NA; Louis V. Caziarc to A. P. Eckel et al., December 4, 1867, LS, 2MD, RG 393, NA.

35. Henry R. Bryan et al. to Asst. Adjt. Genl., 2MD, December 10, 1867, and Edward W. Hinks to J. D. Flanner, January 25, 1868, both in LR, 2MD, RG 393, NA; E. R. S. Canby to Chief of Staff Headquarters of the Army, January 6, 1868, LS, 2MD, RG 393, NA.

36. Rumor had it either that Nethercutt was the victim of a political assassination ordered by carpetbagger Sheriff Colgrove or that he was executed by friends of the Union soldiers hanged at Kinston in 1864, because Nethercutt had commanded one of the local defense battalions from which the condemned men had deserted. The evidence indicates that Nethercutt was simply the victim of cold-blooded murder. The robbers who killed Nethercutt attempted a simi-

lar home invasion ten days later, and no ulterior motives were attached to that crime. Edward W. Hinks to E. R. S. Canby, December 19, 1867, Edward W. Hinks to Louis V. Caziarc, December 23, 1867, and clipping from *New Berne Republican*, December 10, 1867, all in LR, 2MD, RG 393, NA. See also W. Foy to James Fleming, December 9, 1867, with Endorsement of John W. French, February 3, 1868, in ibid; Robert S. Fletcher to Maj. Comdg. Mily. Post of New Bern, N.C., December 12, 1867, Jonathan Worth GP, NCSA.

37. Edward W. Hinks to Louis V. Caziarc, December 23, 1867, and Germain Bernard et al. to Maj. Gen. Miles, [n.d.], both in LR, 2MD, RG 393, NA; King, *Sketches of Pitt County*, 171.

38. Edward W. Hinks to Louis V. Caziarc, December 23, 1867, William A. Cox et al. to E. R. S. Canby, December 16, 1867, Memorandum of Germain Bernard, December 26, 1867, Germain Bernard et al. to Maj. Gen. Miles, December 26, 1867, and Nelson A. Miles to G. Bernard et al., December 31, 1867, all in LR, 2MD, RG 393, NA. See also *Raleigh Daily Sentinel*, December 24, 1867.

39. E. R. S. Canby to Chief of Staff Headquarters of the Army, January 6, 1868, LS, 2MD, RG 393, NA; SO No. 1, 2MD, January 1, 1868, LR, Post of Goldsboro, RG 393, NA.

40. Hinks specified the number of white and black police for each county. Edward W. Hinks to Commanding Officer Post of Goldsboro, January 6, 1868, and Resolutions of Craven County Magistrates, January 21, 1868, both in LR, Post of Goldsboro, RG 393, NA; J. D. Flanner to E. W. Hinks, January 22, 1868, Edward W. Hinks to J. D. Flanner, January 25, 1868, James E. Fleming to E. W. Hinks, February 24, 1868, and Edward W. Hinks to James E. Fleming, February 24, 1868, all in LR, 2MD, RG 393, NA.

41. W. T. Faircloth to Gov. Worth, December 31, 1867, J. J. Van Horn to Jonathan Worth, January 8, 1868, and SO No. 3, Post of New Bern, all in Jonathan Worth GLB, NCSA.

42. E. F. Cox to Louis E. Granger, February 3, April 1, 1868, LR, 2MD, RG 393, NA; J. E. Fleming to E. W. Hinks, January 13, 1868, LR, Post of Goldsboro, RG 393, NA.

43. Robert Avery to E. W. Dennis, November 12, 1867, and Edward W. Hinks to Louis V. Caziarc, April 1, 28, 1868, both in LR, 2MD, RG 393, NA; Horace James to E. R. S. Canby, December 28, 1867, with Endorsement of O. O. Howard, January 2, 1868, and Robert Avery to L. V. Caziarc, December 7, 1867, all in LR, Post of Goldsboro, RG 393, NA; *Tarboro Southerner* quoted in *Raleigh Daily Sentinel*, May 4, 1868; *Cincinnati Commercial* quoted in *Asheville Weekly Pioneer*, May 21, 1868.

44. Edward W. Hinks to Louis V. Caziarc, April 28, 1868, LR, 2MD, RG 393, NA; *Tarboro Southerner* quoted in *Raleigh Daily Sentinel*, May 4, 1868; King, *Sketches of Pitt County*, 175–76.

45. *New Bern Journal of Commerce* and *Tarboro Southerner* quoted in *Raleigh Daily Sentinel*, May 1, 4, 1868. For an account that reversed the roles of Carney and the

soldiers, see the extract from the *Cincinnati Commercial* in the *Asheville Weekly Pioneer*, May 21, 1868.

46. John Mulloy to Comdg. Officer Post of Morganton, March 22, 1868, LR, 2MD, RG 393, NA.

47. S. L. Fremont to Edward R. S. Canby, June 1, 1868, and Henry B. Judd to John I. Hubbard, June 3, 1867, both in LR, 2MD, RG 393, NA; S. L. Fremont to Comdg. Officer Goldsboro, N.C., June 1, 1868, and Sylvester Soper to D. B. Wilson, June 4, 1868, both in LR, Post of Goldsboro, RG 393, NA; GO No. 120, 2MD, November 17, 1867, M843, reel 20, GOC, ACNC, RG 105, NA; "Charge and specification against Daniel M. Elkins, citizen, of Columbus County, North Carolina," [ca. April 1868], Jonathan Worth GP, NCSA; Edward R. S. Canby to Chief of Staff Headquarters of the Army, August 31, 1868, in U.S. Congress, "Report of the Secretary of War," 40th Congress, 3rd Session, 353, 366.

48. Circular No. 12, ACNC, June 18, 1867, and Nelson A. Miles to Oliver O. Howard, October 9, 1867; :"Annual Report of the Assist. Commissioner for North Carolina," 5–6, both in Nelson Appleton Miles Papers, MHI; GO No. 145, 2MD, December 6, 1867, M843, reel 20, GOC, ACNC, RG 105, NA; Nelson A. Miles to Louis V. Caziarc, December 5, 1867, LR, 2MD, RG 393, NA.

49. Nelson A. Miles to Louis V. Caziarc, October 14, 1867, and Nelson A. Miles to O. O. Howard, November 18, 1867, both in LR, 2MD, RG 393, NA; Nelson A. Miles to "Dear General," [Oliver O. Howard], October 15, 1867, Oliver Otis Howard Papers, BC.

50. A. H. Galloway to O. O. Howard, December 22, 1867, R.T. Frank to Louis V. Caziarc, January 17, 1868, Endorsement of Nelson A. Miles, January 2, 1868, attached to A. H. Galloway to O. O. Howard, December 22, 1687, and Nelson A. Miles to General [Canby], January 6, 1868, all in LR, 2MD, RG 393, NA. For a biography of Galloway, see Cecelski, "Abraham Galloway," 43–72.

51. GO No. 165, 2MD, December 31, 1867, U.S. Congress, "General Orders: Reconstruction," 84–85; Heyman, "'Great Reconstructor,'" 68–69.

52. Harris, *Holden*, 235–36; Zuber, *North Carolina during Reconstruction*, 15–17; Lancaster, "Scalawags of North Carolina," 305.

53. GO No. 45, 2MD, March 23, 1868, reel 20, M843, GOC, ACNC, RG 105, NA.

54. J. W. Stephens to J. V. Bomford, [April 6, 1868], and James R. Lee et al. to J. V. Bomford, April 6, 1868, both in LR, Post of Raleigh, RG 393, NA; John O'Connell to J. J. Upham, April 17, 18, 1868, both in LS, Post of Raleigh, RG 393, NA; Zipf, "'Whites Shall Rule,'" 499–534; McGee, "North Carolina Conservatives and Reconstruction," 244–45, 253–55.

55. SO No. 70, April 14, 1868, and Edward W. Hinks to Louis V. Caziarc, April 29, 1868, both in LS, Post of Goldsboro, vol. 3, RG 393, NA; Charles H. Hall to R.T. Frank, April 12, 1868, Isaac A. Rosekrans to Louis E. Granger, April 9, 1868, J. H. Dewell to Louis E. Granger, April 19, 1868, Hiram E. Stilley to I. A. Rosekrans, April 26, 1868, William Stilley to E. W. Hinks, April 26, 1868, W. Tear to D. B.

Wilson, April 28, 1868, D. Heaton to Brig. Genl. Hinks, April 11, 1868, SO No. 86, Post of Goldsboro, SO No. 128, 2MD, June 2, 1868, R. W. King to E. W. Hinks, April 21, 1868, W. H. Hillery et al. to General Hinks, April 25, 1868, C. W. Dodge to Louis E. Granger, April 11, 1868, and William H. Doherty to Louis E. Granger, April 11, 14, 1868, all in LR, Post of Goldsboro, RG 393, NA; Edward W. Hinks to Louis V. Caziarc, April 18, 1868, LR, 2MD, RG 393, NA.

56. GO No. 61, 2MD, April 6, 1868, GOC, ACNC, RG 105, NA; Special Instructions, Post of Raleigh, April 15, 1868, LS, Post of Raleigh, RG 393, NA.

57. Alexander E. Drake to L. V. Caziarc, May 13, 1868, LR, 2MD, RG 393, NA; Heitman, *Historical Register*, 1: 382.

58. Alexander E. Drake to L. V. Caziarc, May 13, 1868, and W. H. Bailey to Col. Drake, April 18, 1868, both in LR, 2MD, RG 393, NA.

59. Thomas Wilhelm to H. M. Houston, April 10, 1868, and John O'Connell to H. M. Lazelle, April 18, 1868, both in LS, Post of Raleigh, RG 393, NA; H. M. Lazelle to Thomas Wilhelm, April 23, 1868, LR, Post of Raleigh, RG 393, NA.

60. Trelease, *White Terror*, 70.

61. Edward R. S. Canby to Chief of Staff, Headquarters of the Army, August 31, 1868, in U.S. Congress, "Report of the Secretary of War," 40th Congress, 3rd Session, 340; Simpson, *Let Us Have Peace*, 239; Harris, *Holden*, 242.

62. Edward R. S. Canby to Governor of North Carolina, July 9, 1868, in Raper and Mitchell, *Holden Papers*, 1: 330–31; Edward W. Hinks to Sheriff of Hyde County, May 3, 1868, and Edward W. Hinks to Louis V. Caziarc, April 24, 1868, both in LS, Post of Goldsboro, vol. 1, RG 393, NA; William H. Doherty to D. B. Wilson, April 29, 30, 1868, Affidavit and Petition of Matchet Taylor, April 27, 1868, Affidavit of Henry Pool, April 27, 1868, Vergel Crumpler et al. to Edward W. Hinks, May 15, 1868, Sylvester Carter et al. to Edward W. Hinks, May 15, 1868, and Affidavit of H. Killett, May 15, 1868, all in LR, Post of Goldsboro, RG 393, NA; William H. Doherty to Louis E. Granger, April 19, 1868, and Report of Joseph S. Sanderlin, Coroner of Camden County, April 19, 1868, both in reel 14, M843, LR, ACNC, RG 105, NA; J. C. Wright to Charles A. Nelson, April 22, 1868, Charles Alexander Nelson Papers, NYPL; Zipf, "'Whites Shall Rule,'" 531.

63. John Dawson et al. to Edward R. S. Canby, May 1, 1868, with Endorsement of E. R. S. C[anby], [n.d.], Samuel J. Person et al. to Edward R. S. Canby, May 1, 1868, and Edward Kidder et al. to Edward R. S. Canby, April 30, 1868, all in LR, 2MD, RG 393, NA.

64. *Wilmington Post*, May 1, 1868, clipping enclosed in Edward Kidder et al. to Edward R. S. Canby, April 30, 1868, LR, 2MD, RG 393, NA; *Wilmington Morning Star*, May 1, 12, 1868; *Wilmington Daily Journal*, May 12, 1868.

65. *Wilmington Daily Journal*, May 12, 1868; *Raleigh Daily Sentinel*, May 2, 18, 1868; Jonathan Worth to J. V. Bomford, May 1, 1868, in Hamilton, *Worth Correspondence*, 2: 1189; J. V. Bomford to Jonathan Worth, May 4, 1868, Jonathan Worth GLB,

NCSA; J. V. Bomford to Kemp P. Battle, June 4, 1868, Battle Family Papers, SHC-UNC; Bishir, "'Strong Force of Ladies,'" 464–67.

66. *Wilmington Morning Star*, September 26, 1867.

67. *Land We Love* (Charlotte) 3 (June 1867): 177–78.

68. McKinney, *Zeb Vance*, 276–78.

8. North Carolina Rejoins the Union

1. Foner, *Reconstruction*, 333–36.

2. Edward R. S. Canby to Chief of Staff, Headquarters of the Army, May 4, 1868, in U.S. Congress, "Letter from the Secretary of War Transmitting Reports Relative to the Condition of the Second Military District," 2–4; Heyman, "'Great Reconstructor,'" 72–73.

3. U.S. Grant to E. M. Stanton, May 6, 1868, and Edwin M. Stanton to S. Colfax, May 6, 1868, both in U.S. Congress, "Letter from the Secretary of War Transmitting Reports Relative to the Condition of the Second Military District," 1–2; GO No. 117, 2MD, June 26, 1868, reprinted in *North Carolina Daily Standard* (Raleigh), July 15, 1868; Harris, *Holden*, 244; Zuber, *Jonathan Worth*, 286.

4. Jonathan Worth to W. W. Holden, July 1, 1868, and Edward R. S. Canby to W. W. Holden, July 3, 1868, both in Raper and Mitchell, *Holden Papers*, 1: 317–18; Edward R. S. Canby to C. O. Goldsboro, July 3, 1868, LR, Post of Goldsboro, RG 393, NA; Zuber, *Jonathan Worth*, 287.

5. William M. Coleman to G. A. Williams, July 14, 1868, George A. Williams to E. R. S. Canby, July 14, 1868 (two telegrams), and George A. Williams to L. V. Caziarc, July 14, 1868, all in LR, 2MD, RG 393, NA; W. W. Holden to E. R. S. Canby, July 16, 1868, in Raper and Mitchell, *Holden Papers*, 1: 339; *North Carolina Daily Standard* (Raleigh), July 15, 1868.

6. E. R. S. Canby to Commanding Officer Post of Raleigh, N.C., July 14, 1868 (two telegrams), E. R. S. Canby to Governor Holden, July 15, 1868, William D. Haywood to E. R. S. Canby, July 14, 1868, and William M. Coleman to E. R. S. Canby, July 14, 1868, all in LR, 2MD, RG 393, NA; W. W. Holden to E. R. S. Canby, July 16, 1868, in Raper and Mitchell, *Holden Papers*, 1: 339; Harris, *Holden*, 248.

7. Edward R. S. Canby to Commanding Officer Post of Raleigh, N.C., July 16, 1868, LS, 2MD, RG 393, NA; W. W. Holden to E. R. S. Canby, July 15, 16, 1868, Edward R. S. Canby to W. W. Holden, July 16, 1868, W. W. Holden to Col. Williams, July 17, 1868, and George A. Williams to W. W. Holden, July 18, 1868, all in Raper and Mitchell, *Holden Papers*, 1: 336, 339, 341, 343–44.

8. Edward R. S. Canby to Chief of Staff, Headquarters of the Army, July 21, 1868, LS, 2MD, RG 393, NA; Edward R. S. Canby to Governor of North Carolina, July 22, 1868, in Raper and Mitchell, *Holden Papers*, 1: 345–46; GO No. 131, 2MD, July 6, 1868, William Lafayette Scott Papers, DU; Heyman, "'Great Reconstructor,'" 74.

9. Heyman, "'Great Reconstructor,'" 77.

10. The Department of the South consisted of the states from the former Second and Third Military Districts: North Carolina, South Carolina, Georgia, Alabama, and Florida. Circular No. 9, ACNC, August 19, 1868, Freedmen's Bureau Orders and Circulars, Nelson Appleton Miles Papers, MHI; W. W. Holden to O. O. Howard, March 26, 1870, Oliver Otis Howard Papers, BC; Harris, Holden, 260.

11. O. O. Howard to Daniel E. Sickles, April 8, 1867, LR, 2MD, RG 393, NA; Schenck, "History of Fort Johnston, North Carolina," NYHS; Powell, Powell's Records, 400; Warner, Generals in Blue, 322–23; Heitman, Historical Register, 1: 708–9; Wooster, Miles and the Frontier Army, 46–47, 50–51; De Montravel, Hero to His Fighting Men, 59–60.

12. R. C. Drum to Commanding Officer District of North Carolina, August 25, 1868, LR, Dist NC, RG 393, NA.

13. Edward R. S. Canby to Adjutant General Department of the South, July 31, 1868, and George G. Meade to E. D. Townsend, August 10, 1868, both in George Gordon Meade Collection, HSPA; Alfred H. Terry to James B. Fry, October 31, 1869, in U.S. Congress, "Report of the Secretary of War," 41st Congress, 2nd Session, 83; Army and Navy Journal (New York), August 29, 1868.

14. William T. Dortch to Andrew Johnson, August 3, 1868, in Graf et al., Johnson Papers, 14: 477; George G. Meade to Adj. Genl. U.S.A., October 13, 1868, George Gordon Meade Collection, HSPA; W. T. Dortch and G. V. Strong to W. E. Pell, August 24, 1868, and William T. Dortch et al. to Jonathan Worth, August 24, 1868, both in Hamilton, Worth Correspondence, 2: 1244–45.

15. Price, Across the Continent, 266–67; Wilmington Journal and Goldsboro News quoted in Raleigh Daily Sentinel, March 16, 1867; E. T. Lamberton to Commanding Officer Fort Fisher, N.C., April 19, 1867, LR, 2MD, RG 393, NA; Dobak and Phillips, Black Regulars, 4.

16. John Sample to Louis E. Granger, March 16, 1868, with Endorsement of Edward W. Hinks, April 7, 1868, and Nelson A. Miles to James V. Bomford, February 29, 1868, both in LR, 2MD, RG 393, NA; Anonymous Soldiers, 40th U.S. Infantry, to Secretary of War, September 14, 1868, LR, Dist NC, RG 393, NA.

17. Court of Inquiry, Charles E. Hargous, Case No. OO-3652; GO No. 12, Dept South, March 8, 1869, and Trial of Charles E. Hargous, both in Case No. PP-143, RG 153, NA.

18. Nelson A. Miles to Adjt. Genl. U.S. Army, September 28, 1867, LS, 40th Inf., RG 391, NA; Heitman, Historical Register, 1: 332.

19. Petition of Citizens of New Bern, undated (ca. February 1868), LR, Post of Goldsboro, RG 393, NA.

20. James E. Fleming to C. E. Compton, July 7, 1868, and D. B. Wilson to C. E. Compton, July 8, 1868, both in LR, Post of Goldsboro, RG 393, NA; Newbern Journal of Commerce quoted in Wilmington Daily Journal, July 9, 1868, and Raleigh Daily Sentinel, July 9, 10, 1868; Newbern Republican quoted in Wilmington Morning Star, July 11, 1868. For a monograph on the scene of the riot, see Mobley, James City.

21. C. E. Compton to D. B. Wilson, July 7, 1868, C. E. Compton to Mayor of New Bern, July 7, 1868, C. E. Compton to W. S. Long, July 7, 1868, and D. B. Wilson to W. S. Long, July 11, 1868, all in LS, Post of Goldsboro, vol. 1, RG 393, NA.

22. Walter S. Long to James F. Simpson, July 9, 1868, and John B. White to C. E. Compton, July 16, 1868, both in LR, Post of Goldsboro, RG 393, NA; Heitman, *Historical Register*, 1: 640.

23. GO No. 13, Dept South, March 10, 1869, and Trial of Richard Boston, both in Case No. PP-185, RG 153, NA; GO No. 31, Thomas H. Smith, Dept South, October 20, 1868, Case No. OO-3582, RG 153, NA; C. E. Compton to C. B. Gaskill, October 2, 1868, LR, Dist NC, RG 393, NA; C. E. Compton to AAAG District of North Carolina, October 3, 1868, LS, Post of Goldsboro, vol. 2, RG 393, NA; Jacob F. Chur to Louis V. Caziarc, December 23, 24, 1867, January 9, 1868, all in LR, 2MD, RG 393, NA; Jacob F. Chur to Commanding Officer Company E, 40th Infantry, January 17, 1868, M843, reel 2, LS, ACNC, RG 105, NA; Louis V. Caziarc to N. A. Miles, January 4, 13, 1868, and Mayor's Warrant for Anthony Jackson, January 16, 1868, all in M843, reel 12, LR, ACNC, RG 105, NA; Nelson A. Miles to Jacob F. Chur, November 2, 1868, M843, reel 14, LR, ACNC, RG 105, NA; Sylvester Soper to Adjutant General U.S. Army, July 1, 1868, with Endorsement of L. V. C[aziarc], [n.d.], LR, 2MD, RG 393, NA; *Raleigh Daily Sentinel*, December 24, 1867; *North Carolina Weekly Standard* (Raleigh), October 21, December 9, 1868.

24. *Raleigh Daily Sentinel*, July 11, 1868. Only 11 percent of the enlisted men in the 40th U.S. Infantry were native Tar Heels. For the origins of soldiers in the 40th Infantry, see the appendix to this volume.

25. De Montravel, *Hero to His Fighting Men*, 56.

26. Report of William H. Doherty for August 1868, and Richard Dillon to Jacob F. Chur, August 26, 1868, both in M843, reel 22, Reports, ACNC, RG 105, NA; William M. MacFarland to Jacob F. Chur, July 25, 1868, M843, reel 14, LR, ACNC, RG 105, NA; John W. Hofler to W. W. Holden, August 22, 1868, in Raper and Mitchell, *Holden Papers*, 1: 357.

27. William J. Dawes to Jacob F. Chur, August 24, September 2, 1868, both in M843, reel 14, LR, ACNC, RG 105, NA; J. E. Cook to W. W. Holden, August 22, 1868, W. J. Dawes to W. W. Holden, August 22, 1868, and John W. Stephens to W. W. Holden, August 29, 1868, all in Raper and Mitchell, *Holden Papers*, 1: 358, 359, 364–65.

28. Dixon Ingram to Andrew Johnson, September 13, 1868, in Graf et al., *Johnson Papers*, 15: 53–54; William MacFarland to Nelson A. Miles, August 27, 1868, reel 14, LR, ACNC, RG 105, NA; Affidavit of Duncan Holmes, August 25, 1868, in Raper and Mitchell, *Holden Papers*, 1: 362–63.

29. Richard Dillon to Jacob F. Chur, September 26, 1868, M843, reel 22, Reports, ACNC, RG 105, NA; Richard Dillon to N. A. Miles, September 21, 1868, clipping from *Fayetteville Eagle*, September 24, 1868, enclosed in Richard Dillon to

J. F. Chur, October 12, 1868, and R. C. Drum to N. A. Miles, September 22, 1868, all in LR, Dist NC, RG 393, NA; W. W. Holden to Sheriff of Cumberland County, October 24, 1868, in Raper and Mitchell, *Holden Papers,* 1: 394–95; Harris, *Holden,* 249–51.

30. John H. Everitt to W. W. Holden, August 5, November 1, 15 1868, Henry W. Paschall to W. W. Holden, August 18, 1868, Silas L. Curtis et al. to W. W. Holden, October 11, 1868, and W. W. Holden to J. I. Moore, October 14, 1868, all in Raper and Mitchell, *Holden Papers,* 1: 349, 354–55, 385–86, 389–90, 398, 407–8.

31. W. W. Holden to Maj. General G. G. Meade, September 14, 1868, and R. C. Drum to W. W. Holden, September 15, 1868, both in Raper and Mitchell, *Holden Papers,* 1: 372–73; George G. Meade to R. C. Drum, September 14, 1868, George Gordon Meade Collection, HSPA.

32. R. C. Drum to N. A. Miles, September 16, 1868, LR, Dist NC, RG 393, NA.

33. E. D. Townsend to George G. Meade, August 22, 1868, George Gordon Meade Collection, HSPA; J. C. Kelton to George G. Meade, August 25, 1868, in Circular, Department of Virginia, March 4, 1870, M619, reel 808, LR, AGO, RG 94, NA.

34. Nelson A. Miles to R. C. Drum, September 25, 1868, with Affidavit of Henry Baker, September 24, 1868, and Andrew Geddes to Charles B. Gaskill, September 29, 1868, both in M619, reel 609, LR, AGO, RG 94, NA; R. C. Drum to N. A. Miles, September 29, 1868, in Meade, *Report of Military Operations,* 86–87.

35. Nelson A. Miles to R. C. Drum, October 4, 1868, R. C. Drum to N. A. Miles, October 8, 1868, and George G. Meade to U. S. Grant, October 9, 1868, all in M619, reel 609, LR, AGO, RG 94, NA.

36. Nelson A. Miles to R. C. Drum, October 22,1868, and George G. Meade to Adjt. Gen. U.S.A., October 13, 1868, both in M619, reel 609, LR, AGO, RG 94, NA; R. C. Drum to N. A. Miles, September 24, 1868, and Nelson A. Miles to R. C. Drum, September 25, 1868, both in LS, Dist NC, RG 393, NA.

37. GO No. 27, October 8, 1868, Dept South, in Meade, *Report of Military Operations,* 51; Sefton, *Army and Reconstruction,* 198–99; Foner, *Reconstruction,* 342; Kirkland, "Federal Troops in the South Atlantic States," 239–43.

38. The ten additional stations were Boon Hill (Johnston County), Greenville (Pitt County), Henderson (Granville County), Lumberton (Robeson County), Morganton (Burke County), Nashville (Nash County), Shelby (Cleveland County), Warrenton (Warren County), Williamston (Martin County), and Yanceyville (Caswell County). GO No. 9, Dist NC, October 14, 1868, Orders, Dist NC, Nelson Appleton Miles Papers, MHI; Nelson A. Miles to R. C. Drum, September 25, October 29, 1868, both in LS, Dist NC, RG 393, NA; W. A. Smith to Gen. Miles, October 31, 1868, LR, Dist NC, RG 393, NA; William Smith to Post Commander at Goldsboro, October 31, 1868, LR, Post of Goldsboro, RG 393, NA; George G.

Meade to General Grant, October 6, 1868, and General Orders No. 27, October 8, 1868, Dept South, both in Meade, *Report of Military Operations,* 51–52; *Army and Navy Journal* (New York), October 17, 1868.

39. GO No. 27, Dept South, October 8, 1868, in Meade, *Report of Military Operations,* 51–52; GO No. 10, Dist NC, October 30, 1868, Orders, Dist NC, Nelson Appleton Miles Papers, MHI; Proclamation by W. W. Holden, October 12, 1868, and W. W. Holden to J. L. Moore, October 14, 1868, both in Raper and Mitchell, *Holden Papers,* 1: 386–89.

40. William Walsh to Charles B. Gaskill, October 23, 1868, W. J. Broatch to Asst. Adjt. General District of N. Carolina, November 5, 1868, and Charles Bentzoni to A. A. A. General District of North Carolina, November 10, 1868, all in LR, Dist NC, RG 393, NA; Oscar Eastmond to Jacob F. Chur, November 4, 1868, M843, reel 14, LR, ACNC, RG 105, NA; Cousin H. to Willie, December 7, 1868, William C. Stevens Correspondence, UMI; R. M. Henry to W. W. Holden, November 4, 1868, and Oscar Eastmond to W. W. Holden, November 14, 1868, in Raper and Mitchell, *Holden Papers,* 1: 399–400, 407.

41. Lefler and Newsome, *North Carolina,* 493; Holden quoted in Harris, *Holden,* 252–53; Olsen, "Ku Klux Klan," 354.

42. John B. Gretter to Maj. Logan, November 11, 1868, reprinted in *Greensboro Patriot and Times,* November 12, 1868.

43. GO No.11, Dist NC, November 9, 1868, Orders, Dist NC, Nelson Appleton Miles Papers, MHI; Richard Dillon to Jacob F. Chur, November 7, 1868, and T. D. McAlpine to N. A. Miles, November 8, 1868, both in LR, Dist NC, RG 393, NA; F. W. Liedtke to Jacob F. Chur, November 15, 1868, M843, reel 14, LR, ACNC, RG 105, NA.

44. A shoulder strap was a commissioned officer's emblem of rank. Mrs. H. J. Moore to Gen. Miles, December 28, 1868, in Raper and Mitchell, *Holden Papers,* 1: 441–42; Testimony of Thomas Settle, in U.S. Congress, "Condition of Affairs in the Southern States: North Carolina," xvi; Trelease, *White Terror,* 195; Harris, *Holden,* 281.

45. Act of March 3, 1869, ch. 124, U.S. *Statutes at Large* 15: 318; Alfred H. Terry to James B. Fry, October 31, 1869, in U.S. Congress, "Report of the Secretary of War," 41st Congress, 2nd Session, 84; Sefton, *Army and Reconstruction,* 207–8, 262; Heitman, *Historical Register,* 1: 135; Dawson, *Army Generals and Reconstruction,* 95; Wilhelm, *Eighth U.S. Infantry,* 125.

46. Ruger was a former brigadier general in the U.S. Volunteers. On September 1, 1866, he was mustered out of the Volunteers and thus reverted to his Regular Army rank of colonel. W. T. Sherman to Mary Miles, September 18, 1868, Nelson A. Miles Family Papers, LC; Wooster, *Miles and the Frontier Army,* 54; Sefton, *Army and Reconstruction,* 257.

47. E. F Cox to "Friend Ames," February 1, 1869, William Woods Holden Papers, DU; Affidavit of Thomas F. Williford, August 12, 1870, Anonymous Letter

from Stokes County, N.C., October 23, 1870, and Testimony of John T. Freeman, *Testimony of the Witnesses in the Preliminary Examination of the Lenoir County Prisoners* (New Bern, N.C.: Nason and Stearns, 1869), 50–56, all in M666, reel 1, LR, AGO, RG 94, NA; Testimony of Peter Harden, in U.S. Congress, "Condition of Affairs in the Southern States," 33–34; Bogue, "Violence and Oppression," 213–14, 225; Trelease, *White Terror*, 189–90, 193.

48. Proclamation of William W. Holden, June 6, 1870, William Woods Holden GLB, NCSA; O. A. Williams and W. C. Thomas to W. W. Holden, January 23, 1869, William Woods Holden GP, NCSA; *North Carolina Weekly Standard* (Raleigh), March 17, 1869; Bogue, "Violence and Oppression," 218–19; Trelease, *White Terror*, 192.

49. William Campbell to W. W. Holden, April 14, 1869, William Woods Holden GP, NCSA; Escott, *Many Excellent People*, 155; Trelease, *White Terror*, 114.

50. S. W. Watts to Gov. Holden, August 14, 1869, and L. D. Wilkie to W. W. Holden, October 18, 1869, both in William Woods Holden GP, NCSA; Testimony of George W. Tillou and James P. Parrott, *Testimony of the Witnesses*, iv, 26, 28–31, 33–35; Testimony of James E. Boyd, in U.S. Congress, "Condition of Affairs in the Southern States," vi, 20–21; Testimony of William R. Albright, in *Trial of William W. Holden*, 2: 1915; Albion W. Tourgée to the *National Standard*, "The Ku Klux War in North Carolina," 4, reel 52, Albion Winegar Tourgée Papers, SHC-UNC; Trelease, *White Terror*, 114, 189; Bogue, "Violence and Oppression," 216–17.

51. Tourgée was the superior court judge for the Seventh Judicial District, which included Alamance and Caswell counties. A. W. Tourgée to W. W. Holden, July 3, 1869, William Woods Holden GLB, NCSA; D. D. Colgrove to W. W. Holden, May 29, 1869, William Woods Holden GP, NCSA; Albion W. Tourgée, "Ku Klux War," 8–9, reel 52, Albion Winegar Tourgée Papers, SHC-UNC; Testimony of Peter Harden, in U.S. Congress, "Condition of Affairs in the Southern States," 33; Trelease, *White Terror*, 196–97; Olsen, "Albion Winegar Tourgée," 47.

52. H. A. Badham to W. W. Holden, March 22 (two letters), 23, 1869, Henry M. Ray et al. to W. W. Holden, March 22, 1869, and R. T. Bosher to W. W. Holden, March 28, 1869, all in William Woods Holden GP, NCSA; Testimony of John W. Hardin and William R. Albright, in *Trial of William W. Holden*, 2: 1857, 1895–98; A. W. Tourgée to Emma Tourgée, June 9, 1869, reel 7, Albion Winegar Tourgée Papers, SHC-UNC; A. W. Tourgée to W. W. Holden, July 3, 1869, William Woods Holden GLB, NCSA; Testimony of James E. Boyd, in U.S. Congress, "Condition of Affairs in the Southern States," vi–vii, 36; Bogue, "Violence and Oppression," 226; Trelease, *White Terror*, 194; Troxler and Vincent, *Shuttle and Plow*, 328.

53. Albion W. Tourgée, "Ku Klux War," 3, reel 52, Albion Winegar Tourgée Papers, SHC-UNC; Testimony of William A. Albright, in *Trial of William W. Holden*, 2: 2039; Bogue, "Violence and Oppression," 226–27.

54. Testimony of George W. Tillou, *Testimony of the Witnesses*, 28–29; Trelease, *White Terror*, 190; Bogue, "Violence and Oppression," 215.

55. State senator Colgrove fled the state shortly after Sheriff Colgrove's mur-

der. A third brother, John G. Colgrove, had left the county two years earlier when his farm was destroyed by arson. D. D. Colgrove to W. W. Holden, May 29, 1869, John G. Colgrove to W. W. Holden, June 5, 1869, C. R. Thomas to Gov. Holden, May 31, 1869, E. Hubbs to W. W. Holden, May 29, 1869, M. L. Shepard to W. W. Holden, June 28, 1869, R. T. Berry to W. W. Holden, August 16, 1869, W. W. Holden to R. T. Berry, August 17, 1869, John V. Sherard to Gov. Holden, October 28, 1869, and William J. Clarke to W. W. Holden, November 3, 1869, all in William Woods Holden GP, NCSA; Affidavit of Thomas F. Williford, August 12, 1870, M666, reel 1, LR, AGO, RG 94, NA; Testimony of Thomas Waters, James P. Parrott, George W. Tillou, Ethelbert Hubbs, and David D. Colgrove, *Testimony of the Witnesses*, 12–16, 29, 35–36, 45–46; Testimony of Ethelbert Hubbs and C. R. Thomas, in U.S. Congress, "Condition of Affairs in the Southern States," 58–59; *North Carolina Weekly Standard* (Raleigh), June 9, August 25, 1869; Trelease, *White Terror*, 190–91; Harris, *Holden*, 279–80; Bogue, "Violence and Oppression," 214–15; Massengill, "Detectives of Holden," 462–66, 487.

56. Proclamation of William W. Holden, October 20, 1869, William Woods Holden GLB, NCSA; Harris, *Holden*, 280; Bogue, "Violence and Oppression," 217–18; Trelease, *White Terror*, 191.

57. List of Ku Klux Klan Outrages, 1869–1870, and Testimony of W. G. Turrentine, in U.S. Congress, "Condition of Affairs in the Southern States," xxi, 42, 45; A. L. Murdock to Judge Tourgée, August 7, 1869, reel 7, and Affidavit of John W. McCauley, November 4, 1871, reel 10, both in Albion Winegar Tourgée Papers, SHC-UNC; E. McCroray to Governor Holden, February 13, 1871, William Woods Holden Papers, DU; H. B. Williams to W. W. Holden, September 16, 1869, James B. Mason to W. W. Holden, September 22, 1869, L. B. Long to W. W. Holden, November 11, 1869, and Anonymous to S. S. Ashley, December 1, 1869, all in William Woods Holden GP, NCSA; Trelease, *White Terror*, 195–96.

58. W. W. Holden to A. H. Terry, November 5, 1869, and Alfred H. Terry to Governor Holden, November 5, 1869, both in William Woods Holden GP, NCSA; Alfred H. Terry to James B. Fry, October 31, 1869, in U.S. Congress, "Report of the Secretary of War," 41st Congress, 2nd Session, 86; Wilhelm, *Eighth U.S. Infantry*, 125–26; Sefton, *Army and Reconstruction*, 257, 262; Currey, "Role of the Army," 65.

59. W. W. Holden to General Assembly, November 16, 1869, in *Executive and Legislative Documents before the General Assembly*, 10.

60. Alonzo B. Corliss to H. C. Vogell, December 14, 15, 1869, and H. C. Vogell to O. O. Howard, December 14, 1869, all in William Woods Holden Papers, DU; F. A. Whitney to John Roach, December 2, 1869, and W. S. Worth to J. H. Taylor, December 4, 1869, both in LS, Post of Raleigh, RG 393, NA; W. W. Holden to W. S. Worth, December 2, 1869, and W. W. Holden to A. H. Terry, December 3, 1869, both in William Woods Holden GLB, NCSA; Testimony of Peter Harden, in U.S. Congress, "Condition of Affairs in the Southern States," 34; Escott, *Many Excellent People*, 153; Bogue, "Violence and Oppression," 228–29; Trelease, *White Terror*, 202.

61. H. C. Vogell to O. O. Howard, December 14, 16, 1869, and E. Whittlesey to W. W. Holden, December 18, 1869, all in William Woods Holden Papers, DU; A. J. Stephenson to Brother Vogell, March 23, 1869, William Woods Holden GP, NCSA; Testimony of John W. Long, in *Third Annual Message of W. W. Holden*, 181; Testimony of Daniel Worth, in *Trial of William W. Holden*, 1: 573–74; Joel Asheworth to Governor Holden, October 28, 1870, in U.S. Congress, "Condition of Affairs in the Southern States," lxiv; Escott, *Many Excellent People*, 153.

62. Testimony of Caswell Holt, in U.S. Congress, "Condition of Affairs in the Southern States," 341–45; Testimony of Caswell Holt and John S. Murphy, in *Trial of William W. Holden*, 2: 1318, 1370; Albion W. Tourgée, "Ku Klux War," 11–12, reel 52, Albion Winegar Tourgée Papers, SHC-UNC; Trelease, *White Terror*, 193, 205.

63. "An Act to Secure the Better Protection of Life and Property" [Shoffner Act], in U.S. Congress, "Condition of Affairs in the Southern States," xciv–xcv; Albion W. Tourgée, "Ku Klux War," 3, reel 52, Albion Winegar Tourgée Papers, SHC-UNC; Harris, *Holden*, 281–83.

64. Affidavit of George W. Busbee, December 16, 1871, reel 10, Albion Winegar Tourgée Papers, SHC-UNC; Testimony of James E. Boyd, in U.S. Congress, "Condition of Affairs in the Southern States," xiii–xiv, 21–22; Testimony of James E. Boyd, John A. Moore, and Eli S. Euliss, all in *Third Annual Message of W. W. Holden*, 211, 236–37, 238; Testimony of Eli S. Euliss, in *Trial of William W. Holden*, 2: 1977–78; Trelease, *White Terror*, 203.

65. Testimony of William R. Albright, in *Trial of William W. Holden*, 2: 1886–87, 1926.

66. Contrary to the newspaper accounts, Corliss reported that his men fired no rifle ammunition during the riot. A. W. Corliss to J. F. Ritter, October 24, 1869, LR, Post of Goldsboro, RG 393, NA; *Goldsboro Messenger*, October 25, 1869; *Wilmington Weekly Journal*, October 29, 1869; *Army and Navy Journal* (New York), October 30, 1869.

67. For the percentage of Irish-born soldiers in the 8th Infantry, see the appendix to this volume. H. L. Stevens to W. W. Holden, October 25, 1869, William Woods Holden GP, NCSA; *Goldsboro News* quoted in *North Carolina Weekly Standard* (Raleigh), November 3, 1869.

68. J. M. Hollowell to J. B. Whitaker, September 2, 1869, enclosed in J. B. Whitaker to Adjt. Post of Goldsboro, September 3, 1869, and J. M. Hollowell to Comdg. Officer Garrison of Goldsboro, September 21, 1869, all in LR, Post of Goldsboro, RG 393, NA.

69. For a discussion of the Greensboro petitions, see chapter 7 in this volume. See also Wilhelm, *Eighth U.S. Infantry*, 125–27.

9. Fighting Terrorism

1. H. A. Badham et al. to W. W. Holden, February 28, 1870, William Woods Holden GLB, NCSA; Testimony of Henry Holt, David Allred, Jemima Phillips,

and Peter Hardin, all in *Trial of William W. Holden,* 2: 1194, 1197, 1200, 1241–43, 1365, 1930–31.

2. Testimony of William R. Albright, in *Trial of William W. Holden,* 2: 1900–1901, 1916–18; Troxler, "Wyatt Outlaw," 413, 416; Nelson, "Red Strings and Half Brothers," 39, 43–47.

3. Affidavit of James M. Stockard, December 17, 1871, reel 10, Albion Winegar Tourgée Papers, SHC-UNC; Testimony of Henry Holt, Mary Holt, and Jemima Phillips, all in *Trial of William W. Holden,* 1192, 1194, 1299, 1364–67.

4. H. A. Badham et al. to W. W. Holden, February 28, 1870, William Woods Holden GLB, NCSA; Affidavit of George A. Fawcett, December 22, 1871, reel 10, Albion Winegar Tourgée Papers, SHC-UNC; C. P. McTaggart to S. B. Hayman, March 4, 1870, and Paul R. Hambrick to E. R. S. Canby, March 14, 1870, both in U.S. Congress, "Condition of Affairs in the Southern States," xci, cxii; Trelease, *White Terror,* 205.

5. H. A. Badham et al. to W. W. Holden, February 28, 1870, William Woods Holden Papers, DU; Testimony of Henry Holt, in *Trial of William W. Holden,* 2: 1198; A. W. Fisher to S. B. Hayman, March 1, 1870, LR, Post of Raleigh, RG 393, NA; Trelease, *White Terror,* 210.

6. S. B. Hayman to Louis V. Caziarc, March 5, 1870, in U.S. Congress, "Condition of Affairs in the Southern States," xcii; George G. Meade to E. D. Townsend, October 27, 1870, in U.S. Congress, "Report of the Secretary of War," 41st Congress, 3rd Session, 42; Sefton, *Army and Reconstruction,* 257; Wilhelm, *Eighth U.S. Infantry,* 130–31.

7. Circular, Department of Virginia, March 4, 1870, C. P. McTaggart to S. B. Hayman, March 4, 1870, and S. B. Hayman to Louis V. Caziarc, March 7, 1870, all in U.S. Congress, "Condition of Affairs in the Southern States," lxxxiii–lxxxvi, xciii; J. N. Andrews to Louis V. Caziarc, March 8, 1870, LS, Post of Raleigh, RG 393, NA.

8. Testimony of James E. Boyd, *State vs. William M. Andrews et al.,* August 31, 1870, Ku Klux Klan Papers, DU; Paul R. Hambrick to W. W. Holden, March 12, 1870, William Woods Holden GP, NCSA; Testimony of James E. Boyd, in *Third Annual Message of W. W. Holden,* 214; C. P. McTaggart to S. B. Hayman, March 6, 1870, in U.S. Congress, "Condition of Affairs in the Southern States," xcii.

9. James A. Graham to William A. Graham, March 16, 1870, in Hamilton et al., *Graham Papers,* 8: 84–85.

10. C. P. McTaggart to S. B. Hayman, March 6, 1870, in U.S. Congress, "Condition of Affairs in the Southern States," xcii–xciii; S. B. Hayman to Louis V. Caziarc, March 15, 1870, LS, Post of Raleigh, RG 393, NA.

11. Proclamation of William W. Holden, March 7, 1870, W. W. Holden to Senators and Representatives in the Congress of the United States from North Carolina, March 14, 1870, and W. W. Holden to J. C. Abbott, March 17, 1870, all in William Woods Holden GLB, NCSA; W. W. Holden to President of the United

States, March 10, 1870, in U.S. Congress, "Condition of Affairs in the Southern States," xciv.

12. Edward R. S. Canby to Assistant Adjutant General Military Division of the Atlantic, March 8, 1870, with Endorsements of George G. Meade and Edward Schriver, and W. W. Holden Executive Order to A. W. Fisher, March 7, 1870, both in U.S. Congress, "Condition of Affairs in the Southern States," xc–xci.

13. Albion W. Tourgée, "Ku Klux War," 13, reel 52, Albion Winegar Tourgée Papers, SHC-UNC; list of victims of Ku Klux Klan outrages in Alamance County, in U.S. Congress, "Condition of Affairs in the Southern States," xix–xx.

14. Paul R. Hambrick to E. R. S. Canby, March 14, 1870, in U.S. Congress, "Condition of Affairs in the Southern States," cxii–cxiv; Heitman, *Historical Register*, 1: 492. See also Paul R. Hambrick to W. W. Holden, March 12, 1870, William Woods Holden GP, NCSA.

15. Pride Jones to W. W. Holden, March 4, 1870, J. W. Norwood et al. to W. W. Holden, March 5, 1870, and W. W. Holden to Pride Jones, March 7, 1870, all in William Woods Holden Papers, DU; Pride Jones to W. W. Holden, March 9, 1870, W. W. Holden to Pride Jones, March 11, 1870, W. W. Holden to Thomas A. Donoho, April 22, 1870, T. A. Donoho to Gov. Holden, May 16, 1870, E. Cobb et al. to W. W. Holden, May 11, 1870, Samuel Allen to W. W. Holden, May 14, 1870, J. W. Stephens to W. W. Holden, May 16, 1870, A. W. Tourgée to W. W. Holden, May 17, 1870, W. W. Holden to W. P. Bynum, May 17, 1870, and W. P. Bynum to W. W. Holden, May 20, 1870, all in William Woods Holden GLB, NCSA; Testimony of Pride Jones, and "Ku Klux Outrages in Wayne Co., N.C." [January 1870?], both in U.S. Congress, "Testimony Taken by the Joint Committee to Inquire into the Condition of Affairs in the Late Insurrectionary States," 1–7; Trelease, *White Terror*, 206, 211.

16. SO No. 59, Department of Virginia, April 26, 1870, LR, Post of Raleigh, RG 393, NA; W. W. Holden to Irvin McDowell, May 7, 1870, Irvin McDowell to W. W. Holden, May 7, 1870, and Irvin McDowell to W. W. Holden, May 10, 1870, all in William Woods Holden GLB, NCSA; W. W. Holden to Irvin McDowell, May 9, 1870, William Woods Holden GP, NCSA; W. W. Holden to Irvin McDowell, May 9, 1870, C. McKeever to Commanding Officer Post of Raleigh, May 10, 12, 1870, and Irvin McDowell to W. W. Holden, May 12, 1870, all in U.S. Congress, "Condition of Affairs in the Southern States," lxxxii, lxxxvi; Wilhelm, *Eighth U.S. Infantry*, 132.

17. Testimony of N. M. Roan and W. H. Stephens, both in *Third Annual Message of W. W. Holden*, 91–92, 95–96; Testimony of W. H. Stephens, in *Trial of William W. Holden*, 2: 2127–28; Proclamation of William W. Holden, May 25, June 6, July 28, 1870, and W. W. Holden to N. A. Ramsey, May 7, 1870, all in William Woods Holden GLB, NCSA; Statement of John G. Lea, reprinted in Zuber, *North Carolina during Reconstruction*, 30–32; *North Carolina Weekly Standard* (Raleigh), June 1, 1870; Trelease, *White Terror*, 213–15; Harris, *Holden*, 284–85.

18. Act of May 31, 1870, ch. 114, in U.S. Congress, *Statutes at Large* 16: 140.

19. Testimony of R. C. Badger, in Holden, Memoirs, 187–99; W. W. Holden to President of the United States, March 10, 1870, in U.S. Congress, "Condition of Affairs in the Southern States," xciv; Harris, Holden, 287–88; Trelease, White Terror, 215–16.

20. William. J. Clarke to Governor, June 18, 1870, William Woods Holden GP, NCSA; Testimony of R. C. Badger, in Holden, Memoirs, 194; Harris, Holden, 289.

21. R. T. Frank to C. McKeever, October 2, 1870, in U.S. Congress, "Condition of Affairs in the Southern States," lxxi–lxxii; George B. Rodney to R. T. Frank, July 10, 1870, LR, Post of Raleigh, RG 393, NA; Irvin McDowell to R. C. Drum, October 8, 1870, in U.S. Congress, "Report of the Secretary of War," 41st Congress, 3rd Session, 48.

22. Affidavit of Wyatt Prince, December 21, 1870, R. T. Frank to C. McKeever, October 2, 1870, John H. Coster to Royal T. Frank, June 22, 1870, and C. McKeever to R. T. Frank, July 13, 1870, all in U.S. Congress, "Condition of Affairs in the Southern States," lxiv, lxxii, lxxxvii; R. T. Frank to J. W. Powell, July 8, 1870, and R. T. Frank to C. McKeever, July 11, 1870, both in LS, Post of Raleigh, RG 393, NA; North Carolina Weekly Standard (Raleigh), July 13, 1870.

23. R. T. Frank to C. McKeever, July 15, 19, October 2, 1870, and C. McKeever to R. T. Frank, July 18, 1870, all in U.S. Congress, "Condition of Affairs in the Southern States," lxviii–lxix, lxxii, lxxxviii.

24. R. T. Frank to C. McKeever, July 19, October 2, 1870, in U.S. Congress, "Condition of Affairs in the Southern States," lxix, lxxii.

25. William L. Scott to Ella, July 18, 1870, and William L. Scott to "My dear Payne," July 18, 1870, both in William Lafayette Scott Papers, DU; W. W. Holden to George W. Kirk, August 3, 1870, William Woods Holden GLB, NCSA; Testimony of George W. Kirk, in U.S. Congress, "Condition of Affairs in the Southern States," 5; Deposition of John G. Albright, August 24, 1870, in Hamilton et al., Graham Papers, 132–34; Trelease, White Terror 216–18; Harris, Holden, 293–94.

26. G. W. Kirk to W. W. Holden, August 7, 1870, and Robert Hancock Jr. to William J. Clarke, August 7, 1870, both in William Woods Holden Papers, DU; Trelease, White Terror, 218; Harris, Holden, 294.

27. W. W. Holden to President of the United States, July 20, 1870, U. S. Grant to Secretary of War, July 22, 1870, and Irvin McDowell to R. T. Frank, July 25, 1870, all in M619, reel 808, LR, AGO, RG 94, NA; U. S. Grant to W. W. Holden, July 22, 1870, William Woods Holden GLB, NCSA.

28. Detachments of the 4th Artillery were also posted at Fort Macon and Fort Johnston, but they were not part of the District of North Carolina. GO No. 10, Dept East, July 27, 1870, and Endorsement of George G. Meade, August 10, 1870, attached to Henry J. Hunt to Chauncey McKeever, August 4, 1870, both in M619, reel 808, LR, AGO, RG 94, NA; Henry J. Hunt to Assistant Adjutant General Dept East, January 2, 1871, in U.S. Congress, "Condition of Affairs in the Southern States," lxxv; George G. Meade to E. D. Townsend, October 27, 1870,

and Irvin McDowell to R. C. Drum, October 8, 1870, both in U.S. Congress, "Report of the Secretary of War," 41st Congress, 3rd Session, 43, 48; Heitman, *Historical Register*, 1: 556; Warner, *Generals in Blue*, 242.

29. W. W. Holden to President of the United States, July 20, 1870, M619, reel 808, LR, AGO, RG 94, NA; George W. Kirk to W. W. Holden, August 1, 1870, William Woods Holden Papers, DU; GO No. 10, AGO, State of North Carolina, July 27, 1870, and GO No. 13, AGO, State of North Carolina, July 28, 1870, both in Josiah Turner Jr. Papers, SHC-UNC.

30. George W. Kirk to Gov. Holden, July 24, 1870, William Woods Holden GP, NCSA; George B. Rodney to R. T. Frank, July 30, 1870, in U.S. Congress, "Condition of Affairs in the Southern States," lxxvii.

31. Confessions of J. W. Simms, James F. Hopkins, and William Quackenbush, August 1, 1870, Confession of J. J. Younger, August 17, 1870, and Confession of J. C. Whitesell, September 6, 1870, all in M666, reel 1, LR, AGO, RG 94, NA; Confession of Clement C. Curtis and fifteen others, July 28, 1870, Confession of W. S. Bradshaw, July 30, 1870, and George B. Rodney to R. T. Frank, July 30, 1870, all in U.S. Congress, "Condition of Affairs in the Southern States," lv–lvii, lxviii; James E. Boyd to People of North Carolina, July 29, 1870, and Confession of John A. Moore, August 16, 1870, both reprinted in *North Carolina Weekly Standard* (Raleigh), August 3, 24, 1870.

32. Frank G. Smith to J. W. Powell, August 8, 1870, in U.S. Congress, "Condition of Affairs in the Southern States," lxxx; Rufus Knight to Lieut. Powell, August 9, 1870, M619, reel 808, LR, AGO, RG 94, NA; W. W. Holden to George W. Kirk, August 3, 1870, William Woods Holden GLB, NCSA.

33. Joseph C. Abbott and John Pool, "Memorandum Relating to North Carolina," June [1872], Joseph C. Abbott Letters, William E. Chandler Papers, NHHS; Wilson Carey to W. W. Holden, November 3, 1870, William W. Holden Papers, DU; S. N. Benjamin to C. H. Morgan, August 11, 1871, and E. L. Huggins to S. N. Benjamin, August 9, 1871, both in M666, reel 12, LR, AGO, RG 94, NA; Testimony of Caswell Holt and A. L. Ramsour, in U.S. Congress, "Condition of Affairs in the Southern States," 343–44; *North Carolina Weekly Standard* (Raleigh), September 7, 21, 1870; Harris, *Holden*, 297–98; Trelease, *White Terror*, 223; Zuber, *North Carolina during Reconstruction*, 41; Bogue, "Violence and Oppression," 251.

34. Henry J. Hunt to Assistant Adjutant General Dept East, January 2, 1871, Henry J. Hunt to Chauncey McKeever, August 10, 1870, Hosea Wynn and Casey Davids to General Hunt, September 11, 1870, and Henry J. Hunt to Hosea Wynn and Casey Davids, September 11, 1870, all in U.S. Congress, "Condition of Affairs in the Southern States," lxxv, lxxviii–lxxix.

35. Henry J. Hunt to Chauncey McKeever, August 10, 1870, in U.S. Congress, "Condition of Affairs in the Southern States," lxxxix; William J. Clarke to H. J. Hunt, August 8, 1870, Henry Jackson Hunt Papers, LC; C. B. Throckmorton to

James W. Powell, August 8, 1870, and C. N. Warner to James W. Powell, August 9, 1870, both in M619, reel 808, LR, AGO, RG 94, NA.

36. C. B. Throckmorton to James W. Powell, August 8, 1870, with Endorsements of R. T. Frank, August 8, 1870, Henry J. Hunt, August 10, 1870, and Irvin McDowell [n.d.], and C. N. Warner to James W. Powell, August 9, 1870, both in M619, reel 808, LR, AGO, RG 94, NA.

37. George B. Rodney to J. W. Powell, August 14, 1870, in U.S. Congress, "Condition of Affairs in the Southern States," lxxx.

38. R. T. Frank to C. McKeever, October 2, 1870, in U.S. Congress, "Condition of Affairs in the Southern States," lxxii.

39. R. M. Pearson to W. W. Holden, July 18, 1870, W. W. Holden to R. M. Pearson, July 19, 1870, and W. W. Holden to President of the United States, August 7, 1870, all in William Woods Holden GLB, NCSA; North Carolina Weekly Standard (Raleigh), August 10, 1870; Harris, Holden, 295–96.

40. Henry J. Hunt to Assistant Adjutant General Dept East, January 2, 1871, in U.S. Congress, "Condition of Affairs in the Southern States," lxxv.

41. Opinion of A. T. Akerman, August 8, 1870, enclosed in William W. Belknap to W. W. Holden, August 8, 1870, and SO No. 14, Adjutant General's Office, State of North Carolina, August 11, 1870, both in William Woods Holden GLB, NCSA; Harris, Holden, 296; Trelease, White Terror, 221–22.

42. E. D. T[ownsend] to Maj. Gen. Meade, September 9, 1870, GO No. 14, Dept East, September 13, 1870, Henry J. Hunt to C. McKeever, September 16, 1870 (two letters), and Special Orders No. 228, Dept East, November 12, 1870, all in M619, reel 808, LR, AGO, RG 94, NA; George G. Meade to E. D. Townsend, October 27, 1870, and Irvin McDowell to R. C. Drum, October 8, 1870, both in U.S. Congress, "Report of the Secretary of War," 41st Congress, 3rd Session; 43, 48; Chauncey McKeever to R. T. Frank, October 18, 1870, and Chauncey McKeever to Evan Thomas, October 28, 1870, both in LR, Post of Raleigh, RG 393, NA; Wilhelm, Eighth U.S. Infantry, 134.

43. Third Annual Message of Governor W. W. Holden, November 22, 1870, and various affidavits of Klan victims, all quoted in U.S. Congress, "Condition of Affairs in the Southern States," xxvii, lviii–lxv; Harris, Holden, 296–97; Trelease, White Terror, 222.

44. U.S. Congress, "Condition of Affairs in the Southern States," xxx; Moore, History of North Carolina, 2: 372–82; Trelease, White Terror, 224–25; Harris, Holden, 311–12.

45. Trelease, White Terror, 225.

46. Senate Resolution, December 16, 1870, Henry J. Hunt to Assistant Adjutant General Dept East, January 2, 1871, and R. T. Frank to C. McKeever, January 9, 1871, all in U.S. Congress, "Condition of Affairs in the Southern States," lxxv–lxxvi, lxxxi–lxxxii.

47. W. W. Holden to U. S. Grant, January 1, 1871, and U. S. Grant to Senate of

the United States, January 17, 1871, both in U.S. Congress, "Condition of Affairs in the Southern States," ii, xxxi, liv; Trelease, *White Terror*, 386–87. The documents Holden sent to Grant are in U.S. Congress, "Condition of Affairs in the Southern States," and in M666, reel 1, LR, AGO, RG 94, NA.

48. Act of February 28, 1871, ch. 99, U.S. Congress, *Statutes at Large* 16: 433; Act of April 20, 1871, ch. 22, U.S. Congress, *Statutes at Large* 17: 13; U. S. Grant to Senate and House of Representatives, March 23, 1871, in Simon, *Grant Papers*, 21: 246; A. T. Akerman to B. D. Silliman, November 9, 1871, Amos T. Akerman Papers, UVA; Foner, *Reconstruction*, 454–55.

49. Proclamation of the President of the United States, March 24, 1871, in Simon, *Grant Papers*, 21: 257–58; Simpson, *Reconstruction Presidents*, 155; Trelease, *White Terror*, 269–70.

50. Trelease, *White Terror*, 337–39; Bogue, "Violence and Oppression," 256; Jolley, "Ku Klux Klan in Rutherford County," 2.

51. G. W. Logan to T. R. Caldwell, December 27, 1870, Tod Robinson Caldwell GLB, NCSA; Tod R. Caldwell to G. W. Logan, January 5, 1871, Tod Robinson Caldwell GP, NCSA; Trelease, *White Terror*, 343; Warner and Yearns, *Biographical Register*, 153–54.

52. G. W. Logan to Tod R. Caldwell, April 9, 1871, Tod Robinson Caldwell GP, NCSA; Tod R. Caldwell to U. S. Grant, April 20, 1871, Tod Robinson Caldwell GLB, NCSA; Testimony of James M. Justice, in U.S. Congress, "Testimony Taken by the Joint Committee," 146.

53. J. B. Carpenter to U. S. Grant, May 10, 1871, and C. H. Morgan to Adjutant General Dept East, June 9, 1871 (first letter), both in M666, reel 14, LR, AGO, RG 94, NA; Affidavit of J. B. Carpenter, April 13, 1871, reprinted in *Raleigh Daily Sentinel*, May 1, 1871; Jolley, "Ku Klux Klan in Rutherford County," 41–42.

54. Deposition of Aaron Biggerstaff, May 14, 1871, Tod Robinson Caldwell GP, NCSA; C. H. Morgan to Adjutant General Dept East, May 14, 1871, M666, reel 12, June 9, 1871 (first letter), M666, reel 14, and September 15, 1871, M666, reel 44, all in LR, AGO, RG 94, NA; Testimony of Joseph G. Hester, in U.S. Congress, "Testimony Taken by the Joint Committee," 16; Boatner, *Civil War Dictionary*, 565; Heitman, *Historical Register*, 1: 724.

55. Testimony of Joseph G. Hester and J. B. Carpenter, both in U.S. Congress, "Testimony Taken by the Joint Committee," 16, 30–31; C. H. Morgan to Adjutant General Dept East, May 14, 17, 1871, both in M666, reel 12, LR, AGO, RG 94, NA.

56. Deposition of Aaron Biggerstaff, May 14, 1871, Tod Robinson Caldwell GP, NCSA; Testimony of Joseph G. Hester, in U.S. Congress, "Testimony Taken by the Joint Committee," 16; C. H. Morgan to Adjutant General Dept East, May 17, 1871, M666, reel 12, LR, AGO, RG 94, NA.

57. C. H. Morgan to Adjutant General Department of the East, May 17, 1871, M666, reel 12, LR, AGO, RG 94, NA; Testimony of William R. Howle and Edwin

A. Hull, both in U.S. Congress, "Testimony Taken by the Joint Committee,"51–53, 59, 62–64.

58. Testimony of William R. Howle, in U.S. Congress, "Testimony Taken by the Joint Committee," 64; W. R. Howle to Gen. Morgan, May 4, 1871, LR, Post of Raleigh, RG 393, NA; C. H. Morgan to Adjutant General Dept East, September 15, 1871, M666, reel 44, and H. C. Cushing to C. H. Morgan, May 7, 1871, M666, reel 12, both in LR, AGO, RG 94, NA.

59. H. C. Cushing to C. H. Morgan, May 7, 1871, and C. H. Morgan to Adjutant General Dept East, May 11, 1871, both in M666, reel 12, LR, AGO, RG 94 NA.

60. C. H. Morgan to Adjutant General Dept East, June 9, 1871 (first letter), M666, reel 14, LR, AGO, RG 94, NA; Testimony of J. B. Eaves, in U.S. Congress, "Testimony Taken by the Joint Committee," 178–79.

61. C. H. Morgan to Adjutant General Dept East, September 15, 1871, M666, reel 44, John Pool to the President, June 16, 1871, C. H. Morgan to Adjutant General Dept East, June 17, 19, 1871, and F. V. Greene to C. H. Morgan, June 21, 1871, all in M666, reel 12, LR, AGO, RG 94, NA; Testimony of James M. Justice, in U.S. Congress, "Testimony Taken by the Joint Committee," 115–22, 149, 158, 418–20; James M. Justice to Gov. Caldwell, June 12, 1871, Tod Robinson Caldwell GP, NCSA.

62. C. H. Morgan to Adjutant General Dept East, June 18, 1871, M666, reel 14, LR, AGO, RG 94, NA.

63. C. H. Morgan to Adjutant General Dept East, September 15, 1871, M666, reel 44, S. T. Carrow and R. T. Bosher to F. V. Greene, June 17, 1871, and F. V. Greene to C. H. Morgan, June 21, 1871, both in M666, reel 12, LR, AGO, RG 94, NA; D. H. Starbuck to A. T. Akerman, June 17, 1871, M1345, reel 1, SCF N.C. Eastern District, RG 60, NAII.

64. V. K. Hart to C. H. Morgan, July 31, 1871, LR, Post of Raleigh, RG 393, NA; C. H. Morgan to Adjutant General Department of the East, June 19, July 15, 20, 1871, V. K. Hart to C. H. Morgan, July 17, 1871, George G. Meade to H. W. Halleck, June 22, 1871, M666, reel 12, and C. H. Morgan to Adjutant General Department of the East, September, 15, 1871, all in M666, reel 44, LR, AGO, RG 94, NA; Irvin McDowell to Richard C. Drum, October 9, 1871, in U.S. Congress, "Report of the Secretary of War," 42nd Congress, 2nd Session, 54; Hamilton, *Shotwell Papers,* 2: 470–71, 536–37.

65. V. K. Hart to C. H. Morgan, July 5, 1871, C. H. Morgan to Adjutant General Dept East, July 7, 8, 15, 1871, E. D. Townsend to Genl. Barry, July 22, 1871, and Irvin McDowell to C. H. Morgan, August 1, 1871, all in M666, reel 12, LR, AGO, RG 94, NA; Irvin McDowell to Richard C. Drum, October 9, 1871, in U.S. Congress, "Report of the Secretary of War," 42nd Congress, 2nd Session, 54–55.

66. Robert M. Douglass to G. W. Logan, August 2, 1871, G. W. Logan to Col. Morgan, August 7, 1871, Nathan Scoggins to Col. Morgan, August 7, 1871, V. K. Hart to C. H. Morgan, August 7, 1871, and C. H. Morgan to G. W. Logan, August

9, 1871, all in M666, reel 12, LR, AGO, RG 94, NA; V. K. Hart to C.H. Morgan, August 27, 1871, LR, District of Raleigh, RG 393, NA; J. S. McEwan to Attorney General, October 18, 1871, M1345, reel 1, SCF, N.C. Eastern District, RG 60, NAII; Sefton, *Army and Reconstruction*, 225; Stewart, "'When Darkness Reigns,'" 457.

67. C. H. Morgan to Adjutant General Dept East, August 11 (telegram), 23, 30, September 13, 28, 1871, and S. T. Carrow to C. H. Morgan, August 21, 1871, all in M666, reel 12, LR, AGO, RG 94, NA; Irvin McDowell to Richard C. Drum, October 9, 1871, U.S. Congress, "Report of the Secretary of War," 42nd Congress, 2nd Session, 55.

68. Four men were convicted of participating in two raids. U.S. Congress, "Testimony Taken by the Joint Committee," 417, 453, 469; C. H. Morgan to Adjutant General Dept South, November 25, 1871, M666, reel 12, RG 94, NA; "Statement B" in D. H. Starbuck to George H. Williams, February 24, 1872, M1345, reel 1, SCF, N.C. Eastern District, RG 60, NAII; Bogue, "Violence and Oppression," 263; Trelease, *White Terror*, 346, 400, 402.

69. Nathan Scoggins to C. H. Morgan, October 16, 1871, LR, Post of Raleigh, RG 393, NA; C. H. Morgan to Adjutant General Dept East, October 22, 1871, M666, reel 12, C. H. Morgan to Adjutant General Dept South, September 22, 1872, and Evan Thomas to Asst. Adjutant General Dept South, September 23, 1872, M666, reel 98, all in LR, AGO, RG 94, NA; C. H. Morgan to Evan Thomas, October 22, 1871, LR, Post of Charlotte, RG 393, NA; R. A. Shotwell to Capt. McEwan, October 16, 1871, Confessions of Randolph A. Shotwell et al., October 16, 1871, J. S. McEwan to Attorney General, October 18, 1871, and D. H. Starbuck to George H. Williams, March 18, 1872, all in M1345, reel 1, SCF, N.C. Eastern District, RG 60, NAII; G. W. Logan to Attorney General, March 2, 1872, M1345, reel 2, SCF, N.C. Western District, RG 60, NAII; Lewis Merrill to Gov. of North Carolina, August 7, 1871, Tod Robinson Caldwell GP, NCSA.

70. Albion Howe to W. F. Stewart, December 31, 1871, and C. H. Morgan to Adjutant General Dept South, January 4, 1872, both in U.S. Congress, "Testimony Taken by the Joint Committee," 591–92.

71. C. H. Morgan to Adjutant General Dept East, July 27, 1871, Irvin McDowell to C. H. Morgan, August 1, 1871, M666, reel 12, and C. H. Morgan to Adjutant General Dept East, September 15, 1871, M666, reel 44, all in LR, AGO, RG 94, NA.

72. C. H. Morgan to Adjutant General Dept East, July 29, 1871, GO No. 108, Post of Raleigh, July 30, 1871, Edwin S. Curtis to C. H. Morgan, August 9, 1871, E. L. Huggins to S. N. Benjamin, August 9, 1871, and S. N. Benjamin to C. H. Morgan, August 11, 1871, M666, reel 12, C. H. Morgan to Adjutant General Department of the East, September 15, 1871, and Irvin McDowell to Richard C. Drum, October 9, 1871, M666, reel 44, all in LR, AGO, RG 94, NA.

73. Abbott and Pool, "Memorandum," June [1872], William Edgar Chandler Papers, NHHS; Ashe, *History of North Carolina*, 2: 1139–40; Moore, *History of North Carolina*, 2: 392–94.

74. C. H. Morgan to Adjutant General Dept East, September 28, 1871, M666, reel 12, LR, AGO, RG 94, NA; Affidavit of Gabriel Rialls, October 5, 1871, Tod Robinson Caldwell GP, NCSA.

75. Affidavit of Gabriel Rialls, October 5, 1871, and E. H. McQuigg to Gabriel Rialls, October 5, 1871, both in Tod Robinson Caldwell GP, NCSA.

76. Edward Field to C. H. Morgan, October 3, 1871, M666, reel 12, LR, AGO, RG 94, NA; E. H. McQuigg to Tod R. Caldwell, October 5, 1871, Tod Robinson Caldwell GP, NCSA.

77. Edward Field to C. H. Morgan, October 3, 1871, C. H. Morgan to Adjutant General Dept South, November 25, 1871, and C. H. Morgan to T. R. Caldwell, October 10, 1871, M666, reel 12, C. H. Morgan to Adjutant General Dept South, M666, reel 98, all in LR, AGO, RG 94, NA.

78. C. H. Morgan to Adjutant General Dept South, November 25, 1871, M666, reel 12, and C. H. Morgan to Adjutant General Dept South, September 22, 1871, M666, reel 98, both in LR, AGO, RG 94, NA; J. S. McEwan to A. T. Akerman, November 24, 28, 1871, Confessions of Sampson B. West et al., November 22–23, 1871, and Confessions of Abel Bass et al., November 24–25, 1871, all in M1345, reel 1, SCF, N.C. Eastern District, RG 60, NAII; J. S. McEwan to F. G. Smith, November 22, 1871, LR, Post of Fayetteville, RG 393, NA.

79. C. H. Morgan to Adjutant General Dept South, November 25, 1871, September 22, 1872, both in M666, reel 12, LR, AGO, RG 94, NA.

80. N. J. Riddick to John Scott, December 6, 1871, in U.S. Congress, "Testimony Taken by the Joint Committee," 419; Returns for the Annual Report of the Attorney General, District of North Carolina, January 1, 1872, M1345, reel 1, SCF, N.C. Eastern District, RG 60, NAII; Swinney, "Suppressing the Ku Klux Klan," 280–83; Bogue, "Violence and Oppression," 272, 277.

81. W. A. Albright to A. W. Tourgée, December 23, 1871, and A. W. Tourgée to U. S. Grant, December 28, 1871, both in reel 9, Albion Winegar Tourgée Papers, SHC-UNC; Trelease, White Terror, 408–9.

82. Evans, To Die Game, 4–15, 34–41.

83. Irvin McDowell to Richard C. Drum, October 9, 1871, in U.S. Congress, "Report of the Secretary of War," 42nd Congress, 2nd Session, 52.

84. C. McKeever to Evan Thomas, November 29, December 1, 1870, and Evan Thomas to Chauncey McKeever, December 30, 1870, all in U.S. Congress, "Condition of Affairs in the Southern States," lxxii, lxxxix–xc.

85. Lumberton Robesonian paraphrased in Wilmington Morning Star, January 14, 1871; Evans, To Die Game, 146–49.

86. C. H. Morgan to Evan Thomas, February 5, 1871 (two letters), both in Tod Robinson Caldwell GP, NCSA; C. H. Morgan to Adjutant General Dept East, February 5, 1871, LR, Post of Raleigh, RG 393, NA.

87. GO No. 58, Post of Raleigh, May 17, 1871, and C. H. Morgan to Adjutant

General Dept East, September 15, 1871, both in M666, reel 12, RG 94, NA; Evans, *To Die Game*, 182–83.

88. R. McMillan to Gov. Caldwell, July 15, 1871, Tod R. Caldwell to U. S. Grant, July 17, 1871, with Endorsement of C. H. Morgan, August 5, 1871, and C. H. Morgan to Adjutant General Dept East, July 18, 1871 (with newspaper clippings), all in M666, reel 12, LR, AGO, RG 94, NA.

89. C. H. Morgan to Adjutant General Dept East, August 1 (with newspaper clippings), 9, October 15 (with newspaper clippings), 1871, Endorsement of Tod R. Caldwell, August 9, 1871, John H. Coster to C. H. Morgan, August 15, 1871, John Mendenhall to C. H. Morgan, October 2, 1871, with Endorsement of C. H. Morgan, October 4, 1871 M666 reel 12, and John Mendenhall to Assistant Adjutant General Dept South, September 21, 1872, M666, reel 98, all in LR, AGO, RG 94, NA; Irvin McDowell to Richard C. Drum, October 9, 1871, in U.S. Congress, "Report of the Secretary of War," 42nd Congress, 2nd Session, 55; John Mendenhall to C. H. Morgan, August 27, 1871, LR, Post of Raleigh, RG 393, NA.

90. C. H. Morgan to Adjutant General, Dept South, September 22, 1872, M666, reel 98, LR, AGO, RG 94, NA.

91. Evans, *To Die Game*, 220–21, 234–41.

92. Miller, *Revenuers and Moonshiners*, 50; Stewart, "'When Darkness Reigns,'" 458–68.

93. S. H. Wiley to P. W. Perry, August 14, 1871, newspaper clipping enclosed in C. H. Morgan to Adjutant General Dept East, August 30, 1871, M666, reel 12, C. C. Vest to Pinkney Rollins, April 10, 1871, J. B. Eaves to Pinkney Rollins, April 20, 1871, and Pinkney Rollins to P. W. Perry, April 26, 1871, M666, reel 14, all in LR, AGO, RG 94, NA.

94. P. W. Perry to A. Pleasanton, June 21, 1871, M666, reel 14, LR, AGO, RG 94, NA; "Statement B" in D. H. Starbuck to George H. Williams, February 24, 1872, M1345, reel 1, SCF, N.C. Eastern District, RG 60, NAII; Bogue, "Violence and Oppression," 263; Jolley, "Ku Klux Klan in Rutherford County," 32–33.

95. J. C. Tidball to Asst. Adjut. General Dept South, September 15, 1873, LR, Post of Raleigh, RG 393, NA; P. W. Perry to Irvin McDowell, April 5, 1873, LR, Post of Charlotte, RG 393, NA; C. H. Morgan to Adjutant General Dept South, November 25, 1871, M666, reel 12, and "Detachments from Post of Raleigh, N. C. during the period from Nov. 17, 1871 to September 9, 1872," M666, reel 98, both in LR, AGO, RG 94, NA.

96. J. H. Taylor to P. W. Perry, April 21, 1873, and SO No. 77, April 21, 1877, both in LR, Post of Charlotte, RG 393, NA; H. C. Whitley to George S. Williams, November 24, 1873, and V. S. Lusk to Atty. Gen., December 23, 1873, both in M1345, reel 2, SCF, N.C. Western District, RG 60, NAII; Miller, *Revenuers and Moonshiners*, 70–71, 74; Bogue, "Violence and Oppression," 278.

97. John H. Coster to Commanding Officer Post of Marion, December 10, 1874, LR, Post of Raleigh, RG 393, NA; Irvin McDowell to Assistant Adjutant

General Headquarters of the Army, September 30, 1874, M666, reel 184, RG 94, NA; Irvin McDowell to Assistant Adjutant General Headquarters of the Army, October 19, 1875, M666, reel 242, RG 94, NA; *Army and Navy Journal* (New York), February 3, 1877; Miller, *Revenuers and Moonshiners*, 81; Heitman, *Historical Register*, 1: 547.

98. Heitman, *Historical Register*, 1: 274, 547, 953.

Epilogue

1. Charlotte *Western Democrat*, August 6, 1872.

2. Joseph C. Abbott to Chandler, November 4, 1872, William Edgar Chandler Papers, NHHS; Hamilton, *Reconstruction*, 590–92; Simpson, *Reconstruction Presidents*, 158–62; Barney, *Battleground for the Union*, 300.

3. H. C. Cushing to J. H. Taylor, September 21, 1872, M666, reel 98, LR, AGO, RG 94, NA.

4. Escott, *Many Excellent People*, 166–68; Zuber, *North Carolina during Reconstruction*, 48–50; Barney, *Battleground for the Union*, 325–26.

5. The Raleigh "Grays" militia consisted of the Raleigh Light Infantry and the Raleigh Light Artillery. Newspaper clipping from the *Raleigh Era*, reel 18, Albion Winegar Tourgée Papers, SHC-UNC; *Raleigh Daily Sentinel*, May 31, 1875; *Raleigh Daily News*, June 1, 1875.

6. GO No. 11, Post of Raleigh, RG 393, NA; Newspaper clipping from the *Raleigh Elevator*, reel 18, Albion Winegar Tourgée Papers, SHC-UNC.

7. D. W. Bain to H. A. Allen, August 13, 1875, LR, Post of Raleigh, RG 393, NA; unidentified newspaper clipping, Hamilton et al., *Graham Papers*, 8: 490–91; *Raleigh Daily Sentinel*, August 13, 1875.

8. *Army and Navy Journal* (New York), January 15, 1876.

9. Ibid., June 2, 1877.

10. Zuber, *North Carolina during Reconstruction*, 50–51; McKinney, *Zeb Vance*, 275; Escott, *Many Excellent People*, 169.

11. A detachment of the 18th U.S. Infantry was briefly stationed at Raleigh in May 1877. Returns from U.S. Military Posts, 1800–1916, Raleigh, N.C., March 1866-May 1877, M617, reel 986, RG 94, NA; Thomas H. Ruger to Assistant Adjutant General Division of the Atlantic, October 1, 10, 1877, and Troop Strength Tables, October 24, 1877, all in M666, reel 385, LR, AGO, RG 94, NA; SO No. 176, Dept South, November 6, 1877, LR, Post of Morganton, RG 393, NA; Simpson, *Reconstruction Presidents*, 203–12; Barney, *Battleground for the Union*, 328–30; Sefton, *Army and Reconstruction*, 261–62.

12. Escott, *Many Excellent People*, 169, 181, 184.

13. Ibid., 172.

14. For numbers of Irish- and southern-born troops serving in North Carolina, see the appendix to this volume.

15. Bishir, "'Strong Force of Ladies,'" 476.

16. Mrs. Garland Jones quoted in ibid., 490. For the monograph in question, see Neff, *Honoring the Civil War Dead*, 149–50.

17. Powell, *Powell's Records*, 71; Boatner, *Civil War Dictionary*, 72; Bishir, "'Strong Force of Ladies,'" 469.

18. Alderman, "Memories of 1865–1871," 208, 212.

19. Crowe, "Southern Horizons," 113. See also Davis, "Reconstruction in Cleveland County," 13.

20. Foner, *Reconstruction*, xxiii; Sefton, *Army and Reconstruction*, vii–viii; Franklin, *Reconstruction*, 120–21. For scholars who argue that sectional reconciliation began in earnest after Reconstruction, see Blight, *Race and Reunion*, passim; Foster, *Ghosts of the Confederacy*, 63; O'Leary, *To Die For*, 117, 148; Neff, *Honoring the Civil War Dead*, 4–7.

21. The previous monographs are Kirkland, "Federal Troops in North Carolina"; Kirkland, "Federal Troops in the South Atlantic States"; Bogue, "Violence and Oppression in North Carolina"; Currey, "Role of the Army in North Carolina Reconstruction."

BIBLIOGRAPHY

Manuscript Sources

Alamance County Historical Museum, Burlington, North Carolina [ACHM]
    Military Archival Collection: Redmond F. Laswell Papers
Bentonville Battlefield State Historic Site, Four Oaks, North Carolina [BBSHS]
    Hiram M. Austin Letters
Bowdoin College, Brunswick, Maine: George J. Mitchell Department of Special
    Collections and Archives, Hawthorne-Longfellow Library [BC]
    Oliver Otis Howard Papers
Chicago Historical Society, Chicago, Illinois: Archives and Manuscripts Depart-
    ment [CHS]
    Isaac Newton Arnold Papers
Duke University, Durham, North Carolina: Special Collections, Perkins Library
    [DU]
    William E. Ardrey Papers
    Joseph F. Boyd Papers
    Bedford Brown Papers
    Mary Ann S. M. Buie Papers
    Craven-Pegram Family Papers
    Benjamin S. Hedrick Papers
    William Woods Holden Papers
    John Johnson Diary
    Ku Klux Klan Papers
    MacRae Family Papers
    Methodist Church Papers
    George B. Rodney Letter Book
    William Lafayette Scott Papers
    Daniel Edgar Sickles Papers
    Tillinghast Family Papers
    U.S. Army, Department of North Carolina Papers
    Jordan Vollavey Letter
    Wilkes Family Papers

East Carolina University, Greenville, North Carolina: East Carolina Manuscript
     Collection, J.Y. Joyner Library [ECU]
     Della Barlow Papers, Collection No. 107: John M. Perry Letters
     Elizabeth Fearrington Croom Collection, Collection No. 58: James C. Pass
          Correspondence
     William Blount Rodman Papers, Collection No. 329
Greensboro Public Library, Greensboro, North Carolina: North Carolina Collec-
     tion [NCC-GPL]
     North Carolina Biography File
Historical Society of Pennsylvania, Philadelphia [HSPA]
     Thomas J. Jordan Papers
     George Gordon Meade Collection
Illinois State Historical Library, Springfield [ILHS]
     Thomas J. Henderson Papers
Indiana Historical Society, Indianapolis [INHS]
     Joseph W. and Orville T. Chamberlain Papers
     Dwight Fraser Papers
     Isaiah Hutchison Papers
     John Lewis Ketcham Collection: William A. Ketcham Papers
     Kidd Family Papers: John D. Kidd Letters
     William F. King Papers
     Williamson D. Ward Diary
Kennesaw Mountain National Park, Marietta, Georgia [KMNP]
     Jacob Dolson Cox Diary
Library of Congress, Washington, D.C. [LC]
     John William Draper Papers
     Joseph Roswell Hawley Papers
     Henry Jackson Hunt Papers
     Andrew Johnson Papers
     Nelson Appleton Miles Family Papers
     John McAllister Schofield Papers
     Carl Schurz Papers
     William Tecumseh Sherman Papers
     Daniel Edgar Sickles Papers
     Edwin McMasters Stanton Papers
     Alexander Hamilton Stephens Papers
Mary Moulton Barden Collection, New Bern, North Carolina
     Mary Bayard Clarke Papers
New Hampshire Historical Society, Concord [NHHS]
     William E. Chandler Papers: Joseph C. Abbott Letters
     George F. Towle Diary

New-York Historical Society, New York: Manuscript Department [NYHS]
    A. D. Schenck: "The History of Fort Johnston, North Carolina, 1745–1879"
New York Public Library, New York [NYPL]
    Charles Alexander Nelson Papers
North Carolina State Archives, Office of Archives and History, Raleigh [NCSA]
    Private Collections [PC]
        W. Vance Brown Collection: William J. Brown Correspondence
        Stephen S. Burrill Diary
        Walter Clark Papers
        Calvin J. Cowles Papers
        Fred C. Foard Papers
        Leander S. Gash Papers
        Patterson Papers
    State Agency Records: Governor's Letterbooks [GLB] and Governor's Papers
        [GP]; Provisional Governor's Letterbooks [PGLB] and Provisional Gov
        ernor's Papers [PGP]
        Governor Tod Robinson Caldwell Letterbooks, 1870–1874
        Governor Tod Robinson Caldwell Papers, 1870–1874
        Governor William Woods Holden Letterbooks, 1868–1871
        Governor William Woods Holden Papers, 1868–1871
        Governor Jonathan Worth Letterbooks, 1865–1868
        Governor Jonathan Worth Papers, 1865–1868
        Provisional Governor William Woods Holden Letterbook, 1865
        Provisional Governor William Woods Holden Papers, 1865
University of Michigan, Ann Arbor: Bentley Historical Library [UMI]
    William C. Stevens Correspondence
University of North Carolina, Chapel Hill: Louis Round Wilson Library
    North Carolina Collection [NCC-UNC]
        North Carolina Collection Clipping File
        Reconstruction Scrapbook
    Southern Historical Collection [SHC-UNC]
        David A. Barnes Papers
        Battle Family Papers
        Tod Robinson Caldwell Papers
        Edmund J. Cleveland Diary
        Elizabeth Collier Diary
        Anne Cameron Collins Papers: George P. Collins Letters
        De Rosset Family Papers
        Daniel R. Goodloe Papers
        Bryan Grimes Papers: Charlotte Grimes Reminiscences
        Duncan G. McRae Papers

Pettigrew Family Papers
Ruffin, Roulhac, and Hamilton Family Papers
David Schenck Papers
H. Richardson Smith Papers: Jacob Henry Smith Diary
Cornelia Phillips Spencer Papers
David Lowry Swain Papers
Albion Winegar Tourgée Papers
Josiah Turner Jr. Papers
Harvey Washington Walter Papers
Jonathan Worth Papers
University of Notre Dame, South Bend, Indiana: Archives [UND]
William T. Sherman Family Papers
University of Virginia, Charlottesville: Special Collections, Alderman Library [UVA]
Amos T. Akerman Papers
Barnes Family Papers: Charles F. Barnes Correspondence
University of Washington Libraries, Seattle [UWA]
Manning Ferguson Force Papers
U.S. Army Military History Institute, Carlisle Barracks, Pennsylvania [MHI]
Civil War Miscellaneous Collection [CWMC]
Morris W. Chalmers Letters
Abner Eisenhower Diary
W. C. Hackett Letters
Harrison Nesbitt Letters
Benjamin W. Todd Letters
Charles A. Tournier Diary
William Henry Walling Letters
Civil War Times Illustrated Collection [CWTIC]
Nicholas J. De Graff Diary
Harrisburg Civil War Round Table Collection [HCWRTC]
George Shuman Letters
John S. Miles Papers
Leonard A. Boyd Letter
Nelson Appleton Miles Papers
U.S. National Archives and Records Administration, Washington, D.C. [NA]
Federal Population Census [FPC]
Microcopy [M] 593: 1870 Census
Microcopy 653: 1860 Census
Record Group [RG] 94: Records of the Adjutant General's Office [AGO]
Microcopy 565: Letters Sent by the Adjutant General's Office, 1800–1890
Microcopy 617: Returns from U.S. Military Posts, 1800–1916
Microcopy 619: Letters Received by the Adjutant General's Office, 1861–1870

Microcopy 666: Letters Received by the Adjutant General's Office, 1871–1880

Record Group 105: Records of the Bureau of Refugees, Freedmen, and Abandoned Lands [BRFAL], 1865–1870

Microcopy 843: Records of the Assistant Commissioner of the State of North Carolina [ACNC]

Record Group 107: Records of the Office of the Secretary of War

Records Concerning the Conduct and Loyalty of Certain Union Army Officers, Civilian Employees of the War Department, and U.S. Citizens during the Civil War, 1861–1872

Record Group 153: Records of the Office of the Judge Advocate General

Court-Martial Proceedings

MM-2526: John B. Gilbert

MM-2836: Charles Dorsey and Holland Streeter

MM-2968: Temperance Neely

MM-3114: John S. Bowles

MM-3226: Henry Bird, Charles F. Brown, Dock Leech, Robert Stewart, and Joseph Yokeley

MM-3615: Washington Flood, George Josey, Edward Newson, and Jerry Pruden

MM-3632: Owen Martin and William N. Mott

MM-3643: Aaron Benjamin, Pompey Harkell, Providence James, and Oretus Miller

MM-3721: Aaron Johnson and Edward E. Sherridan

MM-3790: Fred Cannon and William Cannon

MM-3972: John H. Gee

MM-3979: Samuel Alderman, Manuel Davis, Isaac Moore, and George Smallwood

OO-1232: Samuel A. Bartleson and Edward Burns et al.

OO-1433: Archibald Baynes

OO-1514: George A. Pitts et al.

OO-1520: O. G. Sempler and F. N. Cook

OO-1679: Isaac A. Rosekrans

OO-1682: Eliphalet Whittlesey

OO-1782: George O. Glavis

OO-1788: Horace James

OO-2419: John W. Day, Jonas Reidel, Frederick D. Schlachter, and Charles Sinkland

OO-2443: Various Defendants

OO-3652: Charles E. Hargous

PP-143: Charles E. Hargous

PP-185: Richard Boston

Record Group 391: Records of U.S. Regular Army Mobile Units, 1821–1942
    37th U.S. Colored Troops
    40th U.S. Infantry
Record Group 393: Records of U.S. Army Continental Commands, 1821–1920
    (National Archives accession numbers follow entry names and dates)
        General Court-Martial Orders Issued, Department of North Carolina,
        1865–1866, part I, E3305
        Letters Received [LR]
            Department of North Carolina, 1865–1866, part I, E3290 [Dept
            NC]
            District of North Carolina, 1868–1869, 1870, part III, E538 [Dist
            NC]
            District of Raleigh, 1871, part II, E5232
            Post of Charlotte, North Carolina, 1865–1868, 1873, 1877, part
            IV, E194
            Post of Fayetteville, North Carolina, 1867–1868, 1871, part IV,
            E456
            Post of Goldsboro, North Carolina, 1867–1869, part IV, E490
            Post of Greensboro, North Carolina, 1867–1868, part IV, E517
            Post of New Bern, North Carolina, 1865–1868, part IV, E917
            Post of Plymouth, North Carolina, 1865–1868, part IV, E1096
            Post of Raleigh, North Carolina, 1865–1877
            Post of Salisbury, North Carolina, 1867–1868, part IV, E1163
            Post of Wilmington, North Carolina, 1865–1868, part IV, E3180
            Second Military District, 1867–1868, part I, E4111 [2MD]
        Letters Sent [LS]
            Department of North Carolina, 1865–1866 [Dept NC]
            District of North Carolina, 1868–1869, 1870, part III, E535 [Dist
            NC]
            District of Western North Carolina, 1865, part III, E860 [Dist
            WNC]
            Post of Fayetteville, North Carolina, 1867–1868, part IV, E454
            Post of Goldsboro, North Carolina, 1867–1868, part IV, E484, E485,
            and E486
            Post of Greensboro, North Carolina, 1867–1868, part IV, E515
            Post of Morganton, North Carolina, 1867–1868, part V, E368-1
            Post of Raleigh, North Carolina, 1865–1877, part V, E368-1
            Post of Salisbury, North Carolina, 1867–1868, part IV, E1160
            Post of Wilmington, North Carolina, 1865–1868, part IV, E1378
            Second Military District, 1867–1868, part I, E4089 [2MD]
            Station of Plymouth, North Carolina, 1864–1865, part I, E1809

U.S. National Archives and Records Administration II, College Park, Maryland [NAII]

Record Group 60: General Records of the Attorney General's Office Microcopy 1345: Letters Received by the Attorney General, Source-Chronological Files for North Carolina [SCF]

Virginia Historical Society, Richmond [VHS]

Charles Jackson Paine Papers

Primary Sources

Alderman, J. T. "Memories of 1865–1871." North Carolina Booklet 13 (April 1914): 199–213.

Andrew, Sidney. The South after the War: As Shown by Fourteen Weeks of Travel in Georgia and the Carolinas. Boston: Ticknor and Fields, 1866.

Clark, Walter, ed. Histories of the Several Regiments and Battalions from North Carolina in the Great War, 1861–1865. 5 vols. Goldsboro, N.C.: Nash Brothers, 1901.

Conyngham, David P. Sherman's March through the South with Sketches and Incidents of the Campaign. New York: Sheldon, 1865.

Cox, Jacob D. "Surrender of Johnston's Army and the Closing Scenes of the War in North Carolina." In Sketches of War History, 1861–1865: Papers Prepared for the Ohio Commandery of the Loyal Legion of the United States, 2: 247–76. Cincinnati: Robert Clarke, 1888–1908.

Crabtree, Beth G., and James W. Patton, eds. "Journal of a Secesh Lady": The Diary of Catherine Ann Devereux Edmondston, 1860–1866. Raleigh: Division of Archives and History, North Carolina Department of Cultural Resources, 1979.

Crow, Terrell Armistead, and Mary Moulton Barden, eds. Live Your Own Life: The Family Papers of Mary Bayard Clarke, 1854–1886. Columbia: University of South Carolina Press, 2003.

Davis, J. R. "Reconstruction in Cleveland County." Historical Papers Published by the Trinity College Historical Society 10 (1914): 5–31.

Drake, James Madison. The History of the Ninth New Jersey Volunteers. Elizabeth, N.J.: Journal Printing House, 1889.

Eldredge, Daniel. The Third New Hampshire and All about It. Boston: E. B. Stillings, 1893.

Everts, Herrmann. A Complete and Comprehensive History of the Ninth Regiment New Jersey Vols. Infantry. Newark, N.J.: A. Stephen Holbrook, 1865.

Executive and Legislative Documents Laid before the General Assembly of North Carolina, Session 1869–'70. Raleigh: Joseph W. Holden, 1870.

Ford, Annette Gee, ed. The Prisoner: Major John H. Gee, Commandant of the Confederate Prison at Salisbury, North Carolina, 1864–1865. Salt Lake City: Utah Bookbinding, 2000.

Gaskill, J. W. Footprints through Dixie: Everyday Life of the Man under a Musket. Alliance, Ohio: n.p., 1919.

Graf, LeRoy P., Ralph W. Haskins, Paul Bergeron et al., eds. *The Papers of Andrew Johnson.* 16 vols. Knoxville: University of Tennessee Press, 1967–2000.

Grant, Ulysses S. *Personal Memoirs of U. S. Grant.* Reprint. New York: Da Capo, 1982.

Hamilton, J. G. de Roulhac, ed. *The Correspondence of Jonathan Worth.* 2 vols. Raleigh: Edwards and Broughton, 1909.

———. *The Papers of Randolph Abbott Shotwell.* 3 vols. Raleigh: North Carolina Historical Commission, 1929–1936.

Hamilton, J. G. de Roulhac, Max R. Williams, and Mary Reynolds Peacock, eds. *The Papers of William Alexander Graham.* 8 vols. Raleigh: Division of Archives and History, North Carolina Department of Cultural Resources, 1957–1992.

Hamilton, William Douglas. *Recollections of a Cavalryman of the Civil War after Fifty Years, 1861–1865.* Columbus, Ohio: F. J. Heer, 1915.

Hayes, Philip C. *Journal-History of the One Hundred and Third Ohio Volunteer Infantry.* Toledo, Ohio: Commercial Steam, 1872.

Holden, W. W. *Memoirs of W.W. Holden.* Durham, N.C.: Seeman, 1911.

Howard, Oliver O. *Autobiography.* 2 vols. New York: Baker and Taylor, 1907.

Howe, M. A. DeWolfe, ed. *Home Letters of General Sherman.* New York: Scribner's, 1909.

———. *Marching with Sherman: Passages from the Letters and Campaign Diaries of Henry Hitchcock.* Reprint. Lincoln: University of Nebraska Press, 1995.

Johnston, Joseph E. *Narrative of Military Operations during the Civil War.* Reprint. New York: Da Capo, 1990.

King, Myrtle C., ed. *Anna Long Thomas Fuller's Journal, 1856–1890.* Alpharetta, Ga.: Priority, n.d.

Kirwan, Thomas, and Henry Splaine. *Memorial History of the Seventeenth Regiment Massachusetts Volunteer Infantry.* Salem, Mass.: Salem Press, 1911.

Kittinger, Joseph. *Diary, 1861–1865.* Buffalo, N.Y.: Kittinger, 1979.

McKinney, Gordon B., and Richard M. McMurry, eds. *The Papers of Zebulon Baird Vance.* 39 microfilm reels. Frederick, Md.: University Publications of America, 1987.

McMurray, John. *Recollections of a Colored Troop.* Brookville, Pa.: McMurray, 1994.

McPherson, Elizabeth Gregory. "Letters from North Carolina to Andrew Johnson." *North Carolina Historical Review* 28 (April–October 1951): 219–37, 362–75, 486–516.

———. "Letters from North Carolina to Andrew Johnson." *North Carolina Historical Review* 29 (January–April 1952): 104–19, 259–68.

Meade, George G. *Report of Major General Meade's Military Operations and Administration of Civil Affairs in the Third Military District and the Department of the South.* Atlanta: Assistant Adjutant General's Office, Department of the South, 1868.

Miles, Nelson A. *Serving the Republic: Memoirs of the Civil and Military Life of Nelson A. Miles.* New York: Harper, 1911.

Nichols, George Ward, *The Story of the Great March: From the Diary of a Staff Officer.* New York: Harper, 1865.

Padgett, James A., ed. "Reconstruction Letters from North Carolina, Part I: Letters to Thaddeus Stevens." *North Carolina Historical Review* 18 (April 1941): 171–95.

Pinney, N. A. *History of the 104th Ohio Volunteer Infantry from 1862 to 1865.* Akron, Ohio: Werner and Lohmann, 1886.

Price, George F. *Across the Continent with the Fifth Cavalry.* New York: D. Van Nostrand, 1883.

Proceedings in the Case of the United States against Duncan G. McRae, William J. Tolar, David Watkins, Samuel Phillips, and Thomas Powers for the Murder of Archibald Beebee. Raleigh: Published for Robert Avery, 1867.

Raper, Horace W., and Thornton W. Mitchell, eds. *The Papers of William Woods Holden, 1841–1868.* 1 vol. to date. Raleigh: Division of Archives and History, North Carolina Department of Cultural Resources, 2000.

Richardson, James D. *A Compilation of the Messages and Papers of the Presidents.* 10 vols. Washington, D.C.: Government Printing Office, 1896–1899.

Runyan, Morris C. *Eight Days with the Confederates and Capture of Their Archives, Flags, Etc., by Company "G," Ninth New Jersey Vol.* Princeton, N.J.: William C. Zapf, 1896.

Schmitt, Martin F., ed. *General George Crook: His Autobiography.* Reprint. Norman: University of Oklahoma Press, 1986.

Schofield, John M. *Forty-Six Years in the Army.* New York: Century, 1897.

Sherman, William T. *Memoirs.* 2 vols. in 1. Reprint. New York: Da Capo, 1984.

Sherwood, Isaac R. *Memories of the War.* Toledo, Ohio: H. J. Chittenden, 1923.

Simon, John Y., ed. *The Papers of Ulysses S. Grant.* 28 vols. to date. Carbondale: Southern Illinois University Press, 1967– .

Simpson, Brooks D., and Jean V. Berlin, eds. *Sherman's Civil War: Selected Correspondence of William T. Sherman, 1860–1865.* Chapel Hill: University of North Carolina Press, 1999.

Simpson, Brooks D., LeRoy P. Graf, and John Muldowny, eds. *Advice after Appomattox: Letters to Andrew Johnson, 1865–1866.* Knoxville: University of Tennessee Press, 1987.

Spencer, Cornelia Phillips. *The Last Ninety Days of the War in North Carolina.* Reprint. Wilmington, N.C.: Broadfoot, 1993.

Third Annual Message of W. W. Holden, November, 1870. Raleigh: Joseph W. Holden, 1871.

Thompson, B. F. *History of the 112th Regiment of Illinois Volunteer Infantry in the Great War of the Rebellion, 1862–1865.* Toulon, Ill.: Stark County News Office, 1885.

Tourgée, Albion W. *A Fool's Errand, by One of the Fools.* New York: Fords, Howard and Hulbert, 1879.

Trial of William W. Holden, Governor of North Carolina. 3 vols. Raleigh: Sentinel Printing Office, 1871.

U.S. Bureau of the Census. *Population of the United States in 1860: Compiled from the Original Returns of the Eighth Census.* Washington, D.C.: Government Printing Office, 1864.

U.S. Congress. "An Act to Provide for the More Efficient Government of the Rebel States." *Senate Executive Document No. 14.* 40th Congress, 1st Session.

———. "Biographical Directory of the United States Congress, 1774–Present." At http://bioguide.congress.gov.

———. "Condition of Affairs in the Southern States: North Carolina." *Senate Report No. 1.* 42nd Congress, 1st Session.

———. "General Orders: Reconstruction." *House Executive Document No. 342.* 40th Congress, 2nd Session.

———. "Letter from the Secretary of War Transmitting Reports Relative to the Condition of the Second Military District." *House Executive Document No. 276.* 40th Congress, 2nd Session.

———. "Message from the President of the United States: Refugees, Freedmen, and Abandoned Lands." *House Executive Document No. 120.* 39th Congress, 1st Session.

———. "Murder of Union Soldiers in North Carolina." *House Executive Document No. 98.* 39th Congress, 1st Session.

———. "Proceedings of a Military Commission Convened at Wilmington, North Carolina." *Senate Executive Document No. 1237.* 39th Congress, 1st Session.

———. *Report of the Joint Committee on Reconstruction at the First Session, Thirty-Ninth Congress.* Washington, D.C.: Government Printing Office, 1866.

———. "Report of the Secretary of War." *House Executive Document No. 1.* 39th Congress, 2nd Session.

———. "Report of the Secretary of War." *House Executive Document No. 1.* 40th Congress, 2nd Session.

———. "Report of the Secretary of War." *House Executive Document No. 1.* 40th Congress, 3rd Session.

———. "Report of the Secretary of War." *House Executive Document No. 1.* 41st Congress, 2nd Session.

———. "Report of the Secretary of War." *House Executive Document No. 1, Part 2.* 41st Congress, 3rd Session.

———. "Report of the Secretary of War." *House Executive Document No. 1, Part 2.* 42nd Congress, 2nd Session.

———. "Report of the Secretary of War." *House Executive Document No. 1.* 43rd Congress, 2nd Session.

———. "Report of the Secretary of War." *House Executive Document No. 1.* 45th Congress, 2nd Session.

———. *Senate Executive Document No. 16.* 41st Congress, 3rd Session.

———. "Sherman-Johnston." In *Report of the Joint Committee on the Conduct of the War, at the Second Session, Thirty-eighth Congress.* 3: 2–23. Washington, D.C.: Government Printing Office, 1865.

———. "Testimony Taken by the Joint Committee to Inquire into the Condition of Affairs in the Late Insurrectionary States: North Carolina." *Senate Report No. 41, Part 2.* 42nd Congress, 2nd Session.

U.S. Statutes at Large, Volumes 13, 15, and 16.

U.S. War Department. *Annual Report of the Secretary of War Ad Interim and General of the Army, 1867.* Washington, D.C.: Government Printing Office, 1867.

———. *The War of the Rebellion: A Compilation of the Official Records of the Union and Confederate Armies.* 128 vols. Washington, D.C.: Government Printing Office, 1880–1901. [OR]

[Walker, L. A.] *The Surrender in Greensboro.* Originally printed in the *Charlotte Observer,* January 11, 1901.

Wilhelm, Thomas. *Synopsis of the History of the Eighth U.S. Infantry.* David's Island, New York Harbor: n.p., 1871.

Wills, Charles W. *Army Life of an Illinois Soldier.* Washington, D.C.: Globe, 1906.

Yearns, W. Buck, and John G. Barrett, eds. *North Carolina Civil War Documentary.* Chapel Hill: University of North Carolina Press, 1980.

Secondary Sources

Alexander, Roberta Sue. *North Carolina Faces the Freedman: Race Relations during Presidential Reconstruction, 1865–1867.* Durham, N.C.: Duke University Press, 1985.

Angley, Wilson, Jerry L. Cross, and Michael Hill, eds. *Sherman's March through North Carolina: A Chronology.* Raleigh: North Carolina Division of Archives and History, 1995.

Arnett, Ethel Stephens. *Confederate Guns Were Stacked at Greensboro, North Carolina.* Greensboro, N.C.: Piedmont Press, 1965.

Ashe, Samuel A. *History of North Carolina.* 2 vols. Greensboro, N.C.: Charles L. Van Noppen, 1925.

Barney, William L. *Battleground for the Union: The Era of the Civil War and Reconstruction, 1848–1877.* Englewood Cliffs, N.J.: Prentice Hall, 1990.

Barrett, John G. *The Civil War in North Carolina.* Chapel Hill: University of North Carolina Press, 1963.

Bishir, Catherine. "'A Strong Force of Ladies': Women, Politics, and Confederate Memorial Associations in Nineteenth-Century Raleigh." *North Carolina Historical Review* 77 (October 2000): 455–91.

Blight, David W. *Race and Reunion: The Civil War in American Memory.* Cambridge, Mass.: Belknap, 2001.

Boatner, Mark Mayo, III. *The Civil War Dictionary.* New York: David McKay, 1959.

Bogue, Jesse Parker, Jr. "Violence and Oppression in North Carolina during Reconstruction, 1865–1873." Ph.D. dissertation, University of Maryland, 1973.

Bradley, Mark L. "'I Rely upon Your Good Judgment and Skill': The Command Partnership of Robert E. Lee and Joseph E. Johnston in 1865." In Peter S. Carmichael, ed., *Audacity Personified: The Generalship of Robert E. Lee.* Baton Rouge: Louisiana State University Press, 2004.

———. *This Astounding Close: The Road to Bennett Place.* Chapel Hill: University of North Carolina Press, 2000.

Campbell, Jacqueline Glass. *When Sherman Marched North from the Sea: Resistance on the Confederate Home Front.* Chapel Hill: University of North Carolina Press, 2003.

Carbone, John S. *The Civil War in Coastal North Carolina.* Raleigh: North Carolina Division of Archives and History, 2001.

Carter, Dan T. "The Anatomy of Fear: The Christmas Day Insurrection Scare of 1865." *Journal of Southern History* 42 (August 1976): 345–64.

———. *When the War Was Over: The Failure of Self-Reconstruction in the South, 1865–1867.* Baton Rouge: Louisiana State University Press, 1985.

Cecelski, David S. "Abraham Galloway : Wilmington's Lost Prophet and the Rise of Black Radicalism in the American South." In David S. Cecelski and Timothy B. Tyson, eds., *Democracy Betrayed: The Wilmington Race Riot of 1898 and Its Legacy.* Chapel Hill: University of North Carolina Press, 1998.

Chamberlain, Hope Summerell. *Old Days in Chapel Hill, Being the Life and Letters of Cornelia Phillips Spencer.* Chapel Hill: University of North Carolina Press, 1926.

Collins, Donald E. "War Crime or Justice?: General George Pickett and the Mass Execution of Deserters in Civil War Kinston, North Carolina." In Steven E. Woodworth, ed., *The Art of Command in the Civil War.* Lincoln: University of Nebraska Press, 1998.

Connelly, Donald B. *John M. Schofield and the Politics of Generalship.* Chapel Hill: University of North Carolina Press, 2006.

Corbitt, David Leroy. *The Formation of the North Carolina Counties, 1663–1943.* Raleigh: North Carolina Department of Archives and History, 1950.

Crowe, Karen. "Southern Horizons: The Autobiography of Thomas Dixon." Ph.D. dissertation, New York University, 1982.

Currey, Craig Jeffrey. "The Role of the Army in North Carolina Reconstruction." M.A. thesis, University of North Carolina at Chapel Hill, 1991.

Dawson, Joseph G., III. *Army Generals and Reconstruction: Louisiana, 1862–1877.* Baton Rouge: Louisiana State University Press, 1982.

De Montravel, Peter R. *A Hero to His Fighting Men: Nelson A. Miles, 1839–1925.* Kent, Ohio: Kent State University Press, 1998.

Dobak, William A., and Thomas D. Phillips. *The Black Regulars, 1866–1898.* Norman: University of Oklahoma Press, 2001.

DuBois, W. E. B. *Black Reconstruction in America.* Reprint. New York: Free Press, 1992.

Escott, Paul D. "Clinton A. Cilley, Yankee War Hero in the Postwar South: A Study in the Compatibility of Regional Values." *North Carolina Historical Review* 68 (October 1991): 404–26.

———. *Many Excellent People: Power and Privilege in North Carolina, 1850–1900.* Chapel Hill: University of North Carolina Press, 1985.

Evans, W. McKee. *Ballots and Fence Rails: Reconstruction on the Lower Cape Fear.* Chapel Hill: University of North Carolina Press, 1967.

———. *To Die Game: The Story of the Lowry Band, Indian Guerrillas of Reconstruction.* Baton Rouge: Louisiana State University Press, 1971.

Foner, Eric. *Reconstruction: America's Unfinished Revolution.* Reprint. New York: History Book Club, 2005.

Foster, Gaines M. *Ghosts of the Confederacy: Defeat, the Lost Cause, and the Emergence of the New South.* New York: Oxford University Press, 1985.

Franklin, John Hope. *Reconstruction after the Civil War.* Reprint. Chicago: University of Chicago Press, 1994.

Glatthaar, Joseph T. *Forged in Battle: The Civil War Alliance of Black Soldiers and White Officers.* New York: Free Press, 1990.

Gordon, Lesley J. *General George E. Pickett in Life and Legend.* Chapel Hill: University of North Carolina Press, 1998.

Grant, Daniel Lindsay, ed. *Alumni History of the University of North Carolina.* Durham, N.C.: Christian and King, 1924.

Hamilton, J. G. de Roulhac. *Reconstruction in North Carolina.* Reprint. Gloucester, Mass.: Peter Smith, 1964.

Harris, William C. *William Woods Holden: Firebrand of North Carolina Politics.* Baton Rouge: Louisiana State University Press, 1987.

—————. *With Charity for All: Lincoln and the Restoration of the Union.* Lexington: University Press of Kentucky, 1997.

Heitman, Francis B. *Historical Register and Dictionary of the United States Army.* 2 vols. Reprint. Baltimore: Genealogical Publishing, 1994.

Heyman, Max L. "'The Great Reconstructor'": General E. R. S. Canby and the Second Military District." *North Carolina Historical Review* 32 (January 1955): 52–80.

Hill, D. H., Jr. *North Carolina.* Vol. 5 of *Confederate Military History,* edited by Clement A. Evans. Reprint. Wilmington, N.C.: Broadfoot, 1987.

Hogue, James K. *Uncivil War: Five New Orleans Street Battles and the Rise and Fall of Radical Reconstruction.* Baton Rouge: Louisiana State University Press, 2006.

Hollandsworth, James G., Jr. *An Absolute Massacre: The New Orleans Race Riot of July 30, 1866.* Baton Rouge: Louisiana State University Press, 2001.

Inscoe, John C., and Gordon B. McKinney. *The Heart of Confederate Appalachia: Western North Carolina in the Civil War.* Chapel Hill: University of North Carolina Press, 2000.

Jolley, Daniel W. "The Ku Klux Klan in Rutherford County, North Carolina, 1870–1871." M.A. thesis, University of North Carolina at Chapel Hill, 1994.

Keneally, Thomas. *American Scoundrel: The Life of the Notorious Civil War General Dan Sickles.* New York: Doubleday, 2002.

King, Henry T. *Sketches of Pitt County, North Carolina: A Brief History of the County, 1704–1910.* Raleigh: Edwards and Broughton, 1911.

Kirkland, John R. "Federal Troops in North Carolina during Reconstruction." M.A. thesis, University of North Carolina at Chapel Hill, 1964.

—————. "Federal Troops in the South Atlantic States during Reconstruction, 1865–1877." Ph.D. dissertation, University of North Carolina at Chapel Hill, 1967.

Lancaster, James L. "The Scalawags of North Carolina, 1850–1868." Ph.D. dissertation, Princeton University, 1974.

Lefler, Hugh Talmage, and Albert Ray Newsome. North Carolina: The History of a Southern State. Chapel Hill: University of North Carolina Press, 1973.

Lemann, Nicholas. Redemption: The Last Battle of the Civil War. New York: Farrar, Straus and Giroux, 2006.

Longacre, Edward G. A Regiment of Slaves: The 4th United States Colored Infantry, 1863–1866. Mechanicsburg, Pa.: Stackpole, 2003.

Marszalek, John F. Sherman: A Soldier's Passion for Order. New York: Free Press, 1993.

Marvel, William. Andersonville: The Last Depot. Chapel Hill: University of North Carolina Press, 1994.

Massengill, Stephen E. "The Detectives of William W. Holden, 1869–1870." North Carolina Historical Review 62 (October 1985): 448–87.

McFeely, William S. Yankee Stepfather: General O. O. Howard and the Freedmen. Reprint. New York: W. W. Norton, 1994.

McGee, Edward H. "North Carolina Conservatives and Reconstruction." Ph.D. dissertation, University of North Carolina at Chapel Hill, 1972.

McKinney, Gordon B. Zeb Vance: North Carolina's Civil War Governor and Gilded Age Political Leader. Chapel Hill: University of North Carolina Press, 2004.

McKitrick, Eric L. Andrew Johnson and Reconstruction. Chicago: University of Chicago Press, 1960.

Miller, Wilbur R. Revenuers and Moonshiners: Enforcing Federal Liquor Law in the Mountain South, 1865–1900. Chapel Hill: University of North Carolina Press, 1992.

Mobley, Joe A. James City: A Black Community in North Carolina, 1863–1900. Raleigh: North Carolina Division of Archives and History, 1981.

Moore, John W. History of North Carolina. 2 vols. Raleigh: Alfred Williams, 1880.

Morrill, James Roy, III. "North Carolina and the Administration of Brevet Major General Sickles." North Carolina Historical Review 42 (July 1965): 291–305.

Murray, Elizabeth Reid. Wake: Capital County of North Carolina. Raleigh: Capital County, 1983.

Neff, John R. Honoring the Civil War Dead: Commemoration and the Problem of Reconciliation. Lawrence: University Press of Kansas, 2005.

Nelson, Scott Reynolds. "Red Strings and Half Brothers: Civil Wars in Alamance County." In John C. Inscoe and Robert C. Kenzer, eds., Enemies of the Country: New Perspectives on Unionists in the Civil War South. Athens: University of Georgia Press, 2003.

O'Leary, Cecilia Elizabeth. To Die For: The Paradox of American Patriotism. Princeton, N.J.: Princeton University Press, 1999.

Olsen, Otto H. "Albion Winegar Tourgée." In William S. Powell, ed. Dictionary of North Carolina Biography. Vol. 6. Chapel Hill: University of North Carolina Press, 1979–1996.

———. Carpetbagger's Crusade: The Life of Albion Winegar Tourgée. Baltimore: Johns Hopkins University Press, 1965.

————. "The Ku Klux Klan: A Study in Reconstruction Politics and Propaganda." *North Carolina Historical Review* 39 (July 1962): 340–62.

Paludan, Philip Shaw. *Victims: A True Story of the Civil War.* Knoxville: University of Tennessee Press, 1981.

Perman, Michael. *Reunion without Compromise: The South and Reconstruction, 1865–1868.* London: Cambridge University Press, 1973.

————. *The Road to Redemption: Southern Politics, 1869–1879.* Chapel Hill: University of North Carolina Press, 1984.

Pfanz, Harry W. *Gettysburg: Culp's Hill and Cemetery Hill.* Chapel Hill: University of North Carolina Press, 1993.

————. *Gettysburg: The Second Day.* Chapel Hill: University of North Carolina Press, 1980.

————. "Soldiering in the South during the Reconstruction Period, 1865–1877." Ph.D. dissertation, Ohio State University, 1958.

Powell, William H. *Powell's Records of Living Officers of the United States Army.* Philadelphia: L. R. Hamersly, 1890.

Rable, George C. *But There Was No Peace: The Role of Violence in the Politics of Reconstruction.* Athens: University of Georgia Press, 1984.

Reid, Richard. "Raising the African Brigade: Early Black Recruitment in Civil War North Carolina." *North Carolina Historical Review* 70 (July 1993): 266–97.

————. "USCT Veterans in Post–Civil War North Carolina." In John David Smith, ed., *Black Soldiers in Blue: African American Troops in the Civil War Era.* Chapel Hill: University of North Carolina Press, 2002.

Rhea, Gordon C. *The Battles for Spotsylvania Courthouse and the Road to Yellow Tavern, May 7–12, 1864.* Baton Rouge: Louisiana State University Press, 1997.

Richter, William L. *The Army in Texas during Reconstruction.* College Station: Texas A&M University Press, 1987.

Robertson, William Glenn. "The Peach Orchard Revisited: Daniel E. Sickles and the Third Corps on July 2, 1863." In Gary W. Gallagher, ed., *The Second Day at Gettysburg: Essays on Confederate and Union Leadership.* Kent, Ohio: Kent State University Press, 1993.

Sanders, Charles W., Jr. *While in the Hands of the Enemy: Military Prisons of the Civil War.* Baton Rouge: Louisiana State University Press, 2005.

Sefton, James E. *The United States Army and Reconstruction, 1865–1877.* Baton Rouge: Louisiana State University Press, 1967.

Silber, Nina. *The Romance of Reunion: Northerners and the South, 1865–1900.* Chapel Hill: University of North Carolina Press, 1993.

Simpson, Brooks D. *Let Us Have Peace: Ulysses S. Grant and the Politics of War and Reconstruction, 1861–1868.* Chapel Hill: University of North Carolina Press, 1991.

————. *The Reconstruction Presidents.* Lawrence: University Press of Kansas, 1998.

Stark, William C. "History of the 103rd Ohio Volunteer Infantry Regiment, 1862–1865." M.A. thesis, Cleveland State University, 1986.

Stein, A. H. *History of the Thirty-Seventh Regt. U.S.C. Infantry.* Philadelphia: King and Baird, 1866.

Stewart, Bruce E. "'When Darkness Reigns Then Is the Hour to Strike': Moonshining, Federal Liquor Taxation, and Klan Violence in Western North Carolina, 1868–1872." *North Carolina Historical Review* 80 (October 2003): 453–74.

Swinney, Everette. "Suppressing the Ku Klux Klan: The Enforcement of the Reconstruction Amendments, 1870–1874." Ph.D. dissertation, University of Texas, 1966.

Trelease, Allen W. *White Terror: The Ku Klux Klan Conspiracy and Southern Reconstruction.* Baton Rouge: Louisiana State University Press, 1971.

Troxler, Carole Watterson. "'To Look More Closely at the Man': Wyatt Outlaw, a Nexus of Local, National, and Personal History." *North Carolina Historical Review* 77 (October 2000): 403–33.

Troxler, Carole Watterson, and William Murray Vincent. *Shuttle and Plow: A History of Alamance County, North Carolina.* n.p.: Alamance County Historical Association, 1999.

Walker, Jacqueline Baldwin. "Blacks in North Carolina during Reconstruction." Ph.D. dissertation, Duke University, 1979.

Warner, Ezra J. *Generals in Blue: Lives of the Union Commanders.* Baton Rouge: Louisiana State University Press, 1964.

Warner, Ezra J., and W. Buck Yearns. *Biographical Register of the Confederate Congress.* Baton Rouge: Louisiana State University Press, 1975.

Wiley, Bell Irvin. *The Life of Billy Yank: The Common Soldier of the Union.* Reprint. Baton Rouge: Louisiana State University, 1994.

Williams, Lou Falkner. *The Great South Carolina Ku Klux Klan Trials, 1871–1872.* Athens: University of Georgia Press, 1996.

Wooster, Robert. *Nelson A. Miles and the Twilight of the Frontier Army.* Lincoln: University of Nebraska Press, 1993.

Zalimas, Robert J., Jr. "Black Union Soldiers in the Postwar South, 1865–1866." M.A. thesis, Arizona State University, 1993.

———. "A Disturbance in the City: Black and White Soldiers in Postwar Charleston." In John David Smith, ed., *Black Soldiers in Blue: African American Troops in the Civil War Era.* Chapel Hill: University of North Carolina Press, 2002.

Zipf, Karin L. "'The Whites Shall Rule the Land or Die': Gender, Race, and Class in North Carolina Reconstruction Politics." *Journal of Southern History* 65 (August 1999): 499–534.

Zuber, Richard L. *Jonathan Worth: A Biography of a Southern Unionist.* Chapel Hill: University of North Carolina Press, 1965.

———. *North Carolina during Reconstruction.* Raleigh: North Carolina Division of Archives and History, 1969.

Zuczek, Richard. *State of Rebellion: Reconstruction in South Carolina.* Columbia: University of South Carolina Press, 1996.

INDEX